Praise for *Maybe 'I do'*

Kevin Andrews has performed a real service with this engagingly written, data-packed analysis of how changes in marriage and family behavior are affecting children and society's future. The sobering picture he paints is relieved by the author's determination to show that cultural trends can and must be shifted in a more positive direction.

– Mary Ann Glendon is the Learned Hand Professor of Law at Harvard University, and author of *The Forum and the Tower: How Scholars and Politicians Have Imagined the World from Plato to Eleanor Roosevelt.*

Kevin Andrews has written a rare and valuable book that is strongly grounded in the best data, international in its scope, and rich in data-based policy discussion and recommendations. It is thorough, meticulously documented, and heartfelt all at once. Every policy maker, social scientist, and interventionist should read this riveting book.

– Blaine Fowers, Ph.D., author of *Beyond the Myth of Marital Happiness*, Professor of Counseling Psychology, University of Miami.

What a terrific book! With comprehensiveness that would put many scholars to shame, Kevin Andrews masterfully assembles the social science evidence showing why marriage matters. And with wisdom and sincerity that are all too rare in today's politics, he offers a compelling vision for renewing this most vital of our social institutions.

– David Blankenhorn is president of the New York-based Institute for American Values and the author of *The Future of Marriage*.

This is a comprehensive and thoroughly documented book on why marriage matters to adults and children. It will be the new bible for those of us in the western world who need the citations for the latest research and literature. Equally important are the practical and relevant recommendations for policy and programs that Kevin Andrews has put forth. I believe this will be the most important family book of the decade.

– **Bill Coffin** was the Special Assistant for Marriage Education, Administration for Children and Families, U.S. Department of Health and Human Services, 2002-2010.

Kevin Andrews has produced an encyclopedic volume citing research data for the past 40 years that documents the importance of marriage for the married couple, their children and society. He shows that most forms of human suffering-stress in relationships, abuse, physical and emotional ailments, divorce, poverty, school and work performance, violence and crime have their roots in distressed intact and dysfunctional families. The solution is obvious: improve family life rather mitigate the downriver effects of family dysfunction. Everyone interested in the transformation of society should read this book and get the message that society is transformed within by the transformation of intimate relationships.

– **Harville Hendrix**, author *Getting the Love You Want: A Guide for Couples*.

Andrews' clarion call for rebuilding a marriage culture capable of sustaining humanity's most fundamental social institution ought to be heard – and acted upon – throughout the western world).

– **George Weigel** is the Distinguished Senior Fellow, Ethics and Public Policy Center, Washington, D.C.

This important book is essential reading for all those concerned with family policy. Kevin Andrews, a politician with years of experience at the highest levels of the Australian government, demonstrates how changes in family life across the western world in the last 30 years have imperilled the future health, wellbeing and prosperity of western nations with lasting consequences for generations to come. More than this, he offers solutions to begin to turn things around to offer a better future.

This book is essential reading for all who are concerned about issues of social inclusion. With impressive scholarship and careful analysis of all the evidence, Kevin Andrews demonstrates the serious consequences of family instability in terms of the health and wellbeing of children. He shows how new divisions in society are emerging between those children who have the benefit of safe, stable and nurturing two parent families, and those who do not. He also shows how both men and women can be disadvantaged, in different ways, by the modern approach of diffident and conditional commitment to intimate relationships. This is not a book about going back to the past, but one that seeks to chart a pathway to the future; not a conservative book bemoaning a lost age of family stability, but a searing analysis of the need for radical change in family policy.

– Patrick Parkinson, Professor of Family Law, University of Sydney.

This is not your ordinary 'policy' book written by an active politician. Kevin Andrews' *Maybe 'I Do'* is a well crafted, cogent, and remarkably thorough analysis of the social science research on the importance of marriage to couples, their children, and society as a whole. Accurately calling the breakdown of marriage, family, and community the greatest threat to the Western world, Andrews ably identifies public policies that could strengthen families in this 21st Century. Concerned citizens, lawmakers, and scholars alike will greatly benefit from this volume.

– Allan Carlson Ph.D. is the President of the Howard Center for Family, Religion & Society and Founder and International Secretary, The World Congress of Families.

This is a reasoned and thoroughly documented call to take the future of marriage as seriously as we take the future of the economy, education, and health care. I have never seen the case made better for marriage as a public good worth preserving and promoting, and not just a personal life style. 'Maybe I Do' also has a human touch, reflecting the author's many years as an educator of young couples. It's a terrific contribution from a national leader.

– William J. Doherty Ph.D. is professor of Family Social Science, University of Minnesota, and director of the Minnesota Couples on the Brink Project. He is author of *A Strong Marriage*.

Kevin Andrews has produced a remarkable analysis and 'tour de force' of the voluminous research which it's necessary to understand if we are to generate a balanced appreciation of the complex and fundamental role that marriage plays in the lives of individuals, institutions and society. Whatever our views and values with respect to marriage, everyone who believes that we need, both as individuals and societies, to make wise decisions concerning it should read this book. Doing so leads to the conclusion that Andrews advocates: that we need to do much more to support and protect marriage. This is required, first, for the sake of children, who are the voiceless citizens harmed, not just in childhood but throughout their lives, by the demise of marriage. Second, in order to promote the well-being and human flourishing of many adults. And, third, if we hope to pass on to future generations shared values that will found societies in which reasonable people would want to live. Marriage is part of the essence of being human and we have obligations to hold that essence on trust for future generations.

– Margaret Somerville is the Samuel Gale Professor of Law, McGill University, Montreal, Canada.

Kevin Andrews is internationally recognized as a leading marriage and family expert. This book ably presents his wide knowledge and wise advice.

– **David Popenoe**, is the Professor of Sociology Emeritus, Rutgers University, USA.

Kevin Andrews has been at the forefront of the broad cultural debate over marriage for the last two decades and this book displays the fruit of that sustained endeavour. Few leaders in Australasia have the tenacity, intellect and passion to advance the ideas and institutions that make our society strong – and perhaps no institution is more important than that of the intact married family. It is the combination of those qualities with the subject material that makes this such recommended reading.

– **Greg Fleming**, CEO, Maxim Institute, Auckland, New Zealand.

Connor Court Publishing Pty Ltd.
PO Box 1
Ballan VIC 3342
sales@connorcourt.com
www.connorcourt.com

ISBN: 978-1-922168-01-6 (pbk.)

Cover design by Ian James

Printed in Australia

TABLE OF CONTENTS

INTRODUCTION

The purpose of this book is to examine the role and significance of marriage in changing times, to highlight those factors which social scientists believe benefit or detract from marital success, and to examine the ways in which individuals, communities and governments can help to create successful marital unions. The intention of this work is not prescriptive. Not everyone aspires to marriage and family life. Some have other goals for their lives. The purpose is not to suggest that all should wed, but to acknowledge that most people seek a successful marriage and a fulfilling family life in which to raise healthy and happy children. Many social, cultural and economic changes have had an adverse impact on our ability to achieve this goal. By lighting a pathway through the maze of social science research, the purpose is to inform a wider discussion about issues that have a significant impact on people's lives, and to provide individuals and communities with information that will help to make informed choices.

Thousands of social science results indicate that a healthy, stable and happy marriage is an optimal relationship for the psychological, emotional and physical wellbeing of adults and children. Functional families are one of the strongest influences on the growth of human competence, and mental and emotional wellbeing.[1] Stable families are also the bedrock of successful societies. The desire for a healthy family life crosses nations, states and cultures. To be loved and accepted, and to feel a part of something greater than ourselves are amongst the deepest yearnings of the human heart. This yearning is at the core of friendship, family, community and nation. It is what brings people together, from small communities to global movements. It is a powerful motivation for human thriving and surviving.

Human beings crave for connection and ritual.[2] The former reflects our desire to love and to be loved; the latter, our sense of place and perspective, and the need to give meaning to life's events. In *A prayer for my daughter*, the Irish poet, William Butler Yeats, reflected on the significance of ritual: "And may her bridegroom bring her to a house/ Where all's accustomed, ceremonious;/For arrogance and hatred are the wares/Peddled in the thoroughfares."[3]

While the great writers and poets of the past have reflected on love, intimacy and connection, the aspiration for a happy and healthy marriage and resilient family life is universal. Young people of both genders continue to say that "having a good marriage and family life" is "extremely important" to them.[4]

Couples' hopes and dreams for a happy future have not changed over the years, but many other circumstances have. A generation ago, couples wed in their early to mid twenties. By 2012, the average age is 30. Three decades ago, 20 per cent of couples cohabited before marriage; now 60-80 per cent do. More people remain unmarried. Twice the proportion of children is born out of wedlock. Divorce is much more common.

Invariably, couples still believe in faithfulness, and marriage for life. Sadly, a combination of factors has contributed to higher rates of marital dysfunction and breakdown, and single parenthood. For a growing group of people, marriage – even a stable relationship – is unachievable. This has many adverse consequences for individuals, especially children, and society.

The retreat from marriage
The recent retreat from marriage that was meant to free individuals from economic and emotional constraints has failed many people. The changes sprang from well-intentioned, even noble concerns;

they were designed to liberate individuals from stultifying and unhappy marriages, and to free them and their children to enter new and fulfilling relationships. In an era of heightened individualism, available contraception and educational and occupational advances for women[5], the proponents envisaged a culture of loving and committed relationships unhindered by a piece of paper. They hoped for a world of conciliation and consent, built on mutual trust and equality. For some, this has come to pass. Individuals have been able to free themselves from unhappy and destructive relationships. But for many, the changes have wrought economic hardship, emotional anguish, and poor health and educational outcomes.[6] "Freedom from the bonds of matrimony came at a terrible price for many women in terms of adverse financial consequences; it exacted a different kind of toll for divorced fathers,"[7] often alienation from their children and a severing of links with extended family.[8] While adults have some ability to air their concerns and deal with the consequences, many children have been the voiceless losers in this family revolution.

The abandonment of children

Prior to the introduction of Child Support legislation in the 1980s, many former spouses, principally men, had an appalling record of not paying maintenance for their children. In 1988, only 25.6 per cent or 62,000 of the 240,000 sole parent pensioners in Australia were declaring maintenance income. The amount paid was an average of $27 for each child.[9] In the US in the 1960s, "the absent father could all but choose not to pay,"[10] a situation that may have been compounded by no-fault divorce legislation.[11] As recently as 2005, less than half of all custodial parents in the United States received full child support, and 22.8 per cent received none.[12] Indeed, the number of single mothers in receipt of child support increased by just one per cent between 1976 and 1997,[13] largely because the number of never-married mothers increased substantially, compared to the increase in separated and divorced mothers. In Britain, only around half of the three million children growing up in separated families are benefiting from the maintenance system.[14]

In three decades from 1974 to 2006, sole parent families increased from 9.2 per cent to 22 per cent of all families in Australia with children under 15 years of age. Most were the result of separation or relationship breakdown.[15] As around two-thirds of these sought social security benefits, at least for a period, the costs to Australians were huge, rising almost twenty-fold from $160 million in 1973-74 to $2,900 million in just two decades. The Australian experience was similar. In 2006, the 21.2 million children living with 13.6 million custodial parents in the United States represented just over a quarter of all children under the age of 21.[16]

Faced with a barrage of complaints about child support, legislatures in many nations examined the operation of their schemes.[17] Under the systems that operated in many nations, including Australia till the end of the 1980s, financial support for children of separated parents was virtually a voluntary payment. A new expression entered the language: "Deadbeat Dads." It was descriptive of the community attitude to parents who could not or would not meet their obligations to financially support their children.

Soon after my election to Parliament in 1991, I was appointed to a committee to inquire into the operation of the child support system.[18] The Australian Inquiry received the largest number of submissions for an inquiry ever conducted by the Parliament at that time, and more than 150,000 attempts were made by Australians to contact the Inquiry on a special telephone hotline. The Scheme and the Inquiry raised a number of cultural issues.

Cultural attitudes

The level of dissatisfaction with the Child Support Scheme did not merely reflect complaints about the appropriateness of the formula that was applied to determine payments, and the administration of the Agency charged to oversee it. One consequence of the introduction of no-fault divorce legislation[19] was to engender a cultural attitude that partners could simply walk away from marriage upon its ending. Professor Patrick Parkinson notes, "for the majority of divorced men in many countries, the divorce revolution meant walking away from the marriage, or being shown the door, without attribution of blame, but also without continuing responsibilities."[20] Child Support legislation, developed in part as a response to burgeoning welfare bills, challenged that attitude and required ongoing financial responsibility for children. Marriage was legally dissoluble, but parenthood was not.

The Parliamentary Inquiry also touched upon the cultural significance of the family as a bridge between the individual and larger society, what the sociologist, Peter Berger, described as a "mediating structure".[21] The idea of the family as an integral bridge between the individual and society is not new. It was Aristotle's view that if children did not love their parents and family members, they would love no one but themselves. Martin Luther King eloquently stated: "The institution of the family is decisive in determining not only if a person has the capacity to love another individual but in the larger sense whether he is capable of loving ... The whole of society rests on this foundation for stability, understanding and social peace."[22]

What happens to individuals when a significant mediating structure, such as the family, has to deal with a broken marriage? Many former spouses seek new relationships, whether for social or economic reasons or both, but many also portray an alienation they feel as individuals because a structure that gave their lives meaning and identity has been fractured. There may be a sense of relief about the ending of an unsatisfactory relationship, but there is often a sense of confusion, alienation, and loss of identity about their family also. This loss is particularly felt by many children. As Lynne Graham wrote in the *State of the Family Report* for the Australian family services agency, Anglicare, "family breakdown and family dysfunction have a price."[23]

The emotional upheaval subsequent to separation and divorce was evident in thousands of submissions to the Child Support Inquiry. It was also particularly felt by many non-custodial parents, invariably fathers, who complained bitterly about the lack of access to their children. Whatever their relationship with their children may have been beforehand, the sense of injustice that many fathers felt in not being able to maintain a real relationship subsequent to separation was undeniably evident in many of the submissions to the inquiry.

The bipartisan committee agreed that there were inequities in the scheme that should be remedied. Yet within an hour of the release of the report, the then government categorically ruled out any substantial change. The curt response was counterproductive. It was part of the reason why child support has remained a political issue for so long. On regular occasions, Members of Parliament would raise the issue. As a consequence, further inquiries were established, leading ultimately to reforms and the creation of the Family Relationship Centres and the legal concept of shared parenting.[24] Similar discussions and debates have occurred in other countries.[25]

We can draw important lessons from these events. If issues of significant concern to the community are not addressed, they do not disappear. To the contrary they fester and compound until policy makers finally confront them. Secondly, as the Parliamentary Committee travelled around Australia in the early 1990s, it became clear that often children had been the losers from the major upheavals in cultural attitudes and social policy over the preceding two decades.

The sense of alienation and loss was reinforced a few years later during the inquiry into strengthening marriage and relationships, *To have and to hold*, which I chaired. As I wrote in the preface to the findings: "This is a report about strengthening marital relationships. It is about preventing marital distress and the consequent breakdown of relationships. It arises from our concern for children: for their future, their happiness and their ability to form their own loving and fulfilling relationships."[26]

The report called for an alternative to the polarising debate – between those who say that divorce is a right, not to be encumbered in any way; and those who maintain it has led to social breakdown and adverse consequences for both adults and children – by adopting a national strategy to strengthen marriage and relationships.[27] Importantly, it called for a renewed emphasis on prevention.

Prevention

Prevention remains an elusive goal of social policy, but it is worth pursuing. As evidence to the *To have and to hold* inquiry revealed, many people regret their separation and divorce, and wish it had not happened. This is supported by research that shows that many people who work through the difficulties and challenges have a fulfilling relationship a few years later.[28]

It also highlights the fact that every dollar spent on prevention saves many dollars in services later. The Parliamentary Inquiry estimated that the direct cost of marriage and relationship breakdown in 1998 was at least $3 billion per year, and as much as $6 billion when indirect costs were included.[29] This is similar to overseas findings. The Canadian Institute for Marriage and Family found the costs to that country to be around $7 billion a year.[30] The British Relationships Foundation put the cost of family breakdown at £37 billion annually,[31] while the Centre for Social Justice estimated that it was £20 billion per year.[32] A US study concluded that the social costs for more than a million couples' divorcing each year was $33.3 billion – or $125 million for every million people in the country.[33] When family dysfunction and marital breakdown cost a nation billions of dollars a year, prevention deserves greater attention.

A decade later, the trends remain, the process of marital dysfunction has compounded, and more children are at risk. The ranks of the separated and divorced have swelled in the past two decades with a corresponding increase in never-married – and often – single, parents.

The place of children

There are two prevailing views of the marital trends. One is to treat the negative consequences as the unavoidable flotsam of modern relations. This view is reinforced by the powerful social and cultural forces discussed in this book. Some are natural, including the reluctance to be seen interfering in the lives of others. Some are the result of the modern obsession to avoid some questions of common morality. The result is policy inertia.

The other view recognises that while most people survive the adverse consequences, many are disadvantaged significantly. It recognises that a satisfying marriage and a healthy family life remain widely held aspirations. It is compounded by a critical fact: that many children suffer consequences that can last a lifetime.

The former view, which underlies much of the discussion about family over the past half century, including legal issues surrounding divorce, and more recently, same-sex unions, is primarily about adults. Conversely, children are at the heart of the latter view. In the words of the Council on Families in America:

> [T]he institution of marriage was designed less for the accommodation of adults in love than for the proper functioning of society, especially regarding the care of children. Indeed, marriage as an institution is historically based on a fundamental realisation – that all affective ties between men and women, no matter how biologically based they may be, are notoriously fragile and breakable. Because of this fact, an important aspect

of marriage, in both its legal and religious contexts, are the vows of fidelity and permanence that are almost always part of the wedding ceremony. In large measure, these promises are designed to bind males to long-term commitment in order to foster the social institution of fatherhood.[34]

The essential purpose of marriage involves the binding of the father to the mother-child unit. The anthropologist, Bronislaw Malinowski, observed:

> In all human societies the father is regarded by tradition as indispensible ... no child should be brought into the world without a man – and one man at that – assuming the role of sociological father, that is, guardian and protector, the male link between the child and the rest of the community.[35]

Decades after Malinowski's observations, the trends towards a non-marital culture compound in most western nations. While divorce was the driver of these changes in the 1970s and 80s, cohabitation and single-parenthood have been the main engines in the decades since.

Maybe 'I do'

The retreat from a marital culture has been evident in the western world for the past four decades. The data in this book outlines the size of the changes, the impact on adults and children, and more generally communities. It reflects an image of negative trends, as measured by thousands of studies by family scholars and marital researchers across many nations. But there are signs of hope. In some places, the marriage rate has risen, and the divorce rate fallen in recent years. Other studies reveal that, at least for the well-off and educated, marriage and divorce rates are near the levels they were half a century ago. In some nations, birth rates have ceased declining, and have even risen slightly. These signs do not signal a wholesale return to marriage, but they do suggest that individuals and communities still find marriage a fulfilling and desirable aspiration. Nonetheless, there is widespread ambivalence and uncertainty about getting married. This is reflected in the 'not just yet' attitudes to marriage; cohabitation 'until further notice'; and the increasing incidence of non-marital childbearing. Maybe 'I do' reflects an individual and societal ambivalence about marriage.

Common responses

In writing this book, I am aware of the pitfalls that await anyone who questions current orthodoxy. There are a series of common criticisms of proposals to strengthen marriages and families. Some are well-meaning; others designed to dismiss the arguments and stifle discussion. These responses include:

> *We have to move with the times.* This suggestion holds that all social change is progress that improves the welfare and happiness of individuals. This is patently false, as even a cursory reflection of social history reveals.

> *It is a return to the 'bad old days' of fault divorce and prying detectives.* Nothing in this book proposes banning divorce. Nor should anything written here be construed as an argument that people should enter or remain in destructive relationships. But it does recognise that many people regret divorce and relatively little information is available about the negative consequences for the individuals involved and society generally.

> *Marriage is 'just a piece of paper.'* Most people enter marriage believing it to be a life-long commitment. As thousands of studies illustrate, this commitment has profound consequences, especially for children.

> *We shouldn't stigmatise single parents and their children.* Many children are doing well, so it is wrong to publicise the social science research that indicates otherwise, according to this response.[36] We need to be sensitive, but avoiding the issue compounds the problems.[37] Most parents care deeply about their children's wellbeing. Knowing the impact of changes can help

to empower them in their quest to continue to provide for their children's welfare.

It is none of the government's business and *we don't need the government playing 'big brother'*. This is misplaced. It becomes the government's business when children require state care, former partners need welfare to survive and social agencies expend much time, effort and finances on the consequences of marital dysfunction.

It is a male conspiracy to subordinate women. According to some, to question the causes of family breakdown is tantamount to misogamy. The fact that women can participate in the paid workforce and take-up many other opportunities is welcome. But there are also unintended consequences of the many changes of the past few decades, not the least of which is increased female poverty.

This is a right wing, conservative and/or religious argument. To the contrary, hundreds of social scientists of different faiths (and of none) have researched and identified the consequences of the retreat from marriage; and a growing number of liberals and conservatives alike worry about them.

We are unmarried with children and they are fine. Some children will survive separation and divorce or unmarried parenthood without any harm. Some will not. The research indicates that the risk of adverse outcomes for health, well-being, education and employment is clearly higher for these children.

What about 'old fashioned love?' The notion of educating people about marriage and family life strikes a dissonant chord with some people. In a letter to a major newspaper some years ago, a sceptic of education asked "Whatever happened to old fashioned love, the kind that would last through the years?"[38] Surely if couples were only more committed to each other, relationships would last. Regrettably, the evidence is otherwise.

The research is out-of-date, or from elsewhere. Few areas of social science research have been so consistent in their conclusions over such a long time, across many western nations, as is the data on marriage and family.[39]

It is just one study. Hundreds of studies are cited in this book, and for every study cited, there are often many others supporting the same conclusions.

This is a return to the common family structures of the past, with higher levels of de facto relationships and non-marital childbearing. In fact, the incidence of divorce, unwed childbearing and single parenting has reached significantly higher levels over the past few decades.

It is telling people how to live their lives. This work does not suggest that everyone should marry, before they are ready, in the face of serious doubts, under duress, or at all. But it does recognise that many people aspire to marriage, but have little knowledge of what works and what undermines success.

There is a need to move beyond these characterisations to discuss an issue of profound significance to many individuals and societies. Few individuals and families in the modern western world have not experienced the emotional grief and trauma wrought by separation and divorce within their immediate or extended family, or amongst friends or work colleagues. While most people confront their personal challenges with courage and resilience, there is an undeniable personal and communal cost. In a caring society, it should not be ignored.

The greatest threat facing the western world is not climate change or global warming. It is not the continuing financial crisis. Nor is it the threat of radical Islam. The greatest threat is within. It is the steady, but continuing breakdown of the essential structures of civil society – marriage, family and community.

Acknowledgements

This book is built upon my study of and writings about marriage and family for more than two decades.[40] Over that time, I have been fortunate to participate in a series of national and international conferences and meetings. In 1998, I examined some of the data in two publications, *Changing Australia*, which tracked the social, cultural and economic trends in the nation;[41] and in *To have and to hold*, the report of the Parliamentary Inquiry I chaired into strategies to strengthen marriage and relationships. In researching and writing the chair's draft of what became the report of the inquiry, I was able to gather together much of the international social science research then published.

My wife, Margaret, and I have facilitated marriage preparation programs for the past 30 years as part of a team of couples. The program has supported more than 20,000 people on their pathway to marriage. It has brought me into direct discussions with many young couples about their motivations, aspirations, hopes, and fears regarding marriage.

After returning to the families' portfolio in 2009, I was curious to learn if there had been any change in the many adverse consequences of divorce and single parenthood that had been identified in the 1990s. Had the negative trends identified in the research been compounded or ameliorated? Had the policy initiatives taken in the meantime had any impact? In this book, I have drawn liberally upon and updated earlier research with hundreds of subsequent studies.

I have been fortunate also to discuss these issues over many years with some of the foremost family scholars, researchers, practitioners and policy-makers in the world. Where possible, I have drawn upon international experience and examples, but I do not claim this to be a comprehensive study of every development globally. The emphasis is on the English-speaking world – Australia, Britain, Canada, New Zealand and the USA – in particular, partly because of language, and partly because the model of the family which developed in these countries differs in some respects from that which developed on continental Europe,[42] and elsewhere.

I would like to acknowledge and thank the following people for their generosity over many years:

In the USA: Herbert Anderson, David Blankenhorn, Thomas Bradbury, the late Don S Browning, Allan Carlson, Bill Coffin, William Doherty, Patrick Fagan, Mary Ann Glendon, Harville Hendrix, Wade Horn, Jennifer Marshall, John Mueller, David Popenoe, Diane Sollee and Scott Stanley.

In the UK: Catherine Hakim, Jonathan Sacks, Iain Duncan Smith and Philippa Stroud.

In Australia: Alan Craddock, Moira Eastman, Patrick Parkinson and Ruth Weston.

I also wish to acknowledge the many other social scientists, and marriage and family practitioners, particularly members of the Marriage Education Programme Inc., who have shared their experience and expertise with me. I acknowledge the assistance of my personal staff, the staff of the Australian Parliamentary Library and the members and staff of the various Parliamentary Committees with whom I have had the opportunity to examine these issues. I also thank Margaret and Catherine Andrews and Marcella Reiter for their professional comments on the manuscript.

I offer the usual caveat: While I am indebted to many people for their generosity and assistance over the past three decades, the interpretations and conclusions in this book are my own.

Finally, I wish to thank my wife, Margaret, for sharing over 30 years of marriage with me; and our children, Emily, James, Stuart, Catherine and Benjamin, for grounding us in the joys and challenges of married life.

NOTE

When social scientists point to increased risks associated with certain behaviours or family structures, it means there is a higher possibility that the risk will eventuate. To use an analogy, when health professionals point to an increased risk of cancer as a consequence of smoking, it does not mean that every smoker will get cancer; and some non-smokers will suffer the disease. However, the risk of cancer is greater for smokers. Similarly, a risk associated with family structure does not mean that every person will act in a particular way, or that the negative outcome will eventuate for every person in a particular category or circumstance. But a higher proportion of people in the category will bear the predicted consequences.

ONE

PART ONE

MARRIAGE MATTERS

The first society was between man and wife, which gave beginning to that between parents and children. (John Locke)

The fact itself, of causing the existence of a human being, is one of the most responsible actions in the range of human life. To undertake this responsibility – to bestow a life which may be a curse or a blessing – unless the being on whom it is to be bestowed will have at least the ordinary chances of a desirable existence, is a crime against that being. (John Stuart Mill)

For adults, a stable, happy marriage is the best protector against illness and premature death, and for children, such a marriage is the best source of emotional stability and good physical health. (William Doherty)

I do not believe that the real life of this nation is to be found either in great luxury hotels and the petty gossip of so called fashionable suburbs, or in the officialdom of organised masses. It is to be found in the home of people who are nameless and unadvertised, and who, whatever their individual religious conviction or dogma, see in their children their greatest contribution to the immortality of their race. The home is the foundation of sanity and sobriety; it is the indispensable condition of continuity; its health determines the health of society as a whole. (Robert Menzies)

1

THE PURSUIT OF MARITAL HAPPINESS

A happy marriage and family life remain the aspiration of most people. The many thousands of weddings each year are a testament to this ambition. Even where a marriage has ended in separation and divorce, many re-enter marriage or other relationships in the hope that it will work a second or subsequent time.

Functional families are crucial for the raising of children and the stability and well-being of society. Throughout history, the health of the family unit has been a barometer for the health and wellbeing of both individuals and society. Across civilisations and cultures, the family has served the vital functions of providing affection, cooperation and socialisation, and for procreation and the regulation of sexuality. Although a legal contract that creates formal obligations between spouses, marriage is more than a piece of paper that establishes a financial partnership. It is also a personal and a family-making bond.[43]

The lessons that families teach us about the relationships between persons are essential to both our private lives, and to our public relationships:

> It is in the family that we learn to identify ourselves with others or fail to learn to love. It is in family that we learn to give and take with others or fail to learn to be reciprocal. It is in the family that we learn to trust others as we depend on them or learn to distrust them. We learn to form expectations of

others and hold them accountable. We learn to hold ourselves accountable. These lessons of reciprocity, trust, discipline and self-restraint are important to forming of relationships in public life.[44]

Marriage is a relationship within which a community socially approves and encourages sexual intercourse and the birth of children.[45] The demographer, Kingsley Davis, writes: "The genius of [marriage] is that, through it, the society normally holds the biological parents responsible for each other and for their offspring. By identifying children with their parents, and by penalising people who do not have stable relationships, the social system powerfully motivates individuals to settle into a sexual union and take care of ensuing offspring."[46]

In western societies, marriage has evolved as a complex institution, containing at least five dimensions: the natural, religious, economic, social and legal.[47] While romantic love has grown in importance, the procreation of children and the provision of a stable base for their development and education remain the core purpose of marriage.

The political philosopher Jean Bethke Elshtain writes, being a parent is not just another lifestyle choice:

> It is in fact a series of tasks properly conceived as an ethical vocation. And we, as a society, should lighten the burden and smooth the path for parents in order that the complex joys of family life might rise to the surface and in order that the undeniable burdens of family responsibility might be more openheartedly born. In light of the public and social import of the family, we must also recognise that protecting, preserving, and strengthening mothers and fathers and their well-being is a way of affirming our commitment to the individual and to that democratic society that best speaks for the aspirations of individuals. We must re-weave the bonds of democratic community by rebuilding our primary institutions. And we must begin with the institutions of marriage and the family.[48]

Marriage remains popular

Although the pathways into marriage have changed substantially in recent decades, more people remain unmarried, divorce has increased markedly, and attitudes to other forms of relationship liberalised, a committed marriage remains significant for most people.[49]

The *World Values Survey*, collected between 1999 and 2007, found that with the exception of Sweden, the vast majority of adults globally believe a child needs to be raised in a home with both a mother and a father in order to grow up happily. The overwhelming majority of adults also disagree that marriage is outdated.[50] In the US, the majority of young people report that having a good marriage and family life is extremely important to them, but many have low expectations of ever experiencing a healthy romantic relationship or marriage.[51] Regardless of social background, marriage and family life remains a widely shared aspiration. This desire has increased over the past two decades from 77 per cent who said they would choose marriage in 1975 to 80 per cent in 1995.[52]

Teenage views on marriage

The majority of American teens believe it is best to get married, regardless of racial background.[53] Nearly two-thirds of the High School-aged teens in the 2002 *National Survey of Family Growth* agreed with the statement: "It is better for a person to get married than to go through life being single."[54] It seems, perhaps surprisingly, that young males view marriage more favourably than do females, according to results from a University of Michigan *Monitoring the Future* survey. While four in ten male high school seniors agreed that people who marry have happier lives than those who remain single or cohabit, the percentage of females who agreed fell from a similar level in 1976 to 28.5 per cent by 2000.[55] Although teens growing up with both parents tend to have more traditional attitudes towards marriage, cohabitation and divorce, less than half of them approve of divorce as a remedy for a troubled marriage.[56]

The *Australian Temperament Project* revealed that 92 per cent of 17 and 18 year olds hoped to experience a long-term relationship, with 81 per cent hoping to be in such a relationship within five years.[57] Four out of five also hoped to marry in the future. The later *Household, Income and Labour Dynamics in Australia Survey* found that 72 per cent of 18 and 19 year olds who were neither married nor cohabiting at the time expected to marry in the future.[58]

Young adults' attitudes to marriage

The proportion of young American adults who express that having a 'good' marriage has also increased since the 1980s.[59] In a national survey of 11,980 young adults aged 20-24, 83 per cent of unmarried respondents reported that they thought it was important to be married someday, compared with five per cent who considered it unimportant and 12 per cent who felt it was only somewhat important.[60] More than three-quarters of the young adults agreed that love, fidelity and making a life-long commitment were very important to a successful relationship. Other research reveals that 82 per cent of young adults expect to be married for life.[61] A survey of graduate law and MBA students in Michigan found that a large majority identified 'family' as the primary source of long-term meaning in life.[62] This reflects a Gallup survey of women aged 20 to 29 which revealed that 89 per cent considered a good marriage and family life extremely important.[63] A more recent Rasmussen poll found that 78 per cent of American adults rate marriage as at least somewhat important (with 60 per cent considering it very important) and only three per cent saying that it is not at all important.[64] A two parent home was rated as very important by 77 per cent of children.

Similarly, the Australian *Family Values Survey*, and the two earlier *National Social Science Surveys*, found:

- 61 per cent of people thought that husband and wife should do most things as a couple;

- 80 per cent of people agreed that one's really important relationships are in the home;
- 78 per cent agreed that marriage is for life;
- 87 per cent disapproved of marrying thinking that divorce is an option if it does not work out; and
- 70 per cent thought it is too easy to get a divorce.[65]

The surveys also revealed that:
- only 19 per cent of people thought a couple should stay together for the children;
- 53 per cent said it was not acceptable to have children without being married; and
- 32 per cent disapproved of a man and a woman living together without planning marriage.[66]

According to the family researcher, David de Vaus, "the majority of people in the three surveys ... held many traditional family values."[67] Asked about what is important for a successful marriage, the respondents rated faithfulness (9.6 out of 10), good communication (9.5), mutual respect (9.5), and understanding and tolerance (9.1) as the most important characteristics.[68]

The emphasis on faithfulness and commitment was also reflected in the attitudes of couples participating in a national survey of pre-marriage education programs. "The predominant paradigm is very clearly one of relationship caring and sharing," reported the researchers about the participants' attitudes to marriage:

> Couples continually used such concepts as growing together, love, trust, caring, understanding, togetherness, supporting each other, friendship, intimacy, affection and living for each other. Very few responses explicitly referred to the economic, political or sexual dimensions of marriage. Running through the hundreds of responses were five very common though not

discrete themes centred on commitment, companionship in sharing life together, family/children, love between best friends and union under God.[69]

American scholars analysing surveys conducted from the 1960s through the 1990s found a growing commitment to children, marriage and family life.[70] As compared to the 1970s, young Americans in the 1990s were more committed to the importance of a good marriage and family life ... Furthermore, both motherhood and fatherhood are generally viewed as more fulfilling today than they were in the mid 1970s." The findings were reinforced by another study comparing attitudes in 1980 and 2000, which found that "support for the norm of life-long marriage" had significantly reduced divorce proneness and increased marital happiness."[71]

A study of emerging adults – 18-23 year olds – also found that "close relationships, getting married, having children, and enjoying good friends" were the most frequently mentioned goals of a good life.[72] These young adults often combined marriage and family with a few other goals in their responses. There is also some evidence that subsequent generations have less liberal social attitudes about marriage than those born growing-up in the 1960s. A British *Social Attitudes Survey* found that 49 per cent of those who were young in the sixties disapproved of extramarital sex, compared to 56 per cent of youth a decade later.[73] Amongst Asians and Muslims, commitment to marriage remains very high.[74]

Married couples

Amongst married couples, support for marriage increased over the two decades from 1980 to 2000, as Professor Paul Amato and colleagues demonstrated in their analysis of national data.

Support for Marriage

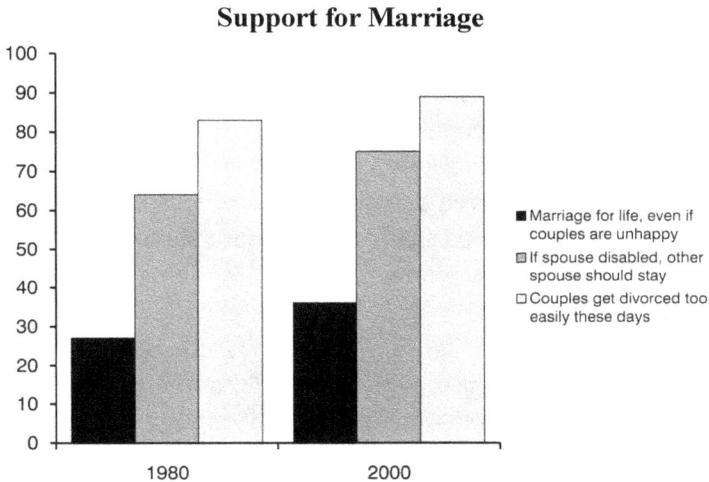

Source: Paul Amato *et al* (2007) *Alone together* [Cambridge MA, Harvard University Press], after 198 (percentages)

A more recent analysis of the *National Longitudinal Study of Adolescent Health* revealed that more than three-quarters of young adults aged 20 – 24 agreed that love (91 per cent of women and 81 per cent of men), fidelity (93 per cent of women and 85 per cent of men) and making a lifelong commitment (82 per cent of women and 72 per cent of men) were very important to a successful relationship.[75] A recent Rasmussen survey found that 45 per cent of adults think it is too easy to get a divorce these days, 35 per cent think it is about right and eight per cent think it too hard. Eighty per cent of Americans believe it's very important for children to grow up in a home with both their parents.[76]

These results are reflected in other surveys. The *National Fatherhood Initiative Marriage Survey* found that large majorities agree that, "all things being equal, it is better for children to be raised in a household that has a married mother and father" (89 per cent), that "fathers are as important as mothers for the proper development of children" (97 per cent), and that "couples who marry should make a lifelong commitment to one another, to be broken only under rare circumstances" (88 per cent). Furthermore, large percentages disagreed with such statements as "marriage is an old-fashioned, outmoded institution" (88 per cent), and "given how long people are living these days, it is unrealistic to expect a couple to remain married to one another for life" (78 per cent). Ninety-four per cent agreed that divorce is a serious national problem, and 71 per cent *disagreed* that "either spouse should be allowed to terminate a marriage at any time."[77]

Happy marriages

The research reflected the experience of life, as well as beliefs about marriage and family. Sixty-nine per cent of the married respondents said their marriages were "very happy" and 88 per cent said they were either "completely satisfied" or "very satisfied" with their marriages.[78] However, other surveys have different conclusions. An alternative measure, known as the *Marital Success Index*, revealed that only 43 per cent of those aged 25 and over were in marriages they reported to be "very happy" with the remaining 57 per cent being either unmarried or in marriages of lesser quality.[79] *General Social Surveys* conducted by the National Opinion Research Center at the University of Chicago have also recorded a 20 percentage point decline in the number of people who reported being "very happy" in their marriage between 1973 and 2002.[80]

Even previously married respondents generally expressed support for marriage, especially for the raising of children. Three-quarters of people agreed that "most couples I know have happy, healthy marriages" and nine out of ten said that they would marry their spouse if they had the chance to do it again.

Similarly, the British *Social Attitudes Survey* has satisfaction with family life growing from 87 per cent of respondents in 2001 to 89.47 per cent in 2006.[81] Only 9.26 per cent of respondents in 2000 and 8.55 per cent of respondents in 2006 thought that marriage was "just a piece of paper". A recent survey of young adults in the UK revealed that 80 per cent expected to marry and have children.[82] In another survey of 2,000 students aged 13-15 in the UK, only four per cent agreed with the statement that 'marriage is old fashioned and no longer relevant'.[83]

It is also the case that the importance of children for a happy marriage has diminished in popular perception. A 2007 study by the US Pew Research Center found that 41 per cent of people considered children very important to a successful marriage, compared to 65 per cent in 1990. Sixty-five per cent of the respondents considered marriage to be for mutual happiness and fulfilment, compared to 23 per cent who said that bearing and raising children is the main purpose of marriage. Yet seven-in-ten thought it important that if a couple have children together, they should marry. A similar proportion believed it important that if a man and a woman intend to spend their life together, they should marry.[84]

Whether single or cohabiting, more than 60 per cent of Americans expected to marry one day. Two-thirds of people were optimistic about the institution of marriage and the family. As the authors of a subsequent Pew report note:

> The decline of marriage has not knocked family life off its pedestal. Three-quarters of all adults (76 per cent) say their family is the most important element of their life, 75 per cent say they are "very satisfied" with their family life, and more than eight-in-ten say the family they live in now is as close (45 per cent) or closer than (40 per cent) the family they grew up in.[85]

Satisfaction varied widely with a person's marital status. Eight in ten married people reported that they were very satisfied with family life, compared to 71 per cent of those living together, 66 per cent of the single and 50 of the divorced or separated. For parents, children remain a very significant source of happiness and fulfilment, matched only by spouses, and situated well above that of jobs, career, friends, hobbies and other relatives. Analysing four waves of the Australian *Quality of Life panel survey*, Bruce Headey and colleagues at the University of Melbourne concluded that "being happily married increases one's life satisfaction, but it is also true that happy people are more likely to maintain happy marriages."[85a]

In another analysis, Charles Murray notes in the US that fifty-eight per cent of white prime-age respondents to the *General Social Survey* reported that they were in very happy marriages, compared to 10 per cent who said their marriages were "pretty happy" and eight per cent who said their marriages were "not too happy:" "Even without asking whether the marriage itself is happy, marriage is still a good bet for achieving happiness."[86] The currently married reported more happiness than the separated, divorced, cohabiting, widowed and never-married.

These surveys show that most teens and adults continue to value marriage despite concerns that the institution is in decline.[87] It is also clear that while the majority of young adults aspire to marriage, they have decided to delay it for a variety of reasons,[88] including 'getting set' financially, and a commitment to individual autonomy.[89] Marriage still matters to most people. Despite the 'bad press' that marriage often receives, it remains a popular aspiration. In the next two chapters, the importance of marriage for the health, well-being and happiness of adults and children will be considered.

SUMMARY

- ♥ Most people aspire to a happy marriage and family.
- ♥ Marriage remains a popular aspiration among young people,
  - ➤ But they are in no rush to tie the knot.
- ♥ Most people hope to have children and believe that it is best that children grow up in a home with two parents.
- ♥ Being a parent is not just another lifestyle choice. It is the means by which happy and healthy children are raised.
- ♥ Most married people are happy in their relationships.

2

HAPPY, HEALTHY AND SECURE ADULTS

Marriage has a significant 'protective effect' on the health, well-being, longevity and happiness of both men and women.[90] As the most common and ubiquitous intimate adult relationship, marriage has more of a bearing on overall happiness in life than any other factor. The University of California Los Angeles psychologists, Thomas Bradbury and Benjamin Karney, write in their encyclopaedic work on relationships, "satisfaction with one's intimate relationship tells us more about someone's overall subjective well-being than does their satisfaction with any other domain in life, including work, finances, friendships, community, and health."[91] In a survey of the factors contributing to overall happiness in life, Bruce Headey and colleagues found that marriage was by far the most significant contributor.[92] The closest other factors were family and health. Other research has revealed that as people approach marriage, their subjective well-being increases,[93] but decreases as they approach divorce.[94]

Decades of research has also clearly established links between health and well-being, and marriage, separation and divorce.[95] Professor William Doherty notes that "for adults, a stable, happy marriage is the best protector against illness and premature death, and for children, such a marriage is the best source of emotional stability and good physical health."[96] A considerable body of research evidence indicates that adults and children are at increased risk for mental and physical problems due to marital distress.[97] "There is both conclusive evidence to show that marriage is a 'healthy environment' associated with lower mortality and morbidity and strong evidence that the process of divorce leaves men, women and children vulnerable to ill-health." As Canadian psychologists observed after a study of over 11,000 men and women, "entry into marriage is associated with lower levels of distress and a transition out of marriage increases psychological distress."[98] Any initiative which aims to prevent ill-health and promote good health should take account of this reality.[99]

In a review of the literature, Professor Linda Waite, observed:

> In a variety of ways and along a number of dimensions, married men and women lead healthier lives than the unmarried. This includes more drinking, substance abuse, drinking and driving and generally living dangerously among single men. Married women more often have access to health insurance. Divorced and widowed men and women are more likely to get into arguments and fights, do dangerous things, take chances that could cause accidents. The married lead more ordered lives, with healthier eating and sleeping habits. Marriage improves both men's and women's psychological well-being. Perhaps as a result, married men and women generally live longer than single men and women.[100]

Marriage has a marked effect on health and welfare. To take just a few examples from the research:[101]

- Married men and women have lower death rates than the unmarried.
- Marriage seems to protect from developing cancer and offers a better chance of survival after diagnosis.
- Premature death rates from cardiovascular disease,[102] pneumonia and hypertension and stroke are all lower for the married.
- The married have fewer mental health problems, and smoke[103] and drink[104] much less than separated or divorced men and women.
- The *National Health Strategy* found that with some exceptions,

the married are at less risk of dying than the never married, widowed or divorced.

- Indeed, marital status has a stronger correlation with death than socio-economic status for most major causes of death.

Furthermore:

- Relationship breakdown is one of the major causes of suicide and the divorced have a three to four-fold increased risk.
- Married people have far higher psycho-social wellbeing.
- Married people express higher levels of satisfaction with their sex lives than cohabiting people.[105]

Recent research provides further evidence of the link between loss, grief and the risk of a heart attack. According to the study of nearly 2,000 adults who survived a heart attack, the risk soared 21 times in the first day after the loss of a loved one, before slowly declining. Previous studies had shown that grieving spouses have higher risks of dying over the long term from heart attacks and strokes.[106]

Indeed, the longer people remain married, the lower the risks they face in developing chronic conditions.[107] While remarriage can mitigate partly the effects of divorce, "those who have married once and remained married are consistently, strongly, and broadly advantaged." "On all the dimensions we examined," Mary Hughes and Linda Waite conclude in a recent study, "currently married persons who have never been divorced or widowed show better health than currently married persons who have ever experienced a marital loss."[108]

These conclusions are not confined to the United States or Britain.[109] In a study of Canadian women aged 25, 60 and 64, scholars found that "married women reported the best health and formerly married women the worst," with never-married women falling between the two.[110] Professor Denis Ladbrook notes that the conclusions drawn from the overseas data are broadly replicable in Australia.[111]

These outcomes are reflected in surveys of happiness. An Australian survey of almost 40,000 people found the married the most happy in the nation. According to one of the researchers, Jonathan Kelley, "it isn't just that happier people marry but when we follow single people over time, we find their happiness is actually boosted by marriage."[112] Both the separated and divorced, and cohabiters had much lower levels of happiness.

HEALTH

Mortality

Virtually every study that has analysed mortality rates by marital status shows that the unmarried have higher death rates, a finding confirmed since the 1930s in every country for which accurate health data exists.[113] In a comparative study of 16 developed countries, Professors Hu and Goldman found that not only is being married associated with increased longevity, but that the excess mortality of the unmarried relative to the married has been increasing over the past two or three decades; and divorced and widowed people in their twenties and thirties have particularly high risks of premature deaths.[114] Swedish scholars replicated the US findings, noting that men living alone, apart from their children experienced "almost four times as great a risk of all-cause mortality, 10 times of death from external violence, 13 times from fall and poisoning, almost five times from suicide, and 19 times from addiction."[115]

Morowitz re-examined earlier data which had documented the health risk of smoking and found that non-smokers who were divorced had only a slightly lower risk of dying from cancer than married men who smoked a pack or more of cigarettes a day.[116] In another study, David Larson found that the age specific death rate for divorced people in the United States is 84 per cent higher than for married people. This translates to a loss of ten years life per divorced man, the equivalent in health terms of smoking a pack of cigarettes a day for the rest of one's life.[117]

In a study of professional women in Wisconsin, Ladbrook found that the pattern of mortality in the US whereby males usually die six years earlier than females was reversed. The main factor accounting for this reversal was the higher ratio of women who were never married, widowed, separated or divorced compared with the married, than was the case with men. A considerably higher percentage of men than women in this category were married and they were living longer than the women in the category.[118]

Marriage seems to protect from contracting cancer and offers better chance of survival after diagnosis. Professor Lilienfield found that nearly every type of terminal cancer inflicted divorced persons of both sexes more frequently than it did the married. Divorced males had double the rate of respiratory cancer, and four-fold increase in buccal cavity and pharynx (throat) cancer, and more than a 50 per cent increase in cancer of the digestive system and peritoneum and urinary tract.[119] In a subsequent study, Goodwin found that married cancer patients did better medically than unmarried cancer patients.[120] Similar results were found by researchers in Norway who suggest that marital status beneficially influences life style: "[T]he married may also tend to avoid unhealthy and risky behaviour because of social control within the family and a feeling of responsibility for spouse and children."[121]

In a study of over 10,000 Finnish women, divorce and/or separation was shown to be the stressful life event most likely to predict breast cancer.[122] Acknowledging that no study had "established a direct link between physiologic changes associated with life events and breast carcinogenesis," the epidemiologists conjectured that stressful life events could cause changes in the hormonal system, which, in turn, elevate the risk of breast cancer.

In addition to cancer, researchers have found a number of other diseases that have contributed to increased mortality among the divorced and separated. Lynch reviewed the mortality data from the

National Center for Health Statistics on all deaths over a two year period and found that the premature death rate from cardiovascular disease, for both white and non-white divorced men, was double that of married men; the premature death rate due to pneumonia for white divorced men was more than seven times that of their married counterparts; and the premature death rate due to hypertension and cardiovascular diseases was double for divorced men compared to their married counterparts.[123] As Fiona McAllister notes in her survey of the literature, "marital status has long been identified as one of the social characteristics associated with heart disease and stroke."[124] She also notes that "as in the case with cancer, there is also evidence of superior survival rates following myocardial infarction among the married, in comparison to other marital status groups."

A study of more than 6,000 white women aged 65 and older in the US found that both higher social network scores and marriage were potent predictors of lower death rates, independent of demographic variables, pre-existing disease and other psychological measures.[125] While the epidemiologists from the University of Pittsburg and the University of California acknowledged that the mechanisms that conferred longer life were poorly understood, the role of marriage was unmistakable: "[I]n this sample, marital status – and not social network scores – was the most consistent predictor of subsequent mortality, and marriage explained most – but not all – of the mortality relationships with social network scores." Another study has linked lower blood pressure readings for the married, compared to their unmarried peers.[126]

Australian studies support these conclusions.[127] In *Health Differentials Among Working Age Australians*, Professor Lee and colleagues identify the health risks of the never married and the divorced and widowed:

There are very large differences in mortality between married/ separated men on the one hand, and never married and divorced/ widowed men on the other. The latter groups have standardised rates over twice the former's ... Separated/divorced/widowed men have more acute symptoms and mental health problems and smoke and drink more, although only the smoking and mental health differences are of comparable magnitude to the mortality differences.

The differences between women in different marital status groups are not quite as extreme as those for men, but the mortality of never-married women is still 80 per cent higher than that of married women, and that of divorced/widowed women over 60 per cent higher. The separated/divorced/widowed women in the surveys also report mental health problems, and smoke, at levels 80 per cent above married women, and they report 20 per cent more acute and chronic symptoms, the latter in contrast to men in the same group who show no excess.[128]

The subsequent 1992 report of the National Health Strategy, *Enough to make you sick,* confirmed the strong correlations between marital status and health outcomes: "With the exception of stomach cancer, brain cancer, pancreatic cancer (in women) and prostate cancer (in men), married individuals aged 25-64 are at less risk of dying from all selected causes of death than never married individuals, widowed/ divorced individuals or both (of the same age)."[129]

Although the National Health Strategy concentrates on inequalities related to low socioeconomic status, Moira Eastman analysed the data to show a striking correlation between marital status and mortality rates for both men and women. Dr. Eastman concludes: *"Enough to make you sick* gives the eight causes of death for which correlations are strongest between low socio-economic status and cause of death. For seven of these causes of death, correlations are even stronger with marital status. That is, the never-married, widowed and divorced have higher death rates on seven of these eight causes of death compared with the married than do the lowest socio-economic bracket compared with the highest socio-economic bracket."[130] The mortality rates of individuals with poor social relationships are higher than those who smoke cigarettes for many years.[131]

More recently, scientists have linked negative social interactions to increased inflammation of tissues and bodily organs, which in turn may trigger illnesses ranging from cancer and heart disease and high blood pressure.[132] Conversely, positive psychological well-being as measured by optimism, life satisfaction, and happiness, are associated with reduced risk of cardiovascular disease, regardless of other factors such as a person's age, socio-economic status, smoking status or body weight, according to researchers at the Harvard School of Public Health.[133]

The effects of marriage on mortality appear to extend also to neighbourhoods. American researchers found in one study that "residents of neighbourhoods where more than 21 per cent of residents aged 18-64 have never been married have higher levels of mortality compared to those neighbourhood where only nine per cent have never been married."[134]

Scholars have wondered why marriage confers significant health effects, particularly for men. Scott Stanley observes that most scholars assume that it is because wives tell their husbands what to do in very important ways:

> I'm pretty sure that one major reason that men live approximately eight years longer if they are married (and are otherwise healthier in various ways) is that their wives tell them what to do and they do some of what their wives tell them.[135]

Suicides and accidents

"Relationship breakdown is one of the major causes of suicide worldwide, and the differential in mortality rates by marital status is huge," notes the One plus One Marriage and Partnership Research Foundation in the UK. "This reflects the experience of loss and depression often associated with divorce and separation."[136] As the British scholar, Fiona McAllister, and her colleagues found, the divorced have a three to four-fold higher risk of suicide than the married.[137]

Dr Moira Eastman notes that "for men and women the divorced/ widowed have suicide rates over three times that of the married and the never married rates are almost three times the rate of the married."[138] UK research reports that those who are separated but not divorced have suicide rates 20 times that of the married.[139] An Australian study at Griffith University of 4000 suicides found that 70 per cent were caused by relationship breakups. Men were nine times more likely to commit suicide than women.[140] A more recent Australian study indicates that the risk of suicide among the divorced, separated and widowed is almost three-quarters again of that found among the married, and climbs even higher among the never-married.[141] An American study found that for every percentage increase in the proportion of divorced women in a county, the suicide rate increased by 7.5 per cent. The pioneering French sociologist, Emile Durkheim, noted: "Divorce is a mechanism that breaks the ties that bind individuals to society ... Accordingly, communities wracked with high divorce rates also tend to have high suicide rates due to weakened regulation and integration."[142]

Professor Ladbrook observes, "marriage, parenting and other social relationships and the obligations that these ties entail actually give a protective solidarity that is less easily available to and accessible by people who live in isolated circumstances."[143] Other researchers, also finding that previously married men and women were more likely to have suicidal thoughts, concluded that there is a "protective effect of marriage."[144]

Family violence and homicides

Family violence by definition involves relationship stress. Although it is difficult to accurately measure family violence, various studies and statistics reveal a considerable problem.[145] An ABS survey, *Crime and Safety in Australia*, indicated that 0.7 per cent of adult women had been victims of assault or threatened at their home. According to a community law reform paper, 3.5 per cent of all police call-outs in the Australian Capital Territory related to domestic incidents, of which one-in-five involved an assault. Victorian police statistics for 1994-95 revealed that there were 13,485 calls to family incidents, of which nearly 14 per cent definitely involved violence against a person. Western Australian police records suggest an annual incident of 109 assaults per 100,000 be males on females and 13 per 100,000 be females on males.

Another ABS survey of 6,300 women aged 18 and over across Australia found that 7 per cent of women had experienced violence in the previous 12 months. When applied to the nation, the survey *Women's Safety*, suggested that 490,000 women (7.1 per cent) had experienced an incident of violence. It indicated that 429,000 women (6.2 per cent) had experienced violence by a man and 110,700 by a woman (1.6 per cent), and 33 per cent of women who experienced violence in the previous 12 months reported incidents by more than one perpetrator. Violence was defined in the survey as any incident involving the occurrence, attempt or threat of either physical or sexual assault.

The National Committee on Violence claims that domestic violence is the most common form of abuse in Australia. According to the National Homicide Monitoring Program, "just under one-half of all female victims of homicide were killed whether directly or indirectly as a result of a dispute between intimate partners." Twenty-two per cent of all Queensland homicides between 1982 and 1987 were spousal murders. In New South Wales, 43 per cent of all homicides between 1968 and 1981 were within the family; and 23 per cent of these occurred between spouses. In 1992, 7,492 violent crimes were reported to South Australian police by females, of which 18.2 per cent have been classified as domestic violence. This represents a rate of 3.4 per 1,000 married, separated and divorced women. Other studies also reveal unacceptably high levels of family violence.

Although separation and divorce are intended to reduce conflict and violence, there is a consistent and regrettable link between the two.[146] Using Federal Bureau of Investigation data, US criminologists have shown that diversification of family structure amongst whites has contributed to white homicide rates.[147] Moreover, "neighbourhoods with larger portions of adults who are less 'invested' in marriage and residential stability are more likely to see higher rates of assault by African-American males."[148]

Married women in the US are also much less likely to serve time in jail than their never-married and separated sisters.[149] Another study by scholars at Harvard and the University of Maryland concluded that "states of marriage causally inhibit crime over the life course."[150] Scholars from the Social Research Center in Baltimore found that less than one-eighth of mothers jailed for drug offences were married or in long-term relationships. Observing an intergenerational effect, they also noted that a majority of the women were "victims of adverse circumstances in their lives related to a breakdown in the integrity of their families of origin and a consequent degradation of the parental guidance and emotional support they received during their early development." Almost two-thirds of the women were born to natural parents who had either separated or had never lived together, four-in-ten had grown up with their mother as sole supporter, and a quarter had no father figure.[151]

There is also some evidence that the incidence of conflict is higher in cohabiting relationships. Australian, Canadian and American researchers have found that "the risk of experiencing violence is higher for a woman living in a *de facto* rather than a married relationship."[152] An American sample of households with teenage children concluded that "stably married couples ... have the lowest rates of Intimate Partner Violence" while "cohabiting couples show the highest rates."[153] A study of battered mothers in Italy and the United States found nearly all the abusers in Italy were present or formers husbands but domestic violence was much more common amongst the unmarried couples in North America.[154] Dr Sotirios Sarantakas in his study *Living Together in Australia* found that there are more cohabitants reporting conflicts (29 per cent) than married, of whom 18 per cent admitted having conflicts of some kind. Furthermore, the study shows that cohabiters, especially women, seem to tolerate in their partner types of behaviour which marriers consider unacceptable.[155] In a review of the literature, Professor Sarantakos also observed that significant family violence occurs against men as well as women.[156] It also seems that the unmarried are less likely to report crime than the married.[157]

Morbidity

Both perceived physical and mental health have been found to be related to marital status in a way similar to mortality.[158] Professor Cox and colleagues suggest a beneficial effect of marriage on psycho-social health (measured by malaise score 'symptoms' including worrying, feeling lonely and having difficulty sleeping) after examining two surveys of health data on the British population.[159] Those who married between the two surveys were more likely to either declare lower malaise scores at both times or to move into a lower category, that is, higher psycho-social well-being, in the follow-up. Of the married women who reported average or high malaise at the first survey, 32 per cent dropped to the low category, as compared with only 10 per cent of those who remained single. Similarly, analysis of the US data indicates that married men and women in all age groups are less likely to be limited in activity (a general health indice) due to illness than single, separated, divorced, or widowed people.[160] Professor Ladbrook observes: "Clearly having someone at home who cares, supervises and calls for help is an enormous advantage over being alone or in an unnoticing or caring social environment when one is ill."[161]

The findings extend to the psychopathology of adults who experience divorce. A US study by Chatav and Whisman concluded that "marital dissolution was associated with a 3.7-fold increased risk for mood disorders, a 2.5-fold increased risk for anxiety disorders, and a 3.3-fold increased risk for substance abuse."[162] Canadian scholars observed that "separated/divorced mothers had the highest frequencies of depression, dysthymia, General Anxiety Disorder, and alcohol abuse" while the "never-married and separated/divorced mothers had equally high frequencies of Post Traumatic Stress Disorder, drug abuse, and antisocial personality disorder."[163]

Marriage also seems to have a protective effect against some pre-existing conditions. A US study revealed that the previously depressed benefit more from marriage than the non-depressed even though their marital quality is slightly worse. The researchers, Adrianne Frech and Kristi Williams, speculate that "marriage may give a depressed person the sense that he or she matters to a spouse and to new social ties, whereas someone who was not depressed prior to marrying may have always felt that he or she matters to others."[164] Even in a vertical society, such as Japan, spousal presence has been shown to be important in "mitigating the presence of depressive symptoms."[165]

These trends extend to other behaviours. Alcohol consumption for example, has been found to be very much higher in the divorced,[166] and that twice as many marriages complicated by alcoholism end in divorce compared to marriages where alcohol problems are absent.[167] All unmarried men and women are more likely to smoke than their married peers, engage in hazardous drinking, suffer more from hypertension and diabetes, with lower survival rates, according to the findings of recent British and Swedish studies.[168] In a study of pregnant women, married women were 3.34 times more likely to abstain from smoking during gestation than their unmarked peers.[169]

A European study also suggests that men and women in intact marriages enjoy a significant level of protection against the debilitating effects of Alzheimer's disease: "There is a substantial and independent association between marital status in mid-life and cognitive function later in life," report the researchers. "People without a partner had twice the risk of developing cognitive impairment and Alzheimer's disease compared to people living with a partner."[170]

The impact of marriage even extends to the chances of being in a motor vehicle accident! In a US study, never-married drivers reported the highest collision rate (13 per cent), almost double that of married drivers (6.6 per cent).[171]

In America at least, the marital advantage extends to hospital care, with elderly patients without a spouse more likely to end up in lower quality hospitals and then require longer stays, perhaps because "the married ... have access to better information and better referral networks: better informed, they are able to make better choices about which hospitals to use and how to use them."[172]

Mental health

Using the idea of human 'flourishing' as a measure of psychological health, American mental health experts examined data from more than 3,000 people across the nation. The results indicated that the married were more likely to be 'flourishing' (20 per cent), compared to 15 per cent of the widowed, 13 per cent of the never married, 12 per cent of the separated, and 10 per cent of the divorced.[173] Conversely, the divorced and separated were more likely to be experiencing "pure depression".

In Australia, marriage itself has been found to be responsible for at least 61 per cent of the positive effect of marriage on the subjective well-being of married men and women: "stable marriage is the most satisfying lifestyle, on average and other things equal" and "divorce without remarriage, or long lasting cohabitation without formal marriage, reduces the life-time sum of subjective well-being by 4-12 per cent for both men and women."[174] Asking themselves the questions, "Does marriage make people happy?" or "Do happy people get married?" Swiss researchers studied more than 15,000 German men and women. They concluded that the selection effects could not fully explain the strong correlation between marriage and happiness, suggesting that factors in the marriage itself affected the outcome.[175]

Similarly, a major international study across 15 countries and more than 34,000 people found that getting married is positive for the mental health of both men and women. The New Zealand scholars, who conducted the study, also found that separation, divorce and widowhood is associated with a substantially increased risk of mental health disorders in both genders, particularly substance abuse for women and depression for men.[176]

Social isolation

People living alone have significant health disadvantages including depression.[177] A thirteen-year Norwegian study of 1,000 households revealed that mothers suffering from high levels of depression over an extended period were disproportionately single-mothers.[178] US studies reached similar conclusions: single-mothers were at increased risk for depression,[179] as did Canadian research.[180] This is consistent with Susan Campbell's studies that women with few symptoms[181] and with low stable depression[182] were more likely to be in stable marriages. According to a British study, divorce and separation have led to increased social isolation for many elderly people.[183]

Unsurprisingly, as Canadian research found, single-mother families not only had higher rates of family dysfunction and maternal depression, they also had "lower scores on social support."[184] A team of US psychiatrists concluded: "Perhaps for mothers, even in marriages of questionable quality, the presence of a partner alleviates some of the pressures and burdens of single-parenting."[185]

Divorced grandparents also report less contact and engaged in fewer shared activities with their adolescent grandchildren.[186]

Children also have a protective effect on adults. As Swedish scholars observe, "children give structure to custodial parents' lives; they provide much needed company and life-meaning, and also access to other adults (neighbours, close kin and friends)."[187]

Marital distress

Marital distress is an important health hazard for adults and children, concludes Professor William Doherty.[188] Marital distress leads to depression and reduces immune system functioning in adults. In addition, chronic marital conflict harms the emotional and physical well-being of children.[189] Scott Stanley and Howard Markman note in their review of the literature that "adults and children are at increased risk for mental and physical problems due to marital distress."[190]

The differences also manifest themselves around the birth of a child. Canadian psychologist, Genevieve Bouchard, found that couples in their first marriage had a more successful transition to parenthood than their peers where one or both of the partners had been in a previous marriage or cohabiting union.[191]

WELL-BEING

Employment

The advantages of marriage extend beyond physical and mental health. Using data collected between 1979 and 2004, researchers from the American and Haifa Universities show that marriage results in a "positive effect of men's motivation" in the workforce, producing behaviours that "signal reliability to employers." The study found that married men worked more hours per year, with a 12 per cent wage gain upon entry into marriage and a 18 per cent gain in continuing marriage, relative to remaining never married.[192]

Wealth

Being married has a significant effect on household wealth. Drawing on 25 years data collected between 1968 and 1992, scholars at Cornell and Washington Universities found that "marriage financially benefits both men and women" and that the benefit is much "more important for women than for men."[193] The study revealed "marriage in early adulthood doubles the odds of affluence." For older individuals, wedlock conferred an even more pronounced advantage. A 15-year study of 9,000 people in the US found that those who married and stayed married built up nearly twice the net worth of people who stayed single.[194]

According to one study, unmarried adults experience a 63 per cent reduction in total wealth relative to those who are married.[195] While acknowledging that there may be a selection effect at play, the researchers consider the possibility that marriage itself causes some of the better outcomes because "it provides institutionalised protection, which generates economies of scale, task specialisation, and access to work-related fringe benefits, which lead to rewards like broader social networks and higher savings rate." The same study suggested that remarriage appears to mitigate, but not eliminate, the harmful financial impact of separation and divorce. Subsequent research indicated that "ever-married women have a poverty rate that is roughly one-third lower than the poverty rate experienced by never-married women."[196] Underlying the significance of family structure, the researchers found that "the deleterious effect associated with a disadvantaged family back ground is completely offset by marrying and staying married" but "for women who marry, but later divorce, poverty rates are substantially higher than for never-married women."

A Canadian poll revealed that divorce had a significant adverse impact on individuals, with 35 per cent going into debt, 22 per cent having to seek financial support from family and friends, 28 per cent having to sell household items or personal assets, and 27 per cent having to sell or redeem financial investments.[197]

Employment and wealth are also linked to the chances of a single woman marrying after the birth of a child, according to a study by US sociologists. The higher the man's earnings, the more likely the couple will marry.[198]

Prior to the 'Global Financial Crisis' and the collapse of much of the US residential property market, Department of Housing and Urban Development economist, Darryl E Getter, concluded that divorce and separation were the economic variables likely to cause a default on home mortgage payments.[199] In Australia it has also been observed that the rate of home ownership for separated fathers and mothers is vastly lower than for parents who are still together.[200]

In another study of poverty levels, US Census Bureau economist, John Iceland, found that "family structure changes – mainly the growth in female-headed families – increased from 1949 through 1990, regardless of the poverty measure used."[201] While the poverty levels stabilised in the 1990s, the changes of the previous two decades had wrought significant damage. Unsurprisingly, "the loss of the wage-earning power of the absent parent, usually the father" is critical to the economic problems for many single-parent families.[202] Often the economic disadvantage extended to the subsequent wealth accumulation of the children of divorce.[203]

Divorce has long been connected with the 'feminisation of poverty'. Beginning with Lenore Weitzman's studies in the mid 1980s,[204] family scholars have observed the adverse consequence of marriage breakdown for many women.[205] While repartnering has allowed women to recover their financial position,[206] their opportunities are often limited.[207] Spousal support after separation and divorce remains very low in many countries.[208]

While it is widely asserted that divorce impoverishes women but enriches men, the latter appears mostly untrue. Using national American data, sociologists have concluded that "most men who separate do not experience gains in their living standards" and that the majority are financial losers from the process.[209] The increased incidence of 'shared parenting' in which children spend more time with both parents has changed the situation for many fathers.[210] Professor Patrick Parkinson notes:

> Whatever the situation may have been in the 1970s and 1980s, the situation now is that many men as well as women suffer from the loss of the other partner's income when relationships breakdown. While the economic impact of separation and divorce on women and men depends greatly on both their preseparation circumstances and their postseparation household composition, it is evident that in most cases both parents will suffer a loss in standard of living as long as both are having to meet the housing needs of the children in their separate households, with the duplication of housing cost, furnishings and appliances, and other such expenses, without suffering a significant loss of living standards.[211]

The negative impact of divorce and subsequent singlehood has also been demonstrated in an Australian study of people aged 55 to 74.[212] Conversely, a study of 100,000 people living in Britain and the US found that a happy marriage is worth an extra $150,000 in the bank.[213]

Being married has also been associated with better welfare outcomes. A study of 128,775 'assistance groups' (households), 95 per cent of which were headed by a mother, in the Tennessee 'First Families' welfare program between 1996 and 2001, found that the married had better outcomes and were less likely to enter the system.[214]

These studies indicate that marriage is good for the health and wellbeing of adults. Conversely, separation and divorce is an express lane to poverty for many people. Children particularly experience this impact, as the next chapter illustrates.

SUMMARY

- ♥ Marriage is a significant factor for the health, well-being and happiness of adults.
- ♥ Married men and women lead more healthy lives than the unmarried.
- ♥ Married men and women have lower mortality rates (including from disease, suicide and accidents) than the unmarried, including separated and divorced men and women.
- ♥ Marriage has a positive impact on the psychosocial health and well-being of adults.
- ♥ The married are less likely to be socially isolated.
- ♥ Marriage is associated with better employment outcomes, increased wealth generation, and higher levels of home ownership.

3

HAPPY, HEALTHY AND
WELL-ADJUSTED CHILDREN

Marriage is above all a protective institution for the wellbeing and welfare of children. A large number of studies have shown that marital disruption has both a short-term and a long-term impact on many children,[215] despite their resilience.[216] They also demonstrate that this impact often extends into adult life with consequences for health, family life, educational performance and occupational status.[217] In few areas of human endeavour has the evidence been so compelling, yet largely the media has ignored it. Few individuals comprehend the heightened risks and systemic disadvantages borne by children who do not grow up in stable, two-parent families.

Attachment and happiness

The sense of security that a child experiences from his or her earliest days is critical to their psychological development.[218] Beginning in the 1950s, the psychiatrist, John Bowlby, and the developmental psychologist, Mary Ainsworth, showed that one's early experiences of attachment are critical for all subsequent relationships. The interactions of children with their parents establish powerful dynamics of security and insecurity, with significant implications for subsequent adult relationships. The happiness of adults whose relationships in their early years were secure can differ greatly from those whose relationships were problematic and insecure. The latter are more likely to demonstrate either an avoidance of attachment in their later, adult relationships, or anxiety about their relationships, with corresponding behaviours. Children who show signs of insecure attachment, such as avoidant or ambivalent behaviours, most often have parents who were unresponsive or inconsistent in their responses to the child.[219] In a recent survey of 36 international studies, Abdul Khaleque and Ronald Rohner from the University of Connecticut concluded that children and adults everywhere – regardless of differences in race, culture, and gender – tend to respond in exactly the same way when they perceived themselves to be rejected by their caregivers and other attachment figures:

> In our half-century of international research, we've not found any other class of experience that has as strong and consistent effect on personality and personality development as does the experience of rejection, especially by parents in childhood.[220]

The circumstances of a child's early life are critical therefore for his or her future relationships and happiness. If those years are marked by insecurity and uncertainty, loss of contact with a parent, shifting 'caregivers' or inconsistent parenting, the child is likely to suffer the impact into his or her adult years.[221] Professor Scott Stanley observes:

> Attachment is an unalterable, important human need and reality, and how attachment systems form in individuals really matters for everything else that really matters.[222]

A child who is raised in an intact, caring family has a great advantage in life.[223] Conversely, as the following discussion indicates, those who do not have this opportunity are at greater risk, from which many suffer lasting consequences.[224]

The impact of divorce on children

Professor Norval Glenn, then editor of the *Journal of Family Issues*, wrote some three decades ago that the views of leading family scholars were beginning to shift from what he described as "continuity-sanguineness" about the condition of the family to "change-concern." He indicated that the scholars were becoming less likely to view current family trends as a process of gradual and even beneficial adaptation, and increasingly likely to view them as new and socially harmful. A decade later he confirmed the outlook: "Not all family social scientists participated in this shift, but it is significant that the most prominent scholars and those most directly involved in the relevant research were most likely to do so."[225]

An example of the shift is the work of Paul Amato. In 1987, while a fellow at the Australian Institute of Family Studies, Professor Amato had written in *Children in Australian Families: The Growth of Competence* that harmful stereotypes such as "staying together for the sake of the children" prevented us from seeing families as they really are. His later US research, published as *A Generation at Risk*, found that only one quarter to a third of divorces end up being better for the children than if the parents had stayed together. By contrast, about 70 per cent of divorces end low-conflict marriages, which would have been better for the children to have continued rather than ending.

Many commentators have observed that children have been the major losers of the social changes of the past three decades. Generally, Gross Domestic Product, health, and educational levels have risen, but consider the evidence of what is happening in many nations:

- Youth suicide has increased markedly.
- Reports of child abuse rise each year.
- Alcohol and drug abuse amongst teenagers has multiplied.
- Violence has increased.
- Welfare beneficiaries are much higher than two or three decades ago.
- Single parent families, even after government benefits, continue to be amongst the poorest groups in the community.

While the causes of these problems are complex, a recurring factor is the breakdown of marriages and the disintegration of family structures. Take two examples. The report of the Prime Ministerial

Taskforce on Youth Homelessness, *Putting Families in the Picture*, found that the majority of young people and families identified conflict in their relationship as the main reason for imminent or early home-leaving by young people.[226] Similarly, the draft *National Action Plan for Suicide Prevention* stated in part: "Young people with suicidal behaviours are less likely to be living with their biological parents and more likely to be from separated, divorced or single parent families or from families where there are interpersonal conflicts."[227]

This is not to say that family problems are the only causes of youth homelessness and suicide. These tragedies can strike any family without apparent reason or cause. Nonetheless, many reports attest to a recurring association between a range of social pathologies and marriage and family breakdown. Conversely, a series of studies reveal that healthy family life is the optimal environment for the wellbeing of both adults and children.

Short term impacts

In the short term, the age of children affected by divorce can relate to changes in behaviour. Professors Richards and Dyson note:

> The most common reactions in children are anger, directed at one or both parents, sadness and depression. In younger children, clinging to parents and 'regressive' reactions like bedwetting are frequently seen while older children may withdraw somewhat from the home and seek relationships elsewhere.[228]

In a subsequent study, the psychologists, Hetherington and Clingempeel, found that while older children and teenagers can disengage from the family situation by going out with friends or establishing supportive relationships with older relatives or family friends, younger children without these opportunities may behave differently.

Conversely, the absence of monitoring by parents and 'overinvestment' by teenagers in peer relationships can lead to behavioural problems in older children. The researchers found in their three-wave study that adolescent children in divorced, lone mother families and in stepfamilies formed through remarriage, consistently scored less-well on indices of behaviour, competence and education than comparable children whose parents were stably married. Over the two-year study period, they noted a decline in the positive relationship between adolescents and stepfathers, and short-term increases in withdrawal and antisocial behaviour towards mothers.[229]

Although finding that family size and healthy family functioning had stronger associations with negative childhood well-being, Canadian research also revealed that "without exception across child outcomes, children living in lone-parent families were reported to experience the highest levels of childhood difficulties, followed by children living in stepfamilies."[230]

In Australia, almost 50,000 children are involved in their parents' divorce each year.[231] If the children involved in all separations, including those by cohabiting couples, are counted, the figure is significantly higher. In the US, over a million children experience divorce annually.[232] Less than half of American children reach the age of 17 in an intact family.[233] Over half of couples divorcing in the UK in 2007 had at least one child aged under 16. This meant that there were over 110,000 children who were aged under 16 when their parents divorced. Twenty per cent of these children were under five years old.[234] By 2010, it was estimated that half of all children would see their parents split-up before age of 16.[235] In Canada, there were 111,626 divorce cases in 2009-2010, with an estimated one-in-two cases involving dependent children.[236] More than 800,000 people who had dependent children with their partners had become separated or divorced between 2001 and 2006, including one-third of whom had been cohabiting.[237]

Long term impacts

It is clear that divorce can also have a long term impact on children.

In Britain, the 1946, 1958 and 1970 cohort studies have provided longitudinal evidence of the impact of divorce. Fiona McAllister writes that the follow-ups at 21, 26, 31 and 36 years of the 1946 cohort "has provided us with robust evidence of a disturbing fact: the experience of divorce as a child can have adverse effects in terms of health, behaviour and economic status thirty years later."[238] There is evidence that the children of parents who divorce when they are less than five years of age are particularly vulnerable.[239] The follow-up studies of the 1958 cohort revealed similar findings, particularly in terms of educational achievement and behaviour.[240] In the Netherlands, scholars from the University of Utrecht concluded that family structure was more important than education in determining whether young adults would obtain employment: "Parental divorce ... may increase the likelihood that children will not learn adaptive interpersonal skills, such as how to reach a compromise and communicate effectively. This, in turn, handicaps their job prospects."[241] Another Dutch study concluded that the effects of divorce on adolescent children were long-term.[242] Canadian research reveals that changes to family structure have been associated with significant increases in child poverty in that country.[243] Overall, divorce tends to have a long-term impact on children who "exhibit higher malaise scores at age 33 than their contemporaries whose parents remained married."[244] The scholarly research also reveals that "single-parent family structure exerts strong, significant effects on early home-leaving behaviour ... for both boys and girls.[245]

Perhaps not unexpectedly, parental divorce also strains ties with grandparents, especially paternal grandparents. Single mothers received less total support from parents and grandparents, including single fathers, and they had the lowest quality relationships with them, according to a recent study.[246]

HEALTH

Marriage is a protective factor for children of all ages. From the earliest days of a child's life, being raised by two biological parents confers significant advantages. The benefits are evident from the beginning of a child's life where a married mother is more likely to breastfed her child.[247] A recent Scottish study also found that after taking into account birth weight, and the mother's age and tobacco use, babies with married mothers are only about half as likely to die of Sudden Infant Death Syndrome (SIDS) than those with single mothers.[248]

Consider a sample of the numerous recent studies. Children living with both parents are healthier generally than those who do not.[249] Parental divorce has been linked to adverse outcomes for children, including adolescent drunkenness.[250] Family failure has been shown to be a prime cause of psychological stress amongst children and adolescents,[251] with links to subsequent criminality.[252] Conversely, strong family involvement helps to protect against gang membership.[253] A study of female gang members in the US found that 57 per cent lived with single mothers, compared to just 21 per cent who resided with both parents. The female gang members were at much higher risk for a range of sexually transmitted diseases[254] and violent behaviours. Other studies discern links to mental health problems.[255]

Teens living in single parent and stepfamilies are more likely to engage in risky behaviours. This includes earlier sexual intercourse,[256] smoking,[257] substance abuse,[258] earlier and dangerous alcohol use,[259] and self-harm.[260] Noting that the incidence of marijuana dependence was almost twice as high for children from non-nuclear families, Florida researchers write:

> Early adolescence is a unique period because it is a time of biological changes linked to puberty as well as changes in

social skills and educational expectations. . . It is also a period
of intensive experimentation and risk-taking, which creates a
context for peer initiation into substance use. For these reasons,
exposure to risk factors [such as a broken home] during early
adolescence may set in motion processes that will affect the
individual during adulthood.[261]

A study of some 5,000 high school students in Mississippi found
that family structure was a significant predictor of carrying guns to
school with youth from single parents and disrupted families most
at risk.[262] In America, at least, "adolescents who lived in a single-
parent home were more likely to report foregone [medical] care than
adolescents living in a two-parent home." This was particularly the
case for teenage daughters.[263] They are also more likely to engage
in various forms of delinquency, ranging from injuring others and
shoplifting to damaging school property on purpose,[264] an outcome
linked to the actual experience of parental divorce rather than
alternative explanations, such as a genetic predisposition.[265] Canadian
research confirmed the patterns identified elsewhere. The Toronto
sociologist, Anne-Marie Ambert, found that 69 per cent of delinquent
boys in the study were from single-parent families, compared to about
a quarter of their peers in the broader society.[266] As a study of auto
theft in the US revealed, the absence of social control in single parent
families, rather than economic disadvantage, was a strong predictor of
the criminal activity.[267]

There is a greater incidence of the development of Attention
Deficit Disorder (ADD),[268] childhood obesity,[269] and depression[270] for
children of divorce. The incidence of teenage anger has been observed
to progress into young adulthood according to a study of American
High School students. The researchers observed a pathological pattern
in which "males in particular tend to move through a sequence of
adaptations, from anger to delinquency to drinking problems, while
females will be more likely to move from anger through delinquency
to symptoms of depression."[271]

Norwegian researchers concluded that parental divorce also contributed to bullying by leaving the adolescents with "less monitoring, often fewer adults to confide in, and sometimes increased aggression because of feelings of loss."[272] Other studies found that youth in single parent and stepfamilies experience greater victimisation than do youth residing with both biological parents.[273]

A significant predictor of subsequent adult psychopathology is family structure.[274] Anxiety amongst many of the children of divorce continues long into adulthood.[275] A series of other studies indicate:

- children of divorced parents seem much more susceptible to psychiatric illness;[276]
- alcohol consumption by women whose parents divorced is far higher than women from intact families;[277]
- the incidence of stomach ulcers and colitis is four times higher for men aged 26 whose parents had divorced before the child was five compared to those who had reached 16 years when their parents divorced;[278]
- vulnerability to eating disorders was twice as high among daughters of single parents;[279]
- children of divorce living with formerly married mothers have a 50 per cent greater risk of developing asthma, and a 20–30 per cent greater risk of injury;[280]
- they are less likely to be vaccinated;[281] and
- parental divorce can be a factor in longevity.[282]

Conversely, paternal involvement in the lives of girls from a young age has been linked to "the development of 'healthy' reproductive functioning in daughters," while father absence for girls at age five has been linked to the early onset of puberty.[283] The researchers found that the "early onset of puberty in girls is associated with negative health and psychological outcomes," including "more emotional problems, such as depression and anxiety" and "alcohol consumption and sexual promiscuity." Given the fact that many separations and divorces occur within the first ten years of marriage, when children are still young, the risks of father absence are significant.

Social skills

Children and young people learn important social skills in healthy, stable families. Conversely, a series of studies show that the social relations and skills of children of divorce can be compromised in a variety of ways, including fear of peer rejection,[284] and fewer childhood friends.[285] In a national study comparing children of divorce with those from intact families, US scholars found that the former group rated worse on peer relationships, hostility towards adults, withdrawal, inattention and aggression.[286]

A diminution of family cohesion and harmony also lead children of divorce to leave home earlier and in greater numbers.[287] Where stepparents are involved, children are more likely to leave home earlier and less likely to return.[288]

Behavioural problems

There is also widespread evidence of increased behavioural problems and delinquency among both boys and girls whose parents have divorced. Even where parental relationships in intact families were poor, a survey of nearly 9,000 teens found a 'consistent premium' for these children, compared to their peers in stepfamilies.[289] A fall in income following divorce has also been found to be "associated with a sequence of events that ultimately impact children's behaviour."[290] "Unlike many of their parents, children do not usually experience an immediate sense of relief when their families break-up," observes Dr David Larson from the National Institute for Healthcare Research. "Rather, most undergo a great amount of emotional distress immediately after the divorce as they try to adjust to their new living arrangements."[291] Analysis of data from the *National Health Interview Survey on Child Health* by Deborah Dawson has shown that children who experienced separation and divorce were two to three times more likely to have been suspended or expelled from school, and three times as likely to be in need of treatment for emotional or behavioural problems. These children also scored higher on measures of antisocial behaviour, anxiety or depression, inattention, hyperactivity, dependency and fearfulness.[292]

Being a member of an intact family, or not, has also been shown to be associated to the tendency of teens to be involved in fights.[293] Although girls are less likely to become delinquent than boys, both boys and girls whose parents have divorced have elevated rates.[294] Conversely, children from intact families are more likely to use their discretionary time constructively.[295]

The impact has been demonstrated from early in a child's life. University of Texas scholars observed that changes in parents' relationship with their partners between birth and the end of kindergarten increase children's behavioural problems in first grade, with parental status at birth either reducing or compounding the instability.[296] A study by psychiatrists at King's College, London, of 3,000 boys and 3,000 girls aged 5-10 found both boys and girls living in single parent families were about three times more likely to display symptoms of Disruptive Behaviour Disorders, than those living in intact families.[297] Canadian doctors were almost twice as likely to prescribe Ritalin to children in the period following their parents' divorce, according to another study.[298] Family income, according to other research, was not significantly associated with delinquency.[299]

The impact of family structure is not confined to English-speaking nations. Turkish studies also reveal that children whose parents divorce suffer from more psychological problems, achieve less academic success, and develop more fearful attachment styles than their peers from intact families.[300]

A number of researchers have also linked some violent and aggressive behaviour in school-age children to marital and family disruption.[301] One reason may be that children exposed to 'intimate partner violence' are "more likely to live in households headed by single parents."[302] This, in turn, may expose them to other risk factors "for aggressive/violent influences, such as frequent changes in the resident father figure, difficulty in securing assistance, and difficulty in providing supervision for children."[303] It is little wonder that, in an Oregon study, it was noted that the combination of children living in poverty, experiencing maltreatment and living in single-parent families, was linked to the need to prioritise the "early identification and management of mental health problems" in schools.[304]

It also appears that parental divorce is linked to "late-onset antisocial behaviour" amongst adolescents, according to a study by researchers from Rutgers University and the University of Minnesota.[305] The study of 358 youths also found a high risk of substance abuse during the transition to young adulthood.[306]

Reflecting on the higher incidence of single-parent families in recent decades, Scottish researchers considered whether studies of delinquency from the 1950s and 60s remain valid. Their results showed little difference to earlier findings: the volume of offending was lowest among children in two-parent families, and considerably higher among children living with their mother and stepfather, or with a single father.[307] New Zealand scholars have also observed that 'family factors' play a major mediating role in the relationship between poverty and crime.[308] The patterns appear to extend to neighbourhoods. An analysis of crime data in England and Wales, the Netherlands and the United States revealed that lone parent households are burgled more frequently than otherwise similar households in each country.[309]

Communities comprising intact families also appear to be the safest environments for adolescents to develop their own autonomy. Conversely, teens seeking to do so in communities with few intact families are at greater risk of antisocial behaviour.[310] Hence the supportive social context in which "schools, neighbourhoods, nuclear families and friendships groups contribute to positive change" assist adolescents in an ordered transition to adulthood.[311]

Mental health

The Western Australian *Child Health Survey* was the largest of its kind in the nation, involving in-depth interviews with 2,790 children aged between four and 16.[312] The survey focused on the three primary spheres of influence that shape children's development: the family, the school, and the community. An object was to establish "at a population level the nature and extent of various protective factors and risk factors that may be operating in the lives of children and just what it is that tips the balance towards moving along a pathway of resiliency or a path of increased vulnerability."[313]

The survey showed that three major risk factors were predominant: discipline style; family type, whether it be an original, step/blended or one-parent family; and the level of family discord present in the household. The following table indicates the risk factors found in the study.

Risks for mental health problems

	P value	Risk (odds ratio)	Confidence interval
Discipline style			
Coercive	<0.0001	3.3	1.9 - 5.6
Detached	0.0004	2.2	1.3 - 3.7
Inconsistent	<0.0001	2.2	1.7 - 3.0
Family type			
Step/blended	<0.0001	2.4	1.6 - 3.6
One parent	<0.0001	2.5	1.8 - 3.5
Level of discord			
High	0.0004	1.7	1.2 - 2.4

Source: WA Child Health Survey

Professor Sven Silburn explained the significance of the findings to the Australian Parliament:

> With the knowledge of just these three factors, one can correctly predict close to 80 per cent of those children with mental health problems. What you see here is the level of risk associated with each style. For example, if you are looking at a child living in a family with a coercive style of parenting, the children are 3.3 times more likely to have a mental health problem than are children living in a family where there is an encouraging style of parenting. Similarly, whether one is living in a step/blended or a one-parent family, there is a very similar level of risk associated with developing a mental health problem in contrast to those children who are living in an original family. In a household where there is a high level of discord, they are 1.7 times more likely.

Because they are adjusted odds ratios, the odds are multiplicative. If you are a child living in a family with a coercive parenting style, for example, in a step/blended household and there is a high level of family discord, the risks of a mental health problem are 3.3 x 2.4 x 1.7.[314]

Although the survey was not a study of divorce, it did provide a "snapshot" of "the average mental health status of children who are living in different family living arrangements at a particular point in time."[315]

American studies have reached similar conclusions. "Adolescents report an increase in depressed mood and rebelliousness and a decrease in self-esteem if their parents divorced or separated," according to the US Agency for Healthcare Research and Quality.[316] Epidemiologists from the University of Maastricht in the Netherlands found that "living in a single parent family and having a life event [such as a serious illness, a parental divorce, or the death of a family member] were the most important predictors of mood and anxiety disorders" in children.[317] Moreover, the diagnoses of children aged five to six corresponded with diagnoses made one and a half years later, suggesting ongoing problems.

In the Netherlands it has been observed that "family factors such as living in a one-parent family and changes in family composition" can be linked to adolescent mental health problems, even after controlling for the influence of other variables. Dutch adolescents living in a one-parent family were more than twice as likely to perceive a need for psychological help, and more than three times likely to be referred for mental health services.[318] Similar outcomes have been reported from Finland.[319] Examining the use of mental health services by Finnish children in 1989 and 1999, scholars from the University of Turku noticed steady levels in mental health pathology amongst children from non-traditional families, but a drop to much lower levels for children in two-parent biological families. By 1999, the difference had grown to a multiple of 3.6.[320]

While the resulting problems for children reflect deficits in economic and parental resources, "regardless of economic and parental resources, the outcomes of adolescents (12-17 years old) in cohabiting families are worse, on average, than those experienced by adolescents in two-biological-parent married families," according to a study of more than 35,000 children in the United States.[321]

Teenage motherhood has been implicated in problematic behaviour of children, but an American study concluded that early "experiences such as divorce or poverty" are more significant than teenage childbearing in determining whether her children will lag in cognitive development or will develop disruptive behaviours.[322]

Youth depression and suicide

Marital disruption has been implicated in youth depression and suicide.[323] A study using data from 18 first-world nations linked family change (based on an index of marriage, divorce, female labour force rates and fertility) negatively with youth suicide and homicide.[324]

A UK study found "increased disorder rates where the father was absent" the family structure.[325] A 10 year study of boys in the US found that the youth who had experienced changes in parental figures were likely to manifest a high level of depression that persisted throughout the study period, when compared to youngsters who had not experienced parental transitions.[326]

In one of the largest studies undertaken, researchers in Sweden, where a quarter of all 17 year olds in 1999 had experienced their parents' separation, compared the situation of 65,085 children living with single parents with 921,257 children living with both parents.[327] The results were significant, even after adjusting for factors including the mental health of the parents, addiction and socio-economic status: "Girls with single parents were more than twice as likely to commit suicide and more than three times as likely to die from an addiction to drugs or alcohol as were girls with two parents. Boys of single parents were more than five-times as likely to die from addiction to drugs or alcohol, more than three-times likely to die from a fall or poisoning, and four-times more likely to die from external violence." Overall, the risk of dying in boys was 50 per cent greater for those living in single parent families, even after adjusting for a range of variables including socio-economic status.

A study of more than 15,000 college students, for whom suicide is the "third leading cause of death among the US college-aged population (18-24 years of age)" concluded that "the single most protective factor was being married."[328] Describing their findings as "a striking effect" other scholars found an increased mortality risk for children of divorce.[329]

Adolescent sexual behaviour

Early sexual activity has been linked to marital disruption and single parenthood.[330] A study by Les Whitbeck and colleagues at Iowa State University found that mothers' post-divorce dating behaviours had a strong bearing on the sexual behaviour of adolescent boys, and indirectly influenced the adolescent girl's sexuality by affecting their sexual attitudes. The mothers' attitudes about the acceptability of sexual permissiveness influenced the daughters' sexual permissiveness and sexual practices.[331] Researchers in another US study concluded "not living with both parents when 14 years old compared to living with both is positively associated with multiple recent partners among white women."[332] Another survey of almost 4,000 adolescents found that "females from households headed by a mother only or a father only were more likely to have initiated sexual intercourse than were adolescents from two-parent households," but "among adolescent males, an increased likelihood of ever having had sexual intercourse was found among those living in a household headed by a father only or [by] neither parent."[333] An Oklahoma study found that teens living with single-parents were less likely to report being virgins (55 per cent) than were teens from two-parent families (70 per cent).[334] A Scandinavian study revealed that children of divorce are likely to engage in sexual activity earlier.[335] Other studies in the US and the UK reached similar conclusions.[336]

In America and New Zealand, it has been observed that early father-absent girls had rates of teenage pregnancy 7-8 times higher, and late father-absent girls rates two-three times higher, than among father-present girls.[337] After taking into account other factors, such as the stress of divorce, and loss of income, an association was observed between earlier onset of father absence and higher rates of both early sexual activity and adolescent pregnancy: "Father presence was a major protective factor against early sexual outcomes, even if other risk factors were present."[338] The sons of divorced parents have also been found to have a higher risk of earlier sexual activity, more sexual partners, and the contraction of sexually transmitted disease.[339]

It would appear from a study involving data from 80 nationally representative American high schools that the circumstances of both the individual and of their school peers is also a factor in early sexual activity. Indeed, the Canadian and American researchers concluded that "role modelling and collective supervision mechanisms associated with the prevalence of single-parent households in a school context seem to be more important than the prevalence of low socioeconomic status of such families."[340] Conversely, regular contact with the extended family, and attachment to a family's history, are negatively related to risky sexual behaviour.[341]

WELL-BEING

Subsequent adult relationships

The experience of separation and divorce, or transient parental interactions in which attachment is less secure and more uncertain can be far-reaching for the subsequent relationships of such children. Trust can be severely weakened or shattered. And once diminished, it can be difficult to rebuild. The repercussions may be in place long before young adults form their own romantic relationships, making dating and forming a romantic partnership more difficult.[342] Daughters of divorced parents in particular report less trust and satisfaction in their relationships,[343] are more cautious in their outlook, and more ready to believe that their partner is unfaithful.[344]

These findings reflect observations about attitudes towards marriage and divorce amongst children whose parents separated. This includes less positivity about marriage[345] and more positivity toward divorce, resulting in less commitment to romantic relationships and lower relationship quality.[346] Other studies reveal that people whose parents divorced may feel that marriage is unpredictable and unstable,[347] less enduring and permanent,[348] and are less likely to insist on lifelong marital commitment,[349] and less likely to think of themselves as parents.[350] Fears that their future relationships will lack love and trust, and will be highly conflicted have also been observed amongst children of divorce.[351]

Children of divorced parents are less likely to marry themselves, and more likely to divorce if they do.[352] They are also more likely to cohabit, and at an earlier age. A series of studies have also revealed the increased risk of lower marital quality for the children of divorce, increased rates of negative behaviours, and lower levels of happiness.[353] By contrast, children from intact marriages have more favourable attitudes towards marriage[354] and less favourable attitudes to divorce.[355]

Educational outcomes

Families are one of the strongest influences on the growth of human competence, mental and emotional wellbeing and physical health. Four decades ago, the *Coleman Report* identified the family rather than the school as the major determinant of learning outcomes for children.[356] The results have been replicated many times.[357] Children of Indochinese refugees, who had missed months, even years of schooling, and had lived in relocation camps, with scant exposure to western culture and little knowledge of the English language, were found to achieve remarkable success. Their stunning success was not found in the schools that they had originally come from or to which they subsequently attended, but attributable to their family environments. This is just one illustration of the powerful impact of stable marriage and family life on the educational outcomes for children.

Children who grow-up in an intact family achieve higher school scores, report significantly less school-related behavioural problems and higher aspirations for tertiary studies.[358] They also receive greater parental nurturance, mentoring and advising.[359] Conversely, children who experience parental divorce before the age of 18 are significantly less likely to complete high school than children in intact households. According to a Canadian study, the high school graduation rates are particularly low among children who are quite young when their parents divorce.[360] Other studies reveal that children whose parents divorce are more likely to drop out of school[361] and less likely to go onto tertiary studies.[362] Young children are more likely to have delayed speech development.[363] Children of divorced parents, especially girls, also tend to miss more classes than their peers from intact families.[364] An Australian study concluded that children whose parents divorce receive about seven-tenths of a year less education that children from intact families, and are much more likely to drop out of school.[365] Other studies reveal the probability of lower grades, lower test scores, and repeating a grade.[366] Social disadvantage in a child's family of origin, such as only having one parent available in the home, has been linked to adverse child-rearing practices which, in turn, partially determine child adjustment problems.[367]

A series of studies that have examined the impact of parental divorce on children have found the educational performance of children is adversely affected.[368] These studies reveal that the adverse educational effects of divorce can occur in children at any age;[369] the chances of attending university decrease for children of divorce;[370] and unemployment and employment in low paying jobs is more prevalent for children of divorced parents.[371] Conversely, a study of more than 12,000 young people between 14 and 21 found that math and reading achievements were higher for children with a married mother.[372] A survey of 5,000 households using the British *Household Panel Study* produced similar results. An adolescent who was raised in a household with two biological parents was more than twice as likely to achieve five passes on the General Certificate of Secondary Education, as well as two A-level passes, than their classmates in other households.[373] Having a paternal role model has also been associated with positive school performance.[374]

Similar trends are evident in Australia. For 18-24 year olds, 62 per cent of those who experienced parental divorce or permanent separation during their childhood completed year 12, compared with 77 per cent of those whose parents did not. The differential extended to educational achievements, after accounting for the effects of age. People who experienced parental divorce or permanent separation were 28 per cent less likely to have a Bachelor degree or higher. The impact extends to personal income. For people in the ten-year age groups from 25 – 34 years up to 45 – 54 years, those who had experienced parental divorce or separation had, on average, a weekly personal income about eight per cent less than those who had not.[375]

Even in a country such as Norway, which has low levels of economic inequality, relatively generous support for lone parents, and a highly subsidised education system, substantial difference between the educational outcomes for children from single and dual parent families have been observed.[376] This is consistent with findings from other nations that, on average, children who experience a family disruption, such as parental divorce, fare poorly across a wide range of adolescent and adult outcomes, including educational attainment, economic security and physical and psychological well-being.[377] A study of three generations of families in Southern California revealed that 56 per cent of third generation males whose parents remained married had college or advanced degrees, compared with only 23 per cent of males whose parents had divorced before the child attained 18 years of age. Likewise, 41 per cent of third generation females had degrees, compared to just 25 per cent whose parents had divorced before the child reached 18.[378] Given other research which shows the achievement gaps between children at the beginning of their schooling persists throughout their education,[379] the negative impact of family dysfunction deserves greater attention.

Family disruption and poorer educational attainment can be particularly important, as the lower educational outcomes may initiate processes that contribute to other disadvantages, including persistent health differences,[380] relationship stability[381] and economic well-being.[382] Adolescent loneliness and diminished life satisfaction have also been linked to parental divorce.[383] It would appear also that generally children can cope with moderate levels of family mobility (less than eight moves) with no discernable impact of school performance if they live with both biological parents.[384]

There is also a risk that negative outcomes extend beyond one generation for educational attainment, marital discord, and poorer quality relationships with mothers and fathers,[385] a finding that Paul Amato and Jacob Cheadle, found remarkable given the fact that fewer than 10 per cent of the grandchildren had been born at the time of their grandparent's divorces.

Financial circumstances

The adverse impact of divorce on the separating partners often has a significant flow-on effect on their children. There is a greater risk of lower occupational status and financial hardship,[386] lower income and living in public housing,[387] homelessness,[388] and the accumulation of fewer assets.[389] The diminution of parents' income has direct economic and material consequences for many children. They are more likely to depend on welfare, especially if pre-divorce family income was low.[390] According to the Organisation for Economic Cooperation and Development, 75 per cent of women who applied for welfare benefits in the US in the late 1980s did so because of a disrupted marriage or relationship.[391] Julia Heath concluded her study by observing that "changes in family structure are by far the major cause of initial spells of poverty among female-headed households."[392] An Australian study found that the extent to which a divorce was detrimental financially on women correlated with the relative levels of education of the former spouses. Mothers with low education, formerly married to a husband with high education, experienced the greatest losses.[393] As a consequence, their children are at greater risk. Hence, the Australian welfare agency,

Anglicare, reported sole parenthood as the number one risk factor for child social exclusion in 2012.[394]

Reflecting on the body of research, Fiona McAllister writes:

> These finding are of great importance, because those sceptical or unaware of the studies of the effects of divorce on children claim that observed differences are the result of economic factors. Accordingly, they argue that children suffer because the standard of their living falls. While it is undoubtedly true that the fall of economic standards has attendant short-comings, for example, change of housing or moving school, it must be recognised that the evidence from research suggests that other factors are in play. Emotional disturbance and stress are particularly notable in the critical early years of childhood.[395]

The consistency of the findings over decades of research is telling. Yet these risks are hardly known by most people, and little time and efforts is devoted to assisting couples and their children make the best choices for their future fulfilment. This subject is discussed again in chapter 11.

Stepfamilies and remarriage

An increasing number of children are growing up in stepfamilies. While many of them are able to make the multiple adjustments necessary to adapt to the new relationships involved, decades of social science research reveal that the risks for these children are significant, as the following discussion illustrates.

A team of British epidemiologists and psychiatrists concluded their survey of psychological morbidity that "many studies have documented an association between marital disruption and a wide range of deleterious effects in children,"[396] and that "studies on the effects of remarriage generally fail to show a beneficial effect." Seeking to explain the negative outcomes of remarriage for many children, scholars from the University of Arizona suggest that "whereas mothers may be hoping that all will go smoothly as they re-partner, adolescents feel disloyal (to their fathers) if they easily accept or see positive aspects in the new partner and his impact on family life."[397] Indeed, young adults from stepfamilies often view their stepfathers poorly.[398] A yearning for their original family and lack of connection with the new one has also been observed in stepfamily children. "The lack of relational history with other family members often fostered feelings of exclusion," and "the lack of a biological bond made becoming a family more difficult," concluded Tamar Afifi and Stacia Keith in their study of stepfamilies.[399] Moreover, "moving from a single-mother family into a cohabitating stepfamily is associated with increased delinquent behaviour and decreased school engagement."[400]

Canadian and American studies reveal that early puberty, which in turn has been associated with substance abuse, earlier sexual activity and mental health problems among both boys and girls, is influenced by the presence of a stepfather in the house.[401] Youth from both single-parent and stepfamilies report significantly greater exposure to victimisation, including child maltreatment, sexual abuse, physical assault and sibling abuse.[402] A recent US Department of Health and Human Service report about the risks to children where a live-in partner joins the household was stark: "Compared to children living with married biological parents, those whose single parent had a live-in partner had more than eight times the rate of maltreatment overall, over 10 times the rate of abuse, and nearly eight times the rate of neglect."[403] Surveying a decade of research, the American psychiatrist, Frank Putman, concluded that "the presence of a stepfather in the home doubles the risk for girls, not only for being abused by the stepfather but also for being abused by other men prior to the arrival of the stepfather in the home."[404] The incidence of later psychological illness was also found to be high amongst those who suffered sexual abuse as a child.

The academic performance of children in stepfamilies is also at risk, according to a study of High School seniors. Students from intact families averaged 17 per cent better outcomes and missed 78 per cent fewer periods than their peers from other families. Females, in particular were more negatively impacted. Surprisingly, perhaps, the study found that "children in remarried households performed no better than children in either single-mother or single-father families."[405] Young people in married and cohabiting stepfamilies have lower college expectations, according to one study,[406] and are less likely to graduate from college.[407]

The differences are also reflected in economic resources of children in single-parent families. Children in two-parent families and stepfamilies, compared to those in single-parent families, have better socioeconomic indicators (higher household income, greater levels of parental education, and lower rates of financial hardship) and better social-capital indicators (higher levels of parental participation in volunteer work and public worship).[408] Partly as a consequence, they are much more likely to be involved in extra-curricular activities.[409] Conversely, divorce reduces the prospects that parents will help their children financially, especially when divorced fathers remarry.[410]

The risk of adverse outcomes for children in stepfamilies has been shown to compound when step-parents cohabit.[411] Parsing data from 13,000 students from grades seven to 12, scholars at Bowling Green State University found that the adolescents from cohabiting stepfamilies more likely to be suspended or expelled from school, commit delinquent crimes, receive low grades in two or more subjects, and score lower on standard tests of cognitive development.

Perhaps the worst outcome for children is a period of multiple transitions involving a revolving process of parents and 'care-givers' in their lives. It significantly increases the risk of a damaging impact on attachment, educational outcomes, and behavioural problems. Just moving residence has an impact on school outcomes.[412]

Other family arrangements

The advantages for children of having both a mother and a father have been demonstrated in recent studies of same-sex families. In Australian research, Professor Sarantakos found that "overall ... children of married couples are more likely to do well at school in academic and social terms, than children of cohabiting and homosexual couples."[413] A series of small subsequent studies indicated no disadvantage for children of same-sex relationships, but as Professor Loren Marks illustrated, none of them compared "large, random, representative sample of lesbian or gay parents and their children with a large, random, representative sample of married parents and their children."[414] This research deficiency was addressed in the *New Family Structures Study* of a large, random sample of young American adults aged 18-39. The study by the University of Texas sociologist, Mark Regernus, included 2,988 people, including 175 adults raised by lesbian mothers and 73 adults raised by gay fathers. Professor Regernus concluded:

> Do children need a married mother and father to turn out well as adults? No, if we observe many anecdotal accounts with which all Americans are familiar. Moreover, there are many cases in the NFSS where respondents have proven resilient and prevailed as adults in spite of numerous transitions, be they death, divorce, additional or diverse romantic partners, or remarriage. But the NFSS also clearly reveals that children appear most apt to succeed well as adults – on multiple counts across a variety of domains – when they spend their entire childhood with their married mother and father, and especially when the parents remain married to the present day.[415]

Intergenerational effects

Beginning with Judith Wallerstein's examination of the effects of divorce on children in California,[416] a series of studies have confirmed the intergenerational impact of divorce. Twenty-five years after their parents divorce, children continue to suffer the emotional repercussions, claimed Wallerstein, the California researcher and author of one of the longest-running studies on the subject. She claimed that the results of the 25 year follow-up of a group of 131 children whose parents were divorcing in northern California in the 1970s provided more evidence that the impact of divorce upon children is both long-lasting and cumulative. While the study does not quantify the effect of divorce by comparing children of broken marriages with those from intact families, it offers descriptive details of their lives based on hundreds of hours of interviews that Wallerstein conducted over 25 years. "Unlike the adult experience, the child's suffering does not reach its peak at the breakup and then level off. The effect of the parents' divorce is played and replayed throughout the first three decades of the children's lives." While this does not necessarily cause them to fail as adults, she says, it does make the normal challenges of growing up even more difficult.[417]

The earlier ten year report by Dr Wallerstein found that many of the children appeared to be troubled, drifting and underachieving. Almost all confronted issues of love, commitment and marriage with anxiety. Often there was a great deal of concern about betrayal, abandonment and feeling unloved. About half of the young men and women in the study involved themselves in short-lived relationships and impulsive marriages which ended in divorce. Wallerstein found that ten years after their parents had divorced, 34 per cent were depressed, could not concentrate at school, had trouble making friends and suffered a wide range of behavioural problems. The remaining children were doing well in some areas but faltering in others. In a magazine article drawn from the book, Wallerstein noted that "it would be hard to find any other group of children – except perhaps the victims of a natural disaster – who suffered such a rate of serious psychological problems."[418]

While Wallerstein's findings attract criticism about methodology because of the unmatched group, her conclusions are supported by other studies. British studies by Professor Kathleen Kiernan indicated that for women whose parents' divorced, those who married were more likely to marry younger and more likely to divorce.[419] Diana Kuh and Mavis MacLean found that at age 36, 16.3 per cent of children from intact homes had divorced, compared to 23 per cent from backgrounds of parental divorce and separation.[420] More recent studies have linked parental divorce to elevated risks of teenage child-bearing,[421] and to distant relationships with their own children.[422] A survey of 600 young adults in Canada revealed problems with intimacy for the children of divorce.[423] Wives who experienced parental divorce whilst a child, and husbands with highly negative family environments, have greater difficulty solving problems and are at risk of declines in marital satisfaction.[424] Another study revealed that "parental education and growing up in an intact family predicted higher scores of adolescent perception of receiving good parenting," which in turn "predicted less psychological disturbance, better interpersonal relations, and more active social participation in early adulthood."[425]

Australian data reveal similar trends. Over one-quarter (26 per cent) of people aged 18-24 whose parents had divorced or separated (in their childhood) were in a *de facto* relationship, compared to 12 per cent of those whose parents had not divorced. Those who experienced the divorce or permanent separation of their parents as a child are also more likely to have entered multiple live-in relationships over the course of their life. Accounting for the effects of age, those who had experienced parental divorce/permanent separation were twice as likely (10 per cent) to have had three or more live-in relationships than those who did not (five per cent). Children of divorce are also less likely to marry or to delay marriage.[426]

Professor Paul Amato has analysed a series of studies of parental divorce and adult well-being. In one study, he concluded that parental divorce increased the risk of being a single-parent more for men than for women; while women had a higher risk of divorce than men.[427] In a subsequent longitudinal study, Amato concluded that parental divorce elevates the risk of offspring divorce by increasing the likelihood that offspring exhibit behaviours that interfere with the maintenance of mutually rewarding intimate relationships.[428] Professor Amato's findings are reproduced in the chart below:

Risk of Divorce

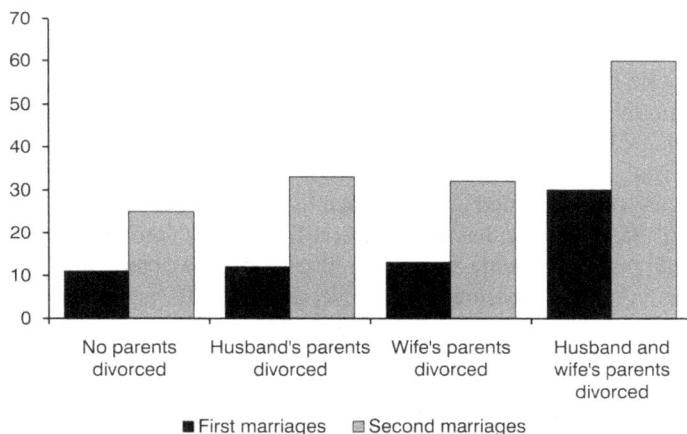

Sources: *Threshold* (1997) 54:15; and *Courier Mail*, November 28, 1996 (percentages).

Even when parents divorce after the children have grown up and moved away from home, it impacts on the parental-child relationship. A study of more than 3,000 young US adults found that weekly contact with parents dropped from 78 per cent for still-married mothers to 62 per cent for divorced mothers, and from 78 per cent for still-married fathers to 44 per cent for divorced fathers.[429]

The possibility of intergenerational effects of divorce was also revealed in a longitudinal study in the UK. Using data from a cohort of the population that has been followed from birth to age 33, researchers were able to trace the effects of parental divorce on indicators of mental health over the entire sweep of the British study – from age seven when behavioural information was first collected, through assessments at ages 11, 16, 23 and 33.[430]

A previous study by Andrew Cherlin found that much of the apparent affect of a parental divorce on children's emotional problems between ages seven and 11 could be attributed to characteristics of the child and family prior to the divorce.[431] The later study suggests that these earlier findings should be modified.

> To be sure, we found evidence that part of the difference in emotional problems between the divorce and no-divorce groups at age 33 can be attributed to predivorce characteristics at age seven ... But as the two groups aged, the difference between the two groups widened ... This widening suggests that the divorce and its aftermath may have effects that persist into adulthood (although some time-varying predisruption characteristics that weren't fully measured may have widened the gap after age seven). If the continuing effect were a result of the divorce rather than unmeasured factors, it would suggest that this childhood event can set in motion a train of circumstances that affects individual's lives even after they have left home, married, and entered the labor force ... The absence of a strong post-disruption effect at age 11 suggests that the long-term effect may emerge only in adolescence or young adulthood. Parental divorce could trigger events such as early child bearing or curtailed education that, in turn, affect adult outcomes.[432]

University of Maryland's Sandra Hofferth and Frances Goldsheilder underline the impact:

> Growing up without two parents has intergenerational consequences. Young men who experienced substantial instability growing up are themselves more likely to experience disrupted fathering and go on to become absent fathers. Girls apparently do not learn appropriate relationship skills if they grow up in families without their fathers, even if the family

structure is stable, and this leads them to rear children in such families themselves.[433]

Reflecting on their findings that young adult daughters of divorced parents find less satisfaction in their romantic relationships and evince a higher level of mistrust toward their romantic partners, California and Texas scholars suggest that these women may have a more realistic understanding of their relationships, but are often unable to advance to deeper involvements, helping to explain their higher divorce rates.[434] Other studies point to higher levels of anxiety amongst women whose parents had divorced[435] and a negative impact of their own ability to make decisions about marriage.[436] While daughters of divorced parents have been shown to have a greater tendency to be overly meek or overly dominant in one study,[437] sons of divorced parents are more inclined to be simultaneously hostile and a 'rescuer' of women to whom they are attracted, rather than open, affectionate and co-operative.[438] Both sons and daughters of divorced parents have been found to have more difficulties with communication and conflict, and resort to aggression and violence, according to other studies.[439]

The effects also extend to the marital stability of the children of divorce. According to the sociologist, Jay Teachman, children born out-of-wedlock and the children whose parent's divorced experience a significantly increased rate of divorces themselves.[440] They are also more likely to cohabit, which, in turn, has been associated with higher levels of separation and divorce.[441] Searching for the reasons why the children of divorced parents are more likely to divorce themselves, Ball State University scholar, Carolyn Kapinus, found a number of factors involved. First, "parents who have favourable attitudes toward divorce transmit these pro-divorce attitudes to offspring." Secondly, fathers have a greater influence on sons' divorce attitudes, whereas parents' gender is not a factor in daughters' divorce attitudes. Thirdly, parental divorce has a positive direct association with daughters' pro-divorce views. Fourthly, post divorce conflicts also play a role, producing negative views of divorce amongst sons, but pro-divorce views amongst daughters. Professor Kapinus suggests that a diminished relationship with a father and the post-divorce conflict "may lead sons to conclude that divorce has negative consequences and should be avoided."[442] Children of divorce would also appear less likely to wed themselves. A survey of data collected over two decades to 1994 revealed that marriage rates for children of divorce had declined dramatically.[443]

In a later study, Professor Teachman found that the divorce of parents is more traumatic than the death of a parent for most children. Surveying data of 4,947 women who married between 1970 and 1989, a Western Washington University study found that the highest correlations with marital risk factors were found where children had lived with a single parent after divorce or in a stepfamily. As remarriage has been associated with more economic resources for the family and children, Teachman theorised that, in contrast to divorce and/or remarriage, "the death of a parent may rally the support of family and friends to an extent exceeding that which occurs following parental divorce."[444]

Children of divorced parents are also more likely to have children at a younger age, which can be a factor in marital instability. Australian data reveals that, after adjusting for age differences, just over one-third of women who had the experience of parental divorce/permanent separation had had a child before the age of 25, including 13 per cent who had their first child as a teenager. In comparison, one-quarter of women who had not had the experience had had a child before the age of 25 years, and only seven per cent had their first child before the age of 20 years.[445]

While children of divorce have been shown in many studies to be at an increased risk of behavioural, psychological and educational problems, research also indicated the resilience of most.[446] At the same time, clinical practitioners continued to observe many of the short and long-term negative effects described in this chapter. This issue has puzzled family scholars for many years.

A study of Dutch young people aged 12-24 found that "even years after the parental divorce, the adolescents and young adults still show increased levels of internalising and externalising problem behaviours, compared to their peers of intact families."[447] While an early US study of resilience factors found that nonfamilial support systems, such as neighbourhood support and school attachment did not buffer adolescents from the effect of low parental support,[448] the issue remained.

Using two linked studies, Lisa Laumann-Billings and Robert E Emery, psychologists at the University of Virginia, sought to resolve the differences, by considering the clinical and research approaches together in examining the "more subtle psychological distress or pain" experienced by children of divorce: "Clinicians often focus on children's frequent distress over parental divorce and may overlook their successful coping – perhaps even among the children they treat. Researchers can suffer from the opposite problem, missing more subtle distress while documenting the resilience of most children from divorced families." Bringing the two approaches together, the American psychologists concluded that both resilience and distress and pain co-exist for many children whose lives have been affected by parental divorce.[449]

Not unexpectedly, medical practitioners often see the consequences of parental divorce in their young patients. Acknowledging that more than one million American children experience their parent's divorce each year, US Pediatricians highlighted the "long searing experience" on children in a special issue of *Pediatrics*.[450] The special clinical report advising doctors on how to assist children experiencing parental divorce noted that "up to half of children show a symptomatic response during the first year after their parents' divorce" Very young children often "show irritability, increased crying, fearfulness, separation anxiety, sleep and gastrointestinal problems, and development regression." Older children, in many cases, "fear they will be abandoned, and have more nightmares and fantasies." They may also grow "moody or preoccupied" and begin to engage in "acting-out behaviour ... School performance may decrease, and they may agonise about their divided loyalties and feel that they should be punished." The editors of the journal pointed to other pathologies, including decreased self-esteem, substance abuse, inappropriate sexual behaviour, depression, and aggressive and delinquent behaviour. Significantly, children of all ages are "likely to feel guilty and responsible for the [parental] separation and feel that they should try to restore the marriage." In addition to providing appropriate treatment, America's leading paediatricians proposed "preserving the intact family where appropriate."

In a subsequent issue of *Pediatrics*, the doctors were clear about the advantages of healthy marriage for children. Marriage is beneficial, they stated, because "people behave differently when they are married. They have healthier lifestyles, eat better, and mother each other's health. Being a part of a couple and a family also increases the number of people and social institutions with which an individual has contact; this ... increases the likelihood that the family will be a successful one."[451]

The role of conflict

The consequences of separation and divorce are not uniform for all people. The researchers, David Demo and Alan Acock note:

> It is simplistic and inaccurate to think of divorce as having uniform consequences for children. The consequences of divorce vary along different dimensions of well-being, characteristics of children (e.g., pre-divorce adjustment, age at time of disruption) and characteristics of families (eg. socioeconomic history, pre- and post-divorce levels of conflict, parent-child relationships

and maternal employment). Most of the evidence reviewed ...
suggests that some sociodemographic characteristics of children
such as race and gender are not as important as characteristics of
families in mediating effects of divorce.[452]

One characteristic that appears important is conflict between
parents. As the UK One plus One Research team noted, the existence
of conflict has been cited as a reason in favour of divorce: better to
separate than to inflict a conflictual relationship on children.[453] More
recent research has raised serious questions about this presumption.

The Exeter study in Britain compared children from intact families
and children whose parents had divorced.[454] The children of divorce
were grouped according to their current situation: single-parent
families, step-families and 're-disrupted families' – meaning families
where the custodial parent had experienced at least one further
relationship breakdown after the original divorce. The intact families
were further divided into 'high conflict and 'low conflict' groups. The
family scholars, Monica Crockett and John Tripp, concluded:

> Previous studies have strongly suggested that it is parental
> conflict rather than actual separation that is associated with poor
> outcomes for children following divorce. This has led some
> commentators to suggest that it is better to resolve a high conflict
> situation by ending the parental relationships than by allowing
> it to continue. This view, while not being widely promoted, has
> gained some credence as 'accepted wisdom', and indeed, many
> of the Exeter families who had divorced believed that their
> decision was in the best interests of their children as well as
> themselves. Data from this study provides some evidence that
> such a 'justification' for divorce may be misunderstanding of
> the reality. It suggests moreover, that parental separation itself
> is one of the major associations with difficulties for children.
> What the data does not show however, and we did not set out to
> demonstrate, is whether the outcomes would have been better if
> parents in unhappy marriages had stayed together 'for the sake
> of the children' instead of separating.

The findings from this pilot study indicate that although *most* children do not exhibit acute difficulties beyond the initial stage of family breakdown, a significant minority of children encountered long term problems. Compared to their matched pairs in intact families, children who had experienced their parents' divorce were more likely to report problems in key areas of their lives, including psychosomatic disorders, difficulties with school work and a low sense of self-esteem. They were more likely to feel confused and uninvolved in arrangements about their future and to have lasting feelings of concern about both their resident and non-resident parents. Parental conflict and financial difficulties are clearly important features of family reorganisation that are associated with adverse outcomes for children. However, in this study it appeared that a more important adverse factor was the loss of a parent and the consequences, which included the risk that history would repeat itself with the breakdown of subsequent parental relationships.

These findings are consistent with studies that have found that adults who have been divorced more than once have poorer physical and mental health than those who have been through one divorce.[455]

Longitudinal studies have been conducted in both the UK and the US. In the UK, the effects of parental divorce during childhood and adolescence on the mental health of young adults (aged 23) were examined using the *National Child Development Study*. Children born in 1958 were assessed at both birth and subsequently followed up at ages seven, 11, 16 and 23 by means of maternal and child interviews, and by psychological, school and medical assessments.[456] The study found that the long-term effects of divorce in childhood on adult emotional adjustment had negative consequences for both men and women. Although the researchers found that in the vast majority of cases, there is substantial recovery following divorce, they noted:

> Our analysis of the clinical cut-off scores showed that in relative terms, divorce was associated with a substantial 39

per cent increase in the risk of psychopathology. An effect of this magnitude in the number of young adults who may need clinical assistance due to parental divorce seems important and worrying.

Interestingly, they found that parental divorce was linked to greater changes in Malaise Inventory scores for better-adjusted children, but these children ultimately showed lower levels of mental health problems in young adulthood than did those from divorced homes who had higher behaviour problems at age seven.

A 15 year intergenerational study by Paul Amato and Alan Booth found that, while children often benefit from divorce when their parents are constantly quarrelsome, they do not from the majority of divorces where parents get along fairly well. The study involved interviews with parents in 1980, 1983, 1988 and 1992; and interviews with their adult children in 1992 and 1995. Amato and Booth noted:

> On the one hand, divorce appears to be a necessary 'safety valve' for children (and parents) in high conflict households. On the other hand, as divorce becomes increasingly normative, people may be leaving marriages that are only moderately unhappy. If the threshold for unhappiness at which parents abandon marriage is declining, then divorce is removing a growing number of children from two-parent homes that still provide many benefits. Although children in these latter situations gain little, they are likely to be exposed to many stresses that frequently follow divorce, such as moving, changing schools, conflict between parents over post divorce arrangements, and declines in household income. According to this latter scenario, most divorces in the past (when marital dissolution was uncommon and occurred only under the most troubling circumstances) freed children from home environments that were especially aversive. In contrast, many divorces today (when marital dissolution is common) subject children to a range of stressful experiences with few compensating advantages.[457]

In these low conflict marriages, "parents do not hate each other," says Professor Amato. "Many are bored, and their marriages could be salvaged." The researchers found that after divorces in low-conflict marriages, the children grow into adults who tend to have increased psychological distress, reduced happiness, fewer ties with kin and friends, and reduced marital quality.[458] This is consistent with other research that linked high levels of social dysfunction prior to a divorce to a greater reduction in child antisocial behaviour after the divorce (while noting that the levels of anxiety and depression are higher for children of divorce than those of intact families).[459] Similarly, other research has shown that the experience of parental separation and divorce is uniformly harmful for children, regardless of how often their parents quarrelled beforehand, but parents remaining together was not a better alternative when the conflict between parents was high.[460]

The findings led Professors Amato and Booth to ask an important question: What proportion of divorces is preceded by a long period of overt interpersonal conflict, and hence, are beneficial to children?

> From our own data we estimate that less than a third of parental divorces involve highly conflicted marriages. Only 28 per cent of parents who divorced during the study reported any sort of spousal physical abuse prior to divorce, 30 per cent reported more than two serious quarrels in the last month, and 23 per cent reported they disagreed 'often' or 'very often' with their spouses. Thus it would appear that only a minority of divorces between 1980 and 1992 involve high-conflict marriage.[461]

Similarly, 85 to 90 per cent of Canadian divorces are deemed to involve low conflict relationships.[462] Paul Amato and Alan Booth observed:

> If divorce today were limited only to high conflict marriages, then divorce would generally be in children's best interest. But the fact that one-half of all marriages today end in divorce

suggests that this is not the case. Instead, with marital dissolution becoming increasingly socially acceptable, it is likely that people are leaving marriages at lower thresholds of unhappiness now than in the past. Unfortunately, these are the very divorces that are most likely to be stressful for children. Consequently, we conclude that the rise in marital disruption, although beneficial to some children, has, on balance, been detrimental to children. Furthermore, if the threshold of marital unhappiness required to trigger a divorce continues to decline, then outcomes for children of divorced parents may be more problematic in the future.[463]

Professors Amato and Booth suggest that "unless marriage becomes a more satisfying and secure arrangement in the future, the outlook for future generations of youth may be even more pessimistic."[464] Fiona McAllister and her co-researchers concluded:

No matter how the associations between marital breakdown, divorce and children's welfare are assessed, it is becoming increasingly clear that the parents' behaviour in their relationship with one another has a vital influence on childrens' current and future well-being. Elements of particular salience for children include: levels of conflict between parents; father absence; changing family structures; economic factors. Marital breakdown and divorce can involve all of these factors in the short and long term.[465]

Cohabitation and children

The negative consequences for children are not confined to single parent families. As the incidence of cohabitation has increased,[466] family scholars have turned their attention to the impact on children.[467]

Children of cohabiting relationships appear to be at higher risks in a number of ways. First, their parents are more likely to separate than married couples. Using data from the Office of National Statistics, the British Bristol Community Trust observed that that three-quarters of all family breakdowns that affect young children involved cohabiting, but unmarried, parents.[468] The *Millennium Cohort Study* of more than 18,000 mothers who gave birth during 2000 and 2001 revealed that after controlling for other factors, including race, education and economic factors, cohabiting parents at the time of their child's birth had more than two and a half times the risk of separating, compared to married parents.[469]

In the US, parental separation by the time a child was age three has been found to be five times greater for children born to cohabiting rather than married parents.[470] Two-thirds of children born to cohabiting parents will see their parents split up before they reach the age ten[471] (and three-quarters by age of sixteen, compared to about one-third of children born to married parents.)[472] Another study found that children, especially white children, born to cohabiting versus married parents have over five times the risk of experiencing their parents' separation.[473]

An Australian study reached similar conclusions. A cohabiting couple had more than seven times the chance of breaking up compared to a married couple who had not lived together before marriage, and more than four times the chance of separation than a couple who had lived together and subsequently married.[474]

The research also indicates that the children of cohabiting parents perform at lower levels than children of married couples. In his survey Professor Sotirios Sarantakos summarised the findings in four areas:[475]

> *Scholastic achievement*: In all measures related to aptitude in language, mathematics, sport, attitudes to school and learning, parent-school relationships, support with homework, sociability, household tasks and educational aspirations of the parents, children of cohabiting couples performed less well than children of married couples.[476] Overall, in the majority of cases, children of married couples do significantly better at school and in the community than children of cohabiting couples.[477]
>
> *Achievement*: There are significantly more children of married couples than of cohabiting couples reporting to have achieved an educational status that is as high or even higher than the expected level. There are also significantly more children of

cohabiting couples than of married couples who report to have
been less successful in the area of employment or who have
been unemployed or could only obtain part-time employment.

Drug use: Children of cohabiting couples appear in larger
proportions than children of married couples among those who
(a) are smoking or have been smoking; (b) have been smoking
earlier in life; (c) have been drinking in larger proportions; (d)
had begun drinking earlier in life; and (e) are using or have used
illicit drugs.[478]

Crime and delinquency: There are significantly more children
of cohabiting couples than children of married couples who
commit criminal offences, or who commit two or more offences.
The findings on delinquency follow the trend identified in the
context of drug use.[479]

More recent studies support the earlier conclusions. A Swedish
study found children of cohabiters were twice as likely to suffer from
psychiatric disorders, diseases, suicide attempts, alcoholism and
drug use.[480] A Norwegian study noted a more precarious economic
situation,[481] while British research observed that children in these
situations were more likely to be unhappy, subject to higher levels of
violence, abuse, debt and alcohol problems, as well as high levels of
anxiety, depression, suicidal thoughts and mental illness.[482]

A recent study of more than 10,000 infants that measured their
emerging literacy from nine months to kindergarten entry found that
children in cohabiting relationships fared worse than those living with
a divorced mother, leading the researcher, Jay Fagan, to conclude that
"several partnerships over a short period of time are disruptive to child
development outcomes."[483] According to Fagan, "the present study
adds to the increasing body of literature showing that cohabitation,
even when stable over a two-year period of time, has negative effects
on children." A recent Australian study tends to confirm other findings:
Children in cohabiting and sole mother families were progressing less
well than those in married families.[484]

Subsequent research has also implicated cohabitation in the dramatic increase in child abuse seen in many western nations. A British study found that, compared to children living with married biological parents, children living with cohabiting but unmarried biological parents are 20 times more likely to be subject to child abuse. A child living with a mother and a cohabiting boyfriend who is not the father is at an increased risk of 33 times, while living with a biological mother alone increases the risk by 14 times.[485]

Some manifestations of relationship dysfunction

Child protection reports

These trends are graphically illustrated in a 2011 Australian report *For Kid's Sake* by Professor Patrick Parkinson.[486] Subtitled "Repairing the social environment for Australian children and young people", it is a wake-up call about significant trends in the social ecology of the nation. Based on social science evidence, Professor Parkinson observes trends of considerable concern in the wellbeing of our children. Describing the dramatic increase in the number of children who have been reported to the various State and Territory child protection systems as the "Canary in the coal mine", the author documents the rise in adolescent mental health and risky behaviours.

The report, using data collected from state child health and welfare reports, found spiraling rates of child abuse and neglect, of children being placed in foster care and of teenage mental health problems, including a dramatic rise in hospitalisation for self-harm. The worrying data included:

- A tripling in the number of children notified for abuse or neglect since 1998.
- A doubling in the number of children in out-of-home care in 12 years.
- A 66 per cent increase in the rate of hospitalisation for self-

harm for 12-14-year-olds between 1996-97 and 2005-06.

- An increase from 28 per cent to 38 per cent in female school students experiencing unwanted sex between 2002 and 2008.
- A doubling in the rate of hospitalisation for alcohol intoxication for women aged 15-24 between 1998-99 and 2005-06.[487]

The graph below illustrates the significant increase in notifications of childhood abuse and neglect in Australia's most populous state, New South Wales, in just five years.

Child abuse and neglect notifications

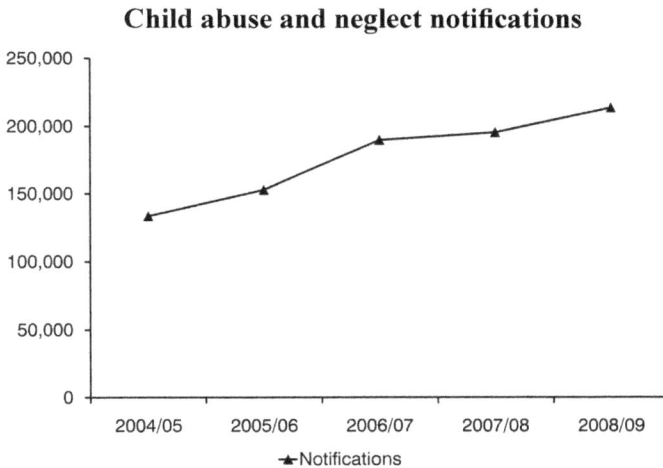

Source: Australian Institute of Health and Welfare, *Child Protection Australia*, 2009-10

While noting that there may be a number of explanations, Professor Parkinson observes that "if there is one major demographic change in western societies that can be linked to a large range of adverse consequences for many children and young people, it is the growth in the numbers of children who experience life in a family other than living with their two biological parents, at some point before the age of 15." Indeed, the number of children who do not reach the age of 15 in an intact family with both of their biological parents have almost doubled within a generation.

Professor Parkinson's conclusions are consistent with available data. In 2010-11, where family type was known, 34 per cent of children who were subject to a substantiated notification (5,660) came from single-parent-female households. This was followed by 32 per cent (5,449) from two parent-intact families. Children from two-parent step or blended families were the subject of 15 per cent of substantiated notifications (2,507). Smaller proportions of children who were subject of substantiated notification came from single parent-male families or from other relatives/kin or foster. Specifically, one per cent came from foster families (167), while five per cent came from single parent-male families (752) and four per cent from other relatives or kin (609).[488] This data probably under-represents the problem. In the related area of child sexual abuse, a survey has found that two-thirds of people are reluctant to report incidents to authorities.[489]

These trends are not confined to Australia. The former Chief Justice of the Supreme Court of Georgia, Leah Ward Sears, noted in 2006 that one in four of every child in the state under the age of 18 had a child support case, 14,000 were in the care of Family and Children Services, and 24,000 admitted to a youth detention centre. Sears added that these figures were typical of every state in the US.[490]

Recent UK data reflects similar patterns. The number of applications for taking children into protective care has soared from 6,689 in 2002-03, the first full year in which figures were collated, to 10,199 in 2011-12. As each application can involve more than one child, and most applications resulted in the children being taken into care, the actual number of children involved is likely to be even higher. More than 65,000 children were being cared for by the state in 2012.[491] The outcomes are particularly grim for children taken into care: 80 per cent of care-leavers are unemployed after two years, just 13 per cent leave school with good grades, and only nine per cent go to university. Half of inmates in young offenders' institutions had been in care, and one-quarter of adults in prison were in care as kids. A quarter of girls in care were pregnant by the time they left, and half of girls in care were single mothers within two years.[492]

A report on the 2011 British riots concluded that poor parenting was one of the major factors behind the violence and destruction that erupted in parts of the country,[493] and 60 per cent of the most dysfunctional families were fatherless.[494]

Child abuse and neglect

The incidence of child abuse and neglect also seems related to relationship dysfunction. A New York study found that children living with single parents – invariably single mothers – are more than twice as likely as children living with both parents to suffer physical abuse. A study for the US Administration for Children and Families found that family structure and living arrangement is the strongest predictor of maltreatment:

> Children living with their married biological parents universally had the lowest rate [of abuse and neglect], whereas those living with a single parent who had a cohabiting partner ... had the highest rate in all maltreatment categories. Compared to children living with married biological parents, those whose single parent had a live-in partner had more than eight times the rate of maltreatment overall, over 10 times the rate of abuse, and nearly eight times the rate of neglect.[495]

The findings are replicated in other studies.[496] The Australian Institute of Health and Welfare concluded 30,615 substantiated cases of child abuse and neglect, involving 26,544 children, were reported in 1994-95. Stepchildren were involved in 21 per cent of cases, although less than four per cent of children lived in stepfamilies. Although 81 per cent of children lived with biological parents, they accounted for only 30 per cent of cases. Dr Neville Turner of the National Children's Bureau of Australia estimates that a child whose mother lives in a *de facto* relationship with a man other than the child's father, or with a husband that is not the child's father, is at least five times more likely to be abused than one who lives with both married parents. South African scholars have also reported family fracture as one of the significant risk factors for child sexual abuse in that country.[497] A study of Brazilian families reached similar conclusions.[498]

Australian data revealed that of 86 homicide victims aged under 15 years from 1989-92, 60 were likely to be killed by parents or *de facto* parents; three by other family members; 12 by acquaintances; and only three by strangers. A NSW study found that a high proportion of child killers are either stepfathers or the mother's *de facto* or boyfriend. Dr Ania Wilczynski found that non-biological parents present "a disproportionate risk for children, particularly in the early stages of their relationship with the child." The proportion of suspected killers in *de facto* relationships was 6.5 times higher than for the general population. The study found that 28 per cent of the child killers had become parents when aged 20 years or younger. Canadian researchers found that children two years of age and younger were 70 to 100 times more likely to be killed by a stepparent than a biological parent.[499]

Regrettably, abuse appears to be transmitted across generations. "Women in clinically abusive relationships had childhood family adversity," concluded researchers from Columbia and Wisconsin-Madison Universities after considering data from 980 men and women aged 24 to 26. "Women who became involved in abusive relationships as adults experienced more caretaker changes in childhood" and "spent more years with a single parents then women who did not become involved in abusive relationships."[500]

Youth homelessness

According to the National Inquiry into Youth Homelessness, family conflict, including violence and abuse, is one of the major factors leading to youth homelessness in Australia.[501] The inquiry found that "at least 20–25,000 youth were homeless." It has been suggested that there are up to 250,000 young people not living with their families, and that approximately 30 per cent of 15-20 year olds are living independently from their families and are vulnerable to drifting in and out of homelessness. According to a Victorian study, there are about 11 in every 1,000 school children who are homeless.

Children aged between five and 18 made more than four million calls to the Kids Help Line between 1991 and 1995. There were 120,744 calls classified as serious, of which 44,554 (36.5 per cent) concerned relationship problems. Half of that number was about family relationships. Most of the callers were under 16, and three quarters of them girls.

A UK survey of 7,300 teenagers aged between 14 and 16 found that of the 84,000 children who run away from home each year, children living with both parents had the lowest rates of absconding. Family conflict was identified as the major reason. Disturbingly, seven out of 10 were not reported missing to the police after they had run away.[502]

Conclusions

Daniel Patrick Moynihan, the US senator, ambassador and statesman, caused widespread consternation when he released a report in 1965 about the disintegration of the negro family in America. Sub-titled "The case for national action", Moynihan's report argued that without jobs, negro men would become alienated as husbands and fathers, leading to family dysfunction and breakdown, increasing out-of-wedlock births and sole parenthood, declining education outcomes and entrenched poverty.[503] Describing the situation as "a tangle of pathology", Moynihan observed:

> From the wild Irish slums of the 19th century Eastern seaboard, to the riot-torn suburbs of Los Angeles, there is one unmistakable lesson in American history; a community that allows a large number of men to grow up in broken families, dominated by women, never acquiring any stable relationships to male authority, never acquiring any set of rational expectations about

the future – that community asks for and gets chaos. Crime, violence, unrest, disorder – most particularly the furious, unrestrained lashing out at the whole social structure – that is not only to be expected; it is very near to inevitable. And it is richly deserved.[504]

The condemnation of Moynihan, later to become a Democrat senator, was fierce. Decades later, his remarks were accepted as commonsense, and pivotal to the war on poverty.[505] What has become clearer over the years is that poverty today is increasingly related to family structure. Hence, using data collected by the National Institute of Child Health and Human Development, scholars from Harvard and Baylor Universities found that "approximately 50 per cent of the time, entry into poverty is caused by events other than "head-of-household earning decreases" citing "changes in family structure" as a prime example.[506]

In a more recent report, *Broken Britain*, the UK Centre for Social Justice concluded that the fabric of society was crumbling, leaving at its margins an underclass, where life is characterised by dependency, addiction, debt and family breakdown. It is an underclass where a child born into poverty today is more likely to remain in poverty than at any time since the late 1960s. The Centre identified five key paths to poverty: family breakdown, serious personal debt, drug and alcohol addiction, failed education, worklessness and dependency.[507]

Social science research reinforces the observations of Pat Moynihan that parental divorce, and fatherless families generate significant health and education problems for children and ongoing social dysfunction. In the five decades since Moynihan made his prescient observations, the incidence of fatherlessness has compounded. Family scholars recently calculated that the probability of children living apart from a father had doubled over three decades.[508]

The consequences for individuals and communities of a fatherless culture have been well-documented.[509] Weak paternal involvement in the lives of children has been consistently linked to adolescent behavioural problems.[510] "Paternal absence appears to be an important predictor of all categories of Separation Anxiety Disorder, even after accounting for other risk factors," including socioeconomic disadvantage, concluded researchers who studied the outcomes for 1,887 pairs of female twins born between 1975 and 1987.[511] Reflecting on the high levels of retaliatory killings in disadvantaged neighbourhoods, American studies show how fatherless and rootless young men often respond to challenges to their manhood through lethal violence which is collectively tolerated and even rewarded.[512] Nor are the adverse consequences confined to the broken relationships between fathers and children. Judith Wallerstein noted that the stress of divorce damages the parental relationship for as many as 40 per cent of divorced mothers.[513]

Thousands of studies consistently indicate that marriage benefits the health and well-being of individuals, and, conversely, that separation and divorce bring with them elevated risks for both former husbands and wives and their children. The extent to which these findings are accepted by social scientists is reflected in the work of a number of leading researchers. Sara McLanahan, herself a single parent, and professor of sociology at Princeton University, concluded her detailed analysis of four major national studies of families – three of them longitudinal:

> Children who grow up in a household with only one biological parent are worse off, on average, than children who grow up in a household with both of their biological parents, regardless of the parent's race or educational background, regardless of whether the parents are married when the child is born, and regardless of whether the resident parent remarries.[514]

Professor McLanahan did not claim that single parenthood was the only reason that some children do poorly: income, parenting patterns, neighbourhood resources, and educational levels are all factors, but they are boosted by the absence of a parent. Unsurprisingly, a combination of factors compounds the adverse effects. As a study of 2,842 Illinois adults found: "high rates of poverty and mother-only families and low-rates of college education and home ownership compromise the ability of residents to create and maintain public order." The sociologists added: "The breakdown of social control and order in disadvantaged neighbourhoods appears to form the major link to individual health."[515]

The non-partisan Council on Families in America, comprising leading scholars of both conservative and liberal inclinations, concluded in their report on marriage:

> The evidence continues to mount, and it points to one striking conclusion: the weakening of marriage has had devastating consequences for the well-being of children. To be sure, television, the movies, and popular music contribute to declining child well-being. So do poor teaching, the loss of skilled jobs, inefficient government bureaucracies, meagre or demeaning welfare programs, and the availability of guns and drugs. But by far the most important causal factor is the remarkable collapse of marriage, leading to growing family instability and decreasing parental investment in children.[516]

The renowned psychologist, Professor Urie Bronfenbrenner concluded: "There has been a progressive disarray at an accelerating rate of the disorganisation of the family in the western world."[517] A series of other official reports and academic studies have reached the same conclusion.[518] In his book, *Men, Mateship, Marriage*, Dr Don Edgar, the former director of the Australian Institute of Family Studies, concludes:

> There is now agreement in all studies on the key divorce effects, though the methodologies vary and there are still many contradictions. Divorce is, above all, disrupting to the lives of children, the continuity of their schooling, friendships and neighbourhood supports. Poverty is a widespread outcome

which is, in itself, a huge disadvantage compared with children in a home with one or two steady incomes. Children are better off economically, psychologically, emotionally with both parents. And fathers (despite their bad press) are an important resource for their children's well-being. Stepfamilies are a high risk, even though, financially, children are better off if the custodial parent re-marries.[519]

Even social scientists that have a more sanguine view of the developments worry about the impact on children. Andrew Cherlin observes:

It's hard to envision how experiencing a series of transitions could be beneficial to children, except as a relief from a series of conflicted relationships. At best, the transitions might do little harm to children.[520]

Professor Cherlin noted that one in five US children had experienced two parental partnerships by age 15, and one in twelve had experienced three or more.[521] Addressing the criticism that while partnership turnover raised the risk of delinquency, but the majority children who experienced it didn't become delinquents, Cherlin noted "even if only a minority have their lives altered, that's still a lot of children."[522] Sara McLanahan, who has studied single parent families for decades,[523] summarised the research: "Marital status at birth is a reasonably good proxy for whether children will grow up in a stable household."[524]

Patrick Fagan and Aaron Churchill stress:

None of the effects applies to each child of every divorced couple, nor has any one child suffered all the effects. . . There is no way to predict how any particular child will be affected nor to what extent, but it is possible to predict divorce's societal effects and how this large cohort of children will be affected as a group. These effects are both numerous and serious.[525]

The reasons why many children suffer from parental divorce are understandable. As a US study comparing divorced and married mothers found, the divorced mothers were significantly more hassled, reported greater numbers of negative life events and significantly greater negative [emotional] affect than did the married mothers. The researchers described a pattern of:

> Overburdened, stressed, depressed, and hassled divorced mothers . . . too preoccupied with more pressing issues such as economic stability and their own general well-being to deal with the daily demands of a preschool child. This inattention to their children's needs may result in less supportive parental behaviours that then provoke increased confrontative and negative mother-child interaction.[526]

In noting these research findings, we must acknowledge the admirable efforts of many single and stepparents, often against difficult odds, who are successfully raising their children and who deserve our support; nor is it to fail to recognise that some married couples are failing the task.[527] One loving parent is better than two parents in chronic high conflict. Nor is it to suggest a return to marriage forms of earlier years; or to suggest that violence and abuse should be condoned. But this should not deter us from advocating programs that seek to strengthen relationships and prevent family breakdown. As the National Council for the Single Mother and her Child said:

> When couples have a chance to explore fully the implications and commitments involved in the steps they are planning they may approach such commitments with more resources to enable them to cope with the demands they will face. The challenge is to encourage the community to see relationship education and counselling as a positive means of enhancing their relationship, rather than somewhere to go when things begin to go wrong.[528]

Given some surveys reveal that 37 per cent of people regret their divorce five years later, and up to 40 per cent believe that it could have been avoided,[529] there is a substantial case for renewed strategies to strengthen marriages and relationships.

In his groundbreaking longitudinal study, *A Generation at Risk*, Professor Paul Amato found that only one quarter to a third of divorces end up being better for the children than if the parents had stayed together. By contrast, about 70 per cent of divorces end low-conflict marriages, which would have been better for the children to have continued rather than ending.[530] This is consistent with other research. University of Chicago scholar, Linda Waite, found that many unhappily married spouses who stayed married reported that their marriages improved within five years.[531]

Marriage and family life require a balance of values. The enhancement of family life for the welfare of children involves the balancing of rights and obligations: between men and women; parents and children; individuals and the community; the present and future generations. In the past the balance was not always right. There was often an overemphasis on women's obligations – to husbands, to children, and to the community – at the expense of individual development. But today, the goal of balance is often replaced by the contemporary libertarian rejection of obligations in the name of individual freedom.

There is a perception that if individuals are happy, satisfied and contended, then so too will be families. While this is partially true, the social science research overwhelming reveals the converse to be true: Lifelong marriages and stable families contribute to the wellbeing of the individual members. In other words, as the family goes, so goes the well being of individual men, women and children.

The consequences of a growing non-marital culture are far-reaching. If more and more children are born to unstable or non-existent relationships between their biological parents, fewer children will have both parents raising them. And fewer will have experienced the support and security fundamental to forming happy and healthy attachments themselves. This will have serious implications for how well these children can attach to other people, and for society more generally.[532]

The bonds of family create moral commitments. Jonathan Sacks observes, "if we have any moral responsibilities at all, then we have moral responsibilities to those we brought into being."[533] It is not a new idea. Nor is it a conservative notion. John Stuart Mill wrote: "The fact itself, of causing the existence of a human being, is one of the most responsible actions in the range of human life. To undertake this responsibility – to bestow a life which may be either a curse or a blessing – unless the being upon whom it is bestowed will have at least the ordinary chance of a desirable existence, is a crime against that being."[534] The commitments of marriage are far-reaching.

SUMMARY

- ♥ The circumstances of a child's early life are critical to his or her future relationships and happiness.

- ♥ For children, a stable, happy marriage is the best source of emotional stability and good physical and mental health.

- ♥ Divorce has both short-term and long-term impacts on children, some which may last a lifetime.

- ♥ Divorce heightens the risks of poor physical and mental health, depression and behavioural problems in children.

- ♥ Subsequent adult relationships, educational performance, and financial circumstances are negatively associated with divorce.

- ♥ Many stepfamilies provide a secure, loving environment for children, but the risks for health, educational and related problems are significantly higher.

- ♥ Divorce can have intergenerational effects on children, affecting their own relationships, health and well-being.

- ♥ While children may benefit from the separation of highly conflicted parents, most divorces involve low conflict marriages, with significant negative effects on children.

- ♥ Children in cohabiting relationships have a significantly increased risk of experiencing the separation of their parents, lower levels of educational achievement, and higher incidence of problematic behaviours.

4

HAPPY, HEALTHY AND
PROSPEROUS SOCIETIES

Successful marriage benefits adults and children. It also benefits society: "as the family goes ... so goes society as a whole."[535] Because individuals gain meaning and identity from their relationships with others, a society dedicated to full and free human development cannot ignore the conditions that are most conducive to the fulfilment of that ideal. For it is in the institutions of civil society – in families, and in voluntary associations such as churches, charitable agencies, even sporting and social clubs – that democratic society is sustained. The Harvard law professor, Mary Ann Glendon, writes:

> The myriad of associations that generate social norms are the invisible supports of, and the *sine qua non* for, a regime in which individuals have rights. Neither the older political and civil rights, nor the newer economic and social rights, can be secure in the absence of the social arrangements that induce those who are disadvantaged by the rights of others to accept the restrictions and interferences that such rights entail.[536]

If we cannot preserve and support the institutions of community in which relationships are developed and nurtured, then we are not merely placing at risk the welfare of many people, particularly the young and the elderly, we are weakening the very foundations of society itself. DH Lawrence observed:

> It is marriage, perhaps, which had given man the best of his freedom, given him his little kingdom of his own within the big

> kingdom of the State ... It is a true freedom because it is a true
> fulfilment, for men, women and children. Do we then want to
> break marriage? If we do break it, it means we all fall to a far
> greater extent under the direct sway of the State.[537]

Civil society embraces those relationships which are independent of the State but provide an environment in which children are formed in the virtues of citizenship and in which adults are encouraged to practise them. Of these institutions, the family is the most important, as it is the first and most critical environment for the development of human competence and virtue. Pope John Paul II noted:

> If the human person is at the centre of every social institution,
> then the family, as the primary place of socialisation, needs to be
> a community of free and responsible persons who are encouraged
> to live marriage as a project of love which contributes to the
> vitality of civil society.[538]

Successful marriage is a key to the central role of transmitting our values to future generations. The psychologist Judith Wallerstein wrote that the good marriage represents us at our civilised best:

> We are at our most considerate, our most loving, our most
> selfless within the orbit of a good family. Only within a satisfying
> marriage can a man and a woman create the emotional intimacy
> and moral vision that they alone can bequeath to their children.[539]

How we support marriage then, as the protective institution of family, particularly the welfare of children, is of profound importance.

The parental relationship is unique in human affairs. Parents committed to each other are by far the most willing to make massive, unbalanced investments in children. Who else is capable and willing to make this investment? The State? Peer groups? Public or private childrearing organisations? The answer, as any parent will tell you, is no-one. No amount of public investment in children can possibly offset the private disinvestment that has accompanied the decline of marriage and the weakening of family ties.[540] Surveying centuries of historical change, the Stanford sociologist, William Goode, noted that "if present social trends continue, other social institutions will function less well," and that "the disintegration of the family is a threat to social cohesion itself."[541]

Modern marriage is often characterised by the expression of romantic love between spouses. Yet survey after survey shows that faithfulness, commitment and companionship in sharing life together are the central aspirations of married couples. These things are at the very core of a vision for marriage as a state of unconditional love, forgiveness and reconciliation, and service between spouses. Indeed, the most recent social science research reveals that couples whose marriages are established on intense levels of romantic bliss are more likely to divorce than those who have a more practical and realistic view of their relationship.

Marriage has an irreplaceable social dimension in the nurturing and socialising of children, by providing them with the economic resources and extended family networks of mutual support and protection. It is in marriage that children have the best chance to experience the domestic virtues, based on respect for human life and dignity, and learn to practice them in understanding, patience and mutual encouragement and forgiveness. As Martin Luther-King said: "The institution of the family is decisive in determining not only if a person has the capacity to love another individual but in the larger sense whether he is capable of loving ... The whole of society rests on this foundation for stability, understanding and social peace."[542] It is in the family that obligations and values are learnt. Two thousand years ago, Aristotle observed that if children do not love their parents and family members, they would love no-one but themselves. The sense of stability and love provided in families is central to the socialisation of individuals.

There is much to celebrate about family life today. There is a renewed recognition that both mothers and fathers play an important role in the lives of their children. There is often a more equitable division of household labour, allowing both parents to contribute to family life and the wider community. There are more opportunities for marriage and parenting education and enrichment programs.

Social capital

It also appears that marriage promotes civic engagement. Married people, for example, vote in disproportionately higher numbers than their percentage of the adult population.[543] Married adults "were 1.3 times more likely than unmarried adults to have volunteered, and married adults averaged 1.4 times more volunteer hours than unmarried individuals," according to a survey of civic contributions in the US.[544] Parents were also found to be almost twice as likely as childless adults to volunteer for charitable activities.

After controlling for economic circumstances, scholars from UCLA and Tulane University found that "children in single-parent families engage in fewer activities with their parents" and that "single parent family structure is associated with fewer links between parents and social circles of children."[545] According to the research, this also related to poorer school performance for the children.

Conversely, "the disintegration of particular institutions (ie churches, families, and schools)" results in communities in which antisocial behaviour, including violence, are much more common.[546] Using the *British Crime Survey*, criminologists from Northwestern University concluded that family disruption predicted both the emergence of unsupervised peer groups in neighbourhoods and a decline in civic involvement.[547]

An Australian study of approximately 2,500 residents of suburban Adelaide noted that marital status was 'positively indirectly associated' with 'informal networks'. The married were more likely to socialise with friends, family, neighbours and work colleagues, and receive more practical, emotional and financial support from others. The advantages extended to 'quality of life' and mental health.[548]

The economic benefits of marriage

Marriage benefits individuals economically. It also benefits society. As a wealth generating institution, married couples create more economic assets on average than singles and cohabiting couples. In studying the effect of marital history on retirement income, researchers found that those who had been continuously married had significantly higher levels of wealth than those who had not: For those who never marry, there was a 75 per cent reduction in wealth; and for those who divorced and didn't remarry, the reduction was 73 per cent.[549]

Through the economies of scale and specialisation that marriage offers, couples receive a wealth bonus.[550] They also tend to invest and save for the future.[551] And because of their responsibilities and societal expectations, married men, on average, earn more than single men with similar education and job experience,[552] whereas the contrary might have been thought true. As the Noble Economics Laureate, Gary S Becker, contends,[553] working longer and more regularly helps a worker to increase productivity to obtain additional income; and this effect flows to the broader economy.[554] According to other US data, twice as many married fathers (32 per cent) worked 45 hours or more per week compared to cohabiting fathers (16 per cent).[555] Similar trends are evident in other nations.[556]

The benefits are not restricted to men. Using an income-to-needs ratio, continuously married women have been found to be significantly better off.[557] The economic benefits are greater for women than they are for men. In the US, households headed by single women have consistently lagged behind those headed by the male, breadwinner households by 43 per cent for the past six decades. The differences are compounded by the fact that dual couple households also have the flexibility to gain a further full-time or part-time income.[558]

Particularly children feel the impact of marriage. Married households have higher incomes when children are present; non-marital household have lower income when children are present. The economist, Robert Lerman, concluded from his studies "the 1971-1989 trend away from marriage among parents accounted for nearly half the increase in income inequality and more than the entire rise in child poverty rates."[559]

The benefits for individual couples multiply and compound in the economy. The increase in income per year for married men, for example, estimated in the US at 0.9 per cent, is almost as much (75 per cent) of the income increase for years of experience on-the-job.[560] The 'marriage premium' – the economic benefits flowing from marriage – has been identified in South Africa,[561] Australia, France, Germany, Israel, Luxembourg, Switzerland, the UK, Norway, the Netherlands, Italy and Canada.[562] However, the 'marriage premium' diminishes in stepfamilies, according to another economic study.[563]

The economic costs of separation and divorce

The retreat from marriage has had profound economic consequences. This occurs in a number of ways. There are the direct costs of divorce, including the courts and associated services. Marital dysfunction and family breakdown often leads to other social problems with significant costs to communities. It is estimated in the UK that each child with untreated behavioural problems costs an average of £70,000 by the time they reach 28 years of age – 10 times the cost of children without behavioural problems.[564] As many non-married parents have little or no independent income, welfare costs have burgeoned. Many people who would otherwise contribute to the economy through their taxes, savings and investments have become dependent upon government for their livelihood. It is partly why welfare reform has been pursued in most nations over the past two decades. Professor Patrick Parkinson observes:

> The costs of family instability are not just borne by individuals. They are, to a significant extent, borne by the taxpayers who provide income support for many parents and their children, pay

substantial administrative costs in ensuring income transfers through the child support system, and bear more of the costs of caring for the elderly than would be necessary if a greater number of marital and quasi-marital relationships remained intact.[565]

Separation and divorce compound the costs of an ageing population, as many people who divorced in the aftermath of the introduction of no-fault laws reach retirement and old-age. Traditionally, the burden of caring for the young and the elderly has fallen disproportionately on women.[566] A consequence of divorce is more women in the workforce, leaving less time to care, and a greater burden on government services. Many divorced individuals also enter retirement themselves with reduced financial resources.[567] As Professor Parkinson notes, "it is only in the last few years that the full impact of the divorce revolution on the aged population of western societies has begun to be felt."[568]

Divorce and non-marital childbearing also increase child poverty.[569] According to one US study, black child poverty rates would have been 28.4 per cent rather than 45.6 per cent, and white child poverty rates 11.4 per cent rather than 15.4 per cent, had family structure not changed between 1960 and 1998.[570]

Much of the cost associated with the profound social changes of the past few decades are borne by the public purse, as households multiply[571] and many individuals are left the poorer and unable to meet the financial demands. More significantly, the growth of a non-married and less child-centred society slows economic growth. Recent American analysis reveals that economic growth in the US is a fraction of the pre-1960s era because of the breakdown of marriage.[572] The combination of proportionately fewer children, and the fact that up to 20 per cent of them are ill-equipped to compete in the modern economy compounds the problem. It is estimated that the GDP growth due to natural population growth is now half what it was four decades ago. Similarly, the contribution of human capital, which ranged from

0.5 per cent to 1.5 per cent of annual Gross Domestic Product growth up until the about 2008, will be wiped out mostly with the retirement of the baby boomers and their replacement with "neglected and undercapitalised generations."[573]

As the proportion of married couples with children decreases as a proportion of all families, the economic impact of marriage declines. This has been the story of the past two decades in the US: after median family income doubled from 1947 to 1977, it has slowed recently;[574] and family income inequality has increased significantly.[575] Hence, median household income of married couples has been estimated to be twice that of divorced households and four times that of separated households.[576] In an age of heightened concern for the environment, US researchers have concluded that separation and divorce has led to less efficient use of energy and resources and bigger expenditure on utilities, largely as a consequence of the increased demand for additional housing.[577]

Describing family breakdown as a pressing social policy problem, Professor Parkinson wonders how long before governments are forced to confront the costs:

> As long as public finances in western societies were healthy, the growing costs of family instability could be absorbed. However, Europe and the United States, in particular, are both facing a crisis in terms of government debt and the affordability of social welfare provision. With an ageing population, and a shrinking tax base, there are very real limits to the capacity of western governments to continue affording to absorb the public costs of private lifestyle decisions.[578]

SUMMARY

- ♥ Marriage promotes civic engagement and social connection.
- ♥ Marriage benefits society as couples generate more wealth, save and invest for the future, and earn more on average than singles.
- ♥ The economic benefits for individual couples multiply and compound in the economy.
- ♥ Conversely, separation, divorce and a non-marital culture costs the economy through lower earnings, reduced taxes, increased welfare and child poverty, and slower economic growth.

PART TWO

THE NEW CULTURE

Men and women of full age, without any limitation due to race, nationality or religion, have the right to marry and to found a family. They are entitled to equal rights as to marriage, during marriage, and at its dissolution.

Marriage shall be entered into only with the free will and full consent of the intending spouses.

The family is the natural and fundamental group unit of society and is entitled to protection by society and the State.

(Universal Declaration of Human Rights)

The breakdown of the social order is not a matter of nostalgia, poor memory or ignorance about the hypocrisies of earlier ages. The decline is readily measurable in statistics on crime, fatherless children, reduced educational outcomes and opportunities, broken trust and the like ... the culture of intense individualism which in the marketplace and laboratory leads to innovation and growth, spilled over into the realm of social norms where it corroded virtually all forms of authority and weakened the bonds holding families, neighbourhoods, and nations together. (Francis Fukuyama)

The fact that we have deconstructed the family – morally, psychologically, economically, politically – is the single most fateful cultural development of our times. (Jonathan Sacks)

5

CHANGING CULTURAL VALUES

The former Director of the Australian Institute for Family Studies, Dr Don Edgar, identified several major factors shaping the 'new marriage':[579]

> First is the certainty of contraception, the careful planning of births and the changing place of children in the marriage.[580]
>
> Second is the new preparation pathway to marriage via multiple relationships, prolonged autonomy as an individual earner, *de facto* living and the resultant confusion about intimacy and commitment.
>
> Third is the growing realisation on the part of women that they cannot and ought not rely upon or be dependants of men. Thus we see improved education, retention of women's career and labour force participation, with consequent changes in the way marriage and family life function.
>
> Fourth is the legal framework progressively enacting equal opportunity, human rights, joint responsibility for men and women fulfilling the obligations of marriage and parenthood. It is a *de facto* 'backward' redefinition of marriage, starting from the end point of divorce, and from combined changes in family law and social security provisions.

These changing values have been reflected in the rise of individualism, the loosening of marital bonds, increasing marital instability, the avoidance of the word 'marriage', and evolving gender relationships.

Individualism

A culture of rights, combined with increasing materialism, has dominated western discussion since the end of World War II.[581] Rights became the dominant language of western culture. This culture was reflected in subsequent changes to our laws. Hence the restrictions on divorce were eased, the right to financial assistance from the State for sole parents enhanced, and the taxation system in many nations gradually skewed against married couples with children.[582] Writing in the American context, the social researcher Daniel Yankelovich observed:

> The quest for greater individual choice clashed directly with the obligations and social norms that held families and communities together in earlier years. People came to feel that questions of how to live and with whom to live were a matter of individual choice not to be governed by restrictive norms. As a nation, we came to experience the bonds to marriage, family, children, job, community, and country as constraints that were no longer necessary. Commitments were loosened.[583]

Hugh McKay traced similar trends in Australia. In his book *Generations: Baby boomers their parents and their children*, he referred to "the emerging boomer philosophy of 'Look after Number One' and 'Do your own thing,' which appeared to offer a conceptual or even intellectual framework for an ethical system devoid of the notion of restraint, or the practice of self-denial."[584] McKay reflects on the impact of this culture on relationships: "Though it was not always recognised as an antisocial movement which carried the potential to destroy relationships, it often turned out in practice to feed self-centredness and to enshrine the idea that personal growth was the way to nirvana (where 'personal growth' often meant not much more than 'feeling good')". A strong sense of individuality was also a feature of the generation born in the 1970s, according to the Australian social researcher.[585]

Deconstructing the family

One of the cultural influences most destructive of marriage and family has been the social philosophy of postmodernism and deconstructionism associated with the French critics Michel Foucault and Jacques Derrida. Although this is not an essay on their works, some reference is necessary to demonstrate that the destruction of marriage and the family is not merely a consequence of their radical social philosophy, it is at its heart.

According to Professor Foucault, there is no objective truth upon which to base social structures, such as marriage and family. Rejecting reason, he argued that knowledge is a set of beliefs constructed to justify power relationships:

> Sexuality (and social structures depending on sexuality like marriage and family) is something we ourselves create – it is our own creation, and much more than the discovery of a secret (unchangeable) side of desire. We have to understand what with our desires, through our desires, go new forms of love, new forms of creation. Sex is not a fatality: it is a (formless) possibility for creative life.[586]

For Foucault, marriage and family are not fixed concepts. They have no meaning beyond the context in which they exist.

Foucault's student, Jacques Derrida, regarded as the founder of deconstructionism, combined Marxist social analysis and Freudian psychological techniques to 'deconstruct' the pillars of western civilisation, including marriage and the family. In *Glas*, Professor Derrida deconstructs the concept of family by affirming the power of sexuality, while at the same time denying sexual difference is truly essential to human existence.[587] Sexual difference does not belong to the existential structure of fundamental human existence (*Dasein*), according to the French philosopher:

> If *Dasein* as such belongs to neither of the sexes, that does not mean that its being is deprived of sex. On the contrary: here one

> must think of a predifferential (non-sexually differentiated), or rather a predual (non-male/female), sexuality . . . a matter here of the positive and powerful source of every possible sexuality.[588]

While Derrida relied, in part, on "Freud's theory that civilisations are essentially neurotic and destroy themselves by restricting sex too much,"[589] the British social scientist, Joseph Unwin, later discredited it.[590] Surveying the major civilisations and societies over 5,000 years of history, Unwin reached the opposite conclusion:

> In human records there is no instance of a society retaining its energy after a complete new generation has inherited a tradition which does not insist on pre-nuptial and post-nuptial continence.[591]

Regardless of their historical legitimacy, the influence of the deconstructionists is evident in writings about modern 'pure' relationships.[592] Beginning in the 1960s, some social scientists published negative views about marriage and family. An example well-known to scholars of the family is Edmund Leach's 1967 Reith Lectures *A Runaway World?* in which he suggested that "far from being the basis of the good society, the family, with its narrow privacy and tawdry secrets, is the source of all our discontents." Indeed, the nuclear family "is the most unusual kind of organisation and I would predict that it is only a transient phase of our society," said Leach. Children "needed to grow up in larger, more relaxed domestic groups centred on the community rather than in mother's kitchen, something like an Israeli kibbutz, or a Chinese commune."[593]

Despite the historical evidence that most people in Britain generally lived in nuclear families and births outside marriage were historically low by today's rates,[594] Leach was not alone in his distaste for marriage and family life. David Cooper and RD Laing saw the intense privacy of the family, with its network of introverted, intense and compulsory relationships as destructive of the individual's self. Cooper described the nuclear family as "the ultimately perfected form of non-meeting;"[595] and Laing claimed that the "initial act of brutality against the average child is the mother's first kiss."[596]

Three decades later, the appeal of the Israeli kibbutz and the Chinese commune have somewhat diminished. Evidence has also continued to mount about the benefits for the health and well-being of stable family life. Despite this, Leach's views continued to be recycled, for example by Anthony Giddens in his 1999 Reith Lectures. Not only are Gidden's ideas reminiscent of Leach's tilt against the family, even the title of his lecture series, *Runaway World*, is familiar.[597]

In words similar to Leach, Professor Giddens asserts that "what most of its defenders in western countries call the traditional family was in fact a late transitional phase in family developments in the 1950s." By defining the traditional family as "both parents living together with their children of the marriage, where the mother is full time housewife, and the father the breadwinner," Giddens constructs a straw man against which to rail. For most families in the western world, two incomes is the norm.

"Romantic love is a modern invention," writes the professor. "Marriage was never in the past based on intimacy." This ignores thousands of years of history. From the *Book of Songs* to Shakespeare and since, authors and poets have written about romantic love and intimacy.

Professor Giddens would replace marriage with "coupling" and "uncoupling" – all done in a "democracy of the emotions." As for children, parents in the past had them only for economic reasons: "One could say that children weren't recognised as individuals." In the end, Giddens is inconsistent. On one page, he refers to "coupling" and "uncoupling" and then to marriage "as a ritual commitment can help stabilise otherwise fragile relationships." But why bother if serial coupling is the path to individual happiness?

Amidst this re-characterisation of relationships, the place of children has been jettisoned. They are seen as 'stressors' on the relationship[598] and a threat to the bond between adults.[599] Instead, the concentration of those theorising about relationships has been on love styles.[600] Analysing this new world of relationships, Professor Dan Cere observes five main ideas:

> First, the distinction between marriage and other intimate relationships is all but eliminated. . . Second the new story tells us of basic human attachment and intimacy needs that must be satisfied. But it also insists that we privately choose the specific 'love styles' with which we seek to gratify those needs ... Third, the new world is very small. It is only big enough for the 'dyad,' the couple ... Children are essentially screened out ... Fourth, the new dyadic relationships are not measured by their capacity to foster any of the traditional virtues, such as courage and self-sacrifice, but instead solely by their capacity to meet what the self views as the self's needs ... Finally ... romantic relationships replace marriage and religion as life's main arenas for the discovery of personal meaning.[601]

Marriage, children and family life are to be replaced by the loving interactions of ever-changing dyad partners. This may reflect life for more people today, but as the social science evidence already canvassed suggests, it is fanciful that such transient relationships provide the base upon which most adults and children will flourish.

A culture of divorce?

Dr Don Edgar has written that in the past few decades marriage has been redefined backwards by reference to divorce. Other commentators have reached similar conclusions. The leading academics and social scientists that comprised the Council on Families in America referred to the divorce revolution in their report *Marriage in America*, by which they meant "the steady displacement of a marriage culture by a culture of divorce and unwed parenthood."[602] There is some evidence to suggest that no-fault divorce legislation has contributed "directly to more divorce and sooner divorces than would have happened otherwise."[603] In most countries, discussion about family relations has centred on the regulation of divorce, to the exclusion of other significant aspects of marriage and family life.

Marital instability

Professor Norval Glenn, a leading sociologist, suggested that the increasing rates of separation and divorce possibly compound marital instability:

> There are strong theoretical reasons for thinking that a decline in the ideal of marital permanence will tend to makes marriages less satisfactory, not just less stable. For instance, the person who enters marriage with the notion that he or she may remain in it only for a few years will not be inclined to fully commit or make the kinds of investments that would be lost if the marriage should end. And if a person constantly compares the existing marriage with real or imagined alternatives to it, the existing marriage will inevitably compare unfavourably in some respects. People are hardly aware of needs that are currently being well served, but they tend to be keenly aware of the needs that are not being satisfied. And since attention tends to centre on needs that are not being especially well met in one's marriage (and there are always some), the grass will always tend to look greener on the other side of the marital fence. Therefore, merely contemplating alternatives to one's marriage may engender marital discontent. Furthermore, persons who still strongly adhere to the ideal of marital permanence may be afraid to commit strongly to their marriages if they perceive a general weakening of the ideal.[604]

Professor Glenn and others have indicated a tendency of many couples to hold back on marital commitments because of the perceived probability of marital disintegration in our society. A second, equally strong tendency, found among couples with stable and long-lasting relationships, is to state that the daily stresses and strains of marriage would probably have led to divorce had the ideal of marital permanence not been such an important part of their relationship. This is confirmed by more recent research, which suggests that attending to the health of one's friends' marriages serves to support and enhance the durability of one's own relationship.[605]

Studies have suggested a decline in marital happiness. In a 1991 study, Professor Glenn reported on a survey of data gathered over a 15 year period from 1973 to 1977 in the US.[606] The evidence "consistently indicates that the probability of attaining marital success, in a first marriage *or* at all, has declined in recent years."[607] The findings ran counter to the expected outcome. As Stacy Rogers and Paul Amato comment in a later study: "This is the opposite of what one would expect if the rise in divorce were due only to the increased ending of unhappy marriages. If divorce removes poor marriages from the pool of married couples, then remaining marriages should be happier now, on average, than in the past."[608]

After discussing possible reasons, including increased expectations of marriage, and the impact of workforce participation, Professor Glenn concluded: "I suspect, however, that underlying any decline in the probability of marital success is a more fundamental change, namely, a decline in the ideal of marital permanence and, perhaps more importantly, in the expectation that marriages will last until one of the spouses dies."[609] Support for Glenn's thesis comes from a recent study. Using a sample from the *National Survey of Families*, Paul Amato examined the experiences of two waves of couples, divorced between 1987-88 and 1992-94. The divorcees from low-conflict marriages reported significant decreases in happiness after divorce for both men and women. In contrast, those from high-conflict marriages reported significant increases in post-divorce happiness, although the level remained below the happiness of men and women that had stayed married. Amato wonders whether "infidelity may be the factor that causes an otherwise stable marriage to unravel relatively quickly" but notes that "the greater social acceptance of divorce, combined with the greater ease of obtaining divorce, has increased the proportion of divorces that occur among couples with average (rather than low) levels of marital quality."[610] Another study of the states in America that passed no-fault divorce legislation in the 1960s and 1970s concluded that no-fault laws resulted in a substantial number of divorces that would not have occurred otherwise."[611]

Stacey Rogers and Paul Amato compared groups in 1980 and 1992 that were identical in terms of age and at similar stages of their marriage and found that members of the younger cohort report less marital interaction, more marital conflict, and more problems in their marriages.[612] Improvements in education and increases in age at marriage in the younger cohort partially offset the rise in marital problems. They also found that marital quality is related to four factors: family economic resources; work/family conflict; gender role attitudes; and premarital cohabitation. Despite the fall in marital quality, Professors Rogers and Amato found that commitment to the idea of life-long marriage appears to be stronger in the younger cohort: "Such a pattern suggests that young married people may be committed to salvaging marriage, and that reports of increased marital tensions and difficulties reflect not the struggles of an outdated social institution, but the inherent difficulties in adapting marriage to a rapidly changing social climate."[613]

Reflecting on the fact that most divorces are initiated by women, Allen Parkman from the University of New Mexico examined what he described as the nonmaterial gifts in marriage – understanding, love and affection, time, sex, how a spouse handled finances, the spouse's domestic role and the spouse's role as a parent – finding that divorced women were less satisfied with these things than their ex-husbands. Mirroring Norval Glenn's thesis, Parkman observed: "The frustration of spouses with their marital outcomes is compounded by unilateral divorce. It discourages gifts during marriage because future reciprocity is uncertain; then, when gifts are not forthcoming, it increases the likelihood of divorce by lowering the transaction costs."[614]

Paul Amato and Danelle DeBoer returned to the apparent intergenerational spread of divorce in a subsequent study of data collected from 2,033 married persons between 1980 and 1997.[615] Finding that "parental divorce approximately doubled the odds that offspring would see their own marriages end in divorce," Amato and DeBoer considered two contrasting hypotheses: that children whose parents have divorced are more likely to divorce themselves because they have been deprived of healthy parental models for developing "the skills and interpersonal orientations that facilitate the maintenance of long-term mutually satisfying intimate relationships;" or that children whose parents divorce are more likely to divorce themselves because that have lost "faith in marital permanence." After testing a number of groups, they concluded:

> Apparently growing up with troubled but continuously married parents predisposes offspring to contemplate divorce in their own marriages. But without a parental divorce to emulate, these thoughts are not generally translated into behaviour.

Accordingly, the undermining of commitment to lifelong marriage is "a primary mechanism underlying the intergenerational transmission of marital instability." Perhaps surprisingly, "divorce was most likely to be transmitted across generations if parents reported a low, rather than a high, level of discord prior to marital dissolution." Professors Amato and DeBoer concluded that divorce in circumstances of low marital discord is likely to be understood by children as evidence of "the nonbinding nature of the marital commitment." Given more recent reports that couples increasingly divorce because of "boredom" with the relationship,[616] this research spells out significant consequences for the children of such marriages.

Avoidance of 'marriage'

Part of the cultural change has been a reluctance to use the word 'marriage' in discussions about relationships in policy formation.[617] Family scholars have listed a number of reasons that have been advanced for the avoidance of the 'M' word:[618]

- The 'M' word brings with it many different kinds of baggage. For feminists, it appears as a smokescreen for re-instituting patriarchy. For single people, gays and lesbians, it raises concerns about discrimination. For conservatives, it can stir up fears of legitimisation of same-sex marriage. For many front line social workers and low-income advocates, it evokes images of domestic violence and abuse.

- Promoting marriage is believed to stigmatise and blame single parents, many of whom are doing a good job under very difficult circumstances.

- The idea of government intruding into marriage makes some people very uncomfortable. For the religious, marriage is a matter between individuals, their god, and faith-based organisations. For the secular, marriage represents a private contract between individuals which they can enter or leave as they please, with minimal interference.

- Many consider marriage a natural, voluntary relationship based on the ideal of romantic love. Love is the cement that binds the couple together and is either present or it isn't. The notion that programs and policies might have anything to do with improving the quality of a couple's relationship or their decision to divorce is viewed with scepticism.

- Many demographers and sociologists have argued that attempts to strengthen marriage are futile since these trends are a result of overwhelming social and world-wide forces that are irreversible. They point out that nothing is permanent any more. Jobs, houses, careers, lifestyles, community residence and education all change constantly throughout our lives. Thus changing partners through 'serial' marriages and creating 'alternative' family forms may be appropriate norms for the future.

- Finally, marriage, divorce and out-of-wedlock childbearing are very personal and often very painful subjects. The overwhelming majority of people have had some direct experience with divorce, either in their own families or in those of their friends. Many have had some acquaintance with unwed pregnancy and/or out-of-wedlock childbearing. Although the stigma attached to these events has lessened, the experience typically remains fraught with pain, disappointment, guilt and feelings of failure.[619]

However, as the scholars and researchers attending the Family Impact Seminar concluded: "Such fears and sensitivities, however real, must not be permitted to stifle debate on a topic of such importance to the vast majority of people and that has such widespread ramifications for society."

Changes in gender roles and the workforce

One of the most profound changes affecting families has been in the relationship between families and work over the past few decades. These changes reflect the participation of women in the paid workforce and the changing face of work, as well as new understandings of gender roles.

The proportion of married women in the paid workforce has increased throughout the industrialised world. In Australia, for example, it jumped from 29 per cent in 1966 to 68 per cent four decades later. Just under half of mothers with children aged four years or under are in the paid labour force. In the UK only 57 per cent of employed people are in traditional employment working full-time for an employer. Twenty five per cent works part-time, 13 per cent are self-employed, and five per cent are contract and casual workers. Sixty per cent of couples with children have both partners in the workforce. In the US, labour force participation by married women with children less than six years of age increased from 18.6 per cent in 1960 to 59.6 per cent in 1993.[620]

The entry of women into the workforce is facilitated by demographic factors, urbanisation, labour-saving domestic appliances, the availability of suitable employment, particularly part-time jobs, education and economic incentives such as higher wages and favourable taxation for two-income couples, the availability of childcare, and a change in attitudes making it acceptable for women to work outside the home.

The long term determinants of female labour supply tend to explain why it was possible for women to enter the workforce last century in increasingly large numbers. Short term determinants explain why women availed themselves of the opportunities provided to work. These include economic pressures to work due to falls in real wages for middle and lower income workers, the loss of employment at middle level for adult males due to economic recession and industrial restructuring, new levels of conspicuous consumption, and increasing costs of housing. The decision by women to enter the labour market is more sensitive to economic incentives than the decision taken by men.

Not only has the participation rate of women in the workforce grown while that of men has declined relatively, the areas of work in which women have been employed are in the fields upon which modern economies are increasingly reliant.[621] While much still needs to be done to ensure equal opportunities for women in the workplace and to provide the flexibility required by women to pursue careers to the same level as men, there is also a growing body of blue collar workers for whom employment is becoming increasingly uncertain.

These changes have also created new tensions for family life and marriages. Many women have to work the double shift, juggling their paid work with family duties.[622] For an increasing number of families, there is no choice about one parent staying at home. While many women enter the paid workforce for career reasons,[623] the Australian social researcher Jeannie Strachan identified three other groups of working mothers: Firstly, "I was once a full-time mother," usually over 40, who had been home most of the school years and has gone back into the workforce "for financial reasons to provide the family with extras, but not for the family's survival." Secondly, "the home at 4.00 p.m. workers." The third group Strachan called "the victim workers – the women who, for whatever reason, have no choice as to whether to work or not, and yet have pre-school age children."[624] A more recent British report also revealed that a majority of mothers were concerned that their work-life balance was wrong, and they did not have enough time for their children.[625]

In her study, *Work-Lifestyle Choices in the 21st Century*,[626] Catherine Hakim, a Senior Research Fellow at the London School of Economics, suggests that women are not a homogenous group, but three distinct groups with different patterns of behaviours and different responses to policies. According to Hakim:

> A minority of women have no interest in employment, careers, or economic independence, and do not plan to work long term unless things go seriously wrong for them. Their aim is to marry as well as they can and give up paid employment to become full-time homemakers and mothers. The group includes highly educated women as well as those who do not get any qualifications.

In contrast, some women actively reject the gender division of labour in the home, expect to work fulltime and continuously throughout life, and prefer symmetrical roles for husband and wife rather than separate roles.

The third group (the so-called "adaptive women") is numerically dominant: women who are determined to combine employment and family work, so become secondary earners. They may work full-time early in life, but later switch to part-time jobs on a semi-permanent basis, and/or to intermittent employment.

In her more recent study, *Models of the family in Modern Societies*, Professor Hakim confirms her theory by examining work preferences in Europe, particularly Spain and the UK.[627] Her conclusions are reflected in numerous surveys and by family and work choices in Australia:

- 24.4 per cent of couple families with children are headed by a couple with one partner working full time and one partner at home full time.
- 25.2 per cent of couple families are headed by a couple with one partner working full time and one working part time.
- Only 27.2 per cent of couple families have both partners working full time.
- In 19.7 per cent of families neither partner has a job.
- Of the families headed by a sole parent, 45.6 per cent are jobless.[628]

Employment status of couple families, Australia 2011

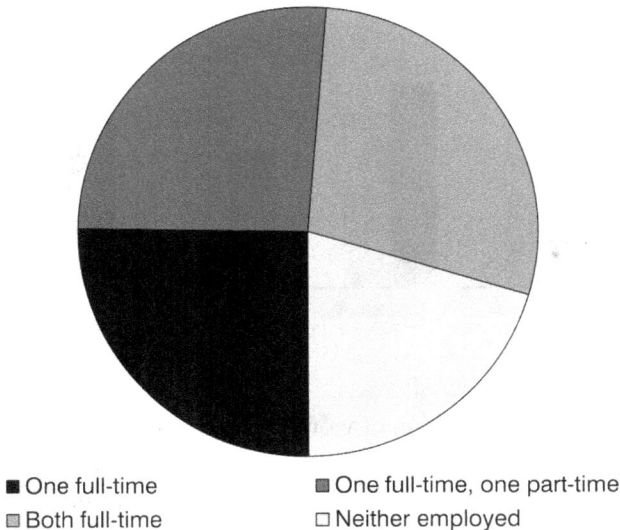

■ One full-time   ▨ One full-time, one part-time
▨ Both full-time   □ Neither employed

The adaptive approach of families to work is also illustrated in the work choices of families with children:

- Of partnered women aged 35-39, 66.7 per cent of those with no children work fulltime, compared to 18.3 per cent who work part-time or who are not in the workforce (14 per cent).
- However, only 25.5 per cent of women with children under 15 work full-time, compared to 40.1 per cent who work part-time or who are not in the labour force (34.3 per cent).
- For those with children over 15, 35.6 per cent work full-time, while 30.4 per cent either work part-time or are not in the labour force (34 per cent).[629]

Labour force participation, Australia 2011 (percentages)

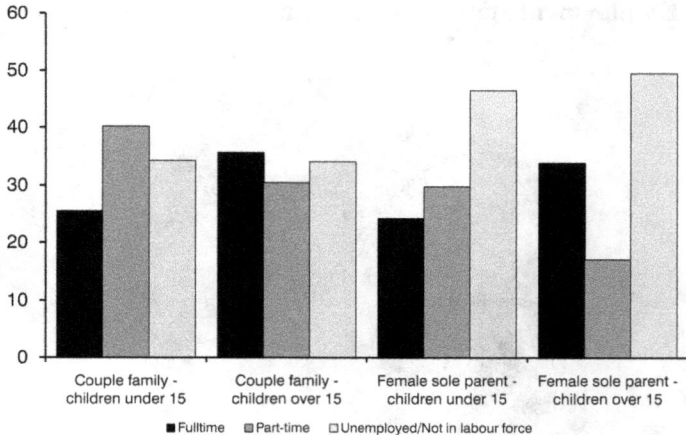

Overall, "the proportion of women employed in part-time jobs rose from 25 per cent to 29 per cent over the decade to December 2005 while full-time employment remained steady at around 37 per cent. Similarly for men, part-time employment increased slightly (from 7 per cent to 10 per cent) and the proportion in full-time employment remained fairly stable (at about 73 per cent)". Part-time employment for women had risen from 17.2 per cent in 1982 to 25 per cent in 1995, while full-time employment had risen from 31.1 per cent in 1982 to 36.8 per cent in 1995.[630] In other words, over more than two decades, full-time work by women grew by 7 per cent and part-time work by almost 12 per cent.

Data from the US reflects similar choices and divisions.[631] A 2007 study by the Pew Research Center found that 19 per cent of mothers with children under 18 claimed that full-time work outside the home was ideal for them, while 80 per cent considered staying at home or part-time work ideal. Interestingly, 70 per cent of the mothers in full-time work preferred to work outside the home part-time or not at all.[632] The choices reflect in part the decisions that women in particular tend to make about child-rearing and market work.[633] An earlier Canadian study also signalled a preference for part-time work by both males and females,[634] and US economists have predicted that the large movement of married women into the labour force in the 1990s would not continue.[635]

These categories are not mutually exclusive. Women who have turned to outside work through financial necessity often also value the sense of identity and purpose and the break from unpaid work it brings. Paid work outside the home became the symbol for women of changing cultural attitudes. But part of the price is tiredness, concern about insufficient time for children, and anger that many men have not recognised or appreciated the costs involved.[636] Studies reveal that women continue to do the majority of housework, even after the significant changes in employment patterns.[637] The consequence is a new tension between the essential family tasks of loving and working.[638]

These changes are placing new pressures on marriage and family life,[639] including elevated conflict[640] infidelity[641] and divorce rates.[642] They have an impact on young couples contemplating marriage and family life. Speaking about the findings of much focus group research, Jeanne Strachan commented: "Young couples today are the first generation since the war to face the reality that they often can't obtain, even with two full-time workers in the house, what their own parents saw as fair and reasonable reward for their hard work."[643] The tension is also reflected by studies in both the Netherlands[644] and the US[645] that full-time female work and higher female incomes are associated with higher divorce rates.

In their study of changing patterns of marriage in America, sociologists at Pennsylvania State University noted the different pictures that emerged for middle class families, in professional positions, with relatively high incomes; and the labor-force participation of working class wives. They found the latter groups vulnerable to work-family strains that translate into lower marital quality: "The increase in the percentage of these couples in the married population, therefore, has placed additional stress on many marriages."[646] Shift work has also been shown to place additional stresses on marriages.[647]

A second consequence is the possible devaluing of marital relationships in favour of relationships in the workplace. Writing in *The Time Bind*, Arlie Russell Hochschild, concluded that "work has become a form of 'home' and home has become 'work'."[648] Professor Hochschild studied the lives of workers in the modern corporation. She reported: "The worlds of home and work have not begun to blur, as conventional wisdom goes, but to reverse places. We are used to thinking that home is where most people feel the most appreciated, the most truly 'themselves', the most secure, the most relaxed. We are used to thinking that work is where most people feel like 'just a number' or a 'cog in a machine.' It is where they have to be 'on', have to 'act', where they are least secure and most harried."

> But new management techniques so pervasive in corporate life
> have helped transform the workplace into a more appreciative,

personal, social sort of world. Meanwhile, at home the divorce rate has risen and emotional demands have become more baffling and complex. In addition to teething, tantrums and the normal developments of growing children, the needs of elderly parents are creating more tasks for the modern family – as are the blending, unblending and reblending of new stepparents, stepchildren, exes and former in-laws.

Professor Hochschild's observations are supported by research that indicates that "couples in which the wife works with many men and few women are more likely to divorce than couples in which the wife works with few women and few men."[649] Although more recent research has found that "the likelihood of finding work a haven versus finding home a haven has declined over time,"[650] Hochschild's observations remain pertinent.

These changes flow through to support for relationships. Professor Hochschild observes: "The modern corporation also tries to take on the role of a helpful relative with regard to employee problems at work and at home. The education and training division offers employees free courses (on company time) in 'Dealing with anger', 'How to give and accept criticism' and 'How to cope with difficult people'. At home of course, people seldom receive anything like this much help on issues basic to family life. There, no courses are being offered on 'Dealing with your child's disappointment in you; or 'How to treat your spouse like an internal customer'."

Australian Professor Denis Ladbrook has reflected on a similar development: "Given the importance to human well-being of both occupations and relationships, it is somewhat incongruous that entry to them is treated so differently by our society. Much preparation and all sorts of protective regulations set parameters on who can do what, in the public domain of occupations, but little preparation and few safeguards are put in place for the private domain of personal and family relationships."[651]

Gender relations

In her 1972 book, *The Future of Marriage,* sociologist Jessie Bernard argued that the modern marriage is best understood, not in the conventional sense as a union between man and woman, but as separate and unequal 'his' and 'hers' marriages, which confer health on men and the opposite on women: "We do not clip wings or bind feet but we do make girls sick. For to be happy in a relationship which imposes so many impediments upon her, as traditional marriage does, a woman must be slightly ill mentally."[652]

Professor Bernard proposed a new order consisting of a range of options about relationships and founded on two bases: The contemporary feminist critique of marriage;[653] and optimism that human beings can accept any kind of relationship if they are properly socialised into it.[654] Bernard asserted: "There is no Ideal Marriage fixed in the nature of things that we will one day discover ... Every age has to find its own ... any form of marriage is transitional between an old one and a new one."[655]

The role of women and the notion of transition remain strong in the critiques of marriage and family.[656] James Wilson has written, "to defend the two parent family is to defend, the critics worry, an institution in which the woman is subordinated to her husband, confined to domestic chores with no opportunity to pursue a career, and taught to indoctrinate her children with a belief in the rightness of the arrangement."[657] However, to identify the advantages to children of being raised in two-parent families is not to defend oppression.

In her survey of health data, the Australian researcher, Moira Eastman, rejected Bernard's thesis: "Despite Bernard's claims, research in a number of countries finds that being married is correlated with markedly better mental and physical health and higher levels of happiness than being never married, separated or divorced and that this is true for both men *and* women."[658] [original emphasis]

While the welcome changes in gender relations of the past few decades have enabled women more equality, especially in the ability to pursue paid work and other interests, significant other changes of the past few decades have had an impact on families and children. Writing in her book *It Takes a Village*, Hilary Clinton observes: "The instability of American households poses great risks to the healthy development of children ... More than anyone else, children bear the brunt of such massive social transitions."[659] The Australian commentator Michael Duffy noted: "It is possible that children have been the great losers of social changes of the past 30 years; as women were oppressed by patriarchal society, children are oppressed by the new order."[660]

Marriage in transition

Another notion prevalent in discussions about family and marriage is one of transition. The National Commission on America's Urban Families wrote: "This opinion is rooted in, and illustrated by, a number of claims that are familiar to many who follow or participate in our public debate on these issues. For example, the family is not getting weaker, it's just 'changing' to something more diverse, and perhaps to something better; we must never fall victim to nostalgia about the good old days of stronger families because family problems always have existed and family change always has been occurring. The real problem facing the society, they say, is not weak families but the forces outside the family that have failed to adjust to the changing realities of contemporary family life. The challenge, they claim, is not to strengthen families; the challenge is merely to adapt the larger society."[661] It has often been claimed that the 'nuclear' family is a modern phenomena,[662] but as Ferdinand Mount illustrated, this is historically inaccurate.[663] Similarly, it has been claimed that high rates of 'illegitimacy' and cohabitation existed previously,[664] which also has been shown to be factually incorrect.[665]

Similar sentiments have been voiced elsewhere.[666] The sociologist

Paul Amato identified a body of scholarly and popular thought that views the changes in terms of marital resilience, rather than marital decline.[667] Writers such as Stephanie Coontz,[668] Judith Stacey and Anthony Giddens see marriage as changing, but robust and not necessarily in decline. Judith Stacey, for example, argues that we face a choice:

> Either we can come to grips with the postmodern family condition by accepting the end of the singular ideal family and begin to promote better living and spiritual conditions for the diverse array of real families we actually inhabit and desire. Or we can continue to engaged in denial, resistance, displacement, and bad faith, by cleaving to a moralistic ideology of *the family* at the same time that we fail to provide social and economic conditions that make life for the modern family or any other kind of family viable, let alone dignified and secure.[669]

Stacey presents a false choice. In many facets of life we are capable of holding aspirations while living with the consequences of not achieving them. Indeed many couples whose marriage fails are committed to having another go. And the great majority of people, across nations, cultures and times, remain attached to the ideal.

The American Commission on Urban Families concluded that the critics miss or evade the main point: "the dimensions and social consequences of the family trend of our time simply are too damaging, obvious, and alarming to be explained away as harmless transition or wished away by warning against nostalgia." Indeed, there are indications that happiness has not increased since the marriage revolution, especially for women.[670] Jonathan Sacks is more pessimistic: "The fact that we have deconstructed the family – morally, psychologically, economically, politically – is the single most fateful cultural development of our times."[671]

While not denying the trends, the 1998 Australian Parliamentary inquiry into marriage was of the opinion that "the passive acceptance of all change involving families is an overly sanguine response to factors that expose many men, women and children to serious emotional trauma, and the nation to an enormous cost."[672] The Committee said that programs of prevention and education are a necessary response to this change.

The postmodernist deconstruction of the family ultimately endangers the wellbeing of individuals. Some commentators, such as Anthony Giddens, have realised the dangers finally: "The obligations of parents to provide for their children, for instance, still stand even if a marriage or relationship breaks down. The traditional left tended to focus much more on rights than obligations; but a society based only on rights will lose all sense of community."[673]

Changing cultural ideas about marriage and family have been reflected in legal developments, as the next chapter illustrates.

SUMMARY

- ♥ Improved contraception, the increase in cohabitation, the move of women into the paid workforce, and a changing legal framework has caused a change in the way marriage is perceived.

- ♥ Rising individualism and the deconstruction of the family have had a significant impact on views about marriage.

- ♥ The increase in marital instability and the redefinition of marriage by reference to divorce has weakened support for marriage.

- ♥ For a variety of reasons, use of the word 'marriage' has been avoided in public and policy discussions.

- ♥ Changing gender relations and the greater entry of women into the paid workforce has impacted on marriage.

- ♥ Some scholars have argued that marriage is in transition which requires adaptation to a new, more fluid form.

6

THE REGULATION OF MARRIAGE
AND DIVORCE

Marriage and the State

Of all the institutions of human society, marriage is ubiquitous. Across civilisations, cultures and historical eras, the pair bond of a man and a woman has been the primary unit of society. David Blankenhorn observes:

> In all or nearly all human societies, marriage is socially approved sexual intercourse between a woman and a man, conceived both as a personal relationship and as an institution, primarily such that any children resulting from the union are – and are understood by society to be – emotionally, morally, practically and legally affiliated with both of the parents.[674]

This is the core of marriage. This conjugal society existed before political institutions and apart from them. The foundation of this society lies in the natural love and obligations of husbands and wives for their biological children.

As a pre-political institution, marriage occupies a discreet sphere of human activity. While many religious believers view marriage in theological terms, the pre-political understanding of marriage is much older. It was Aristotle who rejected the Socratic idea of a breeding elite in which neither parents nor children knew their biological ties.[675] "Whereas in a state having women and children in common, love will be watery; and the father will certainly not say 'my son,' or the son 'my father.' ... Of the two qualities which chiefly inspire regard and affection – that a thing is your own and that is your only one – neither can exist in such as state as this."[676]

The family has served as the main mediating structure between the person and the state, protecting the individual from authoritarian and totalitarian tendencies.[677] From the time of Plato's *Republic* onwards, totalitarian regimes have treated the family with hostility.[678] Hence Marx and Engels were antagonistic towards family,[679] and Hitler proposed that marriage be controlled by the State for its own purposes.[680]

Christian views about marriage were a fusion of the earlier Greek philosophy and later theological perspectives. This is why attempts to label marriage as simply a religious issue are misplaced. Religions recognise and bless marriage, but they did not invent it. The genius of marriage, across cultures and civilisations, has been its ability to link the male into the mother-child bond. It was John Locke who noted that the obligation between husband and wife is ancillary to the relationship that may arise between parent and child.[681] This obligation is not created by the state. Nor can the state remove it. Aristotle observed: "Man is by nature more inclined to live as a couple than to associate politically, since the family is something that precedes and is more necessary than the state."

At the core of this belief is the understanding that the union of a man and a woman is the natural procreative and protective institution for children. This is a belief that has crossed civilisations and cultures throughout history. The paleo-anthropologist, C Owen Lovejoy, demonstrated the natural affinity of men and women to form a lasting pair bond as the key factor in the economic success of the human species.[682]

It is the reason why marriage has been traditionally recognised by the law. Friendships between individuals are not registered. Only marriage, of all human relationships, has generally required registration by the State. The reason, says Richard Stith, is something that everyone knows:

> Sexual relationships between men and women may generate children, beings at once highly vulnerable and essential for the future of every community . . . Lasting marriage receives public approbation . . because it helps to produce human beings able to practice ordered liberty.[683]

Society has an interest, for reasons of self-preservation, to ensure that the relationship for the begetting and protection of children is defined and supported. To the extent that marriage is therefore privileged (and this is less so today than in earlier years), it is because it involves a burden.

When the law has failed to protect the marital relationship, the consequences have been disastrous, particularly for women and children. The treatment of marriage and family in both the Marxist and Post-Modernist eras illustrates the results.

Marxism, marriage and family

Following the belief of Marx and Engels,[684] the Russian Bolsheviks overturned the traditional concepts of marriage and family. Soon after the 1917 revolution, Lenin's new regime introduced unilateral no-fault divorce laws.[685] Two years earlier, Sweden had allowed divorce after separation of the couple for one year.[686] In 1926, the Russian *Family Code* was amended to allow the civil marriage registry to issue a divorce after an *ex parte* application without the knowledge or consent of the other spouse. The legal framework was almost entirely abolished in 1929 when the Russian courts allowed divorce by mutual consent, unilateral decree, or desertion.[687]

The Russian experiment extended beyond divorce law. Both *de jure* and *de facto* relationships were treated equally, with registration of a marriage being only one means of evidencing the union.[688] Cohabitation, mutual spousal support or the joint education of children were other means of proving the marital relationship.[689] The Marxist insistence that women work outside the home limited spousal support post-divorce to just twelve months and only where the woman was unable to work.[690]

Over the next decade, the country experienced a significant increase in divorce, bigamy, abortion and juvenile delinquency. Women and children were the victims of a legal regime that allowed the (mostly) males to dissolve their bonds with the mother and child.[691] Faced with the growing social chaos, the Stalinist authorities restricted access to divorce in 1944.[692] A divorce could only be granted by a court, and reconciliation was to be encouraged. The legal recognition of *de facto* relationships was abolished.

As discussion below illustrates, the West has arrived at a similar legal position to inter-war Soviet Russia, with the free termination of marriage, and the adverse social consequences that result. Professor Patrick Parkinson observes in his recent study of family law and parenthood that "human beings have never worked out a satisfactory way to combine the free terminability of relationships with parenthood in a way that does not lead to disaster or discontent."[693]

The libertarian revolution

Instead of a pro-child, social institution, as it has been regarded historically,[694] some now propose that marriage be based on the gratification or betterment of (two) consenting adults.[695] The self-fulfilment of adults is to replace the social institution centred on the wellbeing of children. This view is particularly evident in the debates about same-sex unions.

In a number of countries, beginning with Denmark in 1989, Norway in 1993, and Sweden in 1994, same sex unions were recognised at law. France followed in 1999 and the Netherlands in 2000. The Dutch laws also allow same sex couples to adopt children. Argentina, Belgium, Canada, Portugal, Spain, South Africa and Sweden also recognise same-sex marriages. Same-sex couples in Germany are able to wed in registry offices and share a common surname. In the United States of America, six states – mostly in the New England region – have allowed same-sex marriage, and 35 States have rejected same-sex unions, the most recent being California. Since 1998, only one state amendment to ban same sex marriage has failed.[696] That was in Arizona in 2006. Two years later, the proposal to ban same-sex marriage was carried. However some Courts have been prepared to find a right to marriage exists for same-sex couples.[697]

This emphasis on adult gratification has a number of profound consequences. First, it overturns the age-old understanding that marriage protects vulnerable children by placing on their biological parents the responsibilities for their moral and practical education and upbringing.[698] It also ignores the overwhelming social science evidence that such as arrangement is optimal for the wellbeing of children and the welfare of society. Seana Sugrue notes the consequences of the state undermining the duty-based and child-focussed nature of marriage: "It increases the likelihood that marital duties, especially to children, will be abdicated and that adults will place their sexual desires above the responsibilities to their children."[699] Don Browning – a liberal in the American sense – wrote:

> Same-sex marriage does not simply extend an old institution to a new group of people. It changes the definition of marriage. It reduces marriage primarily to a committed affectionate sexual relationship. It goes further. It gives this new and more narrow view of marriage all of the cultural, legal, and public supports that accrued to the institution when it functioned to hold together this complex set of goods.[700]

Professor Browning argued that same-sex marriage changes the purpose of the law. It would no longer serve in cooperation with other parts of society to channel behaviour and socialisation to achieve this synthesis of goods: "It will function to extend marriage privileges to a particular group of sexual friendships while excluding many other independent care givers."

At the core of this debate is a central question: What is marriage? The proponents of a revisionist approach seek to appropriate the name 'marriage' for something different: an affectionate, sexual relationship. The apogee of this approach in which the protection of children is minimised and the associations of individuals is maximised was the assertion of the Canadian Law Commission:

> The state's interest in marriage is not connected to the promotion
> of a particular conception of appropriate gender roles, nor is it
> to reserve procreation and the raising of children to marriage.[701]

The emphasis was underscored in the sub-title of the Commission's report, 'Recognising and supporting close personal adult relationships.' The approach downplays the evidence about the protection of children, while appropriating the language of marriage to almost every other type of human relationship, all done in the cause of 'relational equity'. Stephen Heaney observes: "If sexual intercourse between a man and a woman always and naturally led to the same outcome as genital contact between two people of the same sex – that is, pleasure, increased feelings of closeness, even affirmation and love, *and nothing else* – no one would have ever come up with the ideal of marriage."[702]

Redefining marriage will lead to a further weakening of marriage, because the core understanding of the institution would have been changed in the eyes of many people. The law would reinforce the idea that marriage is an emotional union, not a bodily union directed towards the begetting and protection of children.[703] This will tend to increase marital instability. Moreover,

> Because there is no reason that primarily emotional unions any
> more than ordinary friendships in general should be permanent,
> exclusive, or limited to two, these norms of marriage would
> make less and less sense. Less able to understand the rationale
> for these marital norms, people would feel less bound to live

by them. And less able to understand the value of marriage itself as a certain kind of union, even apart from the value of its emotional satisfactions, people would increasingly fail to see the intrinsic reasons they have for marrying or staying with a spouse absent consistently strong feelings.[704]

Redefining marriage also politicises the institution in a novel and dangerous manner, and extends the role of the state beyond its rightful place. Marriage exists independent of state power. It does not require the state to do anything. However, a redefinition of marriage can only occur by state decree. Marriage is no longer a fundamental institution of civil society, but a right, granted by the state. Instead of recognising and supporting the reality that a particular man and woman are parents of a particular child, the state usurps it. It indulges in what Tocqueville described as a "soft despotism" that undermines liberty and freedom. The libertarian, atheist writer, Brendan O'Neill, observes the consequences:

> It's bad for those who are already married because it is part of an inexorable drive to throw open the institutions of marriage and the family to state snooping and bureaucratic remodelling ... From the ferocious patriarchy of the Roman family to the idealised notion of the nuclear family in the 20th century, the institution of marriage and the units it gave rise to were considered deeply private. They shielded people from the scrutiny of the state; they were 'havens in a heartless world', as Christopher Lasch put it. Where we're all subject to moral regulations in the public sphere, through marriage, a public expression of commitment that gives rise to a private unit, people could fashion an institution which they themselves created morality and forged relationships, free from state exertions.[705]

Once marriage becomes a creature of the state, the state can define marriage in any way. If same-sex unions are recognised by civil law, other arrangements can also be recognised.

Once the state can no longer insist that marriage involves a commitment to a member of the opposite sex, there is no ground (other than superstition) for insisting that marriage be limited to one person rather than several.[706]

A consequence will be greater state intrusion into family life. The state will be called upon also to create the social conditions to protect such unions. If the state can define marriage as something new and novel, it can define other arrangements. It can 'educate' people to accept this new arrangement, as has occurred in a series of cases in Canada. Freedoms, including religious freedom, subsequently come under attack. [707] Even the understandings of 'mother' and 'father' are replaced by 'parent 1' and 'parent 2' or some similar language, as the normative foundation of marriage is destroyed.[708]

It has been argued in Australia and elsewhere that people in other relationships, including same-sex relationships, were discriminated against, particularly in relation to their superannuation or pension entitlements. Such discrimination has been removed in Australia.[709] As superannuation is a new form of property, people should be able to dispose of it according to their individual choice. This did not require a redefinition of marriage. The appeal to international human rights conventions has been rejected by a number of tribunals. The European Court of Human Rights, for example, has upheld the view in two cases that there is no right to same sex marriage under the European Convention on Human Rights.[710]

The idea that marriage must be radically redefined in order to protect other forms of relationships is mistaken. Continuing claims of discrimination are spurious, as are attempts to appropriate civil rights language to the cause of same-sex unions. The claims of discrimination fail to address the very nature of marriage.[711]

The case for the legal recognition of same-sex unions is overwhelmingly based on emotive appeals to equality without defining any real inequality. The assertion that redefining marriage will not affect other marriages is misplaced. If the meaning of marriage is centred on adult affection and gratification, to the detriment of raising and protecting children, the new culture would affect all marriages. Otherwise the law has no normative influence. This does not mean that same-sex affection is less than other affections, but it is to recognise the difference between affection and marriage. The case for recognising as marriage, same-sex unions, rests almost entirely on the legal recognition of a committed, affectionate relationship. Neither this affection, nor the desire for community comity is a sufficient basis for re-ordering marriage.[712]

The purpose of marriage

The advent of no-fault divorce reflects developments to laws about the dissolution of marriage that can be traced to the Enlightenment. In his book, *From Sacrament to Contract – Marriage, Religion and Law in the Western Tradition*, John Witte refers to the debates between James Fitzjames Stephen, the prominent Anglican jurist, and John Stuart Mill, the leading utilitarian, in mid-nineteenth century England to introduce a contractarian model of marriage.[713] Many of the ideas espoused by Mill are commonplace today: the equality of men and women; the nurture and education of children rather than the treatment of them as property; the right to sue for divorce at anytime that affection ceases to exist; and the punishment of abuse of children. Similarly, the rise of civil marriage, the removal of the stigma of illegitimacy, the establishment of the notion of the best interest of the child, and the reform of property rights can all be traced to the period of the Enlightenment. Professor Witte observes:

> Most Enlightenment reformers accepted the ideal structure of marriage as a presumptively permanent union of a fit man and a fit woman of the age of consent. Most accepted the classic definition of the goods and goals of marriage: mutual love and affection, mutual procreation and nurture of children, mutual protection from spiritual and civil harms. The primary goal of these Enlightenment reformers was to purge the traditional household and community of its excessive paternalism,

patriarchy, and prudishness, and thus to render the ideal structure
and purpose of marriage a greater reality for all.[714]

Developments since no-fault divorce – private ordering of marriage

Family law has continued to evolve over the past three decades. First,
there has been considerable growth in the use of mediation as an
alternative to litigation. Secondly, there has been the encouragement
for parents to voluntarily enter into plans for the care of their children.
Thirdly, amendments to divorce laws allow couples, both before
and during a marriage, to make binding financial agreements about
property.[715] The notion of marriage as a contractual agreement is
reflected in the language of change. An Australian Attorney-General's
discussion paper on property and family law speaks of marriage as
"an economic partnership as well as a social relationship." These
developments are part of a growing trend towards allowing people
to be able to make their own agreements about their marriages and
the consequences upon their breakdown. Similar developments are
occurring in reforms to child support legislation.

The new developments enable couples to voluntarily determine
some of the arrangements for their own marriage, including their
respective rights and responsibilities should the terms be breached
and the contract broken. This establishes, in theory, a new principle of
responsibility. Currently, many parties to a marriage are barely aware
of the range of financial, social and emotional commitments, much
less have any say as to where ongoing responsibility lies, should one
or other of the parties decide to divorce.

Tamara Metz argues that private ordering be extended to the
'disestablishment' of marriage entirely, that is, that the state should
recognise and support all kinds of caring unions.[716] This is the
approach of the Canadian Law Reform Commission:

> The state's objectives underlying contemporary regulation of
> marriage relate essentially to the facilitation of private ordering:

providing an orderly framework in which people can express their commitment to each other, receive public recognition and support, and voluntarily assume a range of legal rights and obligations.[717]

Despite the reference to private ordering by the Commission, the State's interest in marriage remains, as the protection of the rights of spouses and children still arises.[718] The development of private ordering in family law has been resisted also on the grounds of the suggested power imbalance between parties. The family lawyer, Renata Alexander, writes:

> Private ordering merely replicates existing power imbalances between parties and fails to challenge or redress underlying inequities. It provides informal privatised justice whereby women reach agreements from a base of unequal bargaining power and lack of knowledge of financial matters and legal entitlements. The private and closed context of such agreements precludes any meaningful evaluation of the process or of any outcomes and ensures protection away from public debate and legal scrutiny.[719]

While opponents of private ordering acknowledge that many of the deficiencies they perceive in mediation also exist in litigation, they contend that "only litigation has formal safeguards in terms of public and judicial standards, disclosure and scrutiny."[720]

Provisions in the Australian *Family Law Amendment Act 2000* addressed some of these concerns. The Act allows people to make binding financial agreements about the division of property on marriage breakdown, but there was no requirement to do so. For these agreements to be binding, each party is required to obtain independent legal or financial advice, or both, as to the effect of the agreement before concluding it. Courts are still be able to set aside the agreement in circumstances where, for example, it was obtained by fraud, duress or undue influence, or where there had been a significant change in circumstances that would make it unfair to give effect to the agreement.

While it is possible to discern a trend towards recognising marriage as a private arrangement, the State has retained residual authority, especially to protect a weaker party against fraud or duress, or to act in the best interests of the child. These trends are evident in other aspects of marital law. Hence Courts exercising their equitable powers began to recognise the property claims of *de facto* partners upon the dissolution of their partnerships. Subsequently, legislatures enacted laws to allow *de facto* couples to make property settlements and enter into legally binding domestic arrangements. More recently, many legislatures have extended *de facto* property provisions to same-sex partnerships. Hence in Australia, the Family Court treats the breakdown of a cohabiting relationship of certain duration the same as the breakdown of a legal marriage when resolving maintenance and property issues.[721] New Zealand has gone further, allowing maintenance to be ordered against a natural parent even if the parents had not lived together.[722]

It has also been proposed that the State recognise the internal attitudes to marriage of various religions, such as under sharia law.[723] Although it has been the practice in some Jewish and Christian arrangements for rabbinical and canon law courts to adjudicate aspects of marriage and divorce, these arrangements are in the nature of binding arbitrations or private religious understandings, for example, annulment in the Catholic Church, and have no legal effect.

Problems

John Witte argues that while the changes inaugurated in the first wave of reform – the purging the traditional household of excessive paternalism, patriarchy and prudishness – have been almost universally condoned in the West as salutary, the same judgment cannot be cast for the second transformation of Anglo-American marriage law currently underway:

> The same Enlightenment ideals of individualism, freedom, equality, and privacy, which had earlier driven reforms of

traditional marriage law, are now being increasingly used to reject traditional marriage laws altogether. The early Enlightenment ideals of marriage as a permanent contractual union designed for the sake of mutual love, procreation, and protection is slowly giving way to a new reality of marriage as a 'terminal sexual contract' designed for the gratification of the individual parties.

Professor Witte cites the introduction of unilateral no-fault divorce laws as the embodiment of this trend.

Other developments

In the US, at least 20 states have introduced bills to change divorce laws, either by extending waiting periods, repealing no-fault divorce, mandating counselling, or encouraging pre-marriage education. In Louisiana, the first state to pass such a law, couples can choose between the existing marriage regime based on no-fault divorce, and a new form of covenant marriage. The covenant marriage requires couples to swear that they will live together forever as husband and wife. The partners must disclose to each other 'everything which could adversely affect' their decision to marry. Both must sign a notarised affidavit, swearing they have talked about the nature, purposes and responsibilities of marriage during their premarital counselling. They are legally required to seek marital counselling if problems arise in their marriage. The Florida legislature passed a *Marriage Preparation and Preservation Act* which mandates high school courses on marriage and relationship skill based education, encourages pre-marriage education through financial incentives, and requires parent education and family stabilisation programs upon filing for divorce.

Other nations are also looking beyond divorce. The Blair government announced in its 1998 Green Paper, *Supporting Families*, a proposed 15 day cooling-off period before marriage, and legally binding pre-nuptial agreements in a series of sweeping proposals. The paper also proposed an enhanced role for civil registrars, including new pastoral and counselling functions, and a national parenting and family institute. The Blair Government however had shown a degree of ambivalence about saying it supported marriage.[724] In Ireland, the Commission on the Family proposed a range of measures to support marriage and family life.[725] In neither country has the aspiration been reflected in significant action. A recent report from the UK Centre for Social Justice proposed a three month 'cooling-off' period at the outset of the divorce process.[726] These developments are considered in further detail in chapters ten and eleven.

The future

A tension exists between different approaches to marriage and divorce. It reflects a modern strain between marriage as a private arrangement and the now observed negative effects of marriage dissolution on society, especially children, and an obligation to protect and nurture them. John Witte suggests that "John Stuart Mill's ideal of marriage as "a private, bargained-for exchange between husband and wife about all their rights, goods, and interests" has become a legal reality in contemporary America." He notes however courts do not enforce marital contracts as if they are simple commercial contracts. This raises an important issue. If Mill's ideal of marriage as a freely entered contract is to be fulfilled, it follows that the type of marriage contract available to the parties should not be restricted. Walter Olson makes this point in a discussion about covenant marriage proposals in the US:

> Although the no-fault revolution that began in the 1960s was advertised in some quarters as liberating, it would be a mistake to assume *a priori* that libertarians should find it an improvement over what came before. After all, the modern revolution simply replaced one prescribed-and-invariant marriage contract – one that made it relatively hard to ditch an uncooperative spouse absent proof of serious fault – with a different prescribed-and-invariant contract – one that made it hard to offer or obtain a binding commitment to stick it out in a marriage through better or worse. Some couples entering matrimony undoubtedly prefer

the looser tie, but many others definitely do not, and our current law deprives them of the freedom to strike bargains they'd want to enter in pursuit of genuine security." [727]

A difficulty with the view that marriage is a private arrangement is that other kinds of consensual groupings could also claim legal entitlements if individuals are free to arrange their own marital affairs. In many places this is increasingly the case, leaving only those seeking a legally enforceable life-long marriage unable to do so.

The approach could also lead to a splintering of the law. If private ordering of marriage and family is acceptable, then why should not other individuals and groups be entitled to their own model. Could Catholics utilise canon law instead of the civil law? Should Muslims be entitled to enter marital commitments under the rules of sharia?[728] Should polygamy be available to those who chose such lifestyles? If marriage and family, existing prior to the State, are nonetheless entitled to the protection of the State, a splintering into private arrangements threatens both the unity of the community and the protection of individuals.

This would appear to also open the way for a return to the earlier private notion of marriage in which only the couple themselves knew of the existence of the union. As Reverend Tony Kerin notes that "the most significant development in the history of marriage was the gradual discouragement of clandestine marriage."[729] Many writers have observed that the legal restrictions surrounding marriage, particularly the notions of freedom and consent to marry, and the discouragement of forced marriages, arise from this development.[730]

At least two interpretations can be drawn from legislative and social developments of the past thirty years. One is to consider the development of unilateral no-fault divorce and the judgment by courts to determine issues such as the division of property and the care of children, regardless of the original intention of the parties, as an indication that the contractarian model has been substantially modified, if not discarded, in reality. Even where couples decide not to marry, but to live in a consensual relationship, the law increasingly reaches into their affairs. The reluctance to change no-fault divorce laws can be seen as social support for this new model, which could be described as a paternalistic state model of marriage.

A second and contrary interpretation is to regard a series of other developments as supporting the contractual model. An example is the recent legislation in Louisiana and elsewhere to allow couples to choose from two different versions of marriage. Similarly, the encouragement of binding pre-nuptial financial and property agreements, and the development of agreed parenting and child support plans support a contractual model. It is too early to conclude which model is likely to prevail. Professor Witte remains pessimistic about the outcome:

> It is hard to see the promise of . . . future benefits. . . in the current phase of the legal revolution of marriage ... The rudimentary dispositions on equality, privacy, and freedom offered by courts and commentators today seem altogether too lean to nourish sufficiently the legal revolution of marriage and the family that is now taking place. The elementary deconstructions and dismissals of a millennium-long tradition of marriage and family law and life seem altogether too glib to be taken seriously. Yet the legal revolution marches on. And the massive social, psychological, and spiritual costs continue to mount up. The wild oats sown in the course of the American sexual revolution have brought forth such a great forest of tangled structural, moral, and intellectual thorns that we seem almost powerless to cut it down.

There is considerable evidence to support this view. A review of demographic trends that are outlined in the next chapter reveals a steady displacement of a marriage culture with a culture of divorce and single parenthood. Moreover, it is associated with a series of negative trends, ranging from increased poverty, through lower education outcomes for children, to poorer health and higher morbidity and mortality rates. Indeed, it could be said that James Fitzjames Stephen's warning that private contractualisation of marriage will bring ruin to many women and children, has become a reality.

John Witte concludes: "We seem to be living out the grim prophecy that Friedrich Nietzsche offered a century ago: that in the course of the twentieth century, 'the family will be slowly ground into a random collection of individuals,' haphazardly bound together 'in the common pursuit of selfish ends' – and in the common rejection of the structures and strictures of family, church, state, and civil society." If this is true, then Witte identifies a model antithetical to marriage. Its ethical basis is convenience, its creed is radical individualism, and its goal is immediate personal fulfilment and material prosperity. History suggests however that it is unlikely to sustain either individuals or society for very long.

The fact that the debate about marriage and family life has begun suggests that such an outcome is far from inevitable. Professor Norval Glenn noted that there have been "numerous historical examples of reversals in specific marriage and family trends, including, for instance, in trends towards either permissive or restrictive sex norms."[731]

There are reasons to remain optimistic about the future. The fact that the majority of individuals, no matter their personal experiences, aspire to fulfilling lifelong unions indicates that marriage remains a widely held human goal. Moreover, the majority of people remain married to each other and continue to rate their personal relationship as the most important and fulfilling aspect of their life. Nonetheless, there are measures that could be taken that would re-align the balance between rights and responsibilities and to support marriage generally. These could include further support for families with children in the taxation system; better provision for parents, especially of young children, to take time out of the paid workforce; and more extensive programs of marriage education and enrichment. These ideas are explored in later chapters.

SUMMARY

- ♥ The pair bond of a man and a woman has been the primary unit of society historically.

- ♥ Marriage is a pre-political institution. It is not a creature of the State.

- ♥ The union of a man and a woman is the natural procreative and protective institution for children.

- ♥ Where the State has failed to protect marriage, adverse consequences, particularly for women and children, have resulted.

- ♥ There is an ongoing debate between proponents of marriage as a private contract between consenting adults, and proponents of marriage as the protective institution for children.

PART THREE

THE RETREAT FROM MARRIAGE

The ideal family environment for raising young children has the following traits: an enduring two-biological parent family that engages regularly in activities together, has developed its own routines, traditions and stories, and provides a great deal of contact time between adults and children. Surrounded by a community that is child friendly and supportive of parents, the family is able to develop a vibrant family subculture that provides a rich legacy of meaning and values for children throughout their lives. (David Popenoe)

The real soul mate is the one you are actually married to.
(JRR Tolkien)

Two nations between whom there is no intercourse and no sympathy; who are as ignorant of each other's habits, thoughts, and feelings, as if they were dwellers in different zones, or inhabitants of different planets. The rich and the poor.
(Benjamin Disraeli).

7

THE DECLINE IN MARITAL PERMANENCE

There have been a series of changes in family patterns throughout the industrialised world over the past four decades that indicate a decline in marriage and a weakening of family life. In summary:

- People are marrying less.
- Those couples who marry do so at an older age.
- Pre-marital cohabitation has increased significantly.
- There has been a dramatic increase in divorce.
- The number of children involved in divorce has continued to grow since the early 1970s.
- The rates of remarriage have fallen over the past 30 years.
- Families are having fewer children.
- The proportion of children born out of wedlock has increased dramatically.
- There has been a marked increase in the proportion of single parent families.

In addition to these direct trends:

- Families increasingly have both parents in the paid workforce; and
- In most nations, the population is ageing.

The evidence of these trends is shown in ten nations: Australia,

Canada, France, Italy, Japan, New Zealand, Russia, Sweden, the United Kingdom, and the United States of America.[732] These include the major English-speaking nations, a sample of countries from Europe (France, Italy and Sweden), as well as Japan and Russia for comparison.[733]

People are marrying less.

The crude marriage rate (the number of marriages per 1,000 people) has fallen significantly in most western nations. This is as true of Australia,[734] Canada[735] and New Zealand, as it has been of the nations of Europe and the United States, as the following table indicates.

Crude marriage rate

	1970	1980	1990	2000	2010
Australia	9.3	7.4	6.9	5.9	5.5
Canada	8.8	7.9	7.1	5.1	4.5
France	7.75	6.21	5.06	5.03	3.84
Italy	7.35	5.72	5.61	4.99	3.59
Japan	10.0	6.6	5.8	6.3	5.5
New Zealand	9.2	5.5	6.9	5.4	4.8
Russia	9.7	10.3	8.9	8.7	8.53
Sweden	5.38	4.52	4.73	4.5	5.33
UK	8.46	7.43	6.56	5.19	4.32
USA	10.6	10.6	9.8	8.3	6.8

Note: The crude marriage rate is the number of marriages formed each year as a ratio to 1,000 people. Data has been taken from the nearest year when not available for the last year of a decade in this and following tables. The data in this table and following tables was sourced by the Australian Parliamentary Library.

In just four decades, the marriage rate has halved in much of the Western world.[736]

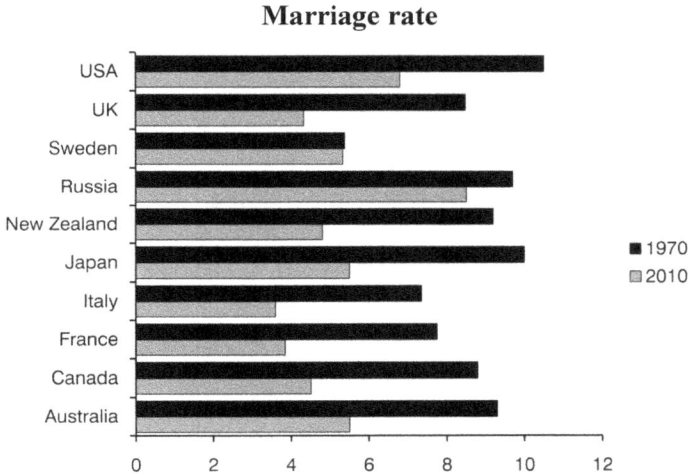

Marriage rate

USA
UK
Sweden
Russia
New Zealand
Japan
Italy
France
Canada
Australia

■ 1970
▨ 2010

0   2   4   6   8   10   12

Some family scholars have suggested that reduced gains from marriage under unilateral divorce has led to a decrease in marriage rates[737] and a decrease or delay in several forms of investment whose returns are at least partly marriage-specific, including having children.[738]

There have been slight increases in the marriage rates in a number of countries in recent years, but it is too early to ascertain whether this is a long-term reversal of the patterns of the past few decades.[739]

Couples marry at an older age

Although men still tend to be older than women when they wed, men and women are increasingly marrying at a later age. In Australia in 1972, one-third of women had married by the time they turned 20, and eight in ten of those reaching 25 had married. By 1991, only 5 per cent of those turning 20 had married, and less than half of those reaching 25 – levels closer to the 1930s. Between 1971 and 2001, the proportion of men aged 25-29 who had never married increased from 26 per cent to 69 per cent, while the proportion of never married women in the same age cohort increased from 12 per cent to 54 per cent.[740]

In the US, the median female college graduate from the early 1950s to the early 1970s was married within a year after college graduation – at 22.5 years old. But by the early 1980s the median female college graduate married at 25 years old.[741] Since then, the average age at first marriage has continued to rise.[742] In 1960, two-thirds of all 'twenty-somethings' in the US were married. In 2008, just 26 per cent were.[743]

Age at first marriage

		1970	1980	1990	2000	2010
Australia	Male	23.4	24.2	26.5	28.5	29.6
	Female	21.1	21.9	24.3	26.7	27.7
Canada	Male			28.3	29.3	30.0
	Female			26.4	27.4	28.1
France	Male		25.1	29.0	30.2	31.6
	Female		23.0	27.0	28.0	29.6
Italy	Male		27.2		30.9	32.8
	Female		24.1		28.1	29.7
Japan	Male	26.9	27.8	28.4	28.8	30.5
	Female	24.2	25.2	25.9	27.0	28.8
New Zealand	Male	22.9	26.8	29.2	29.2	29.9
	Female	20.8	24.5	27.4	27.4	28.2
Russia	Male		24.6	24.8		
	Female		23.1	22.6		
Sweden	Male		29.0		33.1	35.1

	Female		26.4		30.6	32.5
UK	Male		29.2		33.0	33.9
	Female		27.7		31.2	32.3
USA	Male	23.2	24.7	26.1	26.8	28.2
	Female	20.8	22.0	23.9	25.1	26.1

Note: Median age for Australia, New Zealand and USA; Mean age for Canada, France, Italy, Japan, Russia, Sweden and the UK.

With later marriage, young adults are more likely to live at home for extended periods of time.[744] The University of Pennsylvania sociologist, Frank Furstenberg Jr, noted that in 1960, 65 per cent of 30-year-old men and 77 per cent of 30-year-old women had completed five adult transitions, namely, leaving home, finishing school, becoming financially independent, getting married and having a child; whereas by 2000 only 31 per cent of such men and 46 per cent of such women had completed the same transitions.[745]

More couples cohabit before marriage

The increase in pre-marital cohabitation has been one of the most significant developments throughout the western world in the past four decades. According to the Australian Bureau of Statistics, about four out of five couples cohabit before marriage, a figure that has quadrupled in less than four decades. The rise in premarital cohabitation is reflected elsewhere in the world. In the three decades of women born in the US from 1933-42 until those born in 1963-74, the proportion that first cohabited before marriage increased from seven per cent to 64 per cent.[746] Data from England and Wales indicates that about 40 per cent of never-married people aged 16-30 were cohabiting in 2007, with much higher proportion of those in their mid to late twenties.[747]

Premarital cohabitation

	1970	*1980*	*1990*	*2000*	*2010*
Australia	16.0	27.1	56.3	75.9	77.4
UK[748]	5		70		85
USA[749]			30 +	60 +	70

There has also been a significant increase in cohabiters as a proportion of all couples, as the following chart demonstrates.

Cohabiting couples

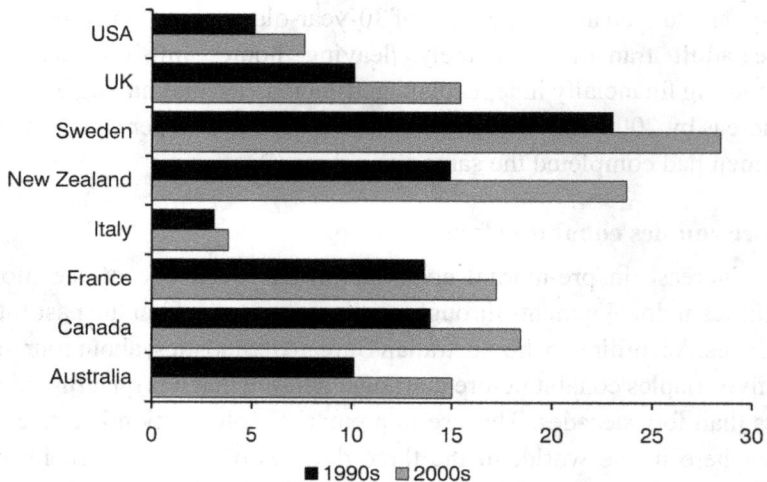

Source: David Popenoe (2008) 'Cohabitation, marriage and child wellbeing' *Threshold* 93: 20-23, Table 1 (percentages).

In the US, more than half of all non-marital births in 2001 were to cohabiters, compared to 38 per cent a decade earlier.[750] While cohabiters with children often aspire to marriage, not many achieve it.[751] In fact, two-thirds of new unmarried mothers with more than one child had at least one child who was fathered by someone other than the father of the new baby.[752]

There has been a recent increase also in what has been described as 'living-apart-together' relationships, that is, people who are a couple but live in different places. Australian data shows that 24 per cent of the officially single population falls into this category, particularly amongst previously married people aged 45 and over.[753] The significant increase in cohabitation is discussed in more detail in chapter 8.

A significant increase in divorce

Divorce rates increased significantly in many countries following the passage of no-fault divorce laws. As President Clinton's Domestic Policy Advisor, Professor William Galston observed: the "divorce epidemic did not just happen. The legal codes ... aided and abetted it through the institution of no-fault divorce."[754]

Crude divorce rate

	1970	1980	1990	2000	2010
Australia	1.0	2.7	2.5	2.6	2.3
Canada	1.37	2.58	1.37	2.32	2.2
France	0.79	1.59	1.86	1.94	2.1
Italy	0.32	0.21	0.48	0.65	0.9
Japan	0.94	1.21	1.27	2.08	2.0
New Zealand	1.11	2.08	2.69	2.5	2.3
Russia	2.62	3.50	3.78	4.31	5.0
Sweden	1.61	2.39	2.26	2.42	2.3
UK	1.18	2.99	2.88	2.58	2.8
USA	4.22	5.19	4.70	4.1	3.4

Note: *The crude divorce rate is the number of divorces each year as a ratio to 1,000 people.*

Divorce rate

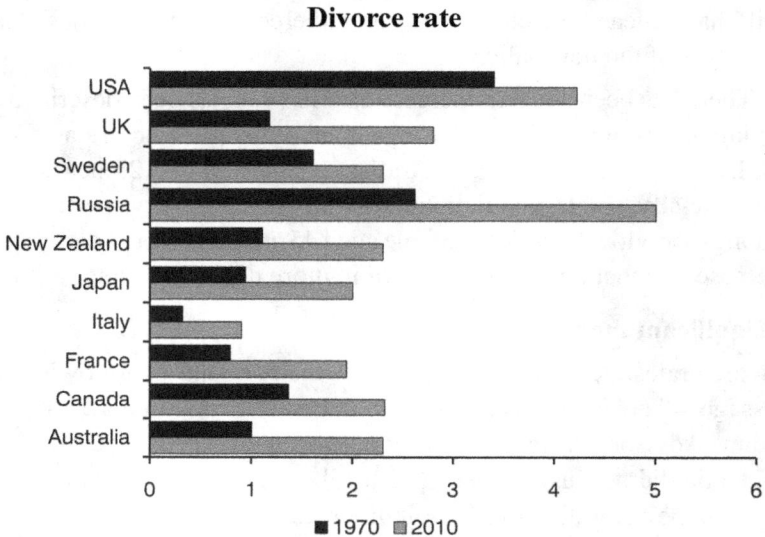

■1970 ■2010

Even in Asia, where divorce was rare, the separation rates have risen significantly in the past decade.[755] In the case of Russia, both marriage and divorce rates are high, partly because couples tend to marry at a young age.[756]

According to a 1995 Australian study, 10 per cent of marriages failed within six years, 20 per cent within 10 years, 30 per cent by 20 years, and a total of 40 per cent by 40 years. More recent data reveals that one quarter of the married couples who separate do so before their third wedding anniversary, and 36 per cent within five years.[757] A British survey found that the three-year marker was a significant time when relationship stress levels peak.[758]

The trends are particularly grim for couples who marry young. Seven out of ten teenage bridegrooms and half of teenage brides are divorced within a decade of their wedding.[759] According to the *Australian Family Formation Study*, the pre-marital experiences contributing most to the risk of marital breakdown are pre-marital cohabitation, having an ex-nuptial child, and leaving home at an early age.[760]

As a consequence, the number of children involved in divorce proceedings has also increased markedly.[761] Nearly half of all divorces involve children. Almost a quarter of Australians aged 18-34 experienced their parent's divorce while a child, compared to less than 10 per cent of people aged 55 and over.[762] Many of the children are very young. An analysis of Australian data, for example, reveals that more than one in five children from single child families involved in divorce were under five years of age, and almost half under 10 years.[763] In Australia alone, almost 50,000 children are involved in their parents' divorce each year.[764] If the children involved in all separations, including those by cohabiting couples, are counted, the figure is significantly higher. In Britain, for example, by the time a child is five years old, the separation rate for couples who were cohabiting when their first child was born is around six times the rate for couples who were married. By the time the child is 16, the separation rate for cohabiting couples is still four times as high.[765] Many of these children of separation and divorce have little or no ongoing relationship with their father.[766]

In the US, over a million children experience divorce each year.[767] Less than half of American children reach the age of 17 in an intact family.[768] Over half of couples divorcing in the UK in 2007 had at least one child aged under 16. This meant that there were over 110,000 children who were aged under 16 when their parents divorced. Twenty per cent of these children were under five years old.[769] By 2010, it was estimated that half of all children would see their parents split up before age of 16.[770] In Canada, there were 111,626 divorce cases in 2009-2010, with an estimated one-in-two cases involving dependent children.[771] More than 800,000 people who had dependent children with their partners had become separated or divorced between 2001 and 2006, including one-third of whom had been cohabiting.[772] As Professor Paul Amato observes, many of these children end up on a "downward trajectory from which they might never fully recover."[773]

While the divorce rates are much higher than they were four decades ago, there has been a slight fall in many countries in recent years,[774] leading some to predict a return to long-term trend rates in the future.[775] Others have suggested that the increase in cohabitation may be a factor in the decrease "as separations that previously occurred while legally married may now occur during premarital cohabitation."[776] The sociologist, David Popenoe, observes that using the divorce rate alone is no longer an accurate measure of relationship breakup, as it does not include the separation of a large number of cohabiting couples: "Relying solely on the divorce rate seriously underestimates the amount of breakup that prevails."[777] Professor Popenoe suggests that the highest family breakup rates in the world are probably in Scandinavia through a combination of high divorce rates and the highest percentage of cohabiting couples. A British study found that three quarters of family breakdown affecting young children now involves unmarried parents.[778]

While there has been a reduction in divorce in some countries in recent years,[779] and an increase in the length of those marriages that end in divorce,[780] it has also been accompanied by an increase in the number of people in longer marriages separating.[781] These changes are reflected partially in the ten-year divorce rates for American women, as the following table shows:[782]

Ten-Year Divorce Rates for Three Generations of US Women

	High School Graduates	College (University) Graduates
1970s	26 per cent	23 per cent
1980s	25 per cent	20 per cent
1990s	19 per cent	16 per cent

The apparent fall in divorce rates measures only one component of the retreat from marriage, as the remainder of this chapter illustrates. There has also been evidence that the global financial crisis resulted in fewer marriages, children and divorces.[783]

More people remain unmarried

The proportion of never married men and women has doubled over the past 25 years. There has also been a dramatic decrease in the number of young married adults.

Females aged 30-34 Ever Married (percentages)

	1976	*1981*	*1991*	*1996*
Australia	93.1	91.4	87.4	77.2
USA	94 (1970)			77 (2003)

In the US, the proportion of 20-24 year old women who had never married doubled between 1970 and 2000, while the proportion of the same age men jumped from 55 per cent to 84 per cent. For women aged 30-34, the proportion tripled from six to 22 per cent, and for men from nine to 30 per cent.[784] In 1970, only one in ten US women aged 25-29 were never married.[785] The historian, Stephanie Coontz, points out that in Europe in 1950, just 10 per cent of households contained just one person, whereas five decades later, they constituted more than a quarter of households in the US, 30 per cent of British households, and 40 per cent of Swedish households.[786]

In Asia, where marriage is near-universal, and cohabitation rare (except in Japan), there is a trend to later and less marriage. A third of Japanese women entering their 30s, and 37 per cent of Taiwanese women aged 30-34 were single in 2010.[787]

The rates of remarriage have fallen

It was a widely-held expectation of the proponents of liberalised divorce laws that many people escaping unhappy marriages would remarry into satisfying and stable new relationships. It has not proven to be the case. Remarriage rates have fallen significantly across the western world. The following table indicates the fall in the remarriage rates for selected age groups in Australia.

Remarriage age specific rates, Australia

		1976	1981	1991	2000
25-29	Bridegrooms	341.8	225.7	130.9	104.4
	Brides	278.0	189.4	142.0	119.2
30-34	Bridegrooms	294.8	194.9	131.2	102.8
	Brides	201.0	135.1	107.3	95.5
35-39	Bridegrooms	239.8	160.4	106.7	83.9
	Brides	136.2	96.3	72.1	63.7
40-44	Bridegrooms	184.6	123.4	80.0	62.1
	Brides	94.0	70.7	49.3	42.2
45-49	Bridegrooms	138.2	95.3	65.9	47.9
	Brides	62.7	45.7	37.9	31.7
50-54	Bridegrooms	98.1	68.7	51.3	41.1
	Brides	31.3	25.9	23.8	21.7

Source: *Australian Bureau of Statistics – per 1,000 population of divorced and widowed as at 30 June each year.*

The Australian remarriage rate has more than halved in the two decades from 1971, falling for males from 246 per thousand divorced persons to 120 by 1991; and for females from 215 per thousand divorced persons to just 101 by 1991. It has since declined further. Curtin University Professor Denis Ladbrook suggests that this reduction in the remarriage rates "probably reflects a rise in cohabitation on the part of men and women who have already been divorced."[788]

The median interval between divorce and remarriage was just 2.8 years for men and 3.2 years for women – much shorter than remarriage following the death of a spouse. "It suggests the possibility of marriages being hastily contracted without adequate time for debriefing the past and rebuilding life securely in the present," says Professor Ladbrook.[789]

In Canada, the proportion of divorced people stating they intend to remarry decreased from 26 per cent to 22 per cent between 1990 and 2006. In contrast, more than six out of 10 divorced Canadians stated that they do not wish to remarry, up from five out of 10 in 1990.[790] An American survey found that 61 per cent of respondents who had been married, but were not at the time of the survey, said they did not want to remarry, including 49 per cent of those aged 35-59 years.[791]

In a 1990 US study, 46 per cent of weddings involved one or both of the partners remarrying. By 2008, this had fallen to 36 per cent.[792] In the UK, 23 per cent of marriages involved a first marriage for one of the partners in 1995, and 19 per cent involved remarriage for both. By 2007, the percentages had fallen to 20 per cent and 17.6 per cent respectively.[793] For New Zealand, the percentage of weddings involving one or more partners remarrying fell from 36 per cent in 1995 to 30.6 per cent in 2010.[794] While many people aspire to remarry, finding a new partner at mid-life can be difficult.[795]

The birth rate has fallen

The birthrate in most western nations, including Australia, Britain, the United States and Canada, has fallen below replacement levels.[796] In a study of global fertility rates, the demographer, Peter McDonald, concluded that if current levels of fertility were maintained, they are so low that they would threaten the future existence of the nations concerned. "In an era in which we have come to understand the momentum of population increase, it is remarkable that we are yet to appreciate that the same momentum applies to population decrease."[797]

It has been estimated by the Institute of Public Policy Research that 90,000 less children are born each year in Britain as a result of women not having the number of children they originally wanted.[798] Data from the Office of National Statistics reveals that a fifth of women turning

45 in 2010 had no children. The childlessness level of 20 per cent for women born in 1956 can be compared with 10 per cent of those born in 1945 and 11 per cent in 1938. The only time in the last century when newborn girls were less likely to grow up to have families was in 1920, a generation whose main childbearing years fell during the Second World War.[799]

It would appear that the fall in fertility is not from a lack of wanting children. According to an Australian study, being in a secure, stable and adequate relationship with a partner and having a secure, stable and adequate income stream are critical preconditions for people to have a child or to have more children.[800]

There has been a welcome increase in birthrates in some nations in recent years. In Australia, for example, a ten-year high was reached in 2005. The reason, according to the demographer, Peter McDonald, was because women had stopped putting off having their first and second children.[801]

Crude birth rate

	1970	1980	1990	2000	2010
Australia	20.6	15.3	15.4	13.0	13.5
Canada	17.4	15.4	15	10.9	11.2
France	17.0	14.0	13.4	13.3	12.8
Italy	16.8	11.3	10.0	9.3	9.5
Japan	18.7	13.5	10.0	9.4	8.5
New Zealand	22.1	16.2	17.5	14.9	14.7
Russia	14.3	15.9	13.4	8.7	12.4
Sweden	13.7	11.6	14.5	10.2	12.0
UK	16.2	13.4	13.9	11.6	12.9
USA	18.4	15.9	16.7	14.7	13.8

Note: *The crude birth rate indicates the number of live births occurring during the year, per 1,000 population estimated at midyear.*

The reduced birthrate and childlessness is also linked to delayed marriage. Using data from Europe, Japan, Australia and the US, Donald Rowland illustrates that since the 1890s, rising childlessness and the incidence of one child families parallels a rising median age of first marriage: "Later ages at marriage bring a greater likelihood of low fecundity and, for some, a strengthened reluctance to have children."[802] Having one or no children also increases the chances that the adults will end up living alone or in an institutional setting.[803]

The increase in cohabitation has also had an impact on the birthrate, as cohabiting couples tend to have fewer children than the married.[804] In countries where cohabitation and out-of-wedlock births are stigmatised, such as in Southern Europe, it would appear the women respond by having fewer children.[805] In both cases, the birth rates have fallen.

A consequence of these changes is that adults spend less of their lives devoted to parenting. In Australia, for example, only 44 per cent of families are couples with children (with 37 per cent being couples without children, and 16 per cent, one parent families).[806] Although Barbara Dafoe Whitehead was writing of the US, her comments are applicable to most of the western world:

> For most of the nation's history, Americans expected to devote much of their adult lives to the nurture and rearing of children. Life with children has been central to norms of adulthood, marriage and the experience of family life. Today however, this historic pattern is changing. Life *without* children is becoming the more common social experience for a growing percentage of the adult population.[807]

Ex-nuptial births have increased

Childbearing outside marriage has increased markedly in the past few decades throughout the western world.

Out of wedlock births

	1970	*1980*	*1990*	*2000*	*2010*
Australia	8.3	13.3	21.9	29.4	34.0
Canada		12.6	24.4	28.3	27.1
France		11.4	31.1	43.6	51.7
Italy		4.3	6.5	9.7	16.2
Japan		0.8	1.1	1.6	2.1
New Zealand	13.3	21.5	34.0	43.2	48.2
Russia	9.6	9.6	13.8	22.8	
Sweden		39.7	47.0	55.3	54.8
UK		11.5	27.9	39.5	43.7
USA	10.7	18.4	28.0	33.2	40.7

Note. *Per cent of babies born outside of marriage or a civil partnership. Russian data is for urban areas only.*

As the table illustrates, the increase in out-of-wedlock births has occurred in many places, rising to more than 40 per cent of all births in many countries. The proportion of ex-nuptial births in Australia has grown markedly since the end of the Second World War when just four in 100 children were born out of wedlock. The proportion doubled to nine in 100 children by 1971 before increasing rapidly to 34 in 100 by 2010. By the end of the 1990s, 65 per cent of ex-nuptial births in Australia were to women in *de facto* relationships who have never married; 18 per cent to never-married solo women; 8.5 per cent to divorced but solo women; and 8.5 per cent to women divorced but in a *de facto* relationship. The proportion of births to teenage mothers fell from 11 per cent of all births in 1971 to five per cent in 1994. However, 90 per cent of teenage births are to unmarried women.

As a growing number of women wed later in life or not at all, an increasing number of them bear children out-of-wedlock.[808] This is reflected in ex-nuptial birthrates in Australia, for example, with rapid growth in the numbers of mothers aged 20-39 years.[809] Twelve per cent of 40-44 year old Australians experienced parents living apart by age 15. For 20-24 year olds, this percentage had jumped to 21.5 per cent.[810]

For women under 30 in the United States, most births now occur outside marriage.[811] Births to women in their twenties accounted for 62 per cent of all non-marital births. Non-marital births to teens rose from 30 per cent in 1970 to 87 per cent in 2009; to women ages 20-24 from nine per cent to 62 per cent; and to women aged 25-29 from four per cent to 34 per cent.[812] Conversely, births to teenagers fell from 49 per cent of all non-marital births in the US in 1970 to 21 per cent by 2009. Overall, 27 per cent of children were living with only one parent, and four per cent with neither, by 2009.[813]

A British study in 2006 predicted that more than half of the nation's children would be born out of wedlock by 2012.[814] In France, Sweden and Norway, a majority of children are already born out-of-wedlock , with Denmark and New Zealand close to equal numbers.[815]

An increase in single parent families
There has been a marked increase in the number and proportion of single parent families.

Single parent families

	1970	1980	1990	2000	2010
Australia	10.7	12.8	12.9	15.1	18.0
Canada		12.7	15.2	23.5	24.6
France		10.2	13.2	17.4	19.8
Italy				7.8	8.0

Japan		4.9	6.5	8.3	10.2
New Zealand			17.2	18.9	18.1
Russia			9.5	8.5	
Sweden		11.2	17.4	21.4	20.7
UK		13.9	19.4	20.7	25.0
USA		19.5	24.0	27.0	28.8

Note: Percentage of total families (including couple only families, except Italy which is percentage of households. Nearest year in some cases.

Single parent families are overwhelmingly headed by women and are amongst the poorest in most places. In their study of poor women in the United States, *Promises I can keep,* Kathryn Edin and Maria Kefalas observed the decoupling of marriage and children. Whereas middle-class women have an interest in avoiding pregnancy and childbirth, their poorer peers see motherhood as providing meaning and purpose in their lives.[816] "Women who bear children outside of marriage are at a considerable disadvantage in the marriage market," concluded sociologists from Ohio State University after surveying the data of more than 100,000 women.[817]

While ex-nuptial births have increased in western nations, the most significant reason for the increase in single-parent households is parental separation after the birth of children.[818] Many scholars have remarked that whereas historically poverty derived from unemployment and low wages; today it derives from family structure.

The population is ageing

By the year 2020, many nations will face a major challenge in providing for an aged population. According to the OECD, the ratio of older people to those in the workforce in 1990 was 19 per cent. By the year 2030, this dependency ratio will double to 38 per cent across the OECD. On current trends, some 40 per cent of people will require long-term care at some stage of their lives.[819] The combination of an ageing population, decreasing marriage and higher divorce rates means that many more elderly people will spend their final years alone.[820]

Population aged 65 and over

	1970	1980	1990	2000	2010
Australia	8.35	9.62	11.19	12.46	13.45
Canada	7.9	9.4	11.3	12.6	14.1
France	12.86	13.93	14.03	16.06	16.79
Italy	11.07	13.36	14.93	18.26	20.35
Japan	7.03	9.05	11.95	17.18	22.69
New Zealand	8.48	9.75	11.08	11.76	13.01
Russia	7.69	10.21	10.2	12.41	12.80
Sweden	13.67	16.29	17.78	17.20	18.24
UK	13.03	14.93	15.70	15.81	16.59
USA	9.84	11.28	12.49	12.38	13.06

Note: As a percentage of the total population

Summary

These trends are evident in most industrialised nations.[821] They reflect profound changes for families and children. Professor David Popenoe summarised the changes as containing five measurable components:

> First, rising rates of divorce and unwed childbearing, which mean the steady disintegration of married, mother-father child-raising unit. Second, the growing inability of families to carry out their primary social functions: maintaining the population level, regulating sexual behavior, socialising children, and caring for family members. Third, the transfer of influence and authority from families to other institutions, such as schools,

peer groups, the media, and the state. Fourth, smaller and more unstable family units. And fifth, the weakening of familism as a cultural value in relationship to other values, such as personal autonomy and egalitarianism.

The sociologist, Andrew Cherlin, suggests American exceptionalism is the reason that the US has one of the highest levels of marriage of any Western nation: "What's different about the United States is the strength of marriage as a cultural ideal."[822] While Americans marry and divorce more frequently than people in many other Western countries, the fact that the trends are repeated in most nations discounts the idea of America being an exception. Similar patterns are replicated in many countries.

These changes are having a profound impact on families. Taken together, the statistics appear to reveal the steady displacement of a marriage culture with a culture of divorce and single parenthood. Birth rates and marriage rates have continued to fall, pre-marital cohabitation has become the norm in most western countries, the median age of first marriage has risen, divorce rates have increased, out-of-wedlock births have grown, as has the proportion of sole-parent families, and the population continues to age. The rates of change vary from country to country, including some welcome reversals in places. However, the deinstitutionalisation of marriage and the consequent trends for less stable families remains significant.[823]

Measuring the decline in marital commitment

United States of America

In 2009, the Institute for American Values and the National Center on African American Marriages and Parenting published the first *Marriage Index*.[824] It measured five leading indicators on the health of marriage and family life in the US: The percentage of adults married, the percentage of married persons "very happy" with their marriages, the percentage of first marriages intact, the percentage of births to married parents, and the percentage of children living with their own married parents. As the following diagram reveals, the index measures a significant decline in the marriage culture.

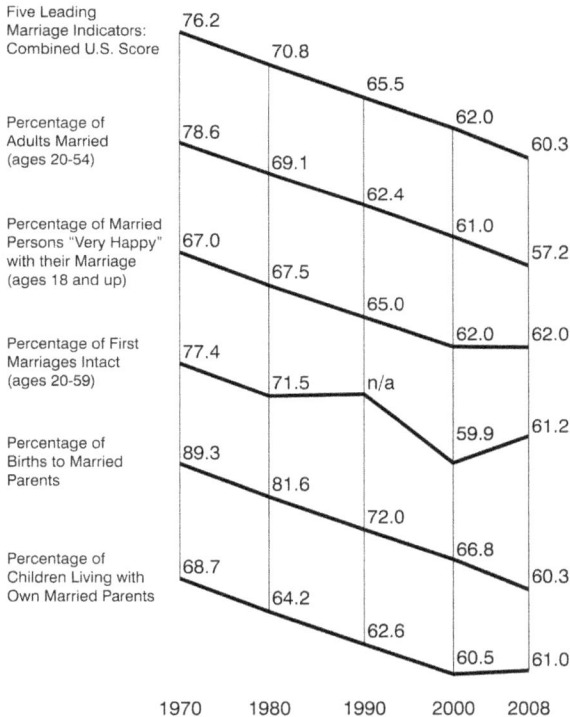

Five Leading Marriage Indicators: Combined U.S. Score
76.2　70.8　65.5　62.0　60.3

Percentage of Adults Married (ages 20-54)
78.6　69.1　62.4　61.0　57.2

Percentage of Married Persons "Very Happy" with their Marriage (ages 18 and up)
67.0　67.5　65.0　62.0　62.0

Percentage of First Marriages Intact (ages 20-59)
77.4　71.5　n/a　59.9　61.2

Percentage of Births to Married Parents
89.3　81.6　72.0　66.8　60.3

Percentage of Children Living with Own Married Parents
68.7　64.2　62.6　60.5　61.0

1970　1980　1990　2000　2008

Source: Institute for American Values, 2008 (percentages)

Australia

The Australian index measures three of the five indicators in the US Index.[825] The measurements of married adults, births to married parents, and children living with married parents show a 30 per cent decline since the early 1970s. The average score fell from 86 in 1971 to just 61 in 2006. This mirrors a similar decline in the US from 76.2 in 1970 to 60.3 in 2008.[826]

The percentage of happily married persons fell, according to the *National Social Science Survey* between 1986 and 1996.[827] It appears that the percentage of first marriages intact has also fallen. While these measures are incomplete for the other two measures used in the US index, both are consistent with the downward trend in the Australian marriage index. The marriage rate has risen slightly in recent years, and the divorce rate has fallen marginally, but the overall downward trend remains.

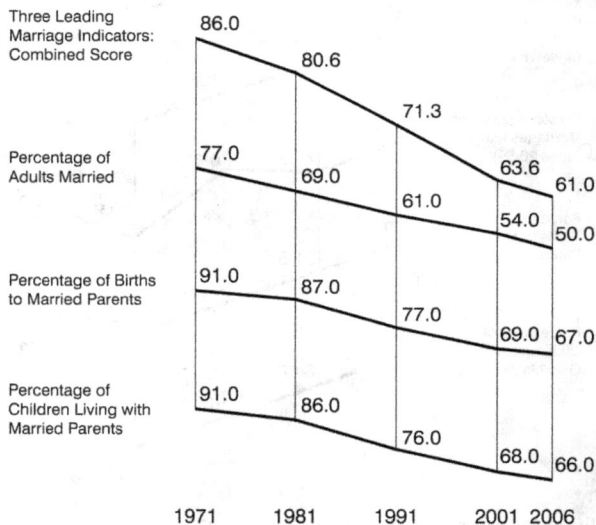

Three Leading Marriage Indicators: Combined Score	86.0	80.6	71.3	63.6	61.0
Percentage of Adults Married	77.0	69.0	61.0	54.0	50.0
Percentage of Births to Married Parents	91.0	87.0	77.0	69.0	67.0
Percentage of Children Living with Married Parents	91.0	86.0	76.0	68.0	66.0
	1971	1981	1991	2001	2006

Sources: ABS Census of Population and Housing, ABS, Births, Australia (percentages)

United Kingdom

A similar pattern emerges in the UK, where scholars at the Jubilee Centre measured domestic data. Although exact comparisons with the US Index were impossible, the British study revealed a similar decline.

1970	*2009*
Percentage of adults married (ages 24-54)	
85.0	54.2
Percentage of married persons satisfied with their marriage	
63.5	61.5*
Percentage of first marriages intact (ages 24-54)	
93.0	68.0
Percentage of births to married parents	
91.7	57.8
Percentage of children living with their own married parents	
92.0	65.0
Combined score	
85.0	61.3

Source: Jubliee Centre (2009) *The UK Marriage Index 2009* [Cambridge, The Centre]
A likely underestimate, according to the UK scholars.

These results are significant for society, as a large body of research suggests that the status of our marriages influences our well-being and productivity, both individually and as a nation.

The causes of marital stability and instability
Understanding the factors that contribute to marital stability and instability for particular couples is important, both for individuals and society. Some are personal and psychological, but others relate to life experiences. Some involve the day-to-day stresses that we all experience.

In a survey of the determinants of marital instability, Australian Institute of Family Studies researcher, Helen Glezer, found that the premarital experiences contributing most to the risk of marital breakdown were: having an ex-nuptial child; pre-marital cohabitation; and leaving home at an early age.[828] While teenage pregnancy has been the subject of considerable attention, American researchers found that the mother's marital status is more significant for subsequent psychological well-being than the age at which she first gives birth.[829] Where a mother has a series of family transitions "with husbands, partners, boyfriends and other relatives moving into and out of the household," her children are also likely to suffer adverse outcomes because of inconsistent parenting environments.[830]

Other studies have implicated exposure to divorce as a child;[831] having pre-marital sex;[832] and marrying as a teenager,[833] as factors contributing to marital instability. These factors can have long term implications. According to Helen Glezer:

> Characteristics of those who experienced marital breakdown compared with those who have not, indicate that like those who have cohabited, they tend to have less traditional family values, are more egalitarian about sex roles, value children less and are more individualistic in their family orientation than those who remain married. . . . family background factors such as growing up in a non religious family, being unhappy at home, leaving home at an early age and coming from a context of non traditional family values are associated with both cohabiting prior to marriage and marital dissolution.

Recent studies suggest there is a significant difference between marrying as a teenager versus marrying in the early twenties.[834] In addition the age-divorce link is most prominent for teens, but much less significant for people in their early twenties.[835]

The fifth wave of the US *National Survey of Family Growth* tracked 4,000 women, then aged 35 to 44. The data revealed that women who had a child out of wedlock were less likely to be married; more likely to be living alone, whether previously married or not; and more likely to cohabit, whether previously married or not. It also found that the women who did not experience unwed childbearing were more likely to have husbands (or male partners, if cohabiting) who were better educated, more likely to be employed, and enjoy higher earnings.[836]

The consequences also extend to men. Using data from the *National Survey of Family Growth*, Daniel Lichter and Deborah Graefe found from a sample of 3,800 men aged 20 to 44 that unwed fathers are about 50 per cent less likely to ever marry than men without unwed first births, even after controlling for other variables such as age, employment, education, race and church attendance.[837]

Concluding their study of 650 divorced Australians, Ilene Woolcott and Jody Hughes noted that most of the men and women in their survey mentioned affective dimensions of the marriage relationship – an umbrella category that could encompass communication problems, incompatibility, changed values and lifestyle desires, and instances of infidelity. "The dominance of relational reasons may reflect the higher expectations of self-fulfilment in marriage and decreasing tolerance of unsatisfying relationships observed by many commentators on marriage and divorce."[838] Conversely, "the mediating effects of demographic or socio-economic factors on attitudes, opportunities and constraints, and patterns of behaviour that may have a profound influence on marital satisfaction and stability, are less likely to have been recognised by respondents as underlying causes for the perceived main reasons for divorce."

Infidelity is cited in many studies as a major cause of separation and divorce. In the US, conservative estimates suggest that "at least one-quarter – and perhaps considerably more – of marital disruptions are preceded by the infidelity of one or the other spouse while the marriage still existed."[839]

A recent US study of parenthood, *When baby makes three*, concluded that married parents are more likely than their childless peers to feel their lives have a sense of meaning and purpose, and that married parents generally experience more happiness and less depression than parents who are unmarried.[840] A Scottish study of 10,000 households over 15 years also found that having children improves married peoples' life satisfaction, and the more they have, the happier they are.[841] Nonetheless, parenthood is typically associated with lower levels of marital happiness. There is also evidence that the gender of children is related to the incidence of divorce, with parents of girls more likely to divorce than parents of boys. The reasons for this effect are unclear.[842]

The US family scholars were able to identify ten aspects of contemporary marriage and parenthood that appears to boost the odds of successfully combining marriage and parenthood. It is probable that these factors are also associated with marital stability. Summarising the findings, they concluded that the top five factors were:[843]

For wives –

"Very happy" in marriage:

1.   Above-average sexual satisfaction
2.   Above-average commitment
3.   Above-average generosity to husband
4.   Above-average attitude to raising children
5.   Above-average social support.

Not prone to separation or divorce:

1.   Above-average commitment
2.   Above-average sexual satisfaction
3.   Both spouses have above-average marital spirituality (e.g., Report God is at the centre of their marriage)
4.   Above-average social support
5.   Wife has above average spirituality.

For husbands –

"Very happy" in marriage:

1.   Above-average sexual satisfaction
2.   Above-average commitment

3. Above-average generosity to wife
4. Above-average attitude towards raising children
5. Both spouses have above-average marital spirituality.

Not prone to separation or divorce:
1. Above-average commitment
2. Above-average sexual satisfaction
3. Both spouses have above-average marital spirituality
4. Both spouses attend religious services weekly or more often
5. Above-average generosity to wife.

In *Should we stay together?,* the marital scholar Jeffry Larson, identified three sets of factors that predict relationship dissatisfaction: Individual traits such as high neurosis, anxiety, depression and impulsiveness; couple traits such as dissimilarity, short acquaintanceship, and pre-marital pregnancy; and context such as younger age, unhealthy family-of-origin experiences, parental divorce and pressure to marry.[844]

The scholarly findings underscore three observations. First, a satisfying sexual union is an integral component of most successful marriages.[845] Secondly, couples who make a regular practice of being generous with each other enjoy markedly higher levels of marital quality and stability.[846] Positive attitudes towards sacrificing for a partner are powerful positives for a successful marriage.[847] Thirdly:

> Commitment is also an exceedingly powerful predictor of marital success among today's young parents. Husbands and wives who prioritise their mutual identity as a couple do much better than their peers who seek to put their own needs first, or who regularly or even occasionally scan the social scene in search of potential new romantic options.[848]

The scholars found that above-average commitment triples the odds of marital happiness for husbands and wives and reduces their divorce proneness sixfold.[849] Conversely, even among spouses who shared the same materialistic values, materialism is negatively associated with marital quality.[850]

Summarising their national study of married couples, Professor Paul Amato and colleagues at Pennsylvania State University observed that "most successful marriages combine gender equality, two incomes, shared social ties, and a strong commitment to marital permanence."[851] Other studies have identified the relative closeness in the ages of partners, and the absence of parental divorce as factors in marital success.[852] Other factors include shared religious practice,[853] and a preparedness to share household chores.[854]

While researchers have long debated selection effects, a study of two large national representative samples in Australia found that marriage itself is responsible for 61 per cent of the positive effect of marriage on the subjective well-being of married men and women.[855] Being happily married increases one's life satisfaction.[856]

SUMMARY

- ♥ There has been a significant decline in marriage over the past four decades:
  - ➢ People are marrying less.
  - ➢ Couples marry at an older age.
  - ➢ Pre-marital cohabitation has increased significantly.
  - ➢ There has been a significant increase in divorce.
  - ➢ The number of children involved in divorce is higher.
  - ➢ The rates of remarriage have fallen.
  - ➢ Families are having fewer children.
  - ➢ The proportion of children born out-of-wedlock has increased dramatically.
  - ➢ There has been a marked increase in the number of single parent families.
- ♥ Families have also been affected by other changes, including the entry of women into the paid workforce, and the ageing of the population.
- ♥ Marital commitment has declined significantly in western nations.
- ♥ Marital instability has been linked to having an ex-nuptial child, pre-marital cohabitation, pre-marital sex, leaving home at an early age, marrying as a teenager, and parental divorce.
- ♥ Factors associated with marital stability include a satisfying sexual union, showing generosity towards a partner, and strong levels of commitment.
  - ➢ Other factors include gender equity, two incomes, shared social ties and a commitment to marital permanence.

8

SOUL MATES AND COHABITATION

The quest for a 'soul mate', that person with whom one can make a deep spiritual and emotional connection for life, is a significant priority for contemporary young adults. An overwhelming majority (94 per cent) of respondents to the 2001 US *State of our Unions* survey agreed that "when you marry you want your spouse to be your soul mate, first and foremost."[857] Over 80 per cent of all women, married and single, in the same survey agreed that it was more important for them to have a husband who can communicate about his deepest feelings than to have a husband who makes a good living. Almost nine out-of-ten single men and women agreed that "there is a special person, a soul mate, waiting for you somewhere out there."

The idea of a special person is not new, but the strength of the belief is a remarkable feature of modern relationships. In part, it reflects many of the cultural and demographic trends already discussed, including a heightened sense of individualism, and strength of romantic attachment. Paradoxically, it reinforces a desire for a deep, committed union at a time when many other forces undermine that possibility. The twenty-something singles who participated in the survey aspired to a life-long marriage, with almost 80 per cent agreeing that a couple should not get married unless they are prepared to stay together for life.

The search for a 'soul mate' also reflects the fear of divorce. Looking at their parents' generation, these young adults reveal that one of their biggest concerns about getting married is the possibility that it will end in divorce. It is a reason why cohabitation has become ubiquitous: "if one wants to marry a soul mate, then one has to live with a prospective spouse '24/7' in order to evaluate his or her emotional fitness for this special kind of relationship."[858]

The rise in cohabitation[859]

The substantial increase in the number of couples living together, both before and as a substitute for marriage, is one of the most significant family trends in recent decades.[860] In the US, the number of cohabiting couples increased fifteen-fold between 1960 and 2009,[861] a pattern replicated in most western nations.[862] The reasons that couples choose to live together can vary greatly. In early studies of the phenomenon, Macklin identified at least five different patterns amongst cohabiters:

- *a temporary, casual convenience* with minimum emotional or physical involvement and limited commitment. The motivation may be more economic or protective than romantic;

- *an extension of an affectionate, steady relationship*, which generally includes being sexually intimate. It is likely to continue as long as the couple enjoy being together;

- *a trial marriage* for couples who are contemplating making their relationship permanent and want to test it out. In this sense, living together becomes part of courtship;

- *a temporary alternative to marriage for people who have determined to marry.* They simply live together until it is professionally or economically feasible to marry;

- *a permanent or semipermanent alternative to marriage.* For some people, such as elderly persons, living together permanently is determined by economic factors. For others, this decision may include negative views on the institution of marriage or the desire to keep love alive by avoiding the security of marriage.[863]

While it is true that there has been an increase in the number of couples in the last category, partially as a result of the increase in divorce, studies indicate that for most people, cohabitation is a pathway to marriage, either with the same partner or another.[864] A 1993 survey by the Australian Bureau of Statistics found that almost 60 per cent of couples enter a cohabiting relationship before marriage, up from 15 per cent of married couples surveyed in 1975.[865] Two decades later, the proportion has risen to over 75 per cent. Similar developments have occurred elsewhere. In the United States, for example, the proportion of couples living together before marriage increased from 11 per cent in the years 1965-74 to 44 per cent in 1980-84 and has continued to increase since.[866] It is now about 70 per cent.[867]

The reasons that individuals begin to cohabit can vary greatly.[868] It can include testing compatibility,[869] wishing to spend time together, and wanting to share financial resources.[870] The purpose of this chapter is to explore the consequences of the significant rise in cohabitation over the past four decades.

The cohabitation pathway

In reviewing the findings of an early (1991) ten year longitudinal survey of cohabitants, Sotirios Sarantakos, found that the vast majority of cohabitants marry, either their partner or another person.[871] Professor Sarantakos discovered:

> The vast majority of the cohabitants abandon cohabitation with its liberal ideology and join matrimony, with the same or another partner. Even those who do stay for some time in cohabitation (i) do not practise fully the liberalistic ideology of cohabitation (for example with regard to freedom, stability, commitment, responsibility, security, and so on); and (ii) establish a relationship that is in structural and organisational terms not different from marriage. In most cases cohabitation is, by no means an alternative to marriage, but rather a normative step leading to marriage. Consciously or unconsciously many cohabitants ... by joining cohabitation, seem to reject the wedding, rather than marriage.[872]

Sarantakos concluded that cohabitation is an extremely unstable system: "This study leaves no doubt about the fact that life is easier in marriage, and that *de facto* unions are more likely to encounter problems than marriages are," he wrote in his seminal work *Living Together in Australia*.[873] This finding has been replicated in other later studies,[874] including by the Australian family scholars, Ruth Weston, Lixia Qu and David de Vaus, who found that cohabiting relationships tend to be short-lived and "separation is almost as likely as marriage" as a result.[875] British research reveals that about 55 per cent of cohabitations lead to marriage, while 45 per cent end in separation.[876] Yet two-thirds of cohabiting couples expect they will marry their partner, according to US research.[877]

It would appear that many couples commence cohabiting after knowing each other for only a short period of time. According to the *Australian Family Formation Study*, a fifth of those in existing *de facto* relationships had been involved in their relationship three months or less before moving in together; a further quarter had known each other four to six months; and an additional seven per cent had known each other for more than two years before they started living together. The same study found that 25 per cent of relationships lasted 12 months, around half ended after two years, and three-quarters ended by four years.[878]

Reflecting on the evidence of relationship instability, Professor Sarantakos commented:

> More recent findings, for instance, relating to the effectiveness of cohabitation as a dyadic relationship and as a socialising agency show clearly that this lifestyle cannot be compared to marriage. Particularly with regard to its role as a child-rearing agency, cohabitation demonstrates serious shortcomings which deserve further consideration.[879]

Subsequent research has confirmed the unstable nature of cohabitation. A study of 906 white men and women born in the Detroit area in 1961 revealed rates of separation for cohabiters nearly five times as high as for married couples, and very low rates of reconciliation.[880] Other studies confirm these findings,[881] especially for people who cohabit with more than one partner prior to marriage.[882] Hence, a British study revealed that couples who lived with each other were 15 per cent more likely to divorce, while couples who had previously lived with a different partner were around 45 per cent more likely to divorce.[883] A study by the UK Office for National Statistics found that 61 per cent of people cohabiting in 1991 were still with the same partner a decade later, compared to 82 per cent of those who were married.[884]

There is recent evidence that cohabitations are now formed under more varied circumstances by different types of people, and fewer cohabitations are transitioning to marriage.[885] Using data from the *National Survey of Family Growth*, Karen Guzzo studied six cohabitation cohorts of people in their twenties over two decades from 1985. In her sample, the proportion of first-time cohabiters fell over the period from over 80 per cent to about 70 per cent amongst 20-24 year olds, and from over 60 per cent to less than 50 per cent amongst 25-29 year olds, but the numbers of second cohabitations increased for each group. Third or subsequent cohabitations remained fairly steady and low amongst the younger group, but more than doubled to over 10 per cent in the 25-29 age group. Professor Guzzo identified an increase in the number of unions which dissolved in the most recent cohorts relative to the cohabitations that formed in 1980-84. She also found that engagement to marry was protective against dissolution for first time cohabiters, but not second-time cohabiters, amongst the 20-24 year olds, but not amongst the 25-29 year olds.

Emerging adults

Recent studies about the attitudes and behaviour patterns of emerging adults – young people aged 18-23 – reveal that the rise in cohabitation is linked to earlier experiences for most people. The sociologists,

Mark Regnerus and Jeremy Uecker, write in their study of how young Americans meet, mate and think about marrying, that their relationships "often lack security and commence sex relatively quickly" and tend to end "typically within a year of commencement":

> Sex within friendships has emerged as a popular – if still minority practice. While the sex may be initially frequent within them, it's short-lived, especially when compared to the more stable sexual access afforded to people in romantic relationships. So while emerging adults don't do commitmentless sex for very long, neither are they adept at keeping relationship commitments for long, either.[886]

Their study is supported by other surveys. In an analysis of the *National Longitudinal Study of Adolescent Health*, scholars at Child Trends found that 31 per cent of 18-25 year olds in the US had sex within four weeks of knowing a partner, with five per cent within a day.[887] Another report found that 25 per cent of women had sex within the first week of dating.[888] A UK poll identified a new culture of a 'friend with benefits', a description of no-strings-attached casual relationships.[889]

This culture of casual relationships and 'hooking up' can have lasting effects for individuals.[890] In their national longitudinal study of more than 3,000 adolescents and young adults, *Lost in transition*, Professor Christian Smith and his fellow sociologists discovered a generation with many regrets:

> Many emerging adults have tested the waters of permissive sexual activity in uncommitted relationships and have, to their surprise, found those waters to be deep and turbulent. More than a few have foundered and struggled to make it back to safety. Their hurt and regrets vary in intensity and longevity. But although their unhappy experiences vary, we can at least say with confidence that the idea that the sexual revolution's promise of easy, safe, uncomplicated, fulfilling, casual sex is being happily lived out by emerging adults today is misleading. Many, in fact, come to grief and thus learn the hard way that sex

is more powerful and potentially problematic than they had ever imagined or been warned.[891]

According to the US scholars, young women bear the brunt of the negative experiences. In societies where women of marriageable age outnumber men, this is compounded. The writer, Kate Bolick, observed in a recent article about the new singles, "when confronted with a surplus of women, men become promiscuous and unwilling to commit to a monogamous relationship."[892] Across the Atlantic, the *Health Survey for England 2010* found that men reported having 9.3 different partners on average while women had an average of 4.7 partners.[893]

As Professor Regnerus and other scholars have shown, these temporary relationships often lead to cohabitation. While unreliable – only about 20 per cent in the US result in marriage, according to one study[894] – cohabitation does serve to "increase exposure to a stable partner, mimic aspects of marriage, and heighten opportunities for sex."[895]

Surprisingly for some, scholars of the emerging generation assert "most of the problems in the lives of youth have their origins in the larger adult world into which youth are being socialised." In this regard, they are "barometers of the condition of the adult world."[896]

Public opinion

There is a widespread belief that cohabitation before marriage is to the advantage of the couple concerned.[897] In national surveys, nearly 60 per cent of American high school seniors indicated they 'agreed' or 'mostly agreed' with the statement "it is usually a good idea for a couple to live together before getting married in order to find out whether they really get along."[898] Fifty-seven per cent of the 20-24 year old respondents to the *National Longitudinal Study of Adolescent Health* agreed that cohabitation, even with no intent for future marriage, was all right.[899]

About half the respondents to the Australian *National Social Science Survey* reported that they would recommend that couples live together and then marry.[900] In a survey for the television program, *A Current Affair*, 55 per cent of respondents said that 'trial' marriage was an appropriate preparation for a life-long relationship.[901] Only 18 per cent of respondents to the 1991 *Australian Family Formation Study*[902] and 32 per cent of respondents to the 1995 *Australian Family Values survey*[903] disagreed with the statement 'It is alright for a couple to live together without planning to marry.' In the *State of our Unions* survey, the majority of young American adults (62 per cent) agreed that living together before marriage is a good way to avoid divorce, and 43 per cent said that they would only marry someone who agreed to live together first.[904]

These views reflect some of the early expert opinion about the trends. Montgomery, for example, stated in 1973 that "couples who live together during courtship will probably make fewer mistakes in selecting marriage partners. Their marriage, in all probability, will be more reasoned and there will be fewer illusions about the person with whom marriage is to take place."[905] These beliefs are regularly aired in the media.

Belief and reality

Summarising the growing social science studies into the effects of cohabitation, family researchers, Scott Stanley and Galena Rhoades, commented: "The belief that cohabiting prior to marriage lowers one's odds of divorce has no evidence going for it, yet it is a strongly held belief,"[906] adding "we know of no published study that shows a benefit of premarital cohabitation for marital outcomes and many published studies showing added risk."[907] Consider some of the findings.

Cohabitation and marital permanence

The Australian Institute of Family Studies *Family Formation Project* found that after five years of marriage, 13 per cent of those who had cohabited would divorce, compared to six per cent of those who had not cohabited. Ten years later, the proportions were 26 per cent for those who had cohabited and 14 per cent for those who had not; and after 20 years: 56 per cent compared to 27 per cent.[908] More recent Australian data confirmed the trends. Using the *Household, Income and Labour Dynamics in Australia* survey of more than 9,000 men and women, University of Queensland researchers found that cohabitation increases the odds of divorce by 41 per cent for men and 31 per cent for women.[909]

These findings have been supported by other research.[910] In a national study of 8,177 ever-married men and women, sociologists David Hall and John Zhao found that "premarital cohabiters in Canada have over twice the risk of divorce in any year of marriage when compared to noncohabiters."[911] A UK Government survey reached similar conclusions. According to research by the UK Office of Population Censuses and Surveys, couples marrying in 1970-74 were 30 per cent more likely to have divorced after five years' marriage if they had cohabited, those marrying in 1975-79 were 40 per cent more likely, and those marrying in 1980-84 were 50 per cent more likely. Another British study revealed that "nearly one in two cohabiting couples split up before their child's fifth birthday, compared to one in twelve married parents" and "three quarters of family breakdown now involves unmarried parents."[912] In 2006, 75 per cent of couples in the UK who had children after they were married had stayed together until their child's 16th birthday, compared to just seven per cent of couples who were unmarried when their child was born.[913]

An analysis of the *British Household Panel Survey* data for 1991-2006, involving 29,065 cases, revealed that prior cohabitation with a spouse is associated with a 60 per cent higher risk of divorce. According to the British scholars, the increased divorce rate was not explained by taking into account the length of time that cohabiters had already lived together.[914]

Allowing for cohabitees' extra years of living together, they are still 20 per cent more likely to be divorced after 15 years of marriage, according to one study.[915] US researchers Larry Bumpass and James Sweet concluded from their survey of the US data that "marriages that are preceded by living together have 50 per cent higher disruption rates than marriages without premarital cohabitation."[916] Another study puts the rate as five times higher.[917] A series of other studies have found a link between cohabitation and marital dissolution.[918] In Sweden, it has been found that cohabiters have a higher risk of divorce even if the period of marriage is counted from the beginning of cohabitation.[919] In their 1990 US research, Jay Teachman and Karen Polonko found that couples who cohabited prior to marriage had a greater chance of marital dissolution. But they also found that for those couples who had only cohabited with their future spouse, the odds of dissolution were no greater than for non-cohabiters.[920]

A subsequent study by Alfred DeMaris and Vininadha Rao found that cohabiting prior to marriage, regardless of the nature of that cohabitation was associated with an enhanced risk of later marital disruption:

> It appears that this association is beginning to take on the status of an empirical generalisation. Contrary to the expectations of many couples who envision that prior cohabitation is a hedge against marital 'failure', those who live together before marrying stand a higher chance of ending their marriage. It only remains to detail the mechanism which makes this association possible.[921]

Recent European studies have confirmed the earlier findings.[922] Dutch sociologists found that "couples who cohabited prior to marriage have a greater risk of divorce" than couples who did not.[923] A Norwegian study concluded that children of cohabiting couples were about two and a half times more likely to experience a parental separation compared to children of married couples. Moreover, the discrepancy had not changed over several decades.[924] In Sweden, where cohabitation is widely accepted and legally supported, children born to cohabiting parents were 75 per cent more likely than children born to married parents to see their parents separate by the time they reached age 15.[925]

The incidence of separation amongst cohabiters is partially hidden, as it is not reflected in official statistics in many places. Professor David Popenoe notes:

> Many ill-matched couples who in earlier years would have gone on to marriage and later divorce, because cohabitation was not possible for them, today cohabit instead. If and when they break up, which they do in large numbers, their break up is, of course, not reflected in the divorce rate.[926]

It has been observed that the association between cohabitation and subsequent marital separation appears to have weakened for more recent birth cohorts,[927] possibly because more couples cohabit than in the past.[928] If more couples cohabit, the total group will reflect not only those who have non-traditional attitudes about marriage, but an increasing number of people with traditional attitudes. A Canadian study, comparing the situation in Quebec, where cohabitation is more common than elsewhere, offered some support for this thesis: In Quebec, cohabiting couple families were 2.5 times more likely to separate than those who married directly, whereas they were five times more likely to do so in the rest of Canada.[929] In one recent study, sociologists Wendy Manning and Jessica Cohen found that being in love and moving closer to a partner is associated with gains in personal well-being and, at least in the short-term, these effects are similar for cohabitation and marriage, but cautioned that differences may have become more difficult to detect, and noted that cohabitation has various meanings, which complicated any analysis.[930] They reiterated previous research[931] that the impact of cohabitation on a subsequent marriage is not a simple or direct relationship, but rather is multifaceted.

Using a national sample, scholars at the US National Center for

Health Statistics examined the marital outcomes for a population of couples over 20 years. They found that women who had never cohabited with their first husband had a significantly higher probability of marriage survival (57 per cent) compared with women who had cohabited with their first spouse prior to marriage.[932] The probability of marriage survival for men who had never cohabited (60 per cent) was similar to men who had cohabited with their first wife after becoming engaged (57 per cent). However, probability of marriage survival for men who had cohabited prior to becoming engaged was significantly lower (49 per cent). A 2005 *National Survey of Marriage in America* also revealed that couples who did not live together had greater chances of marital success, followed by those who lived together whilst engaged and lastly, those who lived together before engagement.[933] These studies suggest that the timing of cohabitation may be an important factor in the risk of subsequent marital separation, at least for men. While the scholars at the National Center for Health Statistics noted that the multivariate models needed to disentangle the complex relationship between premarital cohabitation and the stability of first marriage was beyond the scope of their report, others have suggested reasons, which are discussed below.

Cohabitation and marital happiness

Family scholars have found that couples who cohabit prior to marriage to be significantly lower on measures of marital quality.[934] Alfred DeMaris and Gerald Leslie hypothesised that cohabiters would score higher on communication and couple adjustment in their study. However, they found a negative relationship between cohabitation and satisfaction:

> [C]ompared with noncohabiters, cohabiters scored significantly lower in both perceived quality of marital communication and marital satisfaction. These differences were significant for wives in the area of communication and for both spouses in the area of marital satisfaction. Part of this effect is accounted for

by differences between cohabiters and noncohabiters on sex role traditionalism, church attendance, and other sociocultural variables. However, even after controlling for such differences, having cohabited is associated with slightly lower marital satisfaction for both husbands and wives, although for husbands the effect is not quite significant. The effect persists even after considering the greater amount of time in which cohabiters have been intimately involved and controlling for differences between cohabiters and noncohabiters on commitment to marital permanence.[935]

Recent studies have confirmed the earlier findings that premarital cohabitation is associated with more negative communication in marriage,[936] lower levels of marital satisfaction,[937] less marital happiness,[938] and higher perceived marital instability.[939] While the benefits of union formation tend to diminish over time, social ties to family and friends appear to remain for both cohabiters and the married.[940]

Alfred DeMaris and Gerald Leslie noted:

Rather than acting as a filter that effectively screens out the less-compatible couples, cohabitation appears to select couples from the outset who are somewhat less likely to report high satisfaction once they are married. This may be due to the fact that these individuals expect more out of marriage from the beginning. Alternatively, these may be individuals who adapt less readily to the role expectations of conventional marriage than do more traditional respondents.

Professors Watson and DeMeo concluded their early study of cohabitation noting:

The results of this research cast doubts upon the high hopes which have been held for premarital cohabitation as a means of ensuring the compatibility of prospective spouses, of testing their relationship and, as individuals, of building the interpersonal skills important to successful marriage. It has also been found that the rate of violence is appreciably higher for cohabiting couples who have lived together for one to ten years than for married couples.[941]

The increased risk of violence in cohabiting relationships has been observed in subsequent studies.[942]

The ambiguity of cohabitation

One reason for the lower levels of marital happiness may relate to the commitment of the partners. Analysing the results of a national survey of engaged, married and cohabiting couples, US researchers reported a significantly higher level of commitment or dedication to each other amongst the married couples. The study also found that a man's dedication to his wife was significantly lower among couples that had cohabited prior to marriage compared to couples that had not done so.[943] A more recent study reached a similar conclusion for women who had cohabited, but not for men.[944] A survey using Scandinavian data found that, compared to married couples, cohabiters overall "are less serious, less satisfied, and more often consider to split up from their current relationships."[945]

Lower levels of commitment appear to be reflected in the manner in which cohabiting couples handle money. Using studies and data from Australia, Britain, Germany, Sweden and the United States, Carolyn Vogler found that cohabiting couples function as financially autonomous units, with separate accounts and cheque books.[946]

A recent study from the Netherlands found a difference in interpersonal commitment, measured by the specialisation of labour, purchasing a house and having children, between married and cohabiting couples, and within subgroups of cohabiting couples.[947] Cohabiters with marriage plans were the most likely to marry, but were also most likely to postpone some investments in their relationships, such as having children, because of the symbolic importance of marriage.

Perhaps because many cohabiters have drifted into their relationship, or do not view it as a permanent union, the levels of extra-relational sex were much higher, compared to married peers. A study of 3990 Mexican men found that the cohabiters were almost twice as likely to cheat on their partners.[948]

These findings reflect what Scott Stanley and colleagues at the Center of Marital and Family Studies at the University of Denver have described as "the ambiguity of cohabitation" which "may undermine the ability of some couples to develop a clear and mutual understanding about the nature of their relationships."[949]

Lower levels of commitment may have preceded cohabitation. A survey of the attitudes of young single men in the US revealed reasons why many appear to avoid commitment. The men, aged 25-33, expressed a desire to marry and have children in their lives, but they were in no hurry: "They enjoy their single life and they experience few of the traditional pressures from church, employers or the society that once encouraged men to marry. Moreover, the sexual revolution and the trend towards cohabitation offer them some of the benefits of marriage without its obligations."[950] The psychologist, Ted Huston, also found support for the popular wisdom that "men are slower to invest themselves than women in moving romantic relationships forward."[951] In their summary of their findings, the family scholars, Barbara Dafoe Whitehead and David Popenoe listed ten reasons why men won't commit:

- They can get sex without marriage more easily than in the past.
- They can enjoy the benefits of having a wife by cohabiting rather than marrying.
- They want to avoid divorce and its financial risks.
- They want to wait until they are older to have children.

- They fear that marriage will require too many changes and compromises.
- They are waiting for the perfect soul mate and she hasn't yet appeared.
- They face few social pressures to marry.
- They are reluctant to marry a woman who already has children.
- They want to own a house before they get married.
- They want to enjoy single life as long as they can.

There may be a chemical explanation also to the differences in commitment between men and women. After examining scientific studies about the effect of the chemical oxytocin on bonding and the inducement of trust in humans, Professor Stanley suggests that given the increased prevalence of the chemical in women, it may drive earlier sacrificial behaviours in them, compared to men, whose sacrificial behaviour is a product of long-term commitment.[952] Stanley illustrates the differences in the following diagram.

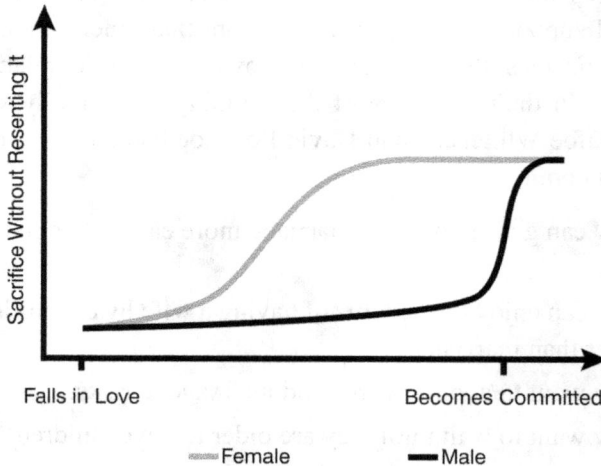

Y-axis: Sacrifice Without Resenting It
X-axis: Falls in Love ... Becomes Committed
Legend: Female ── Male

Professor Stanley adds that if this theory is correct:

The average female is at a disadvantage once the attachment is strong and the oxytocin is flowing, up until the point the male catches up with commitment. Further, since oxytocin levels affect trust, it could be harder for the average woman to see this imbalance for some time, because biology has primed her to see things from a trusting perspective.[953]

Other family scholars have noted ambiguity amongst cohabiters about the meaning of cohabitation.[954] Gender distinctions may be reflected also in changing plans for marriage during the course of the cohabitation:

Among cohabiting couples, men's plans for marriage determine the transition to marriage but, once married, men's plans for marriage may not influence the quality and stability of marriages. It is also possible that women in the most stable marriages may more often retrospectively report engagement at the start of cohabitation, whereas men's retrospective reports of commitment to marriage may be less influenced by the state of the marriage. Men could be less precise reporters of their relationship experiences, and plans for marriage may take a different meaning for men and women. Furthermore, the concepts of being 'engaged' and having 'definite' plans for marriage may seem straightforward, but there is a variation in the interpretation of these terms and differences in couples' interpretation of commitment to marriage or plans for marriage.[955]

Observing the differing levels of commitment between men and women, Scott Stanley hypothesises that attachment triggers committed and sacrificial behaviour in women, whereas a decision to be committed triggers committed and sacrificial behaviour in men. In other words:

Women begin to give their best to men when they are strongly attached. However, men may be less inclined to give fully of themselves unless they have decided that a particular woman is their future.[956]

Men's commitment-phobia may have unintended consequences for women, warn the family scholars: "If this trend continues, it will not be good news for the many young women who hope to marry and bear children before they begin to face problems associated with declining fertility."[957] While men may see marriage as the final step in a process of growing up, there is a potential down side:

> A prolonged period of single life may habituate men to the single life. Some of these men have spent a good part of their adult years living with parents, roommate or alone. They have become accustomed to their own space and routines. They enjoy the freedom of not having to be responsible to anyone else. Like Henry Higgins, they fear losing their solitary pleasures by 'letting a woman into their life.'[958]

There are also consequences for women, which are discussed below and in chapter 12.

The cohabitation effect

In a 1996 article in the *Journal of Marriage and the Family*, Susan Brown and Alan Booth observe that marriages preceded by cohabitation show 'lower levels of marital interaction, higher levels of disagreement and instability ... lower levels of commitment to marriage' and higher levels of divorce than marriages without previous cohabitation experience.[959] Similarly Stephen Nock and others have noted that in many instances, cohabitation is not a relationship with a future, but one that lasts for a period of time and then ends, either through marriage or dissolution; and that cohabitation and marriage differ not only in quantity but also in quality.[960]

Sotirios Sarantakos concluded that:

• Premarital cohabitation does not improve the choice of marital partners; does not offer an enriched courtship where partners get to know each other and gain experience with matters related to marriage; and does not offer an opportunity to test the compatibility of the partners; if cohabiting partners had a chance to live their life over again, almost one-half would not have chosen the same partner; and

- There are more couples with than without premarital cohabitation experience demonstrating a low marital satisfaction and low marital happiness, lack of freedom, interpersonal dependence, domestic violence, marital conflicts and instability.[961]

Professor Sarantakos posited four reasons why cohabitation is inferior to marriage as a dyadic relationship and as a socialising relationship:[962] First, cohabitation often attracts people with little if any resources, skills and attributes required for a successful relationship.[963] Secondly, in cohabitation, mate selection is geared towards finding a 'partner' or a 'friend' rather than a 'spouse'. Consequently, screening mechanisms employed by people looking for a suitable partner are less vigorous in cohabitation than in marriage, and therefore cannot guarantee compatibility, commitment and stability of the relationship. Thirdly, cohabiters are by definition less committed to stable and enduring relationships, and especially to marriage; many also entertain non-traditional beliefs regarding marriage;[964] and fourthly, cohabitation experiences expose couples to liberal attitudes and environments, to modernism and tolerance to alternative beliefs and practices. Drugs, drinking, sexual freedom and social deviance are often tolerated more in a cohabitation environment than a marriage environment.

Recent research supports the earlier studies.[965] Examining communication patterns of newlywed couples, scholars at Penn State University reported that "couples with single and multiple cohabitation experiences displayed poorer communication skills compared with couples with no premarital cohabitation."[966] Searching for reasons why this was the case, they suggest that the "premarital cohabitation experience appears to be a vulnerability spouses bring to the marriage that puts them at risk for poorer marital communication." The researchers link this to the level of commitment the partners bring to the marriage, less motivation to develop healthy communication skills, and lower expectations and poorer skills when they actually transition to marriage.

Therapists and educators have pondered the reasons for the greater chance of marital dissolution amongst couples who cohabited prior to marriage. Kerry James, a Sydney marriage counsellor, noted that "people who do decide not to get married and live together may be unsure of their commitment in the first place, and then they may decide to get married. The lack of certainty about the commitment continues and that's why marriages break down."[967]

Helen Glezer, a senior research fellow at the Australian Institute of Family Studies, observed that "men are more likely than women to believe cohabiting allows them to keep their independence. They perceive it as having economic advantages. It is seen as involving less commitment than marriage and men are more likely to view cohabiting as trial marriage. This suggests that women will be either more romantic or emotionally dependent in *de facto* relationships than men."[968] Jim Pilmer, former Director of Anglican Marriage Education and Counselling Services, Melbourne, observed:

> It's amazing how many people can hide their real identity until they're married. People living together slide into relationships fairly easily without evaluating whether they are right for each other ... Unfortunately many couples get married to make poor relationships work, thinking that when they marry everything will be right – it isn't, it gets worse.[969]

Reviewing three decades of research, Professors Scott Stanley and Galena Rhoades describe the association between cohabitation and the risk for problems in marriage as a 'cohabitation effect'. They summarise this effect as:

- More negative communication in marriage.
- Lower levels of marriage satisfaction.

- The erosion over time of the value/view of marriage and childrearing;
- Higher perceived marital instability;
- Lower levels of male commitment to spouse; and
- Greater likelihood of divorce.[970]

While some research points to selection effects, that is, that couples who are more likely to cohabit are also more likely to exhibit risk factors associated with marital unhappiness and dysfunction,[971] this does not appear to explain all of the risk associated with cohabitation prior to marriage.[972] Nor does the view that, as cohabitation becomes more commonplace, the risks will reduce or disappear, as some of the more recent research continues to show the effect.[973] Paul Amato and his colleagues at Pennsylvania State University point out, "if the selection explanation is correct, then the association between premarital cohabitation and divorce should have grown weaker as cohabitation became more common, because cohabitation became less selective of people with high-risk traits of divorce."[974] Noting the studies that the increased risk associated with premarital cohabitation has remained constant across the decades, they conclude that "to the extent that cohabitation leads to marriages that would not have occurred otherwise, cohabitation may contribute to subsequent marital problems and instability."[975]

A significant difference between marriage and cohabitation is what the sociologist, Andrew Cherlin, describes as "enforceable trust."

> Getting married requires a public commitment to a long-term, possibly life-long relationship. This commitment is usually expressed in front of relatives, friends, and religious congregants ... Cohabiting, in contrast, requires only a private commitment, which is easier to break. As a result, marriage lowers the risk that your partner will renege on promises to act in ways that would benefit you and your children.[976]

While Professor Cherlin suggests the difference in the amount of enforceable trust that marriage brings, compared to cohabitation, is eroding, the higher separation rate for cohabiters evidences a continuing variation.

Sliding vs deciding

Aware of research that indicates that background factors involving a distrust of commitment are relevant in marital breakdown,[977] recent studies at the University of Denver suggest that many couples slide into cohabitation without making a commitment to marriage first.[978]

> Imagine that a person already at risk for marital problems links up with someone else at greater-than-average risk ... [and] they begin to live together. After all they like being around each other, they want to spend more time together, and they both believe that cohabitation can do nothing but improve the odds of things working out well in marriage. They believe they will learn important details about one another that will make their decision about marriage a more informed one. They also think that cohabiting will help them learn and develop patterns that could help them out in marriage. But notice what happens here. Nothing about cohabiting lowers their risk. In fact, cohabiting, for the most part, could only lower the risk for individuals who are committed to breaking up with this person if things are not going as desired. Doubtless some do this. But equally doubtless, for others, what cohabitation did is increase the odds of an already high risk relationship continuing.[979]

Using a national sample of cohabiters, it was found that two-thirds reported that their cohabitation began either because they "slid into it" or it "just sort of happened" rather than saying that they talked about it and discussed it.[980] The top reasons for cohabiting are summarised in the following table.

Reasons for cohabiting

Men	Women

I wanted to spend more time with my partner
46%   44%

It was inconvenient to live apart
24%   22%

I wanted us to take a step up in commitment
13%   16%

We had a child to raise together
7%   13%

I wanted to test out our relationship before marriage
9%   5%

I don't believe in the institution of marriage
0.8%   0.4%

The Denver scholars suggest that the crux of the problem with sliding is that constraints are increased before a clear choice or commitment has been made and usually before information is gathered by the couple that might have led to a different decision.[981] Describing this as 'inertia theory', Professor Stanley suggests that living together triggers forces that make it more likely that a couple will get married, even if the fit between the partners was poor to begin with, or they were otherwise at higher risk.[982] Acknowledging that this is consistent with Professor Norval Glenn's idea of premature entanglements that foreclose adequate searching for the right partner, Stanley and Rhoades describe a process where many couples 'slide' into cohabitation rather than 'decide' to take the step. This pattern is consistent with other research which indicates that the desire to wed is often more intense on the part of one partner.[983] As Glenn put it:

> Cohabitation may often be a form of 'premature entanglement,' which limits the person's ability to circulate 'on the marriage

market' to test his or her desirability on the market and to find a highly suitable partner.[984]

Professor Galena Rhoades and colleagues at the University of Denver tested their theory in a more recent study of cohabiting couples. By examining structural and financial constraints such as holding a lease together, sharing credit card debt, owning a pet together, having a joint bank account, paying for future vacation plans, making home improvements together, or naming one another as a beneficiary (but not having a child together), they found that the longer couples lived together, the more constraints they acquired. As a consequence, regardless of an intrinsic desire to be with their partner – *dedication* commitment – the constraints made it harder to breakup. This association between the constraints and perceived difficulty in ending the relationship was strongest for women.[985]

This is also consistent with the changing nature of courtship. Barbara Dafoe Whitehead illustrates in *Why there are no good men left*, that the "rules, conventions and practices that nearly everyone recognised and many followed" largely have been abandoned.[986] Noting the cultural, ritual and legal differences between a wedding and cohabitation, she observes:

> In marriage, there are multiple and overlapping ways in which the couple's mutual agreement is enacted, announced, proclaimed, contracted, pledged, and celebrated. This is not the case with cohabitation. Unlike the entry into marriage, the entry into a cohabiting relationship requires nothing more than a change-of-address card. Indeed, it is the nature of the cohabiting partnership to mean whatever each of the individual partners wants it to mean, and these separate meanings can be wildly different. She can harbor one set of expectations for the relationship, and he can have another.[987]

This may explain partially why one survey revealed that longer periods of romantic involvement (one to three years), rather than cohabitation, predicted marital success.[988]

The timing of cohabitation may be a critical insight into the attitude of couples to commitment and the prospects of marital permanence. After surveying a sample of more than 1,000 married men and women, Rhoades, Stanley and Markman concluded that premarital cohabitation, when limited to the period after the engagement, is not associated with an elevated risk of marital problems; but that couples who cohabitated prior to the engagement were more likely to have marital problems and less likely to be happy in their marriages.[989] According to the 2001 *National Survey of Fertility Growth*, 34 per cent of couples had entered cohabitation having announced a plan to marry.[990] A National Center for Health Statistics report found that 55 per cent of women and 54 per cent of men were engaged or had definite plans to marry when their cohabitation began.[991] However, British data reveals that the length of cohabitation has more than doubled since the 1980s, suggesting either less urgency about the decision to marry for the 'cohabit-to-marry' group, or a growing group who live together with no immediate intention to marry at all – the 'until-further-notice' group:

> Twenty years later, the 'cohabit-to-marry' group still exist, but tend to take longer about their decision since there is far less societal pressure to marry. There are also more who move in with the hope of marrying but who use cohabitation as a 'trial marriage' to see whether they are suited to each other, as anecdotal evidence suggests. . . . Therefore those more likely to marry are now associated with longer periods of cohabitation.[992]

The British scholars observed that there has been a distinct shift towards 'seeing-how-it-goes' as more couples tend to move in and then decide whether or not to marry

If there are increased risks associated with 'sliding' into marriage, then the shift towards 'seeing-how-it-goes' cohabitation may result in more separations. As discussed earlier, a number of family scholars suggest that couples which cohabit, having decided to marry, are at no greater risk of breakdown, whereas couples who drift from cohabitation to marriage have an increased exposure to unhappiness, separation and divorce,[993] although the survey by the National Center for Health Statistics indicates that significant differences remain.[994] This is valuable information for educators in assisting couples to understand relationship risks, and the knowledge and skills that can help to minimise them. Some implications for couples considering cohabitation are discussed in chapter 12.

Consequences for contemporary marriage

In her two-year study of fifty happily married couples, *The good marriage*, the American psychologist, Judith Wallerstein, identified the "companionate marriage": "Born in the vortex of social change, companionate marriage is the most common type among young people today."[995] Written in 1995 before the notion of a 'soul mate' became common, Wallerstein's description nonetheless reflects many modern unions.

As Professor Paul Amato and colleagues indicate in *Alone Together*, their study of changing marriage patterns in America, the idea of a companionate marriage is not new.[996] The sociologist, Ernest Burgess, described a change from an institutionalised form of marriage to a new model over the first half of the twentieth century. According to Burgess, companionate marriage is characterised by egalitarian rather than patriarchal relationships between spouses:

> Companionate marriage is held together not by bonds of social obligation but by ties of love, friendship, and common interest. And unlike institutional marriage, which emphasises conformity to social norms, companionate marriage allows for an ample degree of self-expression and personal satisfaction.[997]

The notion has an older origin in the thoughts of John Locke, John Stuart Mill and other Enlightenment philosophers who sought to remove the patriarchal nature of marriage.[998] More recently,

Professor Andrew Cherlin, has observed that the ethic of expressive individualism has infected marriage as it has the culture generally.[999] Paul Amato and colleagues write:

> This ethic assumes that people have an intrinsic need to express their innermost feelings, and that close relationships exist primarily to enhance individual satisfaction and maximise personal growth. As these new ideas grew in popularity, self-development and personal fulfilment came to replace mutual satisfaction and successful team effort as the basis of marriage. In individualistic marriage, love is necessary to form a union, but these unions are successful only to the extent that they meet each partner's innermost psychological needs. If these needs are not met, then spouses will jettison the union to seek happiness with alternative partners.[1000]

Judith Wallerstein warned that this type of marriage is perhaps the most difficult to maintain as "each individual's separate path may supersede the togetherness that happy marriage requires, leading to a loss of intimacy and emotional connectedness." It reflects a paradox at the heart of modern relationships.[1001] In searching for personal fulfilment and emotional connection, couples may downplay the other factors necessary for a long-lasting union. Scott Yenor observes:

> As the family loses functions and authority, people seem less committed to it and invest less in it. As they invest less in it, people see themselves more as individuals apart from the family and come together only for an increasingly narrow range of tasks revolving around companionship, affection and offering psychological support ... Persons with independent interests in the relationship ... may renegotiate the terms of marriage to suit changes in interest, ambition, and ability, and leaving the relationship is always an option when it no longer secures the mutual support, companionship, and affection that first brought the couple together.[1002]

This issue is discussed further in chapter 12.

SUMMARY

♥ Young adults are searching for a 'soul mate' with whom to make an emotional connection for life.

♥ The majority of people cohabit before marriage.

♥ About half of cohabiters marry their partner, and the other half separate.

♥ Cohabitation tends to follow earlier experiences of short-lived sexual relationships.

♥ Most people believe cohabitation is a good way to test readiness, compatibility and marital commitment.

♥ There is no evidence that cohabitation lowers risk of divorce – and many studies show higher risks:

  ➢ Couples who cohabit appear to have higher risks of divorce than those who do not; and

  ➢ Cohabitation has been associated with lower levels of marital happiness and commitment.

♥ Social scientists describe these risks as a 'cohabitation effect'.

♥ Cohabiters increasingly fall into two groupings: those who 'cohabit-to-marry' and those who 'cohabit-until-further-notice'.

♥ Many cohabiting couples appear to 'slide' into marriage, rather than make a definite decision to get married:

  ➢ However couples that have decided to marry before they begin to cohabit may not have increased risks of separation.

♥ While the modern 'companionate' marriage is widely preferred, it is also difficult to sustain.

9

THE GROWING MARRIAGE DIVIDE

At the end of the last millennia, scholars in a number of countries began to notice a significant shift in marriage patterns. The Australian demographers, Bob Birrell and Virginia Rapson, at Monash University, were some of the first to observe that men and women were living apart at rates which could hardly have been imagined a decade or so beforehand.[1003] While a major reason for the decline in partnering was the change in cultural attitudes discussed earlier, the fall in full-time work was also a significant factor.

> Men or women who do not possess post-school qualifications are not in the vanguard of this attitudinal revolution, yet the decline in partnership rates was greater for this group of men and women than their allegedly liberated tertiary-trained counterparts.

Noting the increasing number of births to women not in stable relationships, the Australian scholars observed that "many of the fathers do not meet the expectations which mothers require of male providers." This is reflected in other studies. British researchers, reporting on the attitudes of women bearing ex-nuptial births noted some evidence that "women had quite high, traditional standards for prospective partners. They wanted a man who would be a responsible breadwinner and father but their current boyfriends did not live up to this ideal and most of these women preferred to have their baby on their own rather than compromise their standards."[1004]

The significant increase in the number and proportion of sole parents disturbed the scholars. In addition to the increase, they noted that "their family income from all sources (including maintenance) is generally low," and largely from welfare payments.

> The revolution in partnering levels ... has contributed to new social divisions which have barely been recognised let alone debated in the literature. One is the division between families headed by sole parents and those headed by intact couples and another between men who can afford to partner and those who cannot. The two modes of inequality are interrelated. Boiled down to its essence, a sizeable proportion of men have less to offer on a predictable basis as providers than women can earn for themselves in the labour market. Unfortunately, previous relationships, even if on a casual basis, have left many of these women as sole parents and many of the men as embittered isolates resentful about having to pay into a home they have long since departed.[1005]

The Australian scholars re-examined the trends in another study five years later. Their findings reiterated the previous research. In the mid 1980s, the great majority of young men and women "were married and thus likely to have established a secure relationship conducive to raising a family," but this was no longer the case by 2001.[1006] Although the number of *de facto* relationships had increased, overall partnering rates had declined. Most of the decline in partnering amongst women occurred in the ranks of those without university degrees – that is, not amongst the professional women who were thought to have the greatest choice about lifestyle and/or marriage options. The pattern was similar for men: those who were married were predominantly drawn from the better off.[1007] Consistent with these findings, the divorce rates for degree-qualified men and women in their thirties had also declined.

College (university) graduates

According to the scholars, two marriage gaps had emerged. First, there were many more single women with university qualifications than single males with such qualifications. In the US, 36 per cent of women ages 25-29 had attained a bachelor's degree, compared to 28 per cent of men.[1008] In the UK, 50 per cent of women are graduating from university, compared to 40 per cent of men.[1009] This gap had also been identified by the American scholar, Barbara Dafoe Whitehead in her book, *Why there are no good men left: The romantic plight of the new single woman.*[1010] It is compounded in those places where the number of women in their twenties exceeds the number of men. In Australia, for example, there were 1.131 million men aged 20-something, an excess of 16,000 more than the 1.115 million women. By 2006, there were 1.312 million males for 1.309 million females in their 20s. In 30 years, the excess will have shrunk to just 3,000 excess men.[1011]

Applying cold mathematical logic, the Australian demographer, Bernard Salt, calculated that of the 1.343 million women aged 25-34, only 86,000 single, largely heterosexual, well-off, young men were available after excluding those who were already married (485,000), in a *de facto* relationship (185,000), were gay (7,000), a single parent (12,000) or earning less than $60,000 per annum (568,000).[1012] Salt's criteria were selective. The number of eligible young men increases for example, if a lower earning level is used. Equally, a similar calculus could apply to the number of available young women. However, it does highlight the fact that there is not an endless supply of potential partners.

The diminishing pool of potential partners also may compound the ability of people to achieve their marital aspirations:

> Some people who are interested in marrying – particularly those who view themselves as having few assets to offer as a partner or as being situated in mating pools that are populated by few desirable mates – do not feel confident that they will be able to get what they want (or require) in a spouse. This is true even of people who hold relatively low standards for a marriage partner. People's expectancies about their chances of securing a partner whom they would like to marry, in turn, are tied to their marital attitudes and desires and – by extension – to their future entry into marriage.[1013]

The less qualified

The second, larger gap was amongst the unpartnered, less qualified and less affluent men and women, especially aged in their thirties. Nearly half of single women aged in their late twenties and thirties, who did not hold post-school qualifications, were lone parents. "Their family obligations and almost universal reliance on parenting payments limits their availability and interest in re-partnering."[1014]

The big losers from this revolution in partnering are the nation's children. Dr Birrell and his Australian colleagues note:

> The majority [of children] are being brought up in stable and economically comfortable circumstances. However, there is a growing minority, now more than one in five of all children aged less than 15 years, who are experiencing the double disadvantage of living in a family with low financial resources and having only one parent responsible for their day-to-day care.[1015]

The situation in the US reflects the observation by the Australian scholars. For white mothers aged 20-30, 51 per cent of births to the women without a college education were ex-nuptial in 2009, compared to just eight per cent for women with a college degree.[1016] Nine out of ten college-educated women are married when they give birth, compared to 62 per cent with some post-secondary education and just 43 per cent a high school diploma or less.[1017]

These trends have been identified in more recent US research. Using data from the *National Survey of Family Growth*, W Bradford Wilcox at the University of Virginia found that highly educated Americans, who make up 30 per cent of the adult population, now enjoy marriages that are as stable and happy as those four decades ago. However, amongst the middle of American society – a group that represents 58 per cent of the adult population – "divorce is high, nonmarital childbearing is spreading, and marital bliss is in increasingly short supply."[1018] Professor Wilcox suggested four reasons for the attachment to marriage amongst the affluent and highly educated: they have better access to better-paying and more stable work; they are more likely to hold 'bourgeois' virtues such as self-control, a high regard for education, and a long-term orientation; they are more likely to practise religion or be involved in civic activities; and they are increasingly likely to have a pro-marriage attitude.

Scholars at the Brookings Institution in Washington DC also examined the links between income and marriage, finding that men who experienced the most adverse economic changes also experienced the largest declines in marriage:

> For men ages 30-50 in the top 10 per cent of annual earnings – a group that saw real earnings increase over time – 83 per cent are married today, down modestly from about 95 per cent in 1970. For the median male worker (who experienced a decline in earnings of roughly 28 per cent), only 64 per cent are married today, down from 91 per cent 40 years ago. And at the bottom 25th percentile of earnings, where earnings have fallen by 60 per cent, half of men are married, compared with 86 per cent in 1970. While the share of men who have been divorced has increased across the earnings distribution, an increase in the share of men who have never been married is the largest contributor to lower marriage rates.[1019]

In a related study, the Pew Research Center concluded that the 'marriage gap' in the US is increasingly aligned with a growing income gap. Whereas the share of college graduates who were married had declined from 76 per cent in 1960 to 64 per cent by 2008, the proportion of married Americans who had only completed high school (or less) declined from 69 per cent to just 48 per cent over the same period. A similar decline was observed amongst those with some college education (72 per cent to 50 per cent).[1020] The divide also extends to cohabiting couples.[1021]

Economic consequences

Increasingly, the higher educated are marrying partners like themselves. According to the Pew Research Center, only 37 per cent of married, college-educated men had a wife with a bachelor's degree in 1970; by 2007, 71 per cent of them did. As a consequence, marriage now offers fewer people a boost up the economic ladder:

> Stop and think what this means for the growing inequality in Americans' incomes over the next decade or more. If well-educated people with good jobs marry one another, they will have a better shot at saving money and accumulating wealth. Less-educated, lower-income couples may stick together, but their lack of schooling means they're both more likely to struggle to find work, and they'll have sparser resources to fall back on if one of them loses a job.[1022]

Isabel Sawhill from the Brookings Institution notes that Americans with higher education standards are likely, more than ever, to marry someone with similar educational attainment: "Men used to marry secretaries. Now they marry the woman they met in med school."[1023] Poorer women retain the same standards about marriage as their middle class sisters, but often prefer unmarried parenthood if they were unable to afford a mortgage, a car loan, some savings and sufficient funds to pay for a 'decent' wedding.[1024]

The sociologists, Andrew Cherlin and Brad Wilcox observe that declining job prospects for high-school educated young people exacerbate the marriage divide, leaving them to cohabitating relationships, with serious attachment issues for their children.[1025] The scenario they describe today had been observed amongst young black men a generation earlier.[1026]

Divorce

There is also a divorce divide. The economists, Betsey Stevenson and Justin Wolfers, analysis of national data reveals that for the cohort of people born between 1950 and 1955, 34.8 per cent of first marriages of college graduates had ended in divorce, compared to 44.3 per cent of people who had no tertiary education. They noted:

> The higher divorce propensity among those without a college
> degree is too large to simply reflect their earlier entry into
> marriage. Furthermore, conditional on divorcing, those without
> a college degree are less likely to remarry, and if they do remarry,
> they are again more likely to divorce.[1027]

Americans without college degrees were about three times more likely to divorce in the first ten years of marriage, compared to their college-educated peers. College-educated parents were also less likely to rate their future chances of separation and divorce as high.[1028] The American scholar, Kay Hymowitz, went so far as to describe the changes as a new caste system, where poor and uneducated families are more prone to marital breakdown and, increasingly, non marital family forms.[1029] Likewise, family background and community influences are now more important determinants of future earnings and opportunities of children today than four decades ago.[1030]

Evidence from the British millennium cohort study reveals that five per cent of degree-educated mothers separated before their child's third birthday, compared to 42 per cent of mothers without qualifications.[1031] Marriage was the most significant factor in whether the couples stayed together. In another UK study, eight per cent of married parents had split by the time of their child's fifth birthday, compared to 57 per cent of cohabiters and 25 per cent of those who married after the birth of the child.[1032]

A racial divide

The economists also indicate a stark racial divide in family structure in the US: By age 45, nearly one-in-four blacks born between 1950 and 1955 had never married, while the equivalent statistic for whites was one-in-ten. As Charles Murray reveals, the divide amongst white Americans is trending towards their black compatriots. In 2010, 83 per cent of American whites aged 30-49 years old in the upper middle class were married. Yet only 48 per cent of working class whites in the same age group were married.[1033]

In his study *Is marriage for white people?* Ralph Richard Banks, noted that African-American marriage decline is not limited to the poor, but now encompasses middle and upper-middle class groupings, while divorce and non-marital childbearing rates have soared.[1034] Indeed, college-educated black women are no more likely to marry, or stay married, than white women who only completed high school. The African-American Stanford law professor advises:

> Imprisonment numbers, unemployment numbers, under-performance academically, these are crises not just for African-Americans, but for the nation. Many women would do well to expand their options in the same way people of other races have, and look beyond black men in their search for a partner.[1035]

In a similar finding, Australian scholars also observe that the negative impact on relationships of having insufficient work is greater than being overworked.[1036] Changes to work, driven in part by the technological revolution of the past few decades,[1037] have resulted in a 'hollowing-out' of the middleclass, with consequences for marriage and family life.

The growing marriage divide is also evident for women. While marriage rates in the US either held constant or increased for the top 10 per cent of female earners over the past four decades, the bottom 70 per cent of female earners saw their marriage rates decline by more than 15 percentage points.[1038] The divide had been evident for African-Americans for some time;[1039] it now extends to the general population.

Impact on children

The result is a growing 'marriage gap' between moderately and highly educated America, between the well-off and the lower middle class and upper working class.[1040] The consequences of this shift are profound, especially for children:

> For a substantial share of the United States, economic mobility will be out of reach, their children's life chances will diminish,

and large numbers of young men will live apart from the civilising power of married life ...

This means that more affluent Americans are now doubly privileged in comparison to their moderately educated fellow citizens – by their superior economic resources and by their stable family lives.[1041]

In a paper for the National Bureau of Economic Research, University of Michigan scholars, Martha J Bailey and Susan M Dynarski, illustrate that between the late 1980s and 2007, college graduation had increased for high income students, compared to only nine per cent of low income students.[1042] However, college graduation has not necessarily improved the marriage chances for the least advantaged. Scholars at Cornell University found that college attendance lessened the least advantaged men's and women's odds of marriage by 38 per cent and 22 per cent respectively, compared to increasing the odds for wealthy man and women by 31 per cent and 8 per cent: "men and women from the least advantaged backgrounds who attend college appear to be caught between two social worlds – reluctant to 'marry down' to partners with less education and unable to 'marry up' to those from more privileged backgrounds."[1043]

The marriage divide has reached children. As the Brookings scholars indicate, the typical American child is living in a family where resources have not increased for 35 years, largely because more and more kids are being raised in single-parent households.[1044] Half of the nation's children experienced gains in family earnings, while the other half experienced losses: "Children at the 90th percentile of the distribution of family earnings experienced a 45 per cent increase in their family earnings over the past 35 years" but "children at the 25th percentile ... have seen real declines in family earnings of over 20 per cent."[1045]

Conclusion

These changes have profound implications for individuals and society. Increasingly, family structure reflects social inequality. Introducing a special issue of the journal *Social Science Research*, the renowned sociologist of marriage and family, Stephen Nock, summarised the data:

> The 'haves' are generally those in stable marriages. The 'have nots' are generally those who live outside of marriage, especially with children. So vast is the difference, one is tempted to replace the traditional notion of social class with the more descriptive term marriage class. Marriage now divides the population in much the same way social class once did. Indeed, it may do so more profoundly. Neither education nor occupation so clearly discriminate between those at the two ends of the economic spectrum as marital status does. Those with higher levels of education, income, and occupational stability are more likely to be married and vice versa. The poor or precarious are more likely to be single and vice versa.[1046]

Benjamin Disraeli's famous reference to "two nations" was less about poverty as such, and more about the lack of connection he observed between the rich and the poor.[1047] In the past few decades, we have recreated "two nations" – this time between the stably married and those who are not. It is a worrying development.

SUMMARY

- ♥ There has been a decline in partnering rates.
- ♥ College-educated (University-educated) men and women continue to marry at high rates,
  - ➤ But marriage among the less educated with fewer assets has declined significantly.
- ♥ A growing marriage gap has opened up in western nations
  - ➤ The well educated tend to marry each other.
  - ➤ The less educated and poorer tend to marry less, but often have children.
- ♥ These trends extend to divorce.
- ♥ There is also a racial divide in the USA.
- ♥ The trends have adverse consequences for many children who are raised in poorer, single-parent households.

PART FOUR

REBUILDING THE CULTURE OF MARRIAGE

The central conservative truth is that it is culture, not politics, that determines the success of a society. The central liberal truth is that politics can change a culture and save it from itself. (Daniel Patrick Moynihan)

He has an affectionate heart. He must love somebody.
(Jane Austen)

We hold these truths to be self evident: that all men are created equal; that they are endowed by their Creator with certain unalienable rights; that among these are life, liberty, and the pursuit of happiness. (Thomas Jefferson)

The most important career decision you're going to make is whether or not you have a life partner and who that partner is. (Sheryl Sandberg)

Marriage is not meant to make you happy; it is meant to make you married. (Frank Pitman)

10

POLICY RESPONSES

F̲ew people in western nations would dispute that life is more uncertain for our children then a generation ago. The renowned scholar of family studies, Professor Urie Bronfenbrenner commented: "There has been a progressive disarray at an accelerating rate since World War 11 of the disorganisation of the family in the western world."[1048] His remarks reflected the conclusion of the sociologist, David Popenoe, that there has been a significant decline in 'familism' by which he means the family is becoming weaker as an institution.[1049] For Professor Popenoe and others[1050] an interesting question is why some family scholars "think of family decline as a myth and seek to dismiss the idea with such vigour and seeming certainty."[1051] Part of the reason lies with the cultural ideals of individualism, sexual freedom, and social tolerance, as well as the obvious gains in health and wealth for many people. It also lies with two manifestations of modern discussion. One is the concept of "wishful thinking" and the other a tendency for the anecdotal to trump the empirical. These themes are explored further in the next chapter.

The data reveals trends negatively affecting families. What is required is an effective social response to avoid the further fragmentation of families and communities, and the alienation of individuals. Despite the global expansion that lifted millions of people from poverty, many remain trapped in poor circumstances. There is also the chaos created when day to day stability and predictability are lost in family life, particularly for children. The latter trend affects rich and poor alike.

The responses to date fall into four broad categories.[1052]

COUNTERING AGEING

The most significant trend affecting families is the dramatic decline in the birthrates in most of the world, resulting in below-replacement fertility levels and the ageing of the population. Family policies, in the absence of families, is a contradiction. But the changes facing many nations will have a significant impact on families and individuals.

Ageing populations have a serious impact on nations. By the year 2020, many nations will face a major challenge in providing for an aged population. According to the Organisation for Economic Cooperation and Development [OECD], the ratio of older people to those in the workforce in 1990 was 19 per cent. By the year 2030, this dependency ratio will double to 38 per cent across the OECD countries. In Germany, it is expected to soar to 49.2 per cent, in Italy 48.3 per cent, France 39.1 per cent, Austria 44 per cent, Belgium 41.1 per cent, USA 36.8 per cent, and Australia 33 per cent.[1053]

In countries like Australia and the United States, there has been a continuing shift over the past three decades of government resources from couples with children to older people.[1054] This shift in the allocation of resources continues apace. It has been estimated that by 2050, people aged 60 and over are expected to outnumber those under 15 for the first time in known history.[1055] On current trends for both nations, some 40 per cent of the population will require long-term care at some stage of their lives. In Germany, for example, the proportion of the population in the working-age group of 26-59 is only 36.5 per cent, while the proportion aged 60 and over is 35.8 per cent. Demographers predict that the aged would increase to 43.9 per cent of the population by 2010, and 67.2 per cent by 2050. Every one of the two billion people who will be over 60 in 2050 has been born.[1056]

This ageing of the population will have a considerable impact on our nations. Not only will health care costs soar, the need for retirement income and other benefits will fall upon a shrinking proportion of the population. The economic, social and strategic implications of such a massive demographic change will be enormous.

For the past three decades a number of exponents of apocalyptic outcomes have suggested that the world faces a population explosion. Their thesis has been that the human race is breeding itself to a point of unsustainability. But, as the demographer Nicholas Eberstadt has observed:

> The modern population explosion was sparked not because people suddenly started breeding like rabbits, but rather because they finally stopped dying like flies ... it wasn't that fertility rates soared; rather, mortality rates plummeted. Since the start of our century, the average life expectancy at birth for a human being has probably doubled, it may have more than doubled.[1057]

The Western world is facing a population implosion. The *Economist* magazine summarised the trends already observable in 1999:

> In 50 or 100 years' time, however, most countries are more likely to worry about the lack of babies than the excess. For there is now a serious possibility ... that world population growth will stabilise by around 2040 at about 7.5 billion – and then start to decline. . . Repeatedly, the UN's demographers have revised down their population projections ... the number of babies born into the world will fall below the number needed for replacement ... with fertility rates in rapid decline, the debate about the global birth rate is now over when, not whether, it will fall below replacement level.[1058]

Urbanisation, improvements in education, and changing work patterns all contribute to the trends. The UN Population Division has estimated that half of the world's people live in nations where the fertility rate has already fallen below the replacement rate. For the population to remain stable, women must have an average of 2.1 babies each. In 61 countries, there are insufficient births to replace the population. To take just a few examples: In the US, women are having less than two children; in the UK, less than 2; in Japan, 1.4; in Italy, 1.2; in Spain, just 1.15. While the global fertility rate is above replacement levels, and the overall world population will continue to grow over the medium term, the variation between nations is significant.[1059]

In a study of global fertility rates, the Australian demographer Peter McDonald concluded that if the current levels of fertility were maintained in many western nations, they are so low that they would threaten the future existence of the nations concerned:

> In an era in which we have come to understand the momentum of population increase, it is remarkable that we are yet to appreciate that the same momentum applies to population decrease.[1060]

The concentration in media headlines[1061] and other writings[1062] on the total size of the global population continues to mask the depopulation momentum in many nations. "Perhaps people used to living for the here and now may have difficulty appreciating the long-term consequences beyond their immediate horizon," noted the Australian demographers, John Caldwell and Thomas Schindlmayr, in their study of 28 countries where the fertility rate has fallen to less than 1.4.[1063] One of the most rapidly ageing societies in the world, Japan, provides a glimpse of the demographic decline underway. While the Japanese are living longer, the number of young people never marrying has also increased significantly.[1064] The National Institute of Population and Social Security Research forecasts that the population will decline from 127.7 million to 86.7 million by 2060, and fall again to 42.9 million by 2110 "if conditions remain unchanged."[1065]

Professor Eberstadt projects the scenario facing the emerging generation of Japanese:

> Consider, for example, a woman born in 1990, now 22 years old. Given current trends, the Institute estimates her life expectancy

to be around 90, even higher. But children – and family, at least in the current understanding of the term – may very well not be part of her life experience. The projections give her slightly less than even odds of getting married, and staying married to age 50. Her chances of never marrying at all are nearly one in four. Further, these projections suggest she has a nearly two-fifths (38 per cent) chance of ending up childless. Even more astonishing: She has a better-than-even chance of completing life with no biological grandchildren.[1066]

Russia presents a snapshot of a declining population. Since 1992, the nation's population has declined every year (except 1993 and 2010) and on present trends is likely to fall from 143 million to just 107 million by 2050. Without immigration from former Soviet states, the decline would have been more significant. Even though there has been an increase in the birthrate from just 1.2 children-per-woman to 1.6, this is likely to be temporary, as it results mainly from the larger numbers of women born in the 1980s having children. With fewer women born in the 1990s, the upward trend is likely to reverse again.

Concern about population decline is growing. Taiwan's former health minister, Yaung Chih-liang, has warned about 'Taiwan's grand collapse,' caused by four nots – "not marrying, not giving birth, not raising children, and not living."[1067] China also faces a demographic challenge. As a result of the one-child policy and sex-selective abortion, the gender ratio has risen to 120 boys for every 100 girls. The normal gender ratio at birth is about 103 to 105 boys for every 100 girls. From 2000 to 2030, the percentage of men in their late 30s who have never been married is projected to increase five-fold.

Eberstadt observes that having an "army of unmarriageable young men" will have an impact on the country's economy and social cohesion. He believes demographic change will pose two problems specific to China.[1068] Its society has relied heavily on trust relationships within extended-family networks. In a country where fewer and fewer people will have uncles, those networks will rapidly atrophy. The government also relies for its legitimacy on a level of economic performance that demographic trends imperil. He observes: "simply maintaining current national birth totals would require heroic upsurges in maternity."[1069]

Even in the Muslim world, there has been dramatic falls in fertility levels for many countries and subnational populations as traditional marriage patterns and living arrangements are undergoing tremendous change. Professor Eberstadt observes that "fertility decline over the past generation has been more rapid in the Arab states than virtually anywhere else on earth," due largely to changing parental attitudes and desires about family size.[1070]

With increasing numbers of parents having only one child, many people in the future will live in families where intergenerational ties are greatly loosened. For example, if an only child marries an only child, their child will have no aunts, uncles or cousins. This is a likely scenario for many families in the new millennium. The Australian Productivity Commission has warned, "changes of this magnitude are likely to have significant social impacts."[1071]

Although the effects of declining birth rates may not have an immediate impact on our societies, marriage breakdown, an ageing population and declining fertility combine to produce an environment inherently more unstable and antithetical to healthy family life. A study of Chinese High School students demonstrates some of the consequences of low birth rates. Children without siblings "showed significant negative mental health tendencies", including "significantly lower love awareness from family, higher neurotic and social depression, trait anxiety, perceived stressors and interpersonal dependency."[1072]

The economic impact will be significant. Using data from two countries that have experienced population contraction – Russia and North Korea – economist Sanghan Yea states that population decline will have a more damaging impact than we expect presently: "Depopulation not only stops economic growth completely, but also reverses it."[1073] Not only is there less demand for goods and services, the reduction in new entrants to the labor force may decrease flexibility and productivity. The world's working age population grew by 1.3 billion, or 40 per cent, between 1990 and 2010,[1074] but is expected to increase by only about 900 million between 2010 and 2030.[1075]

Full employment may return to nations suffering high levels of unemployment, but many people who live longer will do so in circumstances of isolation and loneliness. Extended families will virtually disappear. A larger, older population, suffering from an increase in chronic disease[1076] will require more care and resources. Most nations are unprepared for the challenges they face.[1077]

Demographic patterns are not easily reversed. Even if nations introduced policies today to address these trends, it would likely take two generations for an impact to be observed. It is also easy for nations in the early stages of fertility decline to be seduced by the phenomenon known as the "demographic dividend."[1078] This occurs when birth rates first fall, allowing more people, especially women, to enter the paid workforce. Individuals are able to spend and invest more, including in the education of fewer children. The phenomena occurred in Japan and other Asian countries from the 1960s, and are occurring in China currently. But the dividend must be repaid. As the population ages, there are fewer workers and the numbers of dependent aged grows, there is a drain on resources. Japan is already experiencing the impact, and China will in the coming two decades, as it enters long-term depopulation.

Moreover, popular ideas and current lifestyle choices mitigate against the acceptance of appropriate policy responses. Having experienced their parents' divorces, the movement of governmental support from families with children to the elderly, high levels of unemployment, the need to have two incomes to achieve what their parent's regarded as a reasonable standard of living, and facing what they perceive as an uncertain future, many young people are postponing or avoiding marriage and delaying children.

The outcome of these changes will be far-reaching and unpredictable. A deceleration of the global workforce; the costs of an ageing population; the existence of youth bulges in many developing and underdeveloped countries; the threat of ethnic and religious conflict; the pressures on immigration, both lawful and unlawful; and the prospect of the rise of totalitarianism as a consequence, will have sweeping impacts on families, communities and nations.[1079] Add to this the pressure of financial instability, and we can begin to recognise the significance of the challenge.

Policy makers have generally adopted three approaches to the ageing of their populations, namely increasing immigration, pronatalist inducements, and family-friendly measures.

Immigration

Faced with the cultural trends of later and fewer marriages and smaller and more unstable families, governments have resorted to immigration to ameliorate the impact of ageing populations. During the past two decades, significant population movements have occurred, generally from less developed and less prosperous nations to richer ones. Driven by labour force shortages, governments first sought to attract increasing numbers of younger, skilled immigrants while maintaining or decreasing the proportion of older family members seeking to reunite with their emigrant children.

Skilled workers, and in particular the human capital they possess, are in high demand in many OECD countries. The competition is immense, with countries such as the UK, US and Canada all operating skilled and economic migration programs. The UK has adopted a points-based system for skilled migrants. It is based on the Australian points based system, which focuses on more effectively targeting foreign workers who have skills that are genuinely in demand. In Canada, a ratio of 60/40 economic and humanitarian migration has been maintained since the early 1990's, with a points based system also applying to skilled migration, and a particular premium placed on tertiary education. And in the United States, which has historically had an abundance of low and unskilled workers coming across the border from Mexico, the Senate in 2005 voted to increase the cap on skilled visas.[1080] As labour shortages grew, many countries extended their programs to the unskilled as well. Some also turned a blind eye to unlawful immigration, as potential immigrants surveyed the economic benefits readily attainable in more prosperous nations.

The Australian Treasury argued that the ageing of the population and higher fertility over the next 35 years would bring down per-capita gross domestic product by more than two per cent. But this would be partly offset by a 0.75 per cent through migrant intake alone, and by a further 0.5 per cent through the age composition of the migrants.[1081] However this claim requires more investigation. A House of Lords Committee[1082] asserted in 2008 that "overall Gross Domestic Product is an irrelevant and misleading criterion for assessing the economic impacts of immigration." The Committee argued that the focus of analysis should rather be on the effects of immigration on income per head of the resident population. By this measure, immigration to Australia, for example, has a very modest impact on living standards according to an Econtech report.[1083]

An Australian longitudinal survey of migrants showed very strong employment outcomes for skilled migrants with an employment rate of over 97 per cent and a participation rate of 94 per cent just 18 months after arrival. Migrants on a spouse visa also had very good outcomes, with unemployment of just five per cent, and participation at 72 per cent. However, there are significant variations. Non-English speaking, unskilled and older migrants have much lower levels of employment and many rely on welfare payments. This is exacerbated by any economic downturn.

There are other limitations on immigration. Settlement issues, especially in larger cities, effectively limit the number of immigrants that a place can house and settle. A worldwide demand for skilled immigrants also restricts the numbers. Moreover, immigration does little to influence the age structure of the population, as immigrants also grow older.

Thirdly, the assumptions about population increase over the next 50 years take little account of any possible reversals of life expectancy. Professor Eberstadt observed:

> Long-term stagnation or even decline in life expectancy is now a real possibility for urbanised, educated countries not at war. Severe and prolonged collapses of local health conditions during peacetime, furthermore, is no longer a purely theoretical eventuality. As we look towards 2025, we must consider the unpleasant likelihood that a large and growing fraction of humanity may be separated from the planetary march toward better health and subjected instead to brutal mortality crises of indeterminate duration.[1084]

In the west, cancer, diabetes, alcoholism and other diseases related to affluent but unhealthy lifestyles continue to strike the population. Obesity amongst children is at record levels. In the world's most populous nations, India and China, family sizes are expected to continue to fall.[1085]

Finally, population issues cannot be isolated from other national trends, including lower levels of marriage, the higher incidence of separation and divorce, and the consequences for children.

Immigration is a lazy, and, ultimately limited, response to the ageing of the population. Changing economic circumstances can result in migration reversals. The exodus of recent migrants from eastern Europe in one example. Elsewhere, guest workers have been sent back to their home countries as economic conditions fluctuate.[1086]

Secondly, although generally younger, the new arrivals also age along with the rest of the population. Only a commitment to a continually larger immigration program can counter this fact. A record annual number of immigrants would be necessary, for example, if Europe was to counter the impact of ageing.[1087] This would result in greater congestion and more dense settlement, neither of which would be popular. According to UN estimates, the magnitude of immigration required to prevent population ageing in Europe would result in a migrant population constituting between 59 and 99 per cent of the population.[1088] Even if theoretically feasible, where would these immigrants come from, and what would be the impact on the existing resident population? We have already witnessed tensions in a number of countries between existing populations and more recent arrivals from other parts of the world. Little wonder that a recent survey of fertility and population ageing in Europe concluded that "the sheer numbers of immigrants that are needed to prevent population ageing in the EU and its Member States are not acceptable in the current socio-political climate prevailing in Europe."[1089] Debates over identity are likely to increase, not decrease, in this century.[1090]

Pronatalist inducements

A number of countries have offered direct incentives to couples who have children and disincentives to those who choose not to have them. These approaches include cash payments for each child, privileged access to state housing, medical or education services, and taxation incentives or disincentives related to children.[1091]

During the past century, a range of direct pronatalist policies were implemented in various countries, ranging from restrictions on family planning and abortion in Romania and Hungary to financial incentives to have more children elsewhere.[1092] While the availability of contraception is widely recognised as one of the causes of the decline in fertility across the EU,[1093] the impact of legislation restricting contraception would appear to have only a temporary impact on birthrates.[1094] A survey of global policies suggests that while it is relatively easy to reduce national birthrates, it is very difficult to reverse a decline. Singapore provides a good case study.

Case Study: Singapore

From the late 1950s, the island state adopted a strong antinatalist program of legalised abortion, voluntary sterilisation and disincentives to have more than two children. The total fertility rate fell from 6.56 in 1957 to just 1.42 in 1986.[1095] By the early eighties, the national government became alarmed about the trend. With falling fertility, especially among better educated women, the government expressed concern about the "quality" of the population.[1096] It subsequently introduced measures to encourage more births, including privileged access to high-quality education, income tax relief, childcare leave and subsidies, part-time work rights in the public service, and housing entitlements.[1097] While the total fertility rate had increased to 1.6 by 1997, it remained below replacements levels. A subsequent decline was a concern to the government.

In 2001, the *New York Times* featured the headline: "Singapore, Hoping for a Baby boom, Makes Sex a Civic Duty." The report continued:

> Here in straight-laced Singapore, it's the new patriotism: have sex. Alarmed by its declining birthrate, this tiny city-state of just four million people is urging its citizens to multiply as fast as they can. "We need more babies!" proclaimed Prime Minister Goh Chok Tong last fall. The world, he said, is in danger of running short of Singaporeans.[1098]

A government office, the Working Committee on Marriage and Procreation, has developed monetary and workplace incentives. The idea is to persuade Singaporeans that having children is a better deal than going without. In what it calls the Baby Bonus Scheme, the government is offering cash to couples who have second and third children. It is extending maternity leave and adding a brief paternity leave for government workers. It is experimenting with flexible working hours to make child rearing easier. It is offering special deals on apartment rentals for young couples.

"Let's get on the love wagon" urged a headline in the *Straits Times*. For a nation where dropping litter or spitting on the footpath is regarded as highly disorderly, it comes as a surprise to read in the same article tips for having sex in the back seat of a car with directions to "some of the darkest, most secluded and most romantic spots for Romeos and Juliets." Subsequently, Singapore's Deputy Prime Minister, Dr Tony Tan, announced that the Government would fund $50 million over five years to educate the public on family life. This includes marriage education and parenting classes. The government also established a service, 'Marriage Central', to dispense advice on married life.[1099] More recently, the government set up an online dating service to boost marriage rates among graduates.[1100] Despite these endeavours, Singapore's fertility rate has fallen to 1.28 according the latest data.[1101] The Singapore study illustrates the point that whereas the birthrate can be reduced significantly within the space of a generation, it is much more difficult to increase it again. Direct pronatalist measures alone seem insufficient to reverse declining birthrates. For this reason, policy makers also have turned to family friendly and economic policies.

ECONOMIC SUPPORT FOR FAMILIES

Most governments have sought to provide economic support for families. Using the rhetoric of 'family friendly policies', measures range from direct taxation and social security benefits, to parental leave, and flexible working hours. These policies often serve the twin objectives of encouraging fertility and supporting families to raise children.

A central motivation is the economic, which involves a recognition of the desirability of higher fertility rates in the western world; the additional costs of raising children; and the advantages to individuals and society of life-long marriages. It is also an important recognition that two economies exist within nations: the market economy, where exchanges take place through money and where competition and efficiency drive decisions; and the home economy, where exchanges take place through the altruistic sharing of goods and services among family members.

Direct economic support for families

Case Study: Australia

In the past two decades Australian governments have taken two approaches to supporting families in the tax system. First, the national government raised the tax free threshold – that is, the level of income before tax is paid – for families with children, especially for families with one parent at home.

The Government's 1996 Family Tax Initiative increased the tax-free threshold by $1000 for each dependent child up to the age of 16 and each dependent secondary student up to 18 years. In addition, single income families including sole parents received a further $2,500 increase in their tax-free threshold if they had a child under five. For a single income family of three children, one of whom is under five years, the tax-free threshold almost doubled.

A taxation reform package passed by the Parliament in 1999 built on these initiatives. Apart from reductions in personal income taxes, and the increase and simplification of family benefits, the tax-free threshold increases under the Family Tax Initiative were doubled. From July 1, 2000, all single income families, including sole parents, with one child under five years had an effective tax free threshold of $13,000, more than double the general threshold of $6,000. The government subsequently introduced significant family tax benefits. The effect of these payments was that for a family earning less than about $42,000 per year, there was a net contribution by the government to them, after taking into account taxes and benefits. In addition, the previous government introduced a baby bonus, which is a payment of $5,000 on the birth of a child. Parents also receive childcare subsidies, depending upon their level of income.

More recently, the Australian government has introduced a paid parental leave scheme which enables mothers (and fathers) to take up to 18 weeks leave from their paid employment at minimum wages following the birth of a child,[1102] and increased the tax-free threshold as part of other changes to the taxation system. The tax provisions are in addition to other support for families, including education, health, childcare and other benefits.

While it is too early to claim conclusively that there is a causal connection between these measures and the stability of families in Australia, recent data is encouraging. The long-term decline in the birth rate appears to have been arrested and rose from 1.72 in 2001 to 1.95 in 2008, before falling to 1.89 in 2010.[1103] The Productivity Commission concluded in 2008 that despite the negative impact on birth rates of rising house prices and the high levels of female participation in higher education and the paid workforce, a combination of a prosperous economy and specific policies contributed to the upturn in fertility in recent years.[1104] This is consistent with studies which indicate that higher taxes increase the marginal cost of children relative to consumption, resulting in declining fertility.[1105]

The marriage rate has risen marginally in the past five years, and the divorce rate has fallen, again reversing long-term trends. However, the marriage rate remains significantly lower – and the divorce rate significantly higher – than it was two decades ago.

Case Study: France

Faced with fertility decline a century before the rest of the West,[1106] France has had a long history of support for families. During the past 30 years, the nation has introduced a series of measures, including unpaid leave (1977), special assistance for low and single-income families (1979-80), housing privileges for larger families (1980), benefits for women with three or more children (1985), and extended parental leave (1987 and 1994).[1107] Although some measures have since been varied – for example extending social legislation to unmarried couples (1998) or limited – and some, such as the 35 hour week and employment protection arguably restrict employment growth, France has generous family provisions.

In particular, France has a deliberate third child policy. Whereas Australia, for example, pays a bonus on the birth of each child, France pays a greater amount for third and subsequent children. This is in addition to parental and maternity leave and childcare and family allowances.

The combination of these policies would appear to have had a mixed impact. The birth rate has stabilised at around 1.9, the second highest in Europe (after Ireland). However, other indicators of marital and family health have declined. The marriage rate has fallen from 7.8 in 1970 to 4.4 in 2006; the divorce rate has risen from 2.05 in 1995 to 2.3 in 2006; out-of-wedlock births have jumped from 11.4 per cent in 1980 to over 50 per cent by 2006; and the proportion of single-parent families has almost doubled to 19.8 per cent since 1980.

Work and family measures

It is often claimed that generous provisions that enable women to enter and remain in the paid workforce contribute to higher fertility levels. Hence Hugo argues that "the international ranking of countries according to their fertility levels matches their ranking on the extent to which they facilitate the employment of mothers in the paid workforce and the extent to which a degree of gender equity applies within the family itself."[1108] Other researchers have reached similar conclusions.[1109] The Scandinavian countries are often cited in this respect. However the approaches have differed amongst the northern European nations.

Case Study: Sweden

Beginning in the 1930s, Sweden introduced policies that enabled women to maintain their position in the paid workforce whilst having children.[1110] In the 1980s, the fertility rate climbed to 2.02, leading some commentators to conclude that the reversal was due to the cumulative impact of public daycare, child benefits, parental leave, parent's rights to part time work and other measures.[1111] These views were reinforced as female labour force participation soared to 81 per cent[1112] and the birth rate rose above replacement levels. The growth was temporary, falling to the lowest rate ever for the country of 1.52 by the end of the century.[1113] It would appear that the birth rate related to the economic cycle, and the impact of the so-called "speed premium" whereby parents were entitled to the same income replacement for a second child born within 30 months of their first, irrespective of the level of income between the two births.[1114] The policy would appear to have resulted in births being brought forward, rather than a permanent increase in the number.

Other indicators of family stability in Sweden reveal trends found elsewhere. Cohabitation before marriage is commonplace. More than half of children are born out-of-wedlock, but the rate born to unmarried women is relatively low. The divorce rate has fallen slightly in recent years.

Case Study: Norway

Another policy approach is that of of the Norwegian Government to pay parents the same amount that childcare centres or kindergartens receive in state subsidies – approximately $US 6,000 per year per child – which enables parents a choice about staying at home with children up to the age of three years.

Further initiatives are necessary to address the competing pressures between family and work in our modern societies. As Janne Haaland Matlary, the former Norwegian Secretary of State, has written:

> In order to strengthen families and have a sustainable population, there is a need for policies that give parents flexibility, time, and an ability to combine child-rearing and careers. At a time when women are as well, or better, educated than men, it is completely unrealistic to expect them to stay at home in longer periods of their lives.[1115]

If the work of Hakim and Strachan, cited earlier is correct, then Norway's approach better reflects the choice that parent's desire. In Australia, for example, most child care is provided informally, by other family members and friends, but this is not subsidised by the state.

If this analysis of family – work choices is correct, policies that impact upon the 60 per cent or more of women who are adaptive in their family – work lifestyles are the most likely to provide the choice that families desire. Hakim argues that the role of government is not to favour any of these families. The goal is government neutrality towards all families.

Policy approaches

These observations suggest a number of policy principles. First, parents should have flexibility and choice in their family and work arrangements. Such choice is not just about the hours worked at any one time, but about the arrangements they make over the course of their lives. While a library of books have been written about the so-called *Time Bind*, to adopt Arlie Russell Hochschild's well-known title, little has been written about the work-family balance over the life course.

The *Early Years* report to the Ontario Government concluded, parenting is a key factor in early child development for families at all socioeconomic levels: "Supportive initiatives for parents should begin as early as possible – from the time of conception – with programs of parent support and education."[1116]

These findings reinforce the need for policies that encourage a better balance between work and parenting, particularly when children are in the early years of life. As to how this goal is best achieved while balancing the needs of children and maintaining the stability of the family remains elusive. Given the continuing high levels of marital dissolution and divorce, policy makers have also turned their attention to family law and marriage support.

DISCOURAGING DIVORCE

From time to time, policy makers have suggested changes to the no-fault divorce laws that exist in many nations today. Professor William Galston, President Clinton's Domestic Policy Advisor, suggested that there should be a modified version of no-fault divorce where children were involved. The UK Centre for Social Justice has proposed a "cooling-off" period at the commencement of divorce proceedings.[1117] "What is a matter of private concern when it is on a small scale becomes a matter of public concern when it reaches epidemic proportions," said a senior Family Division judge, Justice Paul Coleridge, in the UK recently.[1118] "I am not saying every broken family produces dysfunctional children but I am saying that almost every dysfunctional child is the product of a broken family," he said a year earlier.[1119] Others share the concern. "Society is dissatisfied with the way things are now," said Ira Lurvey, past-president of the American Bar Association Family Law Section.[1120]

Apart from the personal trauma, a number of studies have reported the significant costs resulting from separation and divorce. In 1998, an Australian Parliamentary inquiry reported that the direct cost to the nation was more than $3 billion a year, and as much and $6 billion when indirect costs were included.[1121] The Canadian Institute for Marriage and Family found the cost in that country to be around $7 billion a year.[1122] The British Relationships Foundation put the cost of family breakdown at 37 billion pounds annually,[1123] while the Centre for Social Justice estimated that it was 20 billion pounds per year.[1124]

Case Study: USA

In the US, at least 20 states have introduced bills to change divorce laws, by extending waiting periods, repealing no-fault divorce, mandating counselling, and/or encouraging pre-marriage education. In Louisiana, the first state to pass such a law, couples can choose between the existing marriage regime based on no-fault divorce, and a new form of covenant marriage. The covenant marriage requires couples to swear that they will live together forever as husband and wife. The partners must disclose to each other "everything which could adversely affect" their decision to marry. Both must sign a notarised affidavit, swearing they have talked about the nature, purposes and responsibilities of marriage during their premarital counselling. They are legally required to seek marital counselling if problems arise in their marriage.[1125] Two other states, Arkansas and Arizona, have enacted similar laws.

The primary argument for covenant marriage is that it may lower the divorce rate, resulting in stronger, happier marriages and more stable conditions for children. It would appear however, that few couples are attracted to the alternative marriage model. In the first three years of its operation in Arkansas, only 800 of the 112,000 couples who married in the state opted for a covenant marriage.[1126] A decade after its introduction in Louisiana, fewer than five per cent of marriages were entered under them covenant model.[1127] Overall the uptake of covenant marriage is less than two per cent across the three states.[1128]

It has been suggested that covenant marriage's lack of mainstream popularity has to do with couples associating constraints with it instead of attractions.[1129] Professor Steven Nock concludes:

> At the moment, covenant marriage appeals to a small, distinct group who differ in important ways from the average person approaching marriage. Based on evidence we have at the moment, there is little to suggest that covenant marriage will soon appeal to a larger, more diverse population.[1130]

These results suggest that the objective of strengthening marriage and family by lowering the divorce rate is unlikely to be achieved, at least in the foreseeable future, by the widespread introduction of covenant marriage.

Case Study: Australia

Encouraging couples to identify and resolve their disputes in a non-adversarial manner has been an aspiration of family policy makers for decades. It was the motivation behind the *Family Law Act* and the Child Support legislation. A significant step forward was the establishment of 65 Family Relationship Centres across the nation by the Australian Government in 2004. As the researchers, Lawrie Maloney and Bruce Smyth, wrote, "Spread widely across the country, the Centres would be capable of responding to local needs and at the same time, guide families towards conflict resolution processes that are child focused, dignified and relatively inexpensive." They concluded:

> Despite our imperfect knowledge of how to best manage post-separation disputes, we have learned enough to know that timely, competent and respectful *processes* minimise the chances of disputes solidifying and becoming entrenched. Relationship Centres have the potential to offer this. In addition, the services 'maze' could all but disappear if separating families knew that Relationship Centres were the recommended first port of call and were strongly encouraged to use them.[1131]

The Australian government introduced the Centres following a report into child support, custody and access to children.[1132] Designed to offer early, practical intervention for couples before conflict became entrenched,[1133] the Centres theoretically embrace education as well as counselling and mediation services.[1134] A recent evaluation found that about half of the parents in non-separated families who had serious relationship problems used services to assist in resolving these problems. There was less use of services to support relationships by couples who had not faced serious problems (about 10 per cent). About two-thirds of parents who separated after the 2006 changes had contacted or used family relationship services during or after separation. Separated parents who used services were more likely than separated parents who had not used services to have issues that impacted negatively on their relationships – especially family violence, mental health problems or drug and alcohol misuse issues. Family dispute resolution services frequently deal with high-conflict complex cases.

The researchers concluded that "overall, relationship services clients provided favourable assessments of the services they attended. The considerable increase in the use of relationship-oriented services, both pre- and post-separation, suggests a cultural shift in the way in which problems that affects family relationships are being dealt with." However it appears that the Centres have not served any significant purpose beyond the conciliation of marital separation.

SUPPORTING MARRIAGE

Rising divorce rates and family instability have led churches, community organisations and governments to introduce programs of marriage preparation in many places.

Case Study: Australia

During the 1950s, Christian churches in Australian conducted "Pre-Cana" conferences for engaged couples. These programs tended to be of one day's duration at which a priest or minister, and married couples spoke to the engaged. Recognition of the need for marriage preparation and the provision of it had been pioneered largely by the churches. In 1920, for example, the Lambeth Conference of Bishops of the Anglican Communion recommended that the clergy should regard it as part of their pastoral responsibility, and by 1969 the practice became a canonical duty.[1135]

In the 1940s and 50s, marriage guidance agencies, modelled on the pattern developing in the UK, were established in Australia.[1136] The Marriage Guidance Council had been established in the UK in 1937, the Catholic Marriage Advisory Council in 1946, and the Family Discussion Bureau in 1948.[1137]

The work of marriage guidance (as it was then known) had been scrutinised at the end of the Second World War by the Denning Committee, which had been established to examine "whether any (and if so, what) machinery should be made available for the purpose of attempting a reconciliation between the parties, either before or after proceedings had been commenced."[1138] In their Final Report, the Committee stated:

> We have throughout our inquiry had in mind the principle that the marriage tie is of the highest importance in the interests of society. The unity of the family is so important that, when parties are estranged, reconciliation should be attempted in every case where there is a prospect of success.

The importance of couples adjusting to differences and understanding family backgrounds was recognised when the Australian Parliament first enacted legislation for matrimonial causes in 1959.[1139] In his Second Reading Speech on the *Matrimonial Causes Act* 1959, the Attorney-General, Sir Garfield Barwick said:

> I am conscious that in the early days of married life, particularly amongst younger people, the two personalities which had theretofore no need to consider any one's interest or comfort but

their own, must make many adjustments in accommodation each to the other in married life.[1140]

Provision was made in the *Marriage Act* for grants to marriage counselling agencies for the purposes of conducting programs of marriage preparation.[1141]

The UK Committee recommended that it should "be recognised as a function of the States to give every encouragement and, where appropriate, financial assistance to marriage guidance as a form of Social Service." A subsequent Home Office Committee concluded that:

> ... this work which we believe is better left as far as possible to the initiative of voluntary organisations and which cannot like other forms of social work be undertaken – at any rate at the present time and without further knowledge and experience – by official bodies.[1142]

This approach was adopted in Australia. Since 1960, the Australian Government has provided grants to both church and secular marriage counselling and education organisations.[1143] Sir Garfield Barwick told Parliament:

> I do not hold the view that this work can be done satisfactorily by people who make it no more than a means of livelihood. The work will best be done by those who, as well as being trained, have a sense of vocation and who, to a large extent, volunteer their good offices in this very skilful and sympathetic task.[1144]

The number and quality of services gradually increased over the years along with modest increments of government support. The work of two national umbrella bodies and a number of committed individuals resulted in a network of programs throughout the nation, funded in part by participating couples and in part by the Australian government.[1145] A Parliamentary Committee reviewing divorce laws urged more funding for marriage education in 1992.[1146] Funding was increased again following the publication of the *To have and to hold report*.[1147] That report found that 30 per cent of couples marrying for the first time in Australia undertook some form of marriage education, usually an information awareness and skills training program or a pre-marital inventory lasting in duration between a number of hours and a number of days.[1148] The outcome of these interventions is discussed below.

Challenges

Despite the spread and apparent success of programs of marital education, a number of challenges remain. Critically, in a nation where the majority of weddings are now conducted by civil marriage celebrants,[1149] most couples participating in education programs are referred by a religious marriage celebrant.[1150]

Secondly, far fewer couples marrying for a second or subsequent time utilise the education services. This mirrors the experience in the US, where couples marrying for the first time are almost twice as likely to participate in marital education (52.2 per cent compared to 29.7 per cent) although the risk of divorce is higher for subsequent marriages.[1151]

How to increase participation remains a challenge. Following the *To have and to hold report,* a pilot scheme of education vouchers was introduced, and although successful, was never implemented universally.[1152] Finally there remain concerns about the ability of the marriage education providers to attract sufficient personnel. While the providers charge a fee-for-service in addition to government subsidies, most educators work on a part-time, sessional or voluntary basis.

Case Study: USA

Measures to support marriage and family have been promoted in the United States over the past two decades. During the 1980s and 90s, governments concentrated on welfare reform in an effort to overcome the pernicious effect of long term dependency. Led by family scholars from the beginning of the 1990s, the nation's attention, including that of key policy makers, increasingly turned to the critical role of marital and family stability for the prospects of both children and adults. Building on a series of governmental[1153] and non-governmental[1154] publications over the previous two decades, national and state policy focussed on initiatives to promote and support marriage.

The US government under the Bush–Clinton–Bush Adminis-trations gradually focussed more attention on the growing concerns about family instability, especially the impact on children. Wade Horn, a president of the Fatherhood Foundation, served as US Commissioner for Children in the Bush senior administration. Hilary Clinton wrote about the issue in *It takes a village*[1155] and Bill Clinton's Domestic Policy Advisor, Professor William Galston, suggested a tightening of divorce legislation when children were involved.[1156]

Concerned about the connection between family breakdown, sole parenthood and poverty, US legislators endorsed a preamble to the 1996 welfare laws that stated that "marriage is the essential foundation of a successful society."[1157] More significant was the development of the Healthy Marriage Initiative in 2002 by the Bush Administration.[1158] Regarded by many as the work of Wade Horn, then Assistant Secretary for Children and Families, the Initiative had parallels with the Australian model. Grants to various organisations, including State government agencies and civil sector organisations, were a feature of the Initiative.[1159] Funding to the program has continued under the Obama administration, and in 2010 Congress voted to provide an additional $75 million for marriage education funding in addition to the $100 million annual funding approved in 2005.

Marriage Movement

A significant factor in the renewed focus on marriage and family is the network of individuals,[1160] scholars,[1161] researchers,[1162] think tanks,[1163] and authors[1164] that has been loosely described as "the marriage movement". A series of books, reports, seminars and conferences together with articles in the media have popularised discussions about marriage and family. It is doubtful that the policy programs that have been implemented would have occurred without this significant leadership and contribution from civil society. It is an example of how the groups that stand between the state and the individual can have a major impact on pubic discussion and government action. Significantly, these groups have not waited for government to act. Recognising the limitations of the state, and the realm of activity that exists outside the state, they have driven the national agenda by persuasion and activity. An important part of that activity involves direct community action.

Community Marriage Policies

Like other countries, community organisations of both a religious and secular constitution have offered programs of marital education for many years in the United States. A common connection between the UK, the US and Australia was the work of David and Vera Mace who were closely involved in the establishment of marriage counselling in all three nations.[1165] Their practical work,[1166] and that of other like-minded individuals, has spread throughout the nation.

While many organisations now promote and support marriage,[1167] one of the most significant features has been the success of Community Marriage Policies. Although many churches had implemented policies about preparing couples for marriage,[1168] the idea of a community adopting a uniform policy had not been tried until 1985. That year, Mike McManus, a syndicated columnist for US newspapers, urged a gathering of pastors at Modesto, California, to adopt a common marriage policy for their community.[1169] The following year 96 pastors, priests and a rabbi signed the first Community Marriage Policy. The idea subsequently spread throughout California and then nationally.

By 1999, 226 communities[1170] had adopted the policies which have five key components: Marriage preparation of at least four months, including a premarital inventory and skills training; an annual enrichment retreat for married couples; mentoring for couples with troubled marriages; reconciliation for the separated; and support for stepfamilies and parents in a remarriage.[1171]

A study of the first 114 communities to implement the policies revealed reductions in the divorce rate by more than two per cent a year, compared to the comparison counties.[1172] The authors noted that some well-implemented policies had much stronger results than was reflected in their analysis. This accords with Marriage Savers own data, which shows that divorce rates fell nearly twice as much for cities with the Policies.[1173] The data also revealed that cohabitation rates fell in cities which implemented Community Marriage Policies.[1174] These outcomes commend further study and widespread implementation of Community Marriage Policies.[1175] They also reinforce the benefits of premarital education.

Professor Norval Glenn observed "that four of the frequently chosen reasons for divorce – 'too much arguing,' 'unrealistic expectations,' 'married too young,' and 'inadequate preparation' for marriage – can be addressed quite directly by the kind of premarital education that is being incorporated into healthy marriage initiatives across the country."[1176] Further policy directions are proposed in the next chapter.

SUMMARY

- ♥ There have been four broad policy responses to the trends of family disorganisation.
- ♥ Many nations have implemented measures to counter the ageing of their populations, including:
  - ➢ Increasing immigration, and
  - ➢ Introducing pronatal inducements for couples to have more children.
- ♥ Economic support for families has been provided in most countries, including:
  - ➢ Direct economic support for families, and
  - ➢ Work and family measures.
- ♥ A number of jurisdictions have introduced measures to discourage divorce.
- ♥ Governments, religious bodies and community organisations have sponsored programs of marriage education and support.

11

FROM CULTURE WARS
TO COMMON GROUND[1177]

CULTURE WARS

Discussions about the meaning and future of marriage and family have emerged over the past few decades. The debates have been particularly willing in the United States, partly because of the interplay of the judiciary and the legislatures in America, and partly because of the overt emphasis on values in the American polity. In his 1990 book, *Culture Wars,* the sociologist James Davidson Hunter classified the parties to the family debate then as orthodox or conservatives, and liberals or progressives.[1178]

A series of high profile events, including the decision by Jimmy Carter, when running for the Presidency to promise a White House conference on the family, and the subsequent controversy about a definition; and the attack by Vice-President Dan Quayle on the television sitcom, *Murphy Brown*, in which the main character, a newswoman played by actress Candice Bergen, decided to have a child out-of-wedlock, ignited sharp and often divisive debates. Similar discussions occurred in other nations, especially around the 1994 International Year of the Family.[1179]

These debates are understandable, given the profound cultural changes that have occurred in western societies in a relatively short period of time. As the demographer, Kingsley Davis, observed: "at no time in history, with the possible exception of Imperial Rome, has the institution of marriage been more problematic than it is today."[1180] Slowly however, new voices emerged, led largely by family scholars who scrutinised the consequences of the profound cultural changes in western – and increasingly other – societies.[1181]

An emerging consensus?

Beginning in the early 1990s, family scholars observed the growing incidence of negative outcomes for many adults and children as a consequence of the retreat from marriage. In 1991, the bipartisan National Commission on Children stated in its report, *Beyond Rhetoric,* that "substantial evidence suggests that the quality of life for many of America's children has declined."[1182] The Commission was clear:

> Children do best when they have the personal involvement and material support of a father and mother and when both parents fulfil their responsibility to be loving providers. . . Rising rates of divorce, out-of-wedlock childbearing and absent parents are not just manifestations of alternative lifestyles, they are patterns of adult behaviour that increase children's risk of negative consequences.

A subsequent report to President Bush Snr., *Families First,* was equally stark: "The trend of family fragmentation drives the nation's most pressing social problems: crime, educational failure, declining mental health, drug abuse and poverty. These in turn further fragment families."[1183]

The growing consensus was supported by an increasing number of family scholars, some of whom had believed previously that the societal changes were benign. One of them was Linda Waite, professor of sociology at the University of Chicago and past president of the American Population Association. Her book, *The case for marriage: Why married people are happier, healthier, and better off financially,* published in 2000, not only set out the accumulated evidence, it represented a sharp revision of views by a leading scholar.[1184] The evidence was popularised by Barbara Dafoe Whitehead in an article provocatively titled 'Dan Quayle was right' in the *Atlantic Monthly* magazine.[1185]

Another was Paul Amato. In 1987, while a fellow at the Australian Institute for Family Studies, Amato had written in *Children in Australian families: The growth of competence,* that harmful stereotypes such as 'staying together for the sake of children' prevented us from seeing families as they really are.[1186] Professor Amato's subsequent research, such as the 1997 study, *A generation at risk,* found that only one-quarter to one-third of divorces ended up being better for children than if the parents had stayed together. By contrast, about 70 per cent of divorces end low-conflict marriages which, for children, would have been better continued.[1187] He concluded that for many couples and their children, it would have been better if the spouses had not divorced.

Subsequently Barbara Dafoe Whitehead and the sociologist, David Popenoe, initiated an annual report on *The state of our unions* which summarised the trends about marriage and families in the US. Across the Atlantic, the British government responded to urgings from the Demos thinktank, the Relate relationship agency and others to strengthen family life.[1188] Similarly, Don Edgar, the then director of the Australian Institute of Family Studies, came to the conclusion that stable, intact families matter.[1189]

Many cultural and political conservatives and liberals (in the American sense) were reaching similar conclusions. Professor William Galston, President Clinton's Deputy Domestic Policy Adviser, is a keen advocate of stronger marriages and restrictions on divorce.[1190] Another liberal, David Blankenhorn, did much to promote the need for fathers and resilient marital unions.[1191] Don S Browning promoted a conversation about marriage and family amongst Christians.[1192] In associations of professional therapists and educators, the likes of Bill Doherty and Diane Sollee had a significant impact.[1193]

In communitarian circles, leading scholars such as Amitai Etzioni,[1194] Mary Ann Glendon[1195] and Jean Bethke Elshtain[1196] increasingly spoke about the importance of marriage, community and civil society. Conservative scholars, including Allan Carlson,[1197] and Patrick Fagan,[1198] and libertarians like Charles Murray[1199] also have had an impact on the continuing debate. Many think tanks and other bodies increasingly pointed to the negative fallout from family breakdown,[1200] and some religious communities adopted marriage policies.[1201]

The common ground was reflected in a 2012 article in the *Washington Post* by the senior economic fellow at the Brookings Institution, Isabel Sawhill. Writing about Dan Quayle's 'Murphy Brown' speech, the respected scholar of child poverty observed "twenty years later, Quayle's words seem less controversial than prophetic." Noting if individuals do just three things – finish high school, work full time and marry before they have children – their chances of being poor drop from 15 per cent to two per cent, Sawhill concluded:

> In the end, Dan Quayle was right. Unless the media, parents and other influential leaders celebrate marriage as the best environment for raising children, the new trend – bringing up baby alone – may be irreversible.[1202]

This intellectual thought gradually infused political discussions. In the US, President Clinton stressed the importance of strong families;[1203] and his wife, Hilary, wrote *It Takes a Village*.[1204] President George Bush Jnr appointed the former head of the Fatherhood Foundation, Wade Horn, to implement his Healthy Marriages Initiative.[1205] As a presidential candidate, Barack Obama advocated expanding access to marriage education services to help married couples stay together and encourage unmarried couples living together to form more lasting bonds.[1206]

In the UK, Prime Minister Tony Blair spoke of family life being "the foundation of a strong and stable society" and the importance of marriage.[1207] More recently, Prime Minister David Cameron and his Work and Pensions Secretary, Iain Duncan Smith, have promoted policies to strengthen marriage, including changes to the benefits system and funding for relationship support for couples.[1208] The British government also commissioned reports from two senior Labor MPs, Frank Field and Graham Allen, on addressing poverty and implementing early intervention services.[1209] The Centre for Social Justice, the think tank founded by Iain Duncan Smith, demonstrated the clear connections between family structure and poverty. In Australia, a Parliamentary Committee comprising both sides of politics issued a bipartisan report affirming measures to strengthen marriages,[1210] which the then government supported.

A number of family court judges have also questioned the prevalence of divorce. In the UK, a senior High Court judge, Sir Paul Coleridge, condemned what he called couples' "recycling" attitudes in ending family relationships when they have children to think of, describing the fact that millions of children are being fought over in family courts as a "complete scandal".[1211] Acknowledging that "genuinely intolerable relationships have to be ended with as much dignity as possible", Justice Coleridge nonetheless drew attention to "the endless game of 'pass the partner', in which such a significant portion of the population is engaged. . . the endless and futile quest for a perfect relationship:"[1212]

> What is a matter of private concern when on a small scale becomes a matter of public concern when it reaches epidemic proportions.

Across the Atlantic, some State judges have also raised concerns about the culture of divorce and nonmarital childbearing.[1213]

Despite underlying political differences, a common emphasis about the importance of healthy marriages and intact families began to emerge. This is not to deny the many differences that exist among people with an interest in this subject: rather it is to acknowledge the acceptance by the majority of family scholars and practitioners of the overwhelming social science data, and a recognition of the growing social problems wrought by the retreat from marriage. Nor is it to suggest that various bipartisan proposals have always been adopted: too often the contrary has been the experience.[1214] While there remain some exceptions to this emerging consensus, it is sufficiently broad to form the basis for further policies and programs. In the remainder of this chapter, some principles, goals and policies to further revitalise a culture of marriage are outlined. The final chapter records a discussion of what marital and family scholars suggest individuals could do if they wish to fulfil their personal aspirations for a successful life-long marital union.

COMMON GROUND

The foregoing discussion suggests that there are a series of principles and goals that attract widespread support. Two principles recognise and support the existence of key mediating or bridging structures in society, such as families and voluntary associations.[1215] First, public policy should protect and foster marriage and family; and, secondly, wherever possible, public policy should utilise the family and community organisations, rather than displacing them. These principles arise from a belief that public policy and social programs should support civil society, and that the institutions of civil society, primarily the family, has priority over the political. It is neither a new nor conservative notion. In a 1962 message to the US Congress on public welfare programs, President John F Kennedy stated:

> The goals of our public welfare programs must be positive and constructive. . . It must stress the integrity and preservation of the family unit. It must contribute to the attack on dependency, juvenile delinquency, family breakdown, illegitimacy, ill health, and disability. It must replace the incidence of these problems, prevent their occurrence and recurrence, and strengthen and protect the vulnerable in a highly competitive world.[1216]

This is opposed to the view that family policy is what government does to and for families.[1217] The institutions of civil society, including the family and charitable, religious and service agencies, are important because they are neither created nor controlled by the State. They should not become arms of government for a number of reasons.[1218] A blending of the role of government and the civil sector risks the domination of the government sphere over all others. "Do not forget that every State power tends to look upon all liberty with a suspicious eye," warned the Dutch statesmen, Abraham Kuyper.[1219] "The ancient history of all people replays a shameful spectacle. Despite stubborn, sometimes heroic struggle, the freedom of the spheres dies out and State power – become Caesarian – triumphs."[1220]

When the State directs the activity of civil society, it enfeebles the ability of citizens to take responsibility for their own community and society. The Harvard sociologist, Nathan Glazer, warned of the unintended consequences:

> Aside from these problems of expectations, cost, competency and limitations of knowledge, there is the simple reality that every piece of social policy substitutes for some traditional arrangement, a new arrangement in which public authorities take over, at least in part, the role of the family, of the ethnic and neighbourhood group, of voluntary associations. In doing so, social policy weakens the position of these traditional agents and further encourages needy people to depend on the government for help rather than traditional structures.[1221]

The practical outcome is all too familiar: a one size fits all approach to social problems, ensnared by contractual obligations with service agencies, designed to fit governmental pigeon holes, which rob much of the individual initiative and personal initiative that should motivate charity. Worse, it endangers the vibrancy of institutions that help to form virtuous citizens. The act of giving, whether finances, services or counsel, becomes a professional activity and function of the State, rather than an act of charity and love directed to fellow human beings.

Four goals are proposed:

1. Nations should have an explicit marriage and family policy.
2. They should seek to maintain at least a replacement birth rate.
3. National policy should proclaim the ideal of marital permanence and affirm marriage as the optimal environment for the raising of children.
4. The policy should value family stability and reinforce personal and inter-generational responsibility.

These goals are modest. In previous times, they would be regarded as unremarkable. If achieved now, they would have a profound beneficial impact on societies. The following discussion outlines these goals and some specific programs that may assist in achieving them.

1. A family policy

Despite political rhetoric about families, few nations have a national family policy. Families are treated as welfare recipients, or the aged, or defence force personnel, or public housing occupants, or taxpayers – but not as families. Even where programs have an impact upon families, they are compartmentalised into stages: infancy, childhood, youth, and the aged.

The failure of family policies to emerge as a distinct issue partly reflects the failure to agree on a common definition of 'family'. Daniel Patrick Moynihan responded:

> A nation without a conscious family policy leaves to chance and mischance an area of social reality of the upmost importance, which in consequence will be exposed to the untrammelled and frequently thoroughly undesirable impact of policies arising in other areas.[1222]

The first step to treating families seriously is for governments

and political parties to adopt specific family policies.[1223] The Irish
Commission on the Family added:

> The foundations of family policy, the principles and objectives
> which underlie and guide it need to be set out clearly. What the
> State is trying to achieve for and with families – the strategic
> dimension of family policy – should be clarified and made
> explicit.[1224]

The Commission found that there is a need to strengthen
the institutional framework of family policy so that the various
manifestations of family policy acquire a greater degree of coherence
and rationality. It proposed a series of principles, the first of which is
that "recognition that the family unit is a fundamental unit providing
stability and well-being in our society."

The explicit adoption of family policies encourages governments
to confront two cultural forces which have undermined families and
communities, namely, the lessening of family autonomy, especially
through state programs; and, secondly, the weakening of family
through the growth of unrestrained individualism. A specific policy,
along with expansion of particular programs proposed below, also has a
normative influence within society. If, as reported in an earlier chapter,
the very fact that a community comprises more divorced people and
unmarried parents, has an impact on the likelihood of divorce or single
parenting, policies and programs that affirm marriage and family are
equally likely to have a positive effect.

A marriage and family policy grid

Suggestions have been made from time to time that all legislative
proposals should be accompanied by a Family Impact Statement.
This approach is used in some jurisdictions. While desirable in theory,
Family Impact Statements require a strong framework if they are to
be effective. First, they need to be public, and not confined to the
policy-makers. Ideally, the impact of any proposal should be assessed

by a body independent from the primary policy-maker. Thirdly, a mechanism is necessary for the administration of the policy to accord with the pro-marriage and family intentions. Unless these things are present, a Family Impact Statement is likely to become a *pro forma* requirement to be 'ticked off' and largely ignored.

The adoption of a Marriage and Family Policy Grid could be a useful mechanism for ensuring oversight and compliance with the headline policy.[1225] As many programs are administrative in nature, not requiring specific legislation except the annual Budget process, a Grid could assist both the administrators of programs and the legislators seeking to verify progress. Given the evidence set out earlier in this book, there are at least four areas that a Marriage and Family Policy Grid could cover. These involve the enhancement of stable marriage; the ability of parents to have children; good parenting skills and parental involvement with children; and ongoing involvement by parents with their children when separation occurs.

Marriage and Family Policy Grid

Does the measure:

- Enhance stable marriage?
- Enhance the ability of parents to have children?
- Enhance good parenting skills and parental involvement with children?
- Enhance ongoing involvement of parents with children following separation?

(Columns: Objectives, Legislation, Regulations, Performance Indicators, Evaluation)

A similar approach could also inform the work of organisations and agencies working with families. The US Administration for Children and Families lists five protective factors that organisations working with families should seek to promote: nurturing and attachment; knowledge of parenting and youth development; parental resilience; social connections; and concrete supports for parents.[1226]

2. A replacement birthrate

Population growth in many western nations is declining, and, in some places, very significantly, as the discussion in chapter ten reveals. Even in nations where slight increases in the birth rate had been recorded over the past decade, they have tended to fall again in the shadow of the global financial crisis.[1227] The fact that the global population is continuing to expand should not be a source of complacency in those countries where it is in decline. Otherwise, the consequence of ageing societies will be a weakening of the essential family and community bonds, economic decline, and geopolitical insecurity. Demography is destiny. Steven Kramer writes:

> Countries that fail to take low birthrates seriously do so at their own peril. Time matters. If they wait too long and get caught in the low fertility trap, they could find themselves in an uncharted era of depopulation that will be eerily different from anything before. And escaping that scenario will be difficult, if not impossible.[1228]

Hence, nations should seek to replace their population over the long term. Where fertility rates have fallen to very low levels, this is extremely difficult. Many nations hope that immigration will ameliorate the consequences of low birth rates, but immigration does little to slow the ageing of the population. A natural fertility rate at, or near to, replacement levels, is the best policy to adopt.

The various measures outlined in chapter ten are examples of the approaches taken to population decline over the past few decades.

None of the measures has been totally successful, but some have shown modest improvements in the birth rate. As there are many social, economic and cultural factors at play, governments aspiring to promote the birth rate will have to employ a variety of measures.

Family-work balance

Effective policies need to achieve an optimal balance between the pressures to increase female participation in the paid workforce and the necessity to maintain the fertility rate. Confronted with an ageing population, and its adverse impact on national growth, governments have generally invoked three responses: increased productivity, higher levels of participation in the workforce, and raising fertility. Hence, a recent Australian study suggested that increasing female participation would make a major contribution to future growth.[1229]

If the tension between participation and fertility is not recognised, there is a danger that one objective will be advanced at the expense of the other, with little overall benefit to the nations concerned. Unless policy makers value the critical importance of having and raising healthy, well-adjusted children, other measures are likely to nullify the expected gains. Nations with ageing populations need both more workers and more children. If a consequence of increasing workforce participation is to drive down fertility rates, the hoped-for economic growth will not be sustained.

Increasing the former at the expense of the latter only postpones the problems.[1230] The economist, John Mueller, observes:

> Neither growth of the labor force nor rising productivity owing to technical progress can be assumed, because there can be no growth in the labor force without a prior investment in child-rearing.[1231]

Mueller notes that investments in human capital in one generation determine the return of labor compensation in the next, a return which has historically accounted for two-thirds of economic growth in the United States.[1232]

Economists can identify measures that are likely to increase female workforce participation. These usually include lower marginal tax rates on second family incomes, the need for parental leave following the birth of a child, adequate child care, and flexible work hours.[1233] The idea that the family-work balance is only driven by economic considerations is misplaced. Parents also have their priorities that include the personal care for their own children, particularly when the children are of pre-school and primary school age. Australians, for example, prefer very young children not to be in formal child care.[1234] Even when outside of parental care, young children tend to be cared for by grandparents. Up to the end of primary school, about half of children are cared for informally, usually by other family members.[1235] While some of these decisions reflect economic considerations, scholars at the Australian Institute of Family Studies also note that in many families, "parents prefer the mother to maintain primary care of infants and to limit their employment participation at this time."[1236] This is reflected in the family-work choices that were referred to in chapter five.

Parents require flexibility and choice in their family and work arrangements. Such choice is not just about the hours worked at any one time, but about the arrangements they make over the course of their lives. While a library of books have been written about the so-called *Time Bind*, to adopt Arlie Russell Hochschild's wellknown title, less has been written about the work-family balance over the life course.

The emphasis on short-term paid maternity leave for those in the workforce ignores the reality that parents balance their family and work responsibilities between them over decades, not just a few weeks after the birth of a child. The life course approach is all the more important with the delay in partnering, the increase in longevity and the ageing of the population.[1237]

Financial encouragement for having and raising children should not be work related exclusively. While many employers offer maternity (and some paternity) provisions, and this will increase as the growth in the workforce contracts, the responsibility for encouraging and supporting children should not primarily rest upon them. If children are critical to the future prosperity of nations, encouragement of parenthood and support for families is a national responsibility. It is not primarily an issue of work, but of children. Nor is it an issue that benefits from a 'one size fits all' industrial approach. Ideally, financial benefits should be available to families whether or not they have both parents in the paid workforce. These benefits can be provided in a variety of forms, ranging from general tax concessions for families with children to childcare and parenting payments. This is not only equitable, it recognises the fact that parents want the flexibility to choose their family and work arrangements over the life course. It recognises also, as Adam Smith did, that marrying and having children are central to lasting economic growth and sustained wealth.[1238]

3. Marital permanence and the welfare of children

Reflecting on the mounting social science data, the family scholar, Paul Amato, describes the two approaches to modern marital relationships as a conflict between the institutional and individual view of marriage.[1239] He concludes that policies should support marriage and family:

> One widely replicated finding tilts the argument in favour of promarriage policies. That is, studies consistently indicate that children raised by two happily and continuously married parents have the best chance of developing into competent and successful adults ... Because we all have an interest in the well-being of children, it is reasonable for social institutions (such as the state) to attempt to increase the proportion of children raised by married parents with satisfying and stable marriages.[1240]

Merely decreasing the rate of divorce is insufficient, he adds. The fear shared by Amato and an increasing number of family scholars is well founded. Recent data from Britain, for example, shows that 20 per cent of children from a broken home lose touch with their absent parent within three years and then never see them again.[1241]

The proclamation of the ideal of marital permanence and affirmation of marriage as the optimal environment for the raising of children should be at the core of national policy. But rhetoric is insufficient. There are measures that could be utilised, in addition to the successful initiatives outlined in the previous chapter.

Information, education and skills

In an era in which the old notion of 'buyer beware' has been replaced, at least partially, by 'informed consent' in many interactions, it is remarkable that so few people outside scholarly circles and family practitioners know and understand the consequences for individuals and society of the retreat from marriage. Yet millions of people are affected.

Education about family and marriage is not new. It has long occurred in a myriad of informal ways:

> It occurs in all families and all marriages beginning with the childhood experiences of family life which provide a model for future attitudes and behaviour. We also learn from other sources – friends, school, the media – so that by the time we begin to contemplate a family of our own, we already have formed ideas and developed behaviour patterns that will significantly affect our future relationships. These attitudes and behaviour patterns are further affected by relationships formed during adolescence and the young adult years and by experiences in the workplace.[1242]

While these formative experiences influence our attitudes and behaviours, an increasingly large number of people have incomplete or little experience of healthy marital relationships. Hence, a comprehensive education program is central to a policy to promote marital permanence and the care of children. Marital education programs have been sponsored in a number of countries, as the previous chapter illustrates. But their coverage is inadequate, and their timing restricted. Providing information and skills to a couple a few weeks or months prior to their wedding is useful, but much more could be done.

The UK Social Justice Group proposed five streams: premarital education, antenatal classes, and parenting 0-5s, 5-11s, and teens, as well as specific programs for lone parents, prisoners, military personnel, and parents of children taken into out-of-home care.[1243] A number of the approaches outlined below would help to address the inadequacies that currently exist.

Relationship education in schools

Better education about relationships should start in schools.[1244] With an increasing number of adolescents sexually active, most schools have some form of sex education. Often sterile debates have raged about the type of education that is appropriate and efficacious, as if the only consequence of ignorance is unwanted pregnancy. Yet sexually transmitted diseases are at epidemic levels and infertility rising.[1245] Equally problematic is the number of children whose lives are disrupted by fatherlessness, separation or divorce, and who grow-up in challenging circumstances. The social, mental, physical and economic consequences are significant as indicated in chapter three. Missing also, is the modelling of healthy family life. Judith Wallerstein observed:

> What children of divorce don't observe and have no chance to learn is how to create a long term loving relationship, how to resolve family conflict, how to build trust, when to compromise, when to stand firm, and as they grow, how to choose a lover and how to commit to another with realistic hope that it can last. They tell me wistfully, "I have never seen a man and a woman on the same beam" or "Sometimes I feel like I was raised on a desert island. Combining sex with love is a mystery to me."[1246]

Reflecting Wallerstein, the American educator and author, Marlene

Pearson, writes that this generation of young people "knows a lot about sex, but very little about building quality relationships and true intimacy."[1247] William Galston and Stephen Goldsmith argue:

> Helping young people understand the very nature of relationships has been the missing ingredient in the nation's efforts at delaying sexual activity, avoiding teen pregnancy, and helping prepare young people for successful marriages. Teens hear about biology and body parts, they are instructed on how to reduce the risk of pregnancy and sexually transmitted diseases, but rarely are they given guidance about how to successfully negotiate the minefields of teen and young adult relationships. In short, young people are often told what to avoid, but hardly ever told how to achieve responsible and respectful relationships.[1248]

Pearson suggests that a comprehensive relationship education program should include five themes generally missing today:

- The emotional and social dimension of sexuality.
- Relationship experiences and relationship building.
- Communication and conflict management skills for successful relationships.
- New tacks in pregnancy prevention that address the disconnect between marriage and childbearing and raise awareness about the needs of the child.
- Marriage education that helps teens learn about thirty years of social science evidence on why marriage matters to children, its benefits, findings on marital success and failure, and the skills that improve marriage success.[1249]

Various organisations and groups have responded with programs and resources,[1250] but a more comprehensive approach is required.

Learning to be parents

Parents have a critical role in the education and outcomes for their children.[1251] For an increasing number of people, the ways of parenting that have been modelled traditionally in the family has been lost.

In a report commissioned by the Conservative UK Prime Minister, David Cameron, the senior Labor MP, Frank Field, called for a new approach, noting that the traditional measure of a identifying and supporting those living below an established poverty line failed to take into account those children whose parents remain disengaged from their responsibilities.[1252] Noting research showing the successes individuals achieve during their adult life can be predicted by the level of cognitive and non-cognitive skills they already possess on their first day at school,[1253] and the role of positive and authoritative parenting and the home learning environment, Field observed how an increasing number of children today suffered the absence of what the sociologist Geoffrey Gorer described as the 'tough love' tradition that had been responsible for raising resilient, well-adjusted young people.[1254]

> Many people appear to have lost the simple parenting skills that were once taken for granted. And this means that Britain is now trapped in a vicious downward spiral, in which parents raise feckless children, who are then incapable of raising responsible, productive offspring of their own.[1255]

Field noted that on visits to schools, ranging from those in poor, marginalised areas to better-off regions, young people repeatedly listed how to be taught to be good parents as an aspiration for their education.[1256] Consequently, he proposed raising knowledge about parenting skills within the school curriculum as a first critical component of a new approach to child poverty "if we are to prevent life's wheel of fortune consistently spinning against the interests of poorer children as a class."[1257] Prime Minister, David Cameron, subsequently announced a program to provide new mothers and fathers with £100 that could be used to attend parenting programs conducted by community organisations.[1258]

Pre-marriage education

Pre-marital education needs to be expanded. Despite the positive findings,[1259] and the common sense acknowledgement, that education about marital relationships can be useful, only a minority of couples undertake any formal program or course. Take Australia for which some, albeit incomplete, data exists. The Parliamentary Report, *To have and to hold,* concluded that approximately 30 per cent of couples marrying for the first time in 1996-97 participated in pre-marriage education.[1260] The overwhelming majority of couples who participated were married in a religious setting, reflecting the strong emphasis that various faith groups have placed on preparation for marriage in recent decades. Conversely, very few couples marrying in a civil ceremony experienced marriage education.

As religious practice decreases, more couples choose to be married in civil ceremonies. In Australia, since the introduction of the civil celebrant's program for example, the proportion of weddings in churches, synagogues, mosques, temples or other religious settings has fallen to just thirty per cent.[1261] Many religious faiths encourage couples to participate in marriage education,[1262] but most civil celebrants do not, despite urgings from government and some celebrant organisations to do so.[1263] National data also reveals that 75 per cent of couples living together married in a civil ceremony, compared with 45 per cent of those who lived apart.[1264] The consequence is the overall proportion of Australian couples participating in marriage education is unlikely to have grown since the late 1990s.[1265]

While family scholars and marriage educators develop programs to meet the changing pathways into marriage,[1266] many of those who would benefit are unaware of the assistance available to them, or regard it as unnecessary because of their cohabiting experience. Many couples who have the highest risk for marital problems are less likely to participate in programs.[1267]

Traditionally, marriage preparation programs have catered

for engaged couples, usually – although not exclusively, and not intentionally – from middle class backgrounds. Recent research shows that the specific aspiration to marry is often strongest among those who have the least access to it, particularly those who are in extreme economic disadvantage.[1268] Many of these people are or have been in *de facto* relationships. They are unlikely to come in contact with existing programs, which tend to have the approach to a marriage celebrant, as their connection point with a couple. While many of the existing programs represent the 'gold standard' in premarital education,[1269] new approaches are also necessary if more couples are to obtain the benefits of information and skills that may be of assistance to them.

As a consequence, family scholars and marriage educators have been devising novel ways to reach out to individuals and couples in different circumstances. These include use of the internet and social media,[1270] and dating agencies.[1271] Building on the Bush Administration's efforts to connect welfare reform and intact families, Scott Stanley and colleagues designed an educational program specifically tailored for individuals struggling with economic disadvantage.[1272]

There is also evidence that the positive impact of pre-marriage education programs reduces after a number of years.[1273] Couples participating in programs exhibit modest improvements in relationship satisfaction[1274] and improvements in observable relationship skills.[1275] This is important, given the significant number of couples who separate within the first few years of the wedding. An Australian study also revealed that some couples will end their engagement as a result of participating in a marriage preparation program,[1276] although the likelihood of pre-marital separation diminishes closer to the wedding. Marriage scholars have responded to these findings by suggesting better targeting of programs,[1277] more post-wedding education opportunities, and continuing research.[1278]

Parenting skills

The birth of a child can be a challenge to a couple's marriage – financially, emotionally, physically and sexually.[1279] In his groundbreaking study of the transition to parenthood, the psychologist, Jay Belsky, found that:

- 12-13 per cent of all new parents become so divided by differences that they begin to lose faith in each other and in their marriage;
- 38 per cent managed to avoid a dramatic marital tailspin during transition but the couples became more polarised;
- 30 per cent overcame enough of their differences to prevent marital decline, but not enough to gain a new sense of closeness; and
- 19 per cent of the couples in the study overcame transition-time marital gaps and divisions to come closer together.[1280]

Later research has countered some of these findings. In his longitudinal study of couples, the University of Texas psychologist, Ted Huston, found that declines in affection with parenthood were comparable to those found among couples who did not have a baby. The study found no evidence that parenthood exacted a toll in terms of marital strife.[1281] Nevertheless, parenthood brought about significant changes in couples' day-to-day lives.

Much time and effort is given to educating parents about the birthing of a child. Little effort is made to assist couple to enhance their relationship at this important transition to parenthood, whether they are married or not. Research indicates that the better the quality of the relationship between biological parents, the better their parenting skills a year after the birth of a child, whether living together or not.[1282] Equally, good co-parenting enhances the involvement of non-resident fathers in the lives of their children.[1283]

The health of a marriage is crucial for the success of children. The psychologists, Carolyn and Philip Cowan, observe:

> You don't have to be a reader of child development research
> to know that the atmosphere in parents' relationships with their
> children will have a lot to do with whether or not they are able
> to provide the kind of secure family environments that foster the
> optimal cognitive, social, and emotional development of their
> children.[1284]

By tracing family relationships in two longitudinal studies, the
Cowans demonstrated that how parents feel about themselves and as
a couple were important influences on the outcome for their children.
When they were successful in helping couples to make positive shifts
in their relationships with their children – and especially in their
relationships *as a couple* – their children reaped the benefits too, by
being more successful in their school work and their relationships.[1285]

> When we followed the children into their first year of school
> at age five ... , we found that the children of parents who had
> the most difficulty managing the transition to parenthood were
> having the most trouble adjusting to school; they were not
> doing as well academically, they were having more trouble
> getting along with other children, and they had more worrisome
> behaviours in terms of acting out, aggressive behaviour, or very
> shy withdrawn behaviour when they were upset.[1286]

A range of resources and programs have been developed to assist
parents in the transition to parenthood.[1287] These include the *Becoming
Parents* program, the *Becoming-a-Family* program, the *Bringing Baby
Home* program, the *Marriage Moments* program,[1288] *And Baby Makes
3*,[1289] and *Ready, Set, Baby*.[1290] A comprehensive marriage and family
policy would encourage all parents to participate in such programs,
which a series of reports have recommended be expanded.[1291]

The US *Building Strong Families* initiative is a program for
unmarried parents. It arose from the Princeton *Fragile Families and
Child Wellbeing* study which suggested that at the time of the birth of
their child, most unmarried parents were still romantically involved
and optimistic about their relationships, but a year later, one-third had

separated and only 12 per cent married.[1292] An evaluation of one of the trial programs, 'Family expectations' in Oklahoma, revealed positive outcomes.[1293] Comprising three components – relationship skills education, family support coordinators, and supportive services – the program resulted in a consistent pattern of significantly positive effects on the quality and status of the couples' relationships, improved co-parenting and more couples living together. About 45 per cent of the couples completed 80 per cent of the 30 hour relationship education classes in the program. The evaluation of the trial sites suggests that an integrated program of skills and support is required to address the needs of unmarried parents.[1294]

Supporting stepfamilies

There has been a significant growth in the number of stepfamilies over the past few decades. It is estimated that 7 per cent of couple families in Australia,[1295] and 10 per cent in the UK are stepfamilies.[1296] In the US, more than 12 per cent of children under 18 years are living in a stepfamily.[1297] While stepfamilies are usually defined to include step and blended families, the official data is likely to underestimate the actual number of reconstituted families.[1298] Estimates suggest that by the time they reach the age of 18, between one-third and one-half of American children will have been part of the stepfamily. Although remarriage rates have fallen, many divorced people enter into subsequent cohabiting relationships. In addition, unmarried childbearing and cohabitation has increased over the past decades.[1299]

Although many couples form lasting and happy stepfamilies, it is well established that the separation and divorce rates for these unions are significantly higher than for first marriages. Second marriages have a 60 per cent divorce rate, and third marriages a 73 per cent divorce rate in the US.[1300] Remarried couples with children have a 50 per cent greater chance of divorce than remarried couples without children.[1301] Equally, cohabitation is a more unstable family system than marriage.

Yet few resources are devoted to educating and supporting couples contemplating remarriage or a new relationship. The 1998 Australian Inquiry reported, for example, that less than one per cent of people participating in relationship education programs were stepfamilies.[1302] Noting that the time of separation is a key transitional point in couples' lives, the Inquiry suggested that Family Courts should play a more proactive role in supporting and encouraging couples to learn new skills to enable them to proceed into more stable marriages or relationships in the future. The Parliamentary Committee recommended that the Family Court use its information sessions, parenting programs and counselling services to educate people about the complexities involved in remarriage and the value in undertaking further education and training.[1303]

That such information, education and skills would be valuable is beyond doubt. Every marital scholar, researcher, educator and therapist who has worked with stepfamilies has noted that stepfamilies are different to other couple relationships, particularly first time families, whether a previously first-time couple relationship, or a single parent relationship.[1304] Ron Deal and David Olson observed in their research:

> A couple's previous marriages (or relationships) and the presence of stepchildren have a significant impact on the long-term viability of the remarriage, but the full weight of this impact doesn't show up until after the wedding. Before the wedding, matters related to ex-spouses and step parenting had limited impact on the couple's level of satisfaction with each other. However, after the wedding, stepfamily issues rose significantly in their impact on couple satisfaction.[1305]

The complexity of stepfamilies arises from many possible events:[1306]

- At least one partner has experienced marriage and parenthood before *or* a partner who *is* a parent has never been married.
- Partners in stepfamilies who have never married or lived with a partner are unaccustomed to family life (apart from their family of origin).

- Adults *and* children come into the relationship at the outset.
- The parent and stepparent often do not have time together alone before having children live with them.
- Stepparents have to live with, care for and/or relate to stepchildren with whom they have no 'history.' There is a lack of bonding.
- Single-parent family life often precedes stepfamily life.
- There is at least one 'intruder' in the stepfamily unit.
- Children often lose contact with a parent from the previous family – sometimes this is a loss of daily contact, other times it is forever.
- Children often have two homes with two sets of rules, conditions, discipline, etc.
- Visiting children/stepchildren have to be accommodated in the stepfamily from time-to-time.
- Family members may experience relocation of home, school, job, activities, etc..
- New responsibilities may emerge.
- Unfinished business from a past marriage (anger, grief, guilt, anxiety) can come into a stepfamily.
- Suspicion and lack of trust between stepparent and stepchildren may exist.
- Surnames of children can be different and create a sense of not belonging.
- There are more people, all at once, having to get used to each other.
- There is no 'legal' relationship between stepparent and stepchild;
- Socioeconomic conditions might change; money can be tight.
- Sibling order might change so the oldest, for example, now could be a middle child.
- There might be less space or territory for each person.
- At least one person has to adjust to living in a different home – with different family rules, etc.

Many therapists and educators who have worked with stepfamilies have observed that there is often unresolved loss and grief in existence.[1307]

A series of 'myths' about stepfamilies have also been identified, such as:

- A stepfamily is created instantly.
- Stepfamilies can function like biological families.
- All stepfamily members will, given time, love one another.
- Relating to stepchildren is the same as relating to biological children.
- All of the children in a stepfamily will automatically get on together.
- Part time stepfamilies where children 'visit' have it easier than full time stepfamilies where children 'live in'.
- The stepfamily is headed by a wicked stepmother or cruel stepfather.
- Stepfamilies formed after the death of a partner have fewer problems than those formed after divorce or separation.
- If stepchildren are treated kindly by their stepparent, they will always respond well.
- The couple can love one another so much that problems creating a stepfamily will be easily overcome.
- Stepfamilies are better off because parents have learned from their mistakes in their first marriages.[1308]

It is little wonder that many stepfamilies confront considerable challenges in creating a happy marital relationship. Despite the difficulties, family scholars have identified positives of living in a stepfamily, especially where the couple have been able to identify the challenges they confront, and are motivated to make their relationship work.[1309] One of the challenges is to recognise that forming a stepfamily is not an event, but a process involving a series of stages, including a fantasy stage, confusion, a stage of chaos and conflict, coming together or stability, and resolution and commitment.[1310] Many people forming stepfamilies are unaware of the extent of the challenges they confront. It is for this reason that much more needs to be done to inform, educate and assist them.

People may not be open to hearing about future relationships at the time of divorce, but at least information that they might return to later could be provided to them. While many enter into subsequent *de facto* relationships, at least those who remarry could be provided also with a range of educational materials. There are many resources and courses offered, some of which are set out in the appendix.[1311] This is far from a comprehensive response, but would be a vast advance on what is provided currently.

More research

A series of studies since the 1970s demonstrated the value of education programs,[1312] and their effectiveness in improving couples' relationships.[1313] A subsequent study found that marriage education produces positive effects on participants' communication skills and relationship quality at both immediate post-assessment and upon later follow-up.[1314] Marriage education has also been shown to function as a universal prevention.[1315] A study across four American states concluded that participation in pre-marriage education was associated with decreased risks of divorce, lower levels of self-reported conflict, higher levels of marital satisfaction and higher commitment between spouses.[1316] Similarly, the National Fatherhood Initiative *Marriage Survey* found that respondents who had premarital counselling/education had more successful marriages than those who did not.[1317]

However, there have been very few randomised controlled studies with long term outcomes. In a recent review of the marital education literature, the University of California psychologists,

Thomas Bradbury and Justin Lavner, observe that "our understanding of how relationships change is incomplete and that our ability to teach couples how to preserve and protect their intimate bonds is not adequate to the task."[1318] They identify six issues that need to be addressed in future research. They suggest shifting interventions away from prescribing behaviours that educators thought would underpin strong relationships to conveying the principles that seem to underlie relationship-sustaining communication; and the need to address the three areas of influence on marital outcomes – personality traits and pre-marital experiences (vulnerabilities); stressful events encountered once married (stressors); and the emotions and communication skills spouses use while adapting to each other (adaptation). Better understanding of which couples are at greater risk, how couples learn and apply knowledge, and the best settings for education will enhance programs. Working with local community organisations[1319] and providing the opportunity for follow-up programs would appear to improve the impact of education initiatives.[1320]

Promoting marriage

Efforts to promote healthy, stable marriages have been embarked upon in a number of countries in recent years. Australian governments have supported a series of campaigns over the past few decades including "How long before your marriage breaks down?" which was aimed at the idealism of 18-25 year olds about marriage;[1321] "Is love enough?";[1322] "Relate";[1323] and "Two equals one"[1324] US campaigns include the "For your marriage" initiative.[1325]

In a British survey, 57 per cent of respondents believed it was right for government to promote marriage.[1326] The US National Fatherhood Initiative *Marriage Survey* found that 86 per cent agreed that all couples considering marriage should get premarital counselling, 57 per cent of the married respondents said they would attend a free marriage education class if one were available, and 73 per cent of the unmarried persons searching for someone to marry said they would attend a free pre-marital education class.[1327] The provision of free marriage education vouchers for couples who had notified their intention to marry was successful in an Australian trial, but the policy was never implemented fully. The Australian Parliamentary Committee that recommended the trial also proposed further campaigns to promote marriage and relationship education.[1328]

Noting the increase in premarital cohabitation, David Popenoe observes that "once established in the culture, cohabitation seems gradually to be corroding the desire of couples to move into marriage,"[1329] citing Canadian research that cohabitation experiences delayed the timing of first marriages by 26 per cent for men and 19 per cent for women.[1330] A promotion campaign would need to address this group of couples.

Raising children in intact families

Given the overwhelming social science evidence about the advantages for children of being raised in stable, intact families, and the corresponding disadvantages of other situations, the State should not be value-neutral about the circumstances in which children are conceived, born and raised. This does not mean that government should force anyone to get married, implement policies that encourage anyone to enter or be trapped in abusive relationships, or promote marriage by withdrawing necessary supports for single-parent or other families.[1331] However, the State should encourage parental responsibility for children. Hence the British government, faced with some 50,000 births each year where the father remains unnamed, has considered forcing birth registration on both parents.[1332]

Acknowledging that cohabitation is not going to disappear, the sociologist, David Popenoe, proposes that efforts should be made "to get more cohabiting couples, when they have children, to shift into marriage and maintain that marriage over the long term."[1333]

Noting that around one in ten married parents split before a child's fifth birthday, compared to one in three cohabiting couples, the UK government stated recently that "marriage should be supported and encouraged."[1334]

Amelioration

The amelioration of the negative consequences of poverty, family dysfunction and social exclusion has been the object of intervention programs for decades. While much attention and considerable resources have been devoted to such programs, they are rarely a panacea for the manifold problems facing many individuals and families in contemporary society. Often the results have been very modest. Perhaps the best example of the limited effects is the US Head Start initiative. Launched by the Johnson administration in 1965, the pre-school program was designed to reduce juvenile delinquency, poverty and dependence. A major review of the impact of the $7 billion a year program found:

> That providing access to Head Start has benefits for both 3-year-olds and 4-year-olds in the cognitive, health, and parenting domains, and for 3-year-olds in the social-emotional domain. However the benefits of access to Head Start at age four are largely absent by 1st grade for the program population as a whole ...[1335]

While some scholars disputed the findings because some of the children in the control group attended preschool programs, including Head Start that were not part of the study,[1336] most acknowledge that the outcomes were, at best, modest,[1337] and others have suggested that not only are the effects of early education short-term, but often yield adverse effects for mainstream children.[1338] While it is easy to understand why legislators continued to fund the program, it is remarkable that the impact of a multi-billion dollar program was not assessed properly for 45 years. The massive investment in programs of alleviation remains a significant reason why prevention programs receive meagre funding.

Most programs of amelioration come too late. In his report on early intervention in the UK, Graham Allen concludes: "The bleak truth is that decades of expensive late intervention have failed. Major social problems have got worse not better: despite heroic frontline efforts tackling the *symptoms*, their *causes* remain unaddressed."[1339] The consequence is the reduced likelihood of achieving a remedy, and expensive palliative measures that often fail to solve the problems that have arisen. A recent survey of child behaviour in the US and the UK reinforces the limitations of welfare programs to ameliorate the negative consequences of divorce. After analysing longitudinal surveys of five to thirteen year old children in both countries, the team of scholars found no evidence that the more developed British welfare state was a substitute for the protective effects of an intact family.[1340]

Amelioration is important, but it is insufficient. A renewed emphasis on prevention and early intervention is likely to be more successful than palliative measures. It is also cost-efficient. Australian research has shown for example, that as much as seven dollars is saved for every dollar spent on marriage counselling. An Australian Institute of Family Studies survey in 1989 found that of those who were in an intact relationship, 81 per cent of women and 78 per cent of men remained together as a result of seeking counselling. Of those who were initially separated, 30 per cent of women and 11 per cent of men had reconciled. Three-quarters said their problem areas, personal life and relationships had improved.[1341]

4. Valuing family stability and reinforcing responsibility

Promoting reconciliation

The weakening of marriage and the increase in divorce over the past four decades has coincided with a retreat from the idea that some couples can be helped to reconcile their differences and maintain their marital relationship before or during family law proceedings. For decades in the US, the conciliation services provided by the courts focussed on the possible reconciliation of marital problems.[1342] Beginning with California in 1969, states throughout the western world removed the legal concept of fault from their divorce laws and replaced it with a notion of the irretrievable breakdown of marriage, usually evidenced by a period of separation of the parties. In the subsequent decades, levels of divorce have risen markedly.

As in the case of Australia's *Family Law Act*, divorce laws were generally constructed on two pillars: First, the centrality or importance of family; and, secondly, the rights *and* obligations of spouses, both during marriage and upon its dissolution. The legislation introduced into the Australian Parliament was based on a series of stated principles, the first of which was that "good family law should buttress, rather than undermine, the stability of marriage." The Parliament had included provisions in the legislation which sought to encourage couples to achieve reconciliation.[1343] The Australian *Family Law Act* provided that in making any adjudication, the Court must have regard to a series of factors, including:

- the need to preserve and protect the institution of marriage as the union of a man and a woman to the exclusion of all others voluntarily entered into for life;
- the need to give the widest possible protection and assistance to the family as the natural and fundamental group unit of society, particularly while it is responsible for the care and education of dependent children;

- the need to protect the rights of children and promote their welfare; and
- the means available for assisting parties to marriage to consider reconciliation or the improvement of their relationship to each other and to the children of the marriage.

Despite the fact that these factors were given considerable weight in the Parliamentary debates preceding the new law, the divorce of the parties remains today the operational basis of the legislation.

In the US, the assumption in family law in the late sixties "was that many divorcing couples could be helped to reconcile, and that the best way to assist them was to assemble a team of legal and mental health professionals."[1344] Other jurisdictions shared this view. Hence the 1975 Australian *Family Law Act* originally required counselling to be undertaken by a couple married for less than two years prior to a divorce hearing.[1345] The Act also provided that counselling and welfare staff be appointed to the Family Court to assist reconciliation and, if unsuccessful, to assist parties to conciliate agreement on property, custody and access issues.[1346] In practice, Family Court counselling is largely directed to conciliation. In 1991, the then Chief Justice of the Court admitted:

> Originally it was thought that the Court would play a role in the promotion of reconciliation but the experience of the past 15 years has been that by the time that a couple approaches the Court, there is little room for reconciliation, and such reconciliations that do occur are of uncertain and doubtful duration.[1347]

From the 1970s, Family Courts moved from reconciliation to the concept of divorce with dignity.[1348] One researcher concluded that "in general, Family Court counselling services appear now to specialise in short-term counselling to resolve disputes over custody and access issues resulting from marriage breakdown."[1349] Mediation also has been promoted widely as an alternative to litigation. In the process, a demarcation line has been drawn in practice between reconciliation therapy and counselling, usually conducted apart from the family law system, and conciliation counselling and mediation once the divorce application has been initiated.[1350]

Under previous legislation, the concept of fault determined the outcome of the divorce application. In cultural terms, partners who walked away from a marriage or caused their spouse to leave risked societal opprobrium. The introduction of unilateral no-fault divorce changed this cultural norm, allowing partners to leave a marriage on the premise that a short period of separation constitutes the irretrievable breakdown of the relationship. Marriage is perceived as a right, including the right to leave it, without corresponding duties. Adults may cope with these arrangements, but the evidence is that children in particular suffer. Professor Parkinson has challenged the view that parenthood is indissoluble,[1351] but the reality is that many parents lose almost all contact with their children following separation and divorce, with all the adverse social and economic consequences detailed earlier.

The abandonment of reconciliation of the relationship in favour of the conciliation of the divorce occurred without any real evidence about its effectiveness. Subsequent research has indicated that a significant number of couples regret their decision to divorce and subsequently believe it could have been avoided.[1352] The majority of both divorced men and women continue to strongly believe in the institution of marriage.[1353] A study by Professor Linda Waite found that many unhappily married couples who stayed married reported that their marriages improved within five years.[1354] This is consistent with the research that shows that marital happiness is 'U-shaped', that is, while it tends to decline during the middle years of a marriage, it tends to increase again as the relationship endures.[1355] Similarly, an Oklahoma study revealed that of the 34 per cent of respondents who had thought their marriage was in trouble, nine out of ten said they were glad they were still together.[1356] Contrary to the view that divorce follows a long period of conflict and misery, recent research has found that most divorced couples report average happiness and low levels of conflict in their marriages in the years before the divorce.[1357] In parsing the results of another national survey, the sociologist, Norval Glenn, observes that "a great deal of the violence that was cited as a reason for divorce grew out of the pre-divorce escalation of conflict and was not long-term."[1358]

Nor does divorce appear to increase happiness. An Australian study of almost 40,000 people found that even the most unhappily married people were, on average, still more content than the divorced group in the sample.[1359] Similarly, a study of 1,700 Dutch men and women who divorced, revealed that 75 per cent said 'growing apart,' 'having not enough attention for each other,' and 'not being able to talk to each other' as a reason for divorce. Growing apart increased to 79 per cent among the more recently divorced. Only 17 per cent named physical violence as a motive for divorce.[1360] Another study of Dutch divorcees since 1949 found that emotional factors, lack of attention to a spouse and longer working hours had surpassed violence and adultery as major factors in a breakup.[1361] An annual survey on divorce in the UK found in 2011 that 'growing apart/falling out of love' to be the most common reason for marriage breakdown, relegating infidelity to second place for the first time.[1362]

The family scholars, Thomas Bradbury and Benjamin Karney, infer that different divorce rates across the world are unlikely to be the result of differing relationship quality from nation to nation: "It seems more likely that across countries, people differ in their standards for ending unsatisfactory marriages."[1363] The consequence, as the family scholars, Paul Amato and Alan Booth, indicate, is that divorces with the greatest potential to harm children because they involve low conflict marriages "occur in marriages that have the greatest potential for reconciliation."[1364] Yet the process of divorce often leaves couples on a treadmill from which they cannot escape. Frank Furstenberg and Andrew Cherlin, observe that "a third of couples had not openly considered the possibility of the marriage breaking up before it actually happened" and "many couples begin the process of separation undecided about its ultimate outcome."[1365] Given the additional fact that a majority of marriages are ended unilaterally, and one partner was surprised that divorce proceedings had been commenced,[1366] Professor Cherlin's claim that we need to find ways to help couples to 'slow down' is persuasive.[1367]

Professor William Doherty and colleagues reported recently that they could find no studies that asked divorcing people if they would be interested in exploring reconciliation via professional services. Two previous studies had suggested that the reconciliation rate ranged from about 10 per cent[1368] to 16 per cent.[1369] The Doherty study came to a similar conclusion: about one in four individual parents indicated some belief that their marriage could still be saved, and in about one in nine matched couples both partners did.[1370] Overall, in about 45 per cent of couples, one or both partners reported holding hopes for the marriage and a possible interest in reconciliation services. While the majority of couples in the study did not indicate an interest in reconciliation, a sizeable number did. A reduction of even five per cent in the divorce rate would be a significant. Professor Paul Amato considers the impact in the US of a reduction in divorce:

> Increasing the share of adolescents living with two biological parents to the 1970 level ... would mean that 643,264 fewer children would repeat a grade. Increasing the share of adolescents in two-parent families to the 1960 level suggests that nearly three-quarters of a million fewer children would repeat a grade. Similarly, increasing marital stability to its 1980 level would result in nearly half a million fewer children suspended from school, about 200,000 fewer children engaging in delinquency or violence, a quarter of a million fewer children receiving therapy, about a quarter of a million fewer smokers, about 80,000 fewer children thinking about suicide, and about 28,000 fewer children attempting suicide.[1371]

There is a need to rebuild the reconciliation pillar of family law. These services could be provided by agencies other than Family Courts, such as the Australian Family Relationship Centres and family relationship organisations. While it was envisaged that the Family Relationship Centres would fulfil this role, they do not appear to have done so, concentrating more on various conciliation and mediation services. This failure needs to be addressed.

In the US, Professor Doherty, and the former Chief Justice of the Georgia Supreme Court, Leah Ward Sears, have proposed 'Second Chances' legislation to reduce unnecessary divorce.[1372] Their proposal includes establishing a waiting period for divorce of at least a year, with a voluntary early notification letter individuals may use to inform their spouses of their intentions without necessarily filing for divorce; and require pre-filing education for parents of minor children considering divorce, with a module on reconciliation and a module on a non-adversarial approach to divorce.[1373]

The idea of waiting periods and earlier intervention where children are involved has attracted support. Hilary Clinton, echoing the words of her husband's Domestic Policy Adviser, William Galston,[1374] said that "divorce should be a little more difficult when you have children... making it a little harder for people who have children to divorce."[1375] A study of divorce in Europe found that about 80 per cent of the increase in divorce rates between 1970 and 1990 could be attributed to the shortening or elimination of waiting periods.[1376] The Minister for Family in the UK Blair Government, Jane Kennedy, proposed delaying divorce until measures to protect the welfare of children had been appropriately settled.[1377]

Legislative requirements alone are unlikely to succeed unless there are also appropriate and timely services available to couples. Doherty and Sears, noting that 46 states in the US have implemented some form of mandatory parenting classes for divorcing couples with minor children,[1378] recommend that the courses be expanded to include content on reconciliation. Specifically, they propose:

- Questions to help individual spouses reflect on their potential interest in reconciliation.
- Research on reconciliation interests among divorcing couples.
- The potential benefits of avoiding divorce for children and adults.
- Resources to assist with reconciliation.
- Information on when the risk of domestic violence should rule out working on reconciliation at this time.[1379]

They also suggest that states require the completion of a four-hour parent education course *before* either spouse files for divorce. "Whether couples ultimately decide to proceed with their divorce or to reconcile, these classes will help them learn more about positive parenting strategies," add Doherty and Sears.[1380] The State of Minnesota has adopted these ideas to launch a 'Couples on the brink' program funded through a surcharge on the State marriage license fee. At the core of the program is a process of discernment counselling, which involves one to five sessions working with the couple together and each partner separately:

> After establishing, via separate phone calls, where each partner is on the divorce decision and interest in discernment counselling, and doing a domestic violence and coercion screen, the first session begins by exploring three narratives: the divorce narrative (what has gone wrong); the repair narrative (how they have tried to fix things); and a possible reconciliation narrative (six months of all-out effort to see if the marriage can be healthy and good for both of them). The specifics of the reconciliation narrative are usually explored with each partner individually, since their attitudes towards potential reconciliation generally differ greatly from the outset.[1381]

If the couple decides to attempt reconciliation, the discernment counsellor switches from the counselling to beginning a six month course of couples therapy and making referrals to additional community resources as necessary. If the decision is to divorce, the counsellor assists the couple to connect with lawyers and other professionals who will support them in achieving a constructive, collaborative divorce.

These proposals are worthy of further discussion and support. In Australia's case, it would involve a return to the original pillars of the *Family Law Act*, and the provision of the appropriate services. The Court can order parties to discuss the arrangements for children post-separation, but there is also a need to educate individuals about the challenges of re-marriage (or re-partnering), especially when children are involved, given the fact that many people enter into new relationships that are at a higher risk of ending than first marriages. While the Family Court provides some services, they are not comprehensive. The Australian Parliamentary Committee recommended that the Court "use its information sessions, parenting programs and counselling services to educate couples about the complexities involved in remarriage and the value in undertaking further relationships education and training."[1382] These proposals need to be revisited.

Recognising marriage in the taxation system

The taxation system should reinforce and support stable families in their critical task of raising children. It is an important recognition that two economies exist within nations: the market economy, where exchanges take place through money and where competition and efficiency drive decisions; and the home economy, where exchanges take place through altruistic sharing of goods and services among family members. Allan Carlson and David Blankenhorn write:

> It is precisely the home economy – acts of unpaid production ranging from parental child care and nursing of the sick and the elderly, to gardening, home carpentry and food preparation – that is the organising principle of family life and the basis of civil society. These little economies are largely undetected in

our measurement of the gross national product, just as they are
usually beyond the reach of tax collectors. But they are vitally
important. If they thrive, the wellbeing of children and society
as a whole improves.[1383]

Society often downplays the importance of raising the next
generation, or celebrates single life at the expense of intact families.
Reflecting on the pressures on contemporary families, Barbara Dafoe
Whitehead and David Popenoe write:

It is hard enough to rear children in a society that is organised
to support that essential social task. Consider how much
more difficult it becomes when a society is indifferent at best,
and hostile, at worst, to those who are caring for the next
generation.[1384]

As there are differences in the manner in which the taxation
system of individual countries has developed over many decades, it is
impossible to offer a simple universal prescription for the appropriate
recognition of the contribution that married couples make to the
wellbeing of individuals and society. However, there are a series
of principles that should inform discussions about the appropriate
taxation and payments measures. First, fiscal approaches should
recognise the unique contribution of healthy and resilient families
to the wellbeing and welfare of individuals, especially children, and
society. At the very least, the taxation and payments systems should
not penalise married parents.[1385] Optimally, it should affirm and
support them. Secondly, and more generally, government should not
usurp the role of parents and the family, unless dysfunction threatens
the life and welfare of individuals. Government should recognise that
the covenanted relationships of love, loyalty, friendship and trust exist
outside the political sphere but are essential to the health of society.
It should respect other spheres of society and not seek to make them
agencies of government. Consequently, government should be limited,
without forgetting that the protection of the poor and the weak are

pivotal political challenges. Whether a proposal will assist those most in need is a critical factor in any assessment.

In keeping with these principles, families should be able to keep as much of their income as possible while allowing for the provision of those functions that individuals, families and communities cannot deliver, or need assistance in the delivery. The alternative – to raise additional revenues by taxation and to return it via welfare payments – is inefficient. The cost of raising taxation and then redistributing it is very significant. According to one estimate, about half of welfare payments are lost in the churn of money through the system.[1386] Inflation also tends to push people into higher taxation brackets and reduce the real value of the payments over time. Moreover, government programs, once commenced, are rarely wound back or abolished. To the contrary, they grow in size and complexity, adding more costs to their administration.

Governments should also seek to eliminate couple penalties in the welfare system that benefits couples living apart rather than together. The UK government, for example, has taken steps to reduce the couple penalty by allowing an enhanced earnings disregard, which allows couples to keep more of their work income.[1387]

While there are various models to achieve an appropriate balance, one model that has been utilised in some nations is income splitting, as the following discussion indicates.[1388]

Income splitting in OECD countries

Seventeen OECD countries (including Australia, Canada and the United Kingdom) use individual taxation. Only four OECD countries (France, Luxembourg, Portugal and Switzerland) use pure joint taxation of earnings. In the Czech Republic, Iceland, the Netherlands, Norway, Poland and Spain, the individual is used as the tax unit but joint taxation is also possible (only capital income of married couples is taxed jointly in Iceland, while in the Netherlands certain parts of income, such as from owner-occupied housing and from savings, can be taxed jointly). In Germany and Ireland, spouses are normally assessed jointly but they have the option of being separately assessed. In the United States, married couples can file their earnings either separately or jointly.

In every country where joint taxation is allowed, income can be split between partners who do not have children.[1389] This is because the general rationale for taxing on a family basis is one of increasing fairness in the taxation of households with different compositions of income.[1390] In other words, why should two different couples with the same aggregate income pay different amounts of tax? Most countries also provide some form of additional assistance to families with children in the form of tax credits or targeted cash transfers.

Germany and the United States provide good examples of the alternative methods of achieving standard 50/50 income splitting, while France, Belgium and Denmark illustrate what variations from the standard model are possible.

In Germany, married partners are generally assessed jointly, but can elect to be separately assessed. The tax liability of jointly assessed married couples is determined by aggregating the total income of each partner and dividing by two. The progressive tax schedule is then applied to this figure, the result of which is multiplied by two to determine the family's total tax liability.

The United States also allows married partners to be assessed jointly or separately, by having a separate tax rate schedule for joint filers. Tax thresholds for joint filers are double those which apply to individuals for joint income up to $63,700 (as of 2007), providing full 50/50 income splitting. Beyond this point the joint filing thresholds are less than double those for individuals. Consequently, it will be better for some couples where both partners earn significant incomes to file separately. The top tax rate (35 per cent) applies from exactly the same income level ($349,700) whether taxpayers file individually or jointly.

France is an example of a well-developed version of joint taxation, whereby taxpayers can split their income not just with their partner, but also with their children and any dependent adults in the family. The system was instituted just after World War II, the intent being to take into account the consumption capacity of each member of the family and to tax it accordingly.[1391] The tax unit is the "fiscal household" (*foyer fiscal*). This means the total family, including children if they are claimed as dependents. Since 2004, a family includes a French civil union (*pacte civil de solidarité*). Unmarried couples always constitute two separate fiscal households, while married persons can, in exceptional circumstances, file separately provided that they live apart.

Income splitting occurs according to the quotient familial or "family share" system. A family is attributed a total number of family shares as follows: two shares are attributed to a married couple (or *pacte civil de solidarité*), one share for a single person, half a share for the first two dependents, and one share for each additional dependent (or for each dependent of a single parent). Total family income is then divided by total family shares. Tax liability is calculated according to the progressive tax rate schedule for one share and then multiplied by the total number of family shares to determine the family's total tax liability.

The tax benefit available for half shares beyond the first two full shares (or one full share for an individual) is limited to €2,159 per half share. The tax benefit from the share attributable to the first dependent of a single parent is limited to €7,472. The benefit from additional dependents is limited to €4,318 (2 x €2,159). These limits have been set on equity grounds, in recognition that the tax benefit of income splitting is greater for households with higher incomes.

Belgium allows partial income splitting similar to that proposed for New Zealand in the 1982 McCaw Report. Spouses are generally taxed separately, but under the marital quotient system (quotient conjugal), a notional amount of income can be transferred between spouses if one earns no more than 30 percent of the couple's combined income. In this case the amount transferred is limited to 30 per cent of total family income less the secondary earner's actual income. This effectively provides 70/30 income splitting. The amount transferred is limited to a maximum of €8,570 (in 2006).

Another alternative is employed in Denmark, where family members are taxed separately, but some unutilised "personal allowances" can be transferred between spouses. The low tax bracket (at central government level) taxes aggregate personal and net positive capital income under 265,500 Kroner at 5.48 per cent. If a married individual cannot use all of his or her 265,500 Kroner "personal allowance", the remainder can be transferred to the spouse. This cannot be done for personal allowances at higher marginal rates.

This discussion illustrates different approaches to income splitting. They have developed as a response to local, domestic forces and recognition of the critical significance of the family for individuals, communities and nations.

SUMMARY

- ♥ The cultural wars over marriage and family in the 1990s have been overtaken gradually by a growing concern about the negative outcomes associated with the retreat from marriage:
  - ➤ Led by family scholars, these discussions have slowly infused policy considerations.

- ♥ Two principles should underpin family policy:
  - ➤ Public policy should protect and foster marriage and healthy families.
  - ➤ Wherever possible, public policy should support, encourage and utilise family and community organisations, rather than displacing them.

- ♥ Four policy goals are proposed:
  - ➤ Nations should have an explicit marriage and family policy.
  - ➤ They should seek to maintain at least a replacement birth rate.
  - ➤ National policy should proclaim the ideal of marital permanence and affirm marriage as the optimal environment for the raising of children.
  - ➤ The policy should value family stability and reinforce personal and inter-generational responsibility.

12

MODERN MARRIAGE AND THE PURSUIT OF HAPPINESS

Having it all?

A high profile female television news anchor wrote a stinging attack a few years ago on mentors from her mother's generation. Approaching 40, 'childless and angry', Virginia Haussegger criticised those who suggested her generation could have it all:

> For those of us who listened to our feminist foremothers' encouragement; waved the purple scarves at their rallies; read about and applauded [feminist leaders and writers]; for all of us who took all that on board and forged ahead, crashed through barriers and carved out good, successful and even some brilliant careers; we're now left – many of us at least – as premature 'empty nesters'.
>
> We're alone, childless, many of us partnerless, or drifting along in 'permanent temporariness' ... to describe that somewhat ambiguous, uncommitted type of relationship that seems to dominate among childless, professional couples in their 30s and 40s ...[1392]

The article provoked a furious response in some quarters, but it also placed in stark relief the modern dilemma of endeavouring to combine career with marriage and family.[1393] Echoing Haussegger, the American writer, Kate Bolick, reviewed single life as she approached 40:

> We took for granted that we'd spend our 20s finding ourselves,
> whatever that meant, and save marriage for after we'd finished
> graduate school and launched our careers, which of course
> would happen at the magical age of 30.[1394]

All social movements have unforeseen or unintended consequences. Often it is not until the next or even later generations that the full impact of change can be seen clearly. Marriage and family is like this. The social revolution that expressed itself in gender equity, liberal divorce laws, uncommitted cohabitation and related changes has had a downside as well as an upside, especially for children. Those in the vanguard of the change – and those later defending it – can miss or ignore the downside. Perhaps it is because they consider their battle unfinished. Perhaps it is because they fear that their achievements will be undermined or reversed. Perhaps they continue to view the world from the same historical perspective, and are less aware of the changed circumstances of the next generation.

Virginia Haussegger, was accurate when she described being told by a medical practitioner that the chances of becoming pregnant for a woman in her late 30s is significantly reduced – and the success rate for IVF is only about one in five. The Genea IVF service reports, "by age 36 a normal woman's chance of conceiving per month is decreased by half" and is less than five per cent by the time she reaches her early forties.[1395]

Chance of conception per month (Age in years)

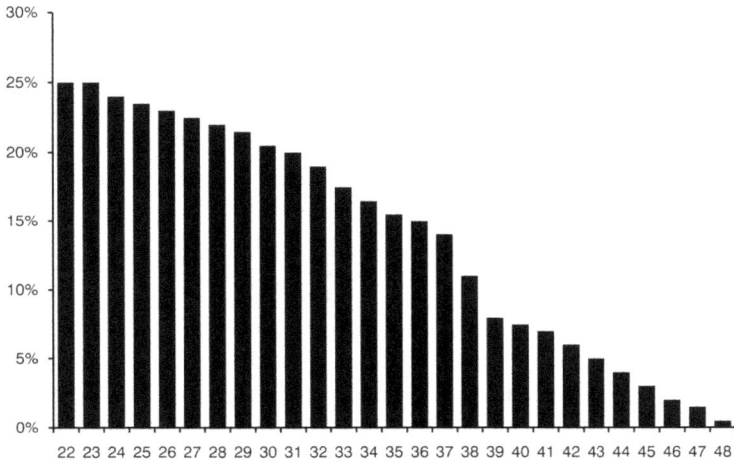

The Service also found that males face a significant decline in fertility from age 35. The decline in fertility led one IVF specialist to advise Australian women to settle for "Mr Not-Quite-Right" or "Mr Not-Too-Bad", saying that women should not be conned into thinking that freezing their eggs offered a "guaranteed family in the fridge"![1396] Even where women have their first child in their 30s, most wish that they had done so a decade earlier,[1397] and a growing number of women in their twenties are seeking sperm donors.[1398]

While Haussegger's attention was focussed on the group of professional women to which she belongs, there are other groups of lower income men and women discussed in chapter nine for whom marriage and family life cannot be considered a given.

Modern dilemmas

At the heart of Virginia Haussegger's critique was a conviction that members of her generation had been duped:

> And none of our mothers thought to warn us that we would need

to stop, take time out and learn to nurture our partnerships and relationships. Or if they did, we were running too fast to hear it.[1399]

Research referred to at the beginning of this book indicated that young people continue to aspire to marriage and family life, and that this view had actually grown over the past few decades.[1400] Equally, younger generations also view marriage as a more voluntary and less obligatory institution. Reflecting on these views, scholars from the Institute for Social Research posed what they described as "the biggest question facing young adults in the future":

> How do people choose among the principles of equality, freedom and family commitment when these highly valued goods become mutually exclusive rather than mutually reinforcing options? How do people take advantage of the freedom to pursue their own individual goals and aspirations while at the same time maintaining family commitments and responsibilities?[1401]

It is a question for individuals and couples throughout the western world. It is as relevant in Australia, Britain, Canada, Europe and elsewhere as it is in America. As the research detailed in this book clearly indicates, the answer that each person decides upon can significantly affect their happiness and the happiness of their children.

The American sociologist, Andrew Cherlin, observes there is unlikely to be a wholesale reversal of the sweeping changes of the past few decades, as the new understandings about relationships and marriage are "deeply rooted in the personal choice-based culture of the current day."[1402] But there is a reappraisal underway, as social scientists examine the mounting evidence of family dysfunction and a new generation of individuals face their own lifetime choices. Many observers also detect the widespread confusion amongst young adults about marriage and family discussed in chapter eight.

There are also signs of a re-appraisal of earlier attitudes. In a reflection on Gen-X and Gen-Y women approaching their 30s, Kerry Rubin and Lia Macko concluded:

> If we didn't start to learn how to integrate our personal, social, and professional lives, we were about five years away from morphing into the angry woman on the other side of a mahogany desk who questions her staff's work ethic after standard 12-hour workdays, before heading home to eat moo shoo pork in her lonely apartment.[1403]

A number of leading professional women have voiced similar sentiments. Facebook's first female board member, Sheryl Sandberg reminded female college graduates that their most important career decision is whether or not they have a life partner and who that partner will be.[1404] Anne-Marie Slaughter, the Princeton professor and Hilary Clinton's former Policy Director, lamented that members of the younger generation had stopped listening, "on the grounds that glibly repeating 'you can have it all' is simply airbrushing reality." Acknowledging her freedoms and opportunities to the previous generation of women, nonetheless she argued that there is a need to reconsider the family-work balance.[1405]

Choices

The notion of 'having it all' is widely promoted in western society. Ever since the long-time editor of *Cosmopolitan* magazine, Helen Gurley Brown, authored a book by that title, the idea that individuals could have whatever they wished for became an increasingly strong cultural belief.[1406] 'Having it all' is a widely held aspiration, but nobody really 'has it all'. Witness the lives of so many celebrities who have fame and fortune, but whose personal lives are a mess. Yet the notion strongly feeds our conscious and subconscious minds, leading us to believe, unwittingly perhaps, that it can be achieved. This is not to imply that individuals should simply put up with their circumstances, especially if difficult, adverse or unjust; rather, it is to recognise that there will always be limitations to the things we can have in life.

Whether we know about it or intend it, some choices limit or rule out others choices. If a person spends limited finances on 'A', then he or she cannot spend them on 'B'. We generally understand this. Hence couples who wed usually understand that the choice of a partner involves the decision not to choose another. The marital scholar, Scott Stanley, observes that "commitment involves making the choice to give up some choices." Some people have difficulties adjusting to their choices, some even endeavour to maintain other options, such as living a single lifestyle whilst married. But most understand that marriage involves taking some other choices off the table.

What is more problematic is an earlier choice that may have a negative effect on later choices, especially if the connection is not apparent. Marriage is one of those later choices that may have already been affected by previous choices. A survey for *Bliss* magazine in the UK, for example, found that 25 year old women had had an average of eight partners, and two-thirds had had a one night stand; but 90 per cent said they would like to get married and expected their marriage to be faithful.[1407] No doubt, a survey of men would reveal similar results. It is not that marriage is being rejected, but people are taking longer to find the right partner. In the meantime, other actions complicate and, in some cases, impinge upon their choices. By moving from one relationship to another, many young people may be undermining their understanding of how to live a committed, faithful relationship.

Wishful thinking

The popular media often promotes the impression that all is fine with marriage and family today. Yet the research increasingly paints a much more opaque picture. This could be due to wishful thinking, and a tendency to sensationalise the novel, at the expense of the run-of-the-mill mainstream. It is compounded by a tendency to prefer the anecdotal over the empirical in our sensate culture.

When a University of Denver study into some of the negative impacts of cohabitation was published, it was featured in many newspapers. One metropolitan paper duly noted the findings, but then quoted a local couple, planning to marry after seven years living together who "dismissed the study's findings". The article featured a large colour photo of the couple.[1408] "There's no negative impact from living together before you get married," they said, directly contradicting the empirical evidence in the accompanying report.

Similarly, a British paper carried the headline "Marriage is overrated and health and happiness benefits for wedded couples are a MYTH" about a scholarly report that actually found the opposite – that when couples are in love, they move closer together and experienced gains in wellbeing, whether cohabiting or married.[1409] Another report asserted that that was no variation in marital stability for couples who had cohabited versus those who had not, ignoring the finding in the research paper upon which the article was based that a significant difference had kicked in by 20 years of marriage.[1410] Yet another writer dismissively asserted, on the basis of anecdotal evidence and one study that examined the expectations of young people, that there were no downsides to cohabitation, ignoring in the process the large body of social science research.[1411]

Apart from the potential to mislead, articles like this continue to disguise some of the challenges of modern relationships. No wonder many individuals have unreal expectations of relationships and often believe they can 'have it all' and that their relationship will be blissfully happy. And no wonder many are greatly disappointed if they discover it is untrue.

Increasing the odds

In a society that highly values informed consent, and has modified the 'buyer beware' rule considerably to protect consumers, it is surprising that many young people are unaware of the factors that enhance or detract from marital success.[1412] According to family scholars, some choices increase the odds of marital success, while others reduce it. Knowing these factors can help individuals avoid poor choices and maximise the chances of marital success.

If a person's goal is successful and happy marriage and the best chance in life for children, family scholars and marital educators have identified optimal pathways. They have also identified a series of beliefs that can detract from marital success. Professor Galena Rhoades and colleagues at the University of Denver write:

> The current research provides many insights for how individuals and couples can be more careful and thoughtful in their relationship behaviour in ways that are protective of themselves and their future aspirations.[1413]

Eight modern myths about marriage and divorce

Myth 1. There is a 50 per cent risk of divorce

It is claimed often that the divorce rate is nearly 50 per cent of all marriages. At best, this is a crude measure; at worst, it is misleading.[1414] Often it is a comparison of the number of weddings and the number of divorces in a year. This is inaccurate, as the divorce figures quoted are a percentage of all marriages, over many years. If it is used as a projection of the number of marriages that are likely to end in divorce before one spouse dies, it is still unreliable, as divorce rates may rise or fall in the future. The divorce rate in a number of countries, including the United States, the United Kingdom, Canada and Australia, has fallen slowly over the past two decades.[1415]

An analysis of 2001 US data revealed that 64.5 per cent of ever married people born from 1940 to 1945 were still in their first marriage; as were 56.6 per cent of those born from 1950 to 1955.[1416] The Australian Bureau of Statistics estimates that two-thirds of the marriages that commenced in 2000-2002 will end through the death of a partner, and only one-third through divorce.[1417] Canadian first marriages have a 67 per cent chance of lasting a lifetime.[1418] Australian data reveals that 82 per cent of people who marry are still married at ages 50-54, and 80 per cent are still married at ages 60-64.[1419]

The risks of divorce vary according to the circumstances of each couple. Here is an analogy. We know that the risk of an automobile accident can be increased or reduced, according to our behaviour. If we speed, drive on bald tyres, or have faulty brakes, the risk increases. If we go through a red light, pass on the crest of a hill, or drive while intoxicated, the risk of an accident is increased. Insurance companies measure these risks. Hence they increase the premium or payment for young drivers who are more likely to engaged in these behaviours because the risk of an accident is higher. Conversely, they reduce the premium for people with a record of safe driving.

The same is true for marriage and divorce. For many people, the risk of divorce is much lower than the often-quoted 50 per cent. Using national health data, American scholars found that various personal and social factors decreased the risk of divorce substantially.[1420]

Risk of divorce

Factors	Percentage decrease in risk of divorce
Making over $50,000 annually (vs. under $25,000)	*- 30%*
Having graduated college (vs. not completed high school)	*- 25%*
Having a baby seven months or more after marriage (vs. before marriage)	*- 24%*
Marrying after 25 years of age (vs. under 18)	*- 24%*
Coming from an intact family of origin (vs. divorced parents)	*- 14%*
Religious affiliation (vs. none)	*- 14%*

Although these risks were calculated for US women only, and there may by some variations from nation to nation, they accord with the multitude of findings previously discussed in this book. Other factors, such as the nature and incidence of cohabitation, may also be relevant. While some of these factors are beyond the control of an individual, such as having divorced parents, others may involve choices. At the very least, knowing about possible risks can help inform personal decisions.

Myth 2. Premarital cohabitation improves the chances of marital success

Despite popular opinion, cohabitation is a problematic pathway to marital success, as the discussion in chapter eight reveals. Three key findings emerge from the social science research. First, cohabitations are short-term relationships which generally do not last more than a few years. Most cohabiting couples separate or marry rather than remain in long-term cohabitation.[1421]

Secondly, it has been insufficiently recognised that the breakdown of a cohabiting relationship is often devastating for at least one of the partners. Professor Christian Smith and his colleagues at Pennsylvania State University observe:

> A significant number of emerging adults appear to have suffered hurtful if not devastating breakups involving romantic partners with whom they thought they were very seriously involved, and often, they assumed, on the road to marriage. Usually, but not always, the most damaged party is the woman involved, not the man.[1422]

The sociologists noted that while young adults want to delay marriage, many of them, particularly women, appear to also seek the intimacy, loyalty and security that only a committed relationship can deliver:

> So in the ill-defined world of romantic relationships that they

inhabit, some emerging adults, who think they have found 'the right' partner who feels the same way that they do, jump in with heart, soul, mind and body. Later, when they are betrayed or dumped, they often discover that their partner did not in fact share their understandings or expectations, or maybe that their partner's feelings or interests gradually changed without them bothering to talk about it.[1423]

If this happens repeatedly, it sets up some young adults "for recurring emotional wallops,"[1424] with possible negative consequences for later relationships. Whereas the grief of a divorce is well recognised,[1425] it is less the case with the ending of cohabiting relationships.

Thirdly, some family scholars suggest that when couples cohabit after having decided to marry, they are at no greater risk of a subsequent marriage breakdown, but couples that drift from cohabitation to marriage have an increased exposure to unhappiness, separation and divorce.[1426] Barbara Dafoe Whitehead observes that because cohabitation conflates courtship and a living together union, there is nothing that ritually marks the entry into a cohabiting relationship:

A couple's decision to cohabit is made privately. Sometimes this decision is thoughtful and purposeful, but very often it is made casually. People can slide into living together, without any serious discussion or mutual understanding as to its meaning, purpose, or likely duration, and without much preparation, other than renting the U-Haul. As a consequence, cohabitation-as-courtship can contribute to confusion, misunderstanding, miscommunication, and faulty assumptions. It is easy for a couple to decide to live together and, at the same time, harbor very different expectations of the relationship.[1427]

Whitehead cautions that cohabitation risks a number of downsides for women in particular, entangling them in a relationship that makes it difficult to see signs that it is not progressing, and even investing time and emotional energy in a stagnating union. Where there are different levels of commitment,[1428] the less committed partner can have more power in the relationships, leaving the other uncertain and constantly seeking signs of reassurance.[1429]

These findings have led some family scholars to advise couples to consider carefully their decision to cohabit. After reviewing the social science research, David Popenoe and Barbara Dafoe Whitehead suggested four principles for couples whose aspiration is a stable, fulfilling, life-long marriage: Consider not living together at all before marriage; Do not make a habit of cohabiting; Limit cohabiting to the shortest possible period of time; and Do not cohabit if children are involved.[1430] Furthermore, Scott Stanley has identified uncommitted cohabitation entered into prior to a decision to marry as problematic for the success of the relationship. In their recent study of *Premarital sex in America*, Mark Regnerus and Jeremy Uecker warn of the downsides of cohabitation, especially for women.[1431]

Marriage and family educators and therapists make similar observations. Reflecting on the fact that seeming to "tell people what to do" invites a rebuff, Rev. Tony Kerin offers a further reason why, in his experience as a marriage educator, cohabitation is complicated for many couples. "Marriages are not," he says "and never have been *prêt-a-porter*. It takes a long time to marry your life to that of your partner." Foreshadowing Scott Stanley's later observations about 'sliding into marriage', Kerin also warns about "commitment creep":

> A couple who commence to cohabit before they are ready for long term commitment often find themselves locked in by the inertia of their circumstances. A relationship that, had they not lived together, would have run its course and dissipated, is given unwarranted encouragement because it takes so much more effort to move out and find new lodgings than to put up with the lacklustre relationship of domestic drudgery which has crept up on them. They are subconsciously more committed to accepting things the way they are than they had deliberately chosen

to be. Eventually the breakup is all the more painful for the dissatisfaction must now overcome this unchosen by creeping commitment.[1432]

Couples are unlikely to know the outcome when they begin to cohabit or necessarily recognise the signs of problems during the course of it. This is why marriage educators have responded to the challenging nature of cohabitation by encouraging individuals to reflect on the decisions they are making, using workshops, inventories and questionnaires.[1433] Professor Sotirios Sarantakos concludes that individuals:

> Need to know more about the advantages and limitations of the alternative lifestyle so commonly used in our community. They need to learn what makes a relationship strong, happy and lasting, and what to expect from the unit they establish. They need to know more about marriage; and they need to know more about cohabitation. For this reason, the role of marriage education and of pre-marital counselling is most significant and the need for constant support in this area is beyond contention.[1434]

The marital researchers, Scott Stanley and colleagues, urge partners to:

> Talk candidly about the meaning of cohabitation, commitment levels (eg, where does each partner see the relationship headed?), and potential constraints to stay together that they might experience during cohabitation.[1435]

Because of the possible ambiguity around the meaning of cohabitation (in the absence of clarity about mutual commitment levels by way of marriage or engagement), they add, there are likely many individuals who discover later rather than sooner that cohabiting did not mean the same thing for their partners as for them.[1436] As discussed in chapter eight, individuals may find it more difficult to break-off relationships because of constraints, even if the partner or the relationship is unsatisfactory. It is for this reason that Professor

Galena Rhoades and her colleagues suggest that it is important to help individuals realise that constraints will likely build up over time and that constraints during cohabitation, regardless of the level of dedication, may make it seem less likely that the relationship will end. Noting that amongst couples who believe in marriage, men are less dedicated than their partners, the scholars suggest because women are more committed, they may be at a disadvantage in terms of relational power:

> Particularly if they are unaware of the difference in commitment, women may wind up making more sacrifices for their relationships than their partners, and these unrequited sacrifices could be detrimental if the relationship ends.[1437]

The educator, Mark Gungor, is more direct about the (generally) different approaches of men and women:

> Women are 'givers' by nature. They love to give; they define themselves by giving. Put a bunch of women together and they'll compliment each other uncontrollably: 'I love your outfit!' 'That colour looks great on you!' Contrariwise, men are takers by nature. They love to take; they define themselves by how much they can 'get.' Put a bunch of guys together and they insult each other: 'Hey ugly!' 'Look who's saying I'm ugly!'[1438]

Gungor is equally direct in his advice to women: "If you want something from a man, you have to learn to ask – to take it."[1439]

The ambiguity about sacrifice and commitment possibly reflects confusion about life cycle transitions. In *Becoming Married*, Herbert Anderson and Robert Fite identify a series of family tasks associated with transitions in the life cycle, such as leaving home, the wedding, the birth of the first child, the last child leaving home, and the death of a spouse.[1440] Anderson and Fite assert that recognition of these life cycle transitions is significant:

> Leaving home is a necessary precondition for the process of

becoming married. Like leaving home, the process of becoming married takes time. It begins before the wedding but is not likely to be completed until much later, when both partners in a marriage discover that the emotional bond between them is deep and sure.[1441]

In this context, the wedding ceremony is the transitional event that publicly inaugurates a new family task of becoming married. But the physical leaving of home does not necessarily mean that emotional separation has occurred. This may partly explain the increasing social science evidence about cohabitation and marital satisfaction. For many couples there may have been a partial leaving and partial cleaving together:

> Nonmarital living together shifts the meaning of the wedding ... People after living together may overlook the work of adjusting to marital roles, which can only be done after the couple's private bond has been granted public status and they have become declared to be husband and wife ... There is no guarantee that couples living together have indeed finished the leaving home agendas. Their experience of living together may have intentionally ignored the marital patterns of either family of origin because they were determined to do it differently from their parents. Moreover, while it is possible that cohabiting couples have developed some skills in relating, marriage generally is more demanding and entails more responsibility and more work than living together.[1442]

While acknowledging that much more needs to be understood about the association between cohabitation and marital risk, a number of family scholars and marital researchers believe enough is now known to incorporate into couple therapy and relationship education programs.[1443] These issues are being addressed by marriage educators. In a series of articles and workshops at conferences, marriage educators have been exploring an appropriate response to the findings of the social science research.[1444] In *Marriage and the Family*, the author of the PREPARE premarital inventory, David Olson, outlines a checklist that can be used with cohabiting couples.[1445] Through this questionnaire, Olson poses issues for cohabiting couples to address when considering their relationship and marriage. A special section for cohabiting couples has also been incorporated into the Facilitating Open Couple Communication, Understanding & Study [FOCCUS] pre-marital inventory.

Similarly, psychologists at the University of Denver have identified a series of questions that couples considering cohabitation or already cohabiting might discuss when contemplating the future of their relationship:[1446]

1. What does/did living together mean to you and mean for the future of your relationship?
2. How did the two of you begin living together? Was it planned, talked about, or something that just sort of happened?
3. Where do you see this relationship going in the future? What sort of timeline do you expect?
4. Do you believe that one of you is more committed than the other? What indicates to you that there is a difference? How will this affect how your future plays out together?
5. How have the two of you made important decisions together in the past?

Acknowledging that both selection and experience effects may be present in a cohabiting couple's relationship,[1447] Australian educators also devised a simple questionnaire that reflects both the research and their experiences of working with many people.[1448] It is appended.

Myth 3. It is preferable to marry later

Many social scientists have observed that most young adults wish to marry, 'but not just yet.' This attitude is reflected in the trends summarised earlier in this book. The median age of marriage has increased significantly over the past few decades throughout the West. A number of reasons have been suggested for the delay, including the fact that education now takes longer for many young adults and the higher costs of establishing a home; a desire to experience life before 'settling down'; as well as the desire to be socially, economically and emotionally ready for a lifelong commitment. Family scholars also point to the fear of divorce, and the knowledge that marrying at a young age is associated with higher levels of marital breakdown.[1449] Australian scholars have noted also both internal and external constraints in finding a suitable partner.

According to the *Young Adults Survey*, nearly three-quarters of men and women who were not in any sort of relationship said that finding a suitable partner was difficult. The internal constraints included "being choosy" and "being cautious." External constraints included time pressures, scarcity of meeting places, remoteness, changing social attitudes, and already having young children.[1450] Paradoxically, time spent doing the things which are perceived to be important before settling down, such as a career, travel, and buying a house, may also diminish the chances of later finding a suitable partner in a tight marriage market.

Marrying very young predicts both divorce[1451] and marital problems.[1452] Analysis by Professor Paul Amato and colleagues of a sample of national US data revealed that there was increased divorce proneness where teens wed.[1453] The sociologists also found that divorce proneness reduced as the age of marriage increased. This factor has spawned a belief that couples who marry at an older age are more mature and therefore more likely to succeed at marriage.[1454] However, recent research suggests there is a significant difference between marrying as a teenager versus marrying in the early twenties.[1455]

The studies raise doubts whether the benefits of delaying marriage extend beyond the mid-twenties. Recent research has found, that all things being equal, marriages commencing between the ages of 22 and 25 show the greatest promise of reporting the highest quality and remaining intact while unions entered into at later ages "fare very well in terms of survival but rather poorly in quality." The scholars conclude, "little or nothing in the way of marital success is likely to be gained by deliberately delaying marriage beyond the mid-twenties."[1456] A recent study of mental health amongst young adults lends support. Using a sample of almost 12,000 people aged 18 to 28, the sociologist, Jeremy Uecker, found that marriage in young adulthood (as distinct from teenage years) was not detrimental to mental health:

> Being in any sort of relationship is good for psychological distress, being marriage or engaged to be married curbs drunkenness, and married young adults, especially those who marry at ages 22 to 26, are more satisfied with their lives.[1457]

Professor Uecker concluded that mental health benefits of marriage are apparent among young adults who have married at a relatively early age. Another national survey of marriage revealed that couples who married between ages 20 and 27 fared better on the *Marital Success Index* than couples who married at younger or older ages.[1458]

This is not to say that marrying late causes lower marital success. Professor Norval Glenn points out that late marriers could tend to have characteristics that cause them both to marry late and to have relatively poor marriages when they do wed. Such characteristics might include unrealistically high standards for a spouse and poor social skills:

> If marrying late does tend to cause poor marital outcomes, it might be the relatively old age itself that has the effect or it might be marrying later than most other people near one's age. Living alone for many years may tend to make persons 'set in their ways' and thus impede their adjustment to marriage, or having a succession of low-commitment relationships, with or without cohabitation, may make it harder for persons to commit to marriage. Marrying later than most of one's age mates gives a person a more limited selection of potential spouses to chose from and may lessen the chances of a good marital match.[1459]

Delayed marriage can have other consequences for couples wishing to have children, including decreasing fertility,[1460] increased low birth weights and preterm delivery.[1461]

Rev. Tony Kerin observes that inertia is often a factor in delayed marriage:

> It is far easier to remain in an unsatisfactory relationship than to go to the trouble of changing one's lifestyle or living arrangements. Where a couple live together this is most pronounced. When faced with insurmountable differences, the sheer dread of having to make alternative living arrangements, move furniture, seek new accommodation and reorganise one's life often sees couples persist in the misery as the lesser of two difficulties.[1462]

Noting that a long courtship by couples who meet in their teens is different to a long courtship by couples meeting in their mid to late twenties, Kerin writes that their failure to move toward marriage may be "a reasoned decision based on their lack of preparedness to commit." In such cases, he counsels the need to differentiate between loyalty and commitment, and encourages marriage educators to help couples, where appropriate, with the painful process of 'breaking up'.

This is not to suggest that everyone should marry in their mid-twenties, before they are ready, in the face of serious doubts,[1463] under duress, or at all.[1464] Rather, it is to reflect the observation of Professor Mark Regernus:

> It's to remind emerging adults who wish eventually to marry that there is a real marriage market out there and that sexual economics affects it, too. All talk of commitment-phobia men, or angst about settling for men who are "good enough", is linked to [social and demographic trends] ... [W]e simply wish to encourage men and women who've met someone who is "marriage material" to think twice before rejecting the notion that they're just not ready for it. Life plans seldom develop exactly as adults anticipate and on the schedule they wish for.[1465]

Myth 4. Marriage is private and natural – there is nothing to learn

"Whatever happened to old fashioned love, the kind that would last through the years", asked a correspondent to a metropolitan newspaper.[1466] In questioning the value of marriage education, he repeated a widely-held notion. Often people think that a relationship is their private business, as if outside influences – whether their own families or the broader society – have no impact or affect upon them. Equally, people often regard relating with another as 'natural' – something we all automatically know how to do.[1467]

The idea is not new. In the famous opening lines of *Anna Karenina*, Tolstoy writes: "All happy families resemble one another; each unhappy family is unhappy in its own way."[1468] The UCLA psychologists, Thomas Bradbury and Benjamin Karney, suggest that Tolstoy was mistaken: People's experiences of intimate relationships vary greatly, according not only to what happens, but importantly the beliefs, values and interpretations that individuals bring to their relationships.[1469] These attitudes may be compounded by a confusion between cohabitation and marriage. Professor Linda Waite writes that people often talk as if marriage were a private, personal relationship:

> But when two people live together for their own strictly private reasons, and carve out their own strictly, private bargain about the relationship, we call that relationship not marriage but 'cohabitation'.[1470]

Marital educators have identified a series of other beliefs that are commonly-held, but misleading:

- If you're in love, a relationship will be good spontaneously and will not require work.
- A relationship, especially marriage, stays the same.
- The less we know about our partner, the more 'romantic' our relationship will be.

- In a significant relationship, emotions always must be intense and positive.
- In marriage, there must be constant sexual attraction.
- My partner must 'complete' me, that is, make up for my weaknesses.
- We will live happily forever.
- Love means never having to say you're sorry.
- My spouse should always understand me.
- If my partner doesn't meet my needs, I'll find someone else.[1471]

Other myths identified by educators include:

- Love is enough.
- There is nothing to learn.
- If you love me, you'll ...
- My mate will (or will not) change.
- I'll do my half.[1472]

A consequence of these beliefs is a reluctance to seek advice. The UK Centre for Social Justice noted:

> Anecdotal evidence we received suggested that most people struggle with the concept of seeking advice on how to manage relationships at home, considering it is only for those who have problems. Seventy-five per cent of all relationship support involves the treatment of problems, such as counselling. . . rather than their prevention.[1473]

There is evidence that preventive programs suffer by association with therapy and counselling, reinforcing the two powerful social taboos in the field of marriage, namely that relationships are entirely private and natural:[1474]

> The notion that marriage is a private relationship and thereby not able to be spoken about publicly or openly, except in a very general sense, does not help couples to learn from and

be supported by other couples. This phenomenon also leads couples experiencing difficulties in their relationships to delay seeking help.

The second myth is the idea of naturism, that is, being married is a natural state, and therefore we know automatically and innately how to 'do it'. No education or enhancement is required if it comes naturally.[1475]

Conversely, as a result of participating in a marriage and relationship education program, couples are more likely to seek professional help if problems arise in their marriage.[1476] A guide to programs and resources is contained in the appendix.

Myth 5. Marital satisfaction necessarily declines over time

There is a widespread belief about a 'honeymoon-is-over' effect in all marriages. This belief was reinforced by a number of studies in the 1990s that indicated a decline in marital satisfaction in the early years of a marriage. One study found that both husbands and wives reported a decline in satisfaction and love over the first two-and-a-half years of their wedded life.[1477] In subsequent research, Professor Lawrence Kurdek concluded that marital quality – measured as attractions to marriage – declines steadily over the first four years of marriage. He also found that depressive symptoms, rather than levels of depression at the start of the marriage, were important for understanding change in marital quality.[1478] As a significant proportion of divorces occur in the early years of marriage, the findings contributed to the popular belief about the honeymoon effect.

More recent research has challenged the premise that marital satisfaction necessarily declines over time. These studies show that marital satisfaction remains highly stable for many couples. In a four-year study of newlyweds,[1479] and a 20-year study of continuously married spouses,[1480] more than two-thirds of the couples studied were found to have highly stable marital satisfaction. The psychologists,

Thomas Bradbury and Justin Lavner, observe: "These findings cast doubt on the inevitability of declines in satisfaction ...".

Myth 6. Conflict destroys marriage

All relationships involve conflict. The renowned marital researcher, John Gottman, observes that all marital conflicts, ranging from mundane annoyances to all-out wars fall into one of two categories, "either they can be resolved, or they are perpetual, which means they will be part of your lives forever, in some form or another."[1481] Professor Gottman discovered the 69 per cent of marital conflicts were of the second type. Despite the perpetual nature of the disagreements, couples who understood that problems were an inevitable part of a relationship were able to cope with them, avoid situations which worsen them, and develop strategies and routines which help to deal with them. It was when couples failed to cope with the inevitable conflicts, and fell into a relationship gridlock, that the pattern endangered the marriage.

Gottman, a professor of psychology at the University of Washington, Seattle, has been studying why marriages succeed or fail for three decades. Trained as a mathematician and research psychologist, he decided to take a scientific approach to the issue. In his Seattle laboratory, he compiled, microsecond by microsecond, behavioural and physiological changes as couples talked to another: "They have examined their facial expressions, monitored how they gadget, and how they gesture. Even breathing patterns and heart rates of couples have been followed as they converse in the laboratory."[1482]

In one study, Gottman and his associates were able to foretell with an astonishing 94 per cent accuracy which couples were headed for divorce three years later, based solely on their views of their marital history and their current perceptions:

> Gathering such information has allowed us to identify the specific processes that lead to the dissolution of a marriage and those that weld it more firmly together.[1483]

Professor Gottman doesn't imply that his findings are foolproof, nor that every couple who experiences certain problems is invariably headed for divorce:

> But being aware that specific patterns and interactions in your marriage are part of a process that leads to divorce – and knowing how to reverse those patterns – may help you back away from that slippery slope.[1484]

According to Gottman, there are three different styles of problem solving into which healthy marriages tend to settle:

> In a validating marriage couples compromise often and calmly work out their problems to mutual satisfaction as they arise. In a conflict-avoiding marriage couples agree to disagree, rarely confronting their differences head-on. And finally, in a volatile marriage, conflict erupts often, resulting in passionate conflicts.[1485]

Gottman rejects the idea that a low level of conflict necessarily equates with marital happiness, and observes that all three styles are equally stable and bode equally well for the marriage's future. The crucial determinant, according to Gottman, is the balance between positive and negative interactions in a relationship: whether the good moments of mutual pleasure, passion, humour, support, kindness and generosity outweigh the bad moments of complaint, criticism, anger, disgust, contempt, defensiveness and coldness. According to Gottman's research, healthy marriages have a ratio of positive moments to negative moments of 5:1. Good moments can be simple: a hug, a smile, a walk in the park that counterbalance the irritants and niggles that exist in all relationships.[1486] In his most recent work, Gottman demonstrates that by building trust through emotional attunement, couples can enhance their relationships.[1487]

This is consistent with other research, including Scott Stanley's observations about commitment which were discussed in chapter eight. Similarly, the psychologist, Benjamin Karney, notes that spouses who are able to make charitable explanations of their partner's disappointing or irritating behaviours can sever the link between specific negative perceptions and the global evaluation of the marriage, leaving the global evaluations more resilient:

> Couples who are able to acknowledge their partner's faults while maintaining positive views of their marriage overall have more stable satisfaction over time and they are far less likely to divorce in the early years of marriage.[1488]

This is consistent with other research which indicates the loss of love and affection early in the marriage as a precursor to divorce.[1489]

Conversely, Gottman posits that certain negative behaviours damage a relationship. Describing these behaviours as the 'Four Horsemen of the Apocalypse', these disastrous ways of interacting – in order of least to most dangerous – are criticism, contempt, defensiveness, and stonewalling:

> What makes the four horsemen so deadly to a marriage is not so much their unpleasantness but the intensive way they interfere with a couple's communication. They create a continuing cycle of discord and negativity that's hard to break through if you don't understand what is happening.[1490]

Professor Gottman has also been vitally interested in strategies to invigorate marriages. His strategies include calming down, soothing talk and speaking non-defensively, humour and validating a partner.[1491]

Other research indicates that certain topics are more causes of conflict than others, ranging from the least frequent – annoying personality styles and traits, friends, intimacy and sex, commitment and expectations for the relationship, and relatives – through the moderately frequent – annoying habits, money and spending, demands relating to work and jobs, leisure and recreation, communicating and listening, and chores – to the most frequent – children.[1492] While reiterating that abusive relationships are unacceptable, these research findings suggest that many couples can improve their marital relations by learning more about the role of conflict in their relationships.

Myth 7. A 'good divorce' is beneficial for adults and children

The idea of a 'good divorce' with minimal distress for the parties, including the children of the marriage, is common.[1493] According to this belief, popularised by Constance Ahrons' 1994 book, *The good divorce*, "adults and children emerge as least as emotionally well as they were before the divorce."[1494] Despite the fact that relationship dysfunction drove the parents apart, the former spouses are sufficiently cooperative according to this thesis "to permit the bonds of kinship – with and through their children – to continue."[1495]

Studies indicate that the separated and divorced are overall less happy than the married: Even the most unhappily married people in a large Australian survey were, on average, still more content than the divorced. According to one of the researchers, Mariah Evans, this is partly because "people in unhappy marriages underestimate the extent to which divorce will disrupt many, many aspects of their lives."[1496] This is borne out by surveys of life satisfaction which reveal much lower levels for the divorced and separated.[1497]

As the many studies outlined in chapter three attest, separation and divorce can have a significant, long-term impact on children.[1498] US Pediatricians highlighted the "long searing experience" on children in a special issue of *Pediatrics*,[1499] and recommended that in addition to providing appropriate treatment, measures aimed at "preserving the intact family where appropriate" should be pursued.

Family relationships after divorce are significant also to the wellbeing of children. Likewise, divorce involving parents in low conflict has been shown to have adverse consequences for them, compared to children from high conflict marriages.[1500] Despite the attractiveness of the belief in a 'good divorce', recent research questions the idea that "positive postdivorce family relationships have substantial benefits for children."[1501] This is apart from the fact that a significant minority of children lose (almost) all contact with one parent following divorce. It has been estimated that one in five children lose all contact with a parent post-divorce in the UK.[1502] A US study found that 36 per cent of post-divorce children were being raised in single-parenting circumstances where "non-resident parents rarely saw their children, had little or no influence on their children's lives, and had little or no communication with the resident parent."[1503] Another study found that half of all children had not seen their father in the past year.[1504] Australian data reveals that one-third of children never stayed with their father post-separation, with 11 per cent never seeing their father and 23 per cent seeing their father only during the daytime.[1505]

Using a national survey and an analysis that grouped post-divorce children into clusters of cooperative parenting (the 'good divorce'), parallel parenting[1506] and single parenting, US sociologists compared the outcome for the three groups. Less than one-third (29 per cent) of the children comprised the 'good divorce' group. Specifically:

> Youth in the good divorce cluster exhibited fewer behaviour problems (as reported by resident parents) and rated their relationships with fathers more positive than did youth in the other two parenting clusters. Adolescents in the good divorce cluster, however, were no better off than were adolescents in the single parenting cluster with respect to self-esteem, school grades, liking school, substance abuse, or life satisfaction. Correspondingly, young adults in the good divorce cluster were no better off than were young adults in the single parenting cluster with respect to substance abuse, early sexual activity, number of sexual partners, cohabiting or marrying as a teenager, and closeness to mothers.[1507]

The researchers conclude that a good divorce is not a panacea for improving children's well-being in post-divorce families:

> Not all children with divorced parents experience long-term problems. But people's willingness to accept the good divorce hypothesis is reason for concern if some parents are lulled into believing that their children are adequately protected from all the potential risks of union disruption.[1508]

The New Zealand family scholar, Jan Pryor, notes although divorce itself is at times preferable to sustaining a toxic marriage, "a 'good divorce' as defined does not ensure optimal outcomes for children."[1509]

Nor does parallel parenting, usually associated with non-resident contact every other weekend, necessarily benefit children. The family scholars, Lisa Laumann-Billings and Robert E Emery, found this typical pattern was the least beneficial in young adulthood, being associated with higher levels of distress than frequent or no contact.[1510] Even for the parents, there are often stark contrasts in how they view their continuing relationship, leading one Australian family scholar to refer to 'his' and 'hers' experiences of separation.[1511]

These findings reflect other research about the diminished parent-child relationship following separation and divorce. Stressed parents face major challenges, often resulting in less caring and more overprotective parenting.[1512] Children can lose trust and feel more distant from parents.[1513] Parental-child relations tend to worsen post divorce according to a series of studies,[1514] even compared to relations in intact, but unhappy families.[1515]

Myth 8. Fathers are dispensable

Fathers are important. Consider the intense bitterness the feminist author, Germaine Greer, expressed towards her father in *Daddy, We Hardly Knew You*. Cut by her father's abandonment of her to go to war, her anguish is intensified by his subsequent failure to want to know her and show affection:

Some children can remember their fathers reciting Urdu poetry or Marlowe, or teaching them to recognise birds or butterflies, to spot trains, to play chess or cricket. But you Daddy dear? Not a curve-ball, not a cover drive, not a card trick. Not a maxim. Not a saw, adage or proverb. Except, "you're big enough and ugly enough to take care of yourself."

Dr Moira Eastman asks in *The Magical Power of Family*, can anyone insist that Greer's choice of theme for her life's work is unrelated to her family experience, especially disillusion with her father? Families have survived and blossomed despite fathers being away at war or work – without the consequences that Greer ascribes to her situation. Nonetheless, mothers and fathers are critical for the welfare of children. In his best-selling book, *The Road Less Travelled*, M Scott Peck observed that children are not deceived by "hollow words" and "mechanical actions". They know by the quantity and quality of time given to them how they are valued. They want "to believe that they are loved but unconsciously they know that their parents' words do not match up to their deeds."[1516]

The view that fathers are superfluous should be, as the Council on Families in America claimed, a major social concern for our society:

First, fathers are vitally important to the task of childrearing. Certainly, we have never met the child who did not say that she or he wanted to be raised by both a father and a mother. And children know whereof they speak. The importance of fathers to childrearing is strongly supported by social science research.

Second, it is extremely important to the larger society that men remain involved in family life. For men, married fatherhood is a civilising force of no mean proportions. Conversely, having a large number of men disconnected from the patterns and satisfactions of family life – and thus much more prone to unhappiness, deviance and crime – has always, and properly, been one of society's worst fears. In too many of our nation's communities today, this fear is becoming a reality.[1517]

As the many studies summarised in chapter three illustrate, a stable, healthy marriage between a husband and wife is optimal for child well-being. Other studies reveal that fathers play an important role in the lives of their children.[1518] In a study of 2,700 adolescents, Columbia University scholar, Marcia L Carlson, found that the higher the level of father involvement, the lower the level of behavioural problems, with adolescents without a father having the highest problem scores. Recent Australian research concluded "adolescent boys engage in more delinquent behaviour if there is no father figure in their lives."[1519] Moreover, "father involvement is more beneficial when the father in coresident" than when the father is living apart from the child.[1520] Another study revealed that teen daughters of married parents are more likely to retain their virginity if they enjoy a close relationship with their fathers.[1521]

After reviewing 16 long-term studies, child health clinicians from Sweden and Australia concluded that the engagement of a father with his children results in improved cognitive skills, fewer behavioural problems among school-age children, less delinquency among teenage boys and fewer psychological problems in young women.[1522] Other research indicates that fathers' impact on their children's behaviour may begin as early as infancy,[1523] and can have a detrimental impact on educational outcomes.[1524] Boys who feel close to their fathers also have better attitudes about intimacy and the prospects for their own married lives than boys who do not.[1525]

After analysing data from three waves of the *National Survey of Children*, American researchers found that fathers matter:

> The level of fathers' involvement influences their children's economic and educational achievement ... Highly involved fathers promote their children's attainment, whereas high involvement and increasing closeness between fathers and adolescents protect adolescents from engaging in delinquent behaviour and experiencing emotional distress ...[1526]

Scholars have also observed that father-infant bonding is not simply a replica of other-infant bonding – that fathers and mothers bring different qualities to the parental relationship.[1527] Child Trends researcher, Suzanne Le Menestrel, observes:

> Warmth, closeness and nurturance are important aspects of a healthy parent-child relationship regardless of whether the parent is a mother or father. But research also suggests that fathers contribute to their children's healthy development in ways that are unique from mothers. For example, in one study of young children's cognitive development, fathers promoted their child's intellectual development and social competence through play, whereas mothers promoted these skills through verbal expressions and teaching activities.[1528]

After analysing a series of international studies, Professor Ronald Rohner concluded that "fatherly love is critical to a person's development."[1529] When fathers are involved, "their children learn more, perform better at school, and exhibit healthier behaviour."[1530] Similarly, "higher levels of father involvement in activities with their children, such as eating meals together, going on outings, and helping with homework, are associated with fewer behavioural problems, higher levels of sociability, and a high level of school performance among children and adolescents.[1531] Even where fathers do not share a home with their children, "their active involvement can have a lasting and positive impact."[1532]

Recent research through the Princeton *Fragile Families and Child Wellbeing Study* underlines the importance of both mothers and fathers. The sociologist, Sara McLanahan, emphasises the need for emotional support between couples: "The better the couple gets along, the better it is for the child."[1533]

What makes marriage work?

David and Vera Mace, pioneering marital educators, stressed three critical components of a successful marriage:

> A commitment to growth, sincerely entered into by husband and wife together; an effective communication system and the necessary skills to use it; and the ability to accept marital conflict and to resolve it creatively.[1534]

Commitment and investment in the relationship have also been identified by scholars and educators,[1535] as has passion and intimacy,[1536] strong feelings of fondness,[1537] and generosity towards a spouse. In her survey of the literature, Robyn Parker notes a recurring theme:

> Couples in enduring marriages report the same sorts of troubles and difficulties as other couples and point out aspects of their own marriages that are less than ideal. In a broad sense, the distinguishing feature of these relationships is the sense of primacy and 'couple-ness': that both spouses are committed to nurturing and sustaining the marriage, and both have the goodwill necessary to learn and engage in the behaviours that keep alive the emotional connection that brought them together in the first place.[1538]

Other observers list similar attributes. The Canadian Olympian and sports psychologist, Nicole Forrester, wrote that men want attraction, independence, fun, sanity and support from a woman.[1539] According to Forrester, the six things women look for in a man are: chivalry, emotional availability, attention to details, genuine and unexpected compliments, honesty and confidence.[1540]

The family scholar, E Mavis Hetherington, observed different types of marriages in her three-decade long study of divorce. Two types – the cohesive marriage in which couples are able to balance togetherness and separateness; and the traditional marriage with the male breadwinner/female homemaker – were found to be the most stable, while three other types – the pursuer-distancer marriage, where most often the women pursues the man who withdraws to avoid confrontation; the disengaged marriage, where two individuals avoid or fear intimacy; and the operatic marriage, which involves emotional highs and lows – involve higher risks of divorce.[1541]

Noting the almost uniform happiness and optimism of newlyweds, and the power of a public commitment, Benjamin Karney, wonders why so many marriages end in separation and divorce. He suggests that it can be difficult to maintain the initial positive feelings "because some disappointments are inevitable in any long-term committed relationship, because some spouses lack the ability to respond to those disappointments effectively, and because even spouses who have the ability may encounter stressful circumstances that prevent them from exercising their abilities when they are most needed."[1542]

There is also research to suggest that the seeds of marital dissatisfaction and breakdown can be found in the courtship days. In his 14 year study of couples, University of Texas psychologist, Ted Huston, observed that the spouses who established stable, happy unions moved through courtship with few hitches and little drama: "The spouses had sweet dispositions, similar interests, and compatible ideas about marital roles. As newlyweds, they were much in love, quite affectionate, and lived together largely in harmony. The look and feel of their marriages held up over time, creating durable, satisfying bonds."[1543] These findings suggest relationship problems during courtship, whether arising from personality differences or compatibility, often presage later marital difficulties.

While acknowledging that adaptive processes, such as teaching skills can be helpful, Professor Karney suggests the public policies also need to support marriages and family life, citing the example of the fall in the divorce rate as a consequence of the Norwegian policy to offer parents financial incentives if they stayed at home to care for their children.[1544]

Professor Karney implies that there is no simple solution, but a combination of information, education, skills and supportive public policies that offer the best hope of halting the retreat from marriage and the restoration of binding intimate relationships. In their encyclopaedic book, *Intimate relationships*, Karney and Thomas Bradbury summarise the practical application of their research in the form of advice about forming and sustaining a healthy, happy and lasting relationship.[1545]

- Relationships can provide us with tremendous benefits, including better mental and physical health. If you want to reap these benefits, you have to **make your relationship a priority** in your life. Few of us are lucky enough to have great relationships without putting forth some real effort, over a sustained period of time.

- Making your relationship a priority means **doing things to make your partner's life better and happier on a regular basis.** Find ways to do this. Making your relationship a priority also means taking active steps to create new experiences and to reflect on the positive experiences that you or your partner has had recently.

- Western models of love and intimacy emphasize intense passion, which can often fade as time passes. This is natural, but you need to create experiences in your relationship to replace it. If you really care about your partner, **work on building a better relationship for the future** instead of lamenting what you no longer have. Good relationships are less like surfing, in which the wave crashes and the ride is over, and more like mountain climbing. Keep moving forward and try to appreciate the new experiences you are creating.

- Never forget that **relationships thrive when partners create security for one another** and eliminate any sense of threat between them. We are driven by our biology to be in relationships, and we are inclined to stay in relationships when we feel understood, validated, and cared for. Expressions of gratitude, kindness, affection, and humour go far in keeping relationships strong. Being hostile, aggressive, selfish, and insensitive are among the very best ways to convince your partner that he or she is not understood, validated, or cared for.

- You cannot understand, validate, or care for your partner very well if you do not spend much time together, in person or otherwise. *Intimate partners benefit from knowing what is going on in one another's lives.* Some of this will involve knowing simply how your partner spent his or her day, and some of this will involve trying to figure out who your partner really is. Even your partner may not know this about himself or herself.

- Whether we realize it or not, we are constantly making choices about what to say and how to behave toward our partner. We and we alone are responsible for the words that come out of our mouth and for the tone that they come out with. Make good choices. *Find ways to open rather than close lines of communication.* Be polite. Apologize when you make a mistake.

- One of the reasons you want to invest in your relationship is that you want it to be healthy and strong in case bad things happen. After all, you do not have complete control over the forces that affect your relationship, and neither does your partner. One of you will get very sick. Somebody you know will die or have a chronic illness. Maybe you will lose your job or your house, through no fault of your own. *Join with your partner to negotiate these challenges.* Later challenges will be easier. Turn to others outside your relationship for support when you need it, and provide it to them when they need it – and even when they don't.

- Practice good mental hygiene. *Think well of your partner.* Give your partner the benefit of the doubt. When you are having a problem in your relationship, focus specifically on that problem and not all the other grievances you might have.

- *Learn how to talk effectively about difficult issues that arise between you.* In the course of any long-term relationship, real problems and challenges will arise. You and your partner will disagree about something really important. You will experience sexual frustrations. You or your partner will feel inadequate as a person and maybe even get depressed. One of you will do or say something that is incredibly insensitive. You might give really serious consideration to ending your relationship. And indeed you might actually end the relationship. Successful couples are imperfect in many ways, but most of them figure out a way to talk about important and difficult issues.

- Disclosures, in particular, are a gift that you and your partner give to one another. Learn to listen for these disclosures from your partner, however trivial they seem to be, and respond to them with interest in a kind and sensitive way. *If you want your relationship to be more than just a friendship, you will need to disclose your thoughts and feelings to your partner.*

- Recognize that your partner is a unique and distinct person, trying to make a go of life just like you are. He or she has goals and quirks, and struggles and uncertainties, joys and sorrows, just as you do. *Help him or her deal with these struggles and uncertainties in a way that you think he or she would want to be helped.* Chances are good that you are not going to change your partner in any fundamental way. You are much better off embracing and accepting your partner as a complete package and trying to understand what makes him or her tick.

- Look out for yourself. *Find a partner you think is mature and healthy, someone whom you will want to care about and who you believe genuinely wants to care about you and your welfare.* Don't be naïve. Some people have accumulated enormous debts, abuse drugs, break the law, or treat their partner badly, and you may not know these things early in your relationship. These can make for difficult relationships. You will either want to avoid these kinds of problems or be prepared to respond when they arise.

- *Recognize that not all relationships are destined to work out.* Even still, relationships that are going to end can be ended constructively and with both partners showing respect toward one another. If your relationship is not going well, take active steps to make it better or to end it well. You will be a better person for having done so. When the going gets rough, have the courage to talk to a therapist (counsellor), either on your own or with your partner.

Karney and Bradbury add: "The best way to take care of yourself, paradoxically, is to take care of someone else, with the hope and faith that your kindness and generosity will be reciprocated." Celebrating the positive events in life, recalling the good times together, and doing small, positive acts of kindness have a powerful impact on a relationship. They are the stuff of friendship.

Modern marriage and the pursuit of happiness

In his reflections on survival in Nazi concentration camps, the psychiatrist, Viktor Frankl, related how one day, when stumbling along a muddy road with other prisoners, a chance comment from a fellow prisoner about their wives sparked a crucial insight:

> Occasionally I looked at the sky, where the stars were fading and the pink light of the morning was beginning to spread behind a dark bank of clouds. But my mind clung to my wife's image, imaging it with uncanny acuteness. I heard her answering me, saw her smile, her frank and encouraging look. Real or not, her look was then more luminous than the sun which was beginning to rise.

> A thought transfixed me: for the first time in my life I saw the truth as it is set into song by so many poets, proclaimed as the final wisdom by so many thinkers. The truth – that love is the ultimate and highest goal to which man can aspire. Then I grasped the meaning of the greatest secret that human poetry and human thought and belief have to impart: The salvation of man is through love and in love.[1546]

There is a yearning in every human heart to be loved and accepted. It has been written about by philosophers and thinkers, and poets and balladeers throughout history. It is this love which brings many people to marriage; and through marriage, that they hope to find happiness.

The "pursuit of happiness," made famous by Thomas Jefferson's memorable words in the American *Declaration of Independence*, is the aspiration of millions of people, including every person who enters into an intimate relationship. When Jefferson wrote of the "pursuit of happiness," he was not thinking of personal betterment or gratification. Nor was he referring to affection and sympathy. The American founders' notion of happiness was about the populace and the nation.[1547] The right that they spoke of was what was required to become fully human, to practice virtues, and to experience a contented life. The connection between virtue and happiness was made by George Washington in his inaugural address to the new nation: "There is no truth more thoroughly established that there exists in the economy and course of nature, an indissoluble union between virtue and happiness."[1548]

In contemporary relationships, our reliance on romantic love and quest for instant gratification seems to have hollowed-out our understanding of happiness. When the romance fades, or the gratification is insufficient, many become bored and restless for new pursuits. Despite the allure of the novel, this has not resulted in greater happiness for many people. For millions, including many children, the opposite has been the consequence.

It is not that romance is not important. It is necessary, but insufficient, to hold together the long-lasting marriage to which individuals aspire:

> The point is not that passionate love isn't an important signal. It surely is – that rush of dopamine is trying to tell us something. But a successful marriage has to endure long past the peak of passion. It has to survive the rigors of adaptation and intimacy, which are features of romantic relationships that don't get valorised in Hollywood, Bollywood or Shakespeare.[1549]

It is like we need a greater level of stimulation to be 'happy.' In the past, simple things like a walk in the park, or a Sunday drive, were considered pleasurable and relationship building. In a world of instant communications and global connections through the internet, facebook, twitter, SMS and the like, we can at once 'connect' to more people, yet remain distant from them. The paradox of modern communication is that many people are living in isolation from each other at a time when connection has never been more accessible. Yet connection, which is celebrated in modern technology, and pursued in romantic love, is not the same thing as a bond.[1550]

Professor Ted Huston observes of his 14 year-long study of a group of couples that: (romantic) love pushes couples down the courtship path; the depth of courtship love foretells couples' experiences as newlyweds; and that the loss of love early in marriage provides clues as to whether a marriage will survive. He adds:

> As important as love is, it is only one of the many factors that propel couples to marriage. . . Although love is an important ingredient of marriage, couples have lasting marriages without being deeply in love and those who fall out of love do not inevitably divorce.[1551]

The historian, Lawrence Stone, notes that individuals have found happiness in many different family forms over time. There is no reason:

> To assume that the family that has emerged in the late twentieth century must necessarily, in all respects, be more conducive to either personal happiness or the public good than the family types that have preceded it. Affective individualism is a theory which lacks any firm foundation in biological, anthropological or sociological data.[1552]

The psychologist, Blaine Fowers, suggests in *Beyond the Myth of Marital Happiness* that our inclination to understand marriage as an emotion-based, private affair is one of the great tragedies of our time. "The romantic approach to marriage" he writes, "has been, in many ways, a noble and exciting experiment, but we now know that it has failed, and we must find another way to strengthen this vital institution."[1523] Summarising the research on happiness, the *New York Times* writer, Tara Parker-Pope observes:

> While the early euphoria of a new marriage does drop, that
> doesn't mean we have become less happy with each other or
> less happy in life. It just means that as individuals, we aren't
> dependent on marriage as a main source of life happiness. And
> people who get married are typically happy people to start with,
> and marriage doesn't change that.[1554]

"Marital happiness creates one kind of attachment between partners, but there are other kinds of ties between partners that are stronger and richer," Professor Fowers writes. He suggests that marriages founded on virtues such as friendship, generosity, loyalty, justice and courage, rather than a therapeutic model, based on unconstrained choice and personal satisfaction, are more likely to succeed. Others have also begun to question the dominant therapeutic approach to marriage.[1555]

Perhaps we should consider again happiness in the broad Aristotelian sense. Condensing the idea of happiness spelt out by Aristotle in *Nicomachean Ethics*, Charles Murray proposes a simple definition: "Happiness consists of lasting and justified satisfaction with life as a whole."[1556] This corresponds with the experience of most people. It stands in stark contrast to the cult of instant gratification that is celebrated in the entertainment industry and held up as an ideal for the populace.[1557] It corresponds with the experience of most parents, who know the joys and challenges of raising children. It is the stuff of satisfaction and contentment in old age. And it is a more realistic approach to marriage than the often-idealistic images presented today.

The pursuit of happiness reflects our deepest human desires to love and be loved. In modern times, 'love' is used in a variety of ways: "I love my spouse", "I love my country", "I love my friends", and even "I love ice-cream". These notions of love have been conflated, without much differentiation. They largely reflect individual, emotional and sensate experiences. By contrast, the ancient Greeks recognised that 'love' had different meanings. They had different words for these meanings. Hence, *agápe* (unconditional love), *éros* (emotional or passionate love), *philía* (friendship or affectionate love), and *storgē* (natural affection like parents for children). The passion of *éros* fuels the romantic attachment that brings a couple together, but without the deepening friendship of *philía*, the relationship is unlikely to thrive. Aristotle taught that friendship was a higher form of love than the emotional. Having children helps to build other loves: the natural affection for family members, and the unconditional generosity and commitment required of successful marriage and parenthood.

Modern western society celebrates the emotional, the sensate, and the sexual – which the Christian writer, CS Lewis, described as *venus*.[1558] Increasingly, however, social scientists stress that the virtues of generosity, commitment, responsibility, and loyalty are required also to sustain marriage. Good communication can only occur if there is a commitment to self-restraint, to listening, by couples. It also requires the restraint involved in judgement, of not saying that which would be destructive of the other person. Equally, self-disclosure requires trust; and vulnerability requires courage.[1559] In this regard, social science reflects an older wisdom about human relationships, as reflected in the Apostle Paul's letter to the people of Corinth:

> Love is always patient and kind; it is never jealous; love is never boastful or conceited; it is never rude or selfish; it does not take offence, and is not resentful. Love takes no pleasure in other people's sins but delights in the truth; it is always ready to excuse, to trust, to hope, and to endure whatever comes. Love does not come to an end.

It was probably this sort of love – the unselfish, generous, patient and giving love – that Viktor Frankl envisaged that day on a muddy road when he imagined his wife smiling upon him.

Many observers have noted also that as marriage has declined as an institution, its symbolic importance has increased.[1560] Fowers observes a modern paradox: "Our deep desire for a happy marriage leads to a strange situation in which marriage is both more valued and more fragile than ever before."[1561] Engagement rituals, including the proposal, and seeking the permission of the bride's father for marriage, are still cherished by many modern couples.[1562] Paradoxically, while the marriage rate has declined over recent decades, the wedding has become an increasingly gala function, sometimes extending to a series of events over one or more days. Prior to the financial crisis, it was reported that the average cost of a wedding in the US was $36,000, similar to the average of $39,000 in Australia.[1563]

Affluence and the pursuit of individualistic goals do not necessarily bode well for marriage and family relationships. A study by scholars at Australia's Murdoch University found a negative relationship between commitment to materialistic goals and the cultivation of satisfactory domestic relationships: "High materialists place possession acquisition foremost in their value hierarchy, ahead of many other values such as family and interpersonal relationships."[1564]

In a study exploring the transition from cohabitation to marriage, Annie Dennis observes "the social achievement of attaining marriage has increased the significance of the wedding ceremony itself as an individual achievement."[1565] This accords with Andrew Cherlin's prediction that in future, that marriage will hold a highly valued, distinguished place rather than being just one relationship among many, but the process towards achievement of marriage will be a long one, often involving prior cohabitation and childbearing.[1566] Whether this 'thin' version of marriage, with all the detriments for the many people who are unable to attain it, is sufficient to sustain families, communities and nations, remains to be determined.

How we preserve marriage – against the cultural and economic pressures that threaten to overwhelm it – as the foundation of healthy family life, the protective institution for children, the crucible of the free market, and the essential condition for democracy, will determine the health and longevity of the critical institutions of the western liberal experiment. The future of individuals, families, communities and nations is tied to the outcome.

SUMMARY

- ♥ The popular notion that individuals can 'have it all' is misleading:
  - ➤ There is a modern dilemma in finding a workable balance between the principles of equality, freedom and family commitment.
  - ➤ Committed marriage involves choosing some things over others.
- ♥ Family scholars have identified a number of myths that can detract from marital success:
  - ➤ There is a 50 per cent risk of divorce.
  - ➤ Premarital cohabitation improves the chances of marital success.
  - ➤ It is preferable to marry later.
  - ➤ Marriage is private and natural – there is nothing to learn.
  - ➤ Marital satisfaction necessarily declines over time.
  - ➤ Conflict destroys marriage.
  - ➤ A 'good divorce' is beneficial for children.
  - ➤ Fathers are dispensable.
- ♥ Family scholars increasingly indicate a number of factors associated with successful marriage. These characteristics include:
  - ➤ Commitment and investment in the relationship.
  - ➤ Passion and intimacy.
  - ➤ Strong feelings of fondness and generosity.
- ♥ Modern society focuses on the emotional, the sensate and the sexual, but social scientists stress increasingly that the underlying values of generosity, commitment, loyalty and responsibility for the other are the important factors in achieving marital happiness.

CONCLUSION

Over four decades of social science research across western nations confirms one clear and unambiguous conclusion: A healthy marriage is the best source of physical and mental health, emotional stability, and prosperity for adults and children. It is also the best bet for attaining happiness and fulfilment.

Why is this important? Young adults who aspire to marriage and family life can know that marriage enhances their prospects of personal happiness. The countless parents who struggle with the everyday challenges that marriage entails, and who make ongoing sacrifices to give their children the best opportunities in life, can be affirmed in the knowledge that their efforts, often unknown and unseen by others, are valuable. The millions of people who put the well-being of their spouses and children ahead of personal gratification can be assured that their efforts are worthwhile. The great majority of couples who innately know that happy and healthy children are their greatest contribution to the future of humanity can be supported in their choice. And policy-makers concerned about the 'pursuit of happiness' and the common good can be reassured that encouraging healthy and stable marriages is beneficial for their societies and national prosperity.

The healthy pair-bond of a man and a woman is the greatest hope of humanity, not just because it is a historically ubiquitous institution,[1567] but also because it's critical role is supported by the mounting social science research. While we read from time to time of sensational reports that marriage and family life is fast disappearing, a lifelong commitment to family remains a popular aspiration, including amongst young people. Marriage and family life remain the optimal conditions for the socialisation and education of children's character and values, without which liberal democracy cannot properly flourish. For these reasons, we cannot ignore the trends affecting families today.

The tragedy of the retreat from marriage is not the billions of dollars it costs each year: it is the personal and emotional trauma which research increasingly indicates affects many children, even into their adulthood; and the consequent diminution of health, educational opportunities, and well-being, including the stability of relationships of children whose parents divorced.

If our desire is for healthy, well-adjusted children and young people who have every opportunity for the best education, who can obtain employment and live fulfilling lives, and who have a reasonable prospect of forming their own sustainable relationships – if we desire a stable and healthy society – then the intact family remains our best bet.

Our choice is clear. We can throw up our hands in despair, unwilling or unable to propose solutions to the retreat from marriage and falling fertility rates, with all the social consequences that follow; or we can take a positive step forward, committed to the aspiration so many people instinctively share, in the hope that with practical support and encouragement, we can build strong nations based on a healthy society with stable married life at its foundation.

APPENDICES

RESOURCES FOR COUPLES

MARITAL INVENTORIES

FOCCUS:

Australia: www.csme.catholic.org.au

UK: www.foccus.org.uk

USA and Canada: www.foccusinc.com

PREPARE:

Australia: www.prepare-enrich.com.au

Canada: www.enrichcanada.ca

New Zealand: www.prepare-enrich.co.nz

UK: www.prepare-enrich.co.uk

USA: www.prepare-enrich.com

RELATE:

International: www.relate-institute.org

WEBSITES AND ONLINE RESOURCES

For Your Marriage: http://foryourmarriage.com

Marriage and Relationship Education links: http://billcoffin.org

Marriage Resource Centre: http://marriageresourcecentre.org

Maybe 'I do': maybeido.com

National Healthy Marriage Resource Center: www.healthymarriageinfo.org

Sliding vs Deciding: www.slidingvsdeciding.blogspot.com.au

Smart Loving: http://smartloving.org

Smartmarriages: www.smartmarriages.com

Smart Stepfamilies: www.smartstepfamilies.com

Stepfamilies: www.stepfamily.org.au

FINDING A MARRIAGE EDUCATION PROGRAM

Australia

The Australian government publishes a list of Family Relationship Education and Skills Training agencies at: www.familyrelationships. gov.au/Services (See Family and Children's Services)

Catholic Society for Marriage Education: www.csme.catholic.org.au

Canada

Canadian Association of Family Resource Programs: www.frp.ca

Parents Matter: www.parentsmatter.ca

New Zealand

Catholic Marriage Preparation: www.catholicmarriage.org.nz (Auckland); and www.wn.catholic.org.nz (Wellington)

The Marriage Course: www.relationshipcentral.org.nz

United Kingdom

Couple Connection: http://thecoupleconnection.net

Marriage Care: www.marriagecare.org.uk

Marriage Preparation Course: www.htp.org.uk

2 in 2 + 1: www.2-in-2-1.co.uk/services

Relate: www.relate.org.uk

United States of America

Smartmarriages: www.smartmarriages.com

BOOKS

For a list of helpful books and resources: www.marriageeducation. com.au/ See the Resources tab.

A LIVING TOGETHER QUESTIONNAIRE FOR INDIVIDUALS AND COUPLES

The experience of cohabitation

While living together may not be viewed initially as permanently bonding, once the decision is made, family and/or societal expectations increase and the slide towards marriage (or 'commitment creep') gains momentum. The personal investment, even in small matters such as domestic living arrangements, has a way of locking people into maintaining the situation. The efforts and energy invested in the relationship is not so easily discarded, and the prospect of breaking up may seem harder than getting married.

Q. *What was your understanding of the initial commitment you made to living together? Has it changed? Has there been an expectation from family and friends that you would/should get married? What made you decide to get married?*

If one partner has a greater expectation than the other does that living together will eventually lead to marriage, this can create an inequality in the relationship.

Q. *Why did you decide to live with your partner? Did you see it as a stepping stone to marriage? Does your partner see it the same as you?*

Couples often believe that a successful living together relationship will guarantee a successful marriage. While cohabiting couples usually develop interpersonal skills, marriage relies on permanent commitment, which is an opposing concept to the 'opt out' clause associated with cohabitation.

Q. *What are the ingredients of a successful marriage? What do you and your partner understand by 'commitment'?*

Having several cohabiting relationships may weaken commitment. If a person is in the habit of leaving relationships, they may become more tolerant of failed relationships.

Q. *Have you had previous cohabiting relationships? If so, why did these relationships end?*

_____

Living in a non-permanent relationship may cause some people to hold back on making a total investment of themselves, out of fear of rejection. This is especially so if there are hurts from a previous relationship.

Q. *Does your partner know you 'warts and all'? Do you feel fully accepted by your partner?*

_____

A wedding does not change personalities and behaviour patterns.

Q. *Are you concerned about any specific personality traits or behaviours? What can you do about seeking help?*

_____

Sex is a powerful physical and emotional bond.

Q. *How much does sex hold your relationship together? What else bonds you together?*

Attitudes and values

Independence and individuality are the opposite of the inter-dependence and sharing that contribute to successful marriage.

Q. *Do you have independent attitudes (e.g., money, possessions) in your relationship? Do you plan for this to change after marriage? How do you plan to share in your marriage?*

_____

Having more individual attitudes means that a person may cohabit (and later marry) primarily for what they will get out of the relationship. Successful marriage requires a significant degree of focussing on the other person.

Q. *Can you identify your partner's physical and emotional needs? How will you fulfil these needs?*

Seeing cohabitation as more like dating than marriage may result in lower expectation of sexual exclusivity in marriage.

Q. *Have you seen your cohabiting as more like dating or more like marriage? Did you discuss faithfulness with your partner when you began living together? Have you discussed your expectations of faithfulness within marriage?*

Choosing a 'partner' for cohabitation may be different from choosing a 'spouse'. Approximately half of all couples who live together, do so after knowing their partner for six months or less. As many cohabiting relationships progress to marriage, insufficient attention may be given to the selection of a suitable marriage partner.

Q. *How long did you know each other before you began living together? Might your relationship have run its course and ended naturally had you not begun living together? How compatible are you with your partner?*

Many people believe that marriage will be the same as living together. If you are living together and one person decides that 'it's not working' he/she can leave. Marriage, however, has 'lifelong commitment' as its basis and is a public, social, emotional and legal promise to family, friends and community. These are opposing concepts, and couples may not be prepared for the psychological and social changes involved.

Q. *In what ways is marriage different from cohabitation? How will you deal with these differences?*

Being afraid of long-term commitment may be a motivation to live together. We live in a society that says if something is broken, it's better to throw it out and get a new one, than try to fix it. Our society also says that we can change and 'outgrow' our marriage. Marriage is a journey where husband and wife grow together (sometimes at different rates), rather than a destination. Marriage is renewable, rather than expendable. Fulfillment is found in working at the relationship so it deepens and matures.

Q. *Did you choose cohabitation because you were uncertain about sustaining a lifelong marriage? Are you ready for a permanent commitment and willing to work through any problems that may arise?*

Being motivated by convenience, peer pressure, or to be seen as independent can lead some people to begin a live-in relationship. For some people, cohabitation is a sign a social status.

Q. *Why did you decide to live together? Did it make you feel more independent in the eyes of family or friends?*

Life events

Leaving home at an early age may expose a person to risk-taking behaviors before they have reached maturity. Risk-taking behaviors can work against establishing enduring and successful relationships.

Q. *Did you leave home at an early age? Did you engage in risk-taking behavior, such as drinking and/or drug use?*

Beginning sexual relationships early in life means that a person is more likely to have lived with one or more people before that have reached 'marrying' age. This can make it more difficult to establish a lifelong marriage.

Q. *At what age did you begin a sexual relationship?*

Having a child may put pressure on a couple, when they may otherwise not have married.

Q. *Do you have any children? If yes, in what ways has this been a motivating factor in your decision to marry? Would you be getting married nonetheless?*

Family background

Having parents who separated or divorced may weaken a person's confidence to build a lifelong marriage. There may be greater acceptance of separation because this is what your parents did.

Q. *Are your parents separated or divorced? If so, what are their attitudes towards marriage? Do you share these attitudes? Are they supportive of your intentions to get married?*

———————

Some people decide not to marry out of fear of divorce. They don't want what has happened to their parents, brother or sister to happen to them.

Q. *Do you have family members or close friends who are separated or divorced? If so, has this discouraged you from getting married? How can you develop the skills necessary to build a lifelong marriage?*

———————

Coming from a non-religious family may mean that people feel less pressure to observe expectations, such as getting married or staying married.

Q. *How important is marriage for you? What messages have you received from your family and friends about the value of marriage? Do you have any friends who are married? Does marriage have a public aspect, or is it simply a private affair?*

———————

ENDNOTES

1 In contrast, rising affluence does not appear to increase happiness: Mihaly Csikszentmihalyi (1999) 'If we are so rich, why aren't we happy?' *American Psychologist* 54: 821-827; and Lisa Ryan and Suzanne Dziurawiec (2001) 'Materialism and its relationship to life satisfaction' *Social Indicators Research* 55: 185-197

2 William Doherty (2000) 'Intentional marriage: Your rituals will set you free' *Threshold* 66: 25-29

3 William Butler Yeats (1919) 'A prayer for my daughter' in Richard J Finneran (ed) (1983) *W.B Yeats The Poems*, [Macmillan, London] 188-190

4 Mindy E Scott *et al* (2009) *Young adult attitudes about relationships and marriage: Times may have changed, but expectations remain high* Child Trends Research Brief [Washington DC, Child Trends], 2; and Barbara Dafoe Whitehead and David Popenoe (2004) *State of our Unions* [Piscataway NJ, National Marriage Project]; See also David de Vaus (1997) 'Family values in the nineties' *Family Matters* 48: 4-10.

5 Don Edgar (1988) 'The new marriage: Changing rules for changing times' *Threshold* 22: 9

6 A series of studies described how divorce had resulted in the 'feminisation of poverty': See for example, James McLindon (1987) 'Separate but unequal; The economic disaster of divorce for women and children' 21 *Family Law Quarterly* 351,for the US; John Eekelaar and Mavis Maclean (1986) *Maintenance after divorce* [Oxford, Oxford University Press] for the UK; and Kate Funder, Margaret Harrison and Ruth Weston (1993) *Settling Down* [Australian Institute of Family Studies, Melbourne] for Australia.

7 Patrick Parkinson (2011) *Family law and the indissolubility of parenthood* [Cambridge, Cambridge University Press]

8 See David Chambers (1982) 'The coming curtailment of compulsory child support' 80 *Michigan Law Review* 1614 for a description of the sense of loss of obligation by fathers following separation.

9 See Joint Select Committee on Certain Family Law Issues (1994) *Child support scheme: An examination of the operation and effectiveness of the scheme* [Canberra, Parliament of Australia], chapter 4

10 Harry Krause (1989) 'Child support reassessed: Limits of private responsibility and public interest' *University of Illinois Law Review* 367, 370

11 Anne C Case, I-Fen Lin and Sara S McLanahan (2003) 'Explaining trends in child support: Economic, demographic and policy effects' *Demography* 40: 171-189

12 Timothy S Grall (2007) *Custodial mothers and fathers and their child support: 2005* [Washington DC, US Census Bureau], 3. See also Irwin Garfinkel, Daniel Meyer and Sara McLanahan (1998) 'A brief history of child support policies in the United States' in Irwin Garfinkel *et al* (eds) (2001) *Fathers under fire: The revolution in child support enforcement.* [New York, Russell Sage Foundation]

13 Elaine Sorensen and Ariel Halpern (1999) *Child support enforcement: How well is it doing?* Discussion Paper [Washington DC, Urban Institute]. Note: the amounts received increased, but not the number of receipients.

14 James Chapman (2012) 'One in five children from broken homes lose touch with one parent for ever' *Daily Mail Online*, January 25

15 ABS (2007) *Australian Social Trends* cat 4102.0

16 Grall (2007) *supra*

17 See for example the Bradley Amendment in the US Congress (1986) *Public Law* 99-509, 42 USC 666 (a) (9) (c)

18 Joint Select Committee on Certain Family Law Issues (1994) *Child Support Scheme: An examination of the operation and effectiveness of the scheme* [Canberra, Parliament of the Commonwealth of Australia]

19 For example: the *Divorce Reform Act* 1969 (England) and the *Family Law Act* 1975 (Australia)

20 Parkinson (2011), *supra*, 213

21 See Peter L Berger and Richard John Neuhaus (1977) *To empower people* [Washington DC, American Enterprise Institute]

22 Martin Luther King (1965) *Speech*, Westchester County, New York

23 Lynne Graham 'A firm footing or falling between the cracks' Anglicare Australia (2010) *In from the edge* (State of the Family Report) [Canberra, Anglicare Australia], 26

24 See: George Brandis (2010) 'Shared parenting' *Australian Polity* 4: 27-29

25 See: Parkinson (2011), *supra*

26 House of Representatives Legal and Constitutional Affairs Committee (1998) *To have and to hold – Strategies to strengthen marriage and relationships* [Canberra, Parliament of the Commonwealth of Australia], i

27 *Ibid.*, ii

28 Linda J Waite *et al* (2002) *Does divorce make people happy? Findings from a study of unhappy marriages* [New York, Institute for American Values]

29 *Ibid.*, 50-51

30 Institute of Marriage and Family Canada (2009) *Private choices, public costs: How failing families cost us all* [Ottawa, The Institute]

31 Relationships Foundation (2008) *When relationships go wrong: Counting the cost of family failure* [Cambridge UK, Relationships Foundation]

32 Centre for Social Justice (2009) *Every family matters* [London, The Centre]

33 David Schramm (2003) *What could divorce be costing your State? The costly consequences of divorce in Utah: The impact on couples, communities and government* [Logan UT, Utah State University]

34 Council on Families in America (1995) *Marriage in America: A report to the nation* [New York, The Council], 11

35 Quoted in Daniel Patrick Moynihan (1986) *Family and Nation* [San Diego CA, Harcourt Brace], 169-70

36 Alex White (2011) 'Marriage breeds better children' *Herald Sun*, Melbourne, November 16

37 Norval D Glenn and Thomas Sylvester (2005) 'The denial: Downplaying the consequences of family structure for children' *Family Scholars Blog* [New York, Institute for American Values]

38 'Whatever happened to old-fashioned love?' (1990) Letter, *The Age* (Melbourne, Australia) June 19

39 The sociologist, David Popenoe, concluded: "... in three decades of work as a social scientist, I know of few other bodies of data in which the weight of evidence is so decisively on one side of the issue: on the whole, for children, two-parent families are preferable to single-parent families and step-families. If our prevailing views on family structure hinged solely on scholarly evidence, the current debate would never have arisen in the first place." David Popenoe (1992) 'The controversial truth: Two-parent families are better' *New York Times* (December 26), 21. Another family scholar, Norval Glenn observed: "To ignore family structure. . is to ignore the huge amount of recent social science evidence, from hundreds of studies, that family structure matters, and matters to an important extent, especially for children but for adults as well. This evidence, while not absolutely conclusive, is about as nearly conclusive as social scientific evidence ever is." Norval Glenn (2008) 'Against family fatalism' *Cato Unbound*, January 21.

40 See, for example: Kevin Andrews (1993) *The provision of family services*, Discussion Paper [Canberra, Liberal and National Parties]; Kevin Andrews (1994) 'Family policy and social cohesion' in K Aldred, K Andrews and P Filing (eds) *The heart of liberalism* [Melbourne, Albury Papers] 355-90; Kevin and Margaret Andrews (1997) 'Strategies to strengthen marriage: The Australian experience' in Theodora Ooms (ed) *Strategies to strengthen marriage: What do we know? What do we need to know?* [Washington DC, Family Impact Seminar]; Kevin and Margaret Andrews (1998) 'Rebuiding a culture of marriage' *The family in America* 12 (10) 1-8 (an abridged version of a presentation to the World Congress of Families, Prague, the

Czech Republic, 1997); and Kevin and Margaret Andrews (1997) *With this ring – Rebuilding a culture of marriage* [Melbourne, Threshold Publishing]

41 Kevin Andrews and Michelle Curtis (1998) *Changing Australia: Social, cultural and economic trends shaping the nation* [Sydney, Federation Press]

42 See: David Willetts (2010) *The pinch – How the baby boomers took their children's future – and why they should give it back* [London, Atlantic Books], 19-20

43 The Marriage Movement (2000) *A statement of principles* [New York, Institute for American Values] 8-9

44 Ernesto Cortes Jr., (1991) 'Reflections on the Catholic tradition of family rights: Catholic social thought' in John Coleman (ed.) *100 years of Catholic social thought* [New York, Orbis Books], 72

45 Council on Families in America (1995) *Marriage in America* [New York, Council on Families] 10

46 K Davis (1985) 'The meaning and significance of marriage in contemporary society' in K Davis (ed) *Contemporary Marriage* [New York, Russell Sage Foundation] 7-8.

47 Council on Families (1995) *supra*.

48 Jean Bethke Elshtain (1996) 'Marriage in civil society' *Family Affairs* 7: 2-5

49 'Worldwide support for families' *Threshold* 63: 30-32 republishing an international survey.

50 Social Trends Institute (2011) *Global family culture* [Barcelona, The Institute]

51 National Center for Health Statistics (2002) *National Survey on Family Growth* [Atlanta GA, Center for Disease Control and Prevention] See also: S Bouchet (2009) *More than jobs – providing disadvantaged teens and young adults with healthy relationships skills as a strategy to reduce poverty and improve child well-being* [Baltimore MD, Annie E Casey Foundation]

52 LD Johnston, JG Bachman and PM O'Malley (1997) *Monitoring the future: Questionnaire responses from the nation's high school seniors, 1995* [Ann Arbor MI, Institute for Social Research]

53 Christine Flanigan, Renee Huffman and Julia Smith (2005) 'Teens attitudes toward marriage, cohabitation and divorce, 2002' *Science Says* [Washington DC, The National Campaign to Prevent Teen Pregnancy]

54 Robert G Wood, Sarah Avellar and Brian Goesling (2008) 'Pathways to adulthood and marriage: Teenagers attitudes, expectations, and relationship patterns' *ASPE Research Brief* [Washington DC, US Department of Human Services]

55 Cited in Scott M Stanley (2005) 'What is it with men and commitment, anyway?' *Threshold* 83: 4-11

56 Robert G Wood *et al* (2008) *supra*

57 Diana Smart (2002) 'Relationships, marriage and parenthood: Views of young people and their parents' *Family Matters* 63: 28-35; and Diana Smart (2008) 'The views of young people about relationships' *Threshold* 93: 24

58 See: Lixia Qu and Grace Soriano (2004) 'Forming couple relationships' *Family Matters* 68: 43-49

59 David Popenoe and Barbara Dafoe Whitehead (1999) 'What's happening to marriage?' *State of our unions: The social health of marriage in America* [The National Marriage Project, Rutgers University NJ]

60 Mindy E Scott *et al* (2009) 'Young adult attitudes about relationships and marriage: Times may have changed, but expectations remain high' *Research Brief 2009-30* [Washington DC, Child Trends]

61 Peter Picard (2009) *What twenty-somethings think about marriage* [Littleton CO, National Healthy Marriage Resource Center], 4

62 Robert M Orrange (2003) 'Individualism, family values, and the professional middle class: In-depth interviews with advanced law and MBA students' *The Sociological Quarterly* 44: 451-480

63 The Gallop Organization (2001) *Young adults' attitudes towards marriage,* cited in Barbara Dafoe Whitehead (2004) *There are no good men left* [New York, Broadway Books] 6

64 '78 per cent rate marriage as important to US society' (2012) [Rasmussen Reports]

65 D de Vaus (1997) 'Family values in the nineties' *Family Matters* 48: 4-10.

66 *Ibid.*

67 *Ibid.*

68 D de Vaus and I Wolcott (eds) (1997) *Australian Family Profiles* [Melbourne, Australian Institute of Family Studies] 16

69 Roger Harris *et al* (1992) *Love, Sex and Waterskiing* [Adelaide, University of South Australia] 84

70 Arland Thornton and Linda Young-DeMarco (2001) 'Four decades of trends in attitudes toward family issues in the United States: The 1960s through the 1990s' *Journal of Marriage and the Family* 63: 1009-1037

71 Paul R Amato *et al* (2003) 'Continuity and change in marital quality between 1980 and 2000' *Journal of Marriage and the Family* 65: 1-22. The study found that other factors, such as cohabitation, longer working hours, and higher education, increased divorce proneness and decreased marital happiness, resulting in nearly identical mean levels of marital happiness for the two periods.

72 Christian Smith, Kari Christofferson, Hilary Davidson and Patricia Snell Herzog (2011) *Lost in transition – The dark side of emerging adulthood* [New York, Oxford University Press], 104-105

73 Alison Park (2001) 'The generation game' in Roger Jowell *et al* (eds) *British Social Attitudes, 17th report 2000/01* [London, National Centre for Social Research], 103

74 'Most believe marriage is for life' (2007) *Threshold* 90: 4-5

75 Mindy E Scott *et al* (2009) *Young adult attitudes about relationships and marriage: Times may have changed, but expectations remain high* Child Trends Research Brief [Washington DC, Child Trends], 2. See also: Lina Guzman *et al* (2009) *Telling it like it is: Teen perspectives on romantic relationships* [Washington DC, Child Trends]

76 'Marriages rated as good or excellent' (2011) *Threshold* 102: 33

77 Norval D Glenn (2005) *With this ring. . . A national survey of marriage in America* [Washington DC, National Fatherhood Initiative], 7

78 *Ibid.*, 14

79 *Ibid.*, 15

80 *Ibid.*, 15

81 www.britsocrat.com

82 *The Observer*, May 28, 2006, cited in David Willetts (2010) *The pinch – How the baby boomers took their children's future – and why they should give it back* [London, Atlantic Books]

83 C Hill (2000) *Sex under sixteen?* [London, Family Education Trust]

84 Paul Taylor, Cary Funk and April Clark (2007) *As marriage and parenthood drift apart, public is concerned about social impact* [Washington DC, Pew Research Center]

85 Pew Research Center (2010) *The decline of marriage and rise of new families* [Washington DC, The Center]

85a Bruce Headey, Ruut Veenhoven and Alex Wearing (1991) 'Top-down versus bottom-up theories of subjective well-being' *Social Indicators Research* 24: 81-100

86 Charles Murray (2012) *Coming apart: The state of white America, 1960 – 2010* [New York, Crown Forum], 256

87 See for example: David Popenoe (1993) 'American family in decline 1960-1990: A review and appraisal' *Journal of Marriage and the Family*, 21: 347-366; James Q Wilson (2002) *The marriage problem: How our culture has weakened families* [New York, Harper Collins]; and Paul R Amato *et al* (2007) *Alone together: How marriage in America is changing* [Cambridge MA, Harvard University Press]

88 Mindy E Scott *et al* (2009) *Young adult attitudes about relationships and marriage: Times have not changed, but expectations remain high* [Washington DC, Child Trends], 4

89 Barbara Dafoe Whitehead and David Popenoe (2000) *Why wed? Young adults talk about sex, love and first unions* [Rutgers NJ National Marriage Project]. See also: Peter Picard (2009), *supra*

90 Chris M Wilson and Anthony J Oswald (2005) 'How does marriage affect physical and psychological health? A survey of the longitudinal evidence' *The Warwick Economics Research Paper Series*, No 728, May 2005

91 Thomas N Bradbury and Benjamin R Karney (2010) *Intimate relationships* [New York, WW Norton and Co], 26

92 Bruce Headey, Ruut Veenhoven and Alex Wearing (1991) 'Top-down versus bottom-up theories of subjective well-being' *Social Indicators Research* 24: 81-100. See also: Norval D Glenn and Charles N Weaver (1981) 'The contribution of marital happiness to global happiness' *Journal of Marriage and the Family* 43: 161-168

93 A Stutzer and B S Frey (2006) 'Does marriage make people happy, or do happy people get married?' *Journal of Socio-Economics* 35: 326-347

94 RE Lucas (2005) 'Time does not heal all wounds: A longitudinal study of reaction and adaptation to divorce' *Psychological Science* 16: 945-950

95 This chapter draws upon the 'To have and to hold' report, *supra*, of which I was the principal author, and which, in turn, drew upon my previous writings.

96 William J Doherty (1997) 'The scientific case for marriage and couples education in health care' *Paper* [Minneapolis MN, University of Minnesota]

97 Andrew J Cherlin and Frank Furstenberg Jr (1994) 'Step families in the United States: A reconsideration' *Annual Review of Sociology* 20: 359-381; J Coie *et al.* (1993) 'The science of prevention: A conceptual framework and some directions for a national research program' *American Psychologist* 48: 1013-1022; JC Coyle, J Kahn and IH Gotlib (1987) *Depression. Family interaction and psychopathology: Theories, methods and findings* [New York: Plenum Press]; CP Cowan and PA Cowan (1992) *When partners become parents: The big life change for couples* [New York, Harper Collins]; F Fincham, J Grych and L Osborne (1993) 'Interparental conflict and child adjustment: A longitudinal analysis' Paper presented at the biennial meeting of the Society for Research in Child Development New Orleans.

98 Lisa Strohschein *et al* (2005) 'Marital transitions and mental health: Are there gender differences in the short-term effects of marital status change?' *Social Science and Medicine* 61: 2293-2303

99 F McAllister (ed) (1995) *Marital breakdown and the Health of the Nation* [London, One plus One]

100 Linda J Waite (1997) 'Why marriage matters' *Threshold* 57: 4-8.

101 There is voluminous literature on the impact of marriage on health outcomes. See, for example, the studies collected in Linda Waite and Maggie Gallagher (2000) *The case for marriage: Why married people are happier, healthier and better off financially* [New York, Doubleday], and the studies cited in House of Representatives Legal and Constitutional Affairs Committee (1998) *To have and to hold* [Canberra, Parliament of Australia] Chapter 3

102 See also Zhenmei Zhand and Mark D Hayward (2006) 'Gender, the marital life course, and cardiovascular disease in late midlife' *Journal of Marriage and Family* 68: 639-657

103 Ossi Rahkonen, Mikko Laaksonen and Sakari Karvonen (2005) 'The contribution of lone parenthood and economic difficulties to smoking' *Social Science and Medicine* 61: 211-216

104 Joseph D Wolfe (2009) 'Age at first birth and alcohol use' *Journal of Health and Social Behavior* 50: 395-409; and C Andre Christie-Mizell and Robert L Peralta (2009) 'The gender gap in alcohol consumption during late adolescence and young adulthood: Gendered attitudes and adult roles' *Journal of Health and Social Behavior* 50: 410-26. It would also appear that alcohol consumption tends to decrease after marriage: 'Marriage singled out as healthier' (2005) *Threshold* 83: 3

105 See also: 'Sexual happiness equals dollars in the bank' (2004) *Threshold* 81: 5

106 'Death of a loved one can truly break a heart' (2012) *The Australian*, January 11, 7

107 Matthew E Dupre and Sarah O Meadows (2007) 'Disaggregating the effects of marital trajectories on health' *Journal of Family Issues* 28: 623-52

108 Mary E Hughes and Linda J Waite (2009) 'Marital biography and health at mid-life' *Journal of Health and Social Behavior* 50: 344-58

109 See Emily MD Grundy and Cecilia Tomassini (2010) 'Marital history, health and mortality among older men and women in England and Wales' *BMC Public Health* 10: 554

110 Penny McDonough, Vivienne Walters and Lisa Strohshein (2002) 'Chronic stress and the social patterning of women's health in Canada' *Social Science and Medicine* 54: 767-782

111 D Ladbrook (1997) 'Why marriage matters: An Australian perspective' *Threshold* 57: 9-10.

112 Cited in Bettina Arndt (2004) 'Better off wed' *The Bulletin*, November 23, 31

113 RH Coombs (1991) 'Marital status and personal well-being: A literature review' *Family Relations* 40: 97; JJ Lynch (1979) *The broken heart* [Sydney, Harper and Row]; and H Carter and P Glick (1970) *Marriage and divorce: A social and economic study* [Cambridge MA, Harvard University Press]

114 Y Hu and N Goldman (1990) 'Mortality differentials by marital status: An international comparison' *Demography* 27(2): 233. See also BD Cox, FA Huppert and MJ Whichelow (1993) *The health and lifestyles survey: Seven years on* [London, Dartmouth Press]; B Burman and G Margolin (1992) 'Analysis of the association between marital relationships and health problems: An international perspective' *Psychological Bulletin* 112: 39–63; and LM Verbrugge (1979) 'Marital status and health' *Journal of Marriage and the Family* 41: 267-285.

115 Gunilla Ringback Weitoft, Bo Burstrom and Mans Rosen (2004) 'Premature mortality among lone fathers and childless men' *Social Science and Medicine* 59: 1449-1459

116 HJ Morowitz (1975) 'Hiding in the Hammond report' *Hospital Practice* August.

117 DB Larson, JP Swyers and SS Larson (1995) *The costly consequences of divorce: Assessing the clinical, economic and public health impact of marital disruption in the United States* [Rockville MD, National Center for Healthcare Research] 46. See also: Carlos Iribarren *et al* (2005) 'Causes and demographic, medical, lifestyle and psychosocial predictors of premature mortality: the CARDIA study' *Social Science and Medicine* 60: 471-482

118 D Ladbrook (1990) 'Sex differentials in premature death among professionals' *Journal of the Australian Population Association* 7: 1-26; 89-115.

119 AM Lilienfield, ML Levin and MJ Kessler (1972) *Cancer in the United States* [Cambridge MA, Harvard University Press]

120 JS Goodwin *et al* (1987) 'The effect of marital status on stage, treatment, and survival of cancer patients' *Journal of the American Medical Association* 258: 3125-3130. See also the series of studies cited in McAllister (1995) *supra.*

121 Oystein Kravdal (2001) 'The impact of marital status on cancer survival' *Social Science and Medicine* 52: 357-368

122 Kirsi Lillberg *et al* (2003) 'Stressful life events and risk of breast cancer in 10,808 women: A cohort study' *American Journal of Epidemiology* 157: 415-423

123 JJ Lynch (1977) *The lonely heart, broken heart, and sudden death* [New York, Basic Books]

124 McAllister (1995) *supra.*

125 Thomas Rutledge *et al* (2003) 'Social networks and marital status predict mortality older women: Prospective evidence from the study of osteoporotic fractures' *Psychosomatic Medicine* 65: 688-694

126 'Aisle lower the blood pressure' (2009) *Threshold* 97: 4

127 'Married live longer – new Australian data' (2008) *Threshold* 94: 3, citing Australian Bureau of Statistics, *Causes of death*, 2006

128 SH Lee *et al* (1987) *Health differentials among working age Australians* [Canberra: Australian Institute of Health]

129 National Health Strategy (1992) *Enough to make you sick: How income and environment affect health* [Melbourne]

130 M Eastman (1997) 'Family variables, health outcomes and national health strategies' *Threshold* 56: 14–25.

131 JS House, KR Landis and D Umberson (1988) 'Social relationships and health' *Science* 241: 540–544.

132 See: Daisy Dumas (2012) 'Could your friends be making you sick? *Daily Mail Online*, January 28, citing a study published in the Proceedings of the National Academy of Sciences journal.

133 Staff Reporter (2012) 'Cheer up ... and save yourself a heart attack: Positive outlook keeps heart healthy, scientists say' *Daily Mail Online*, April 18, citing a study published in *Psychological Bulletin*.

134 Stephanie A Bond *et al* (2002) 'Individual and contextual risks of death among race and ethnic groups in the United States' *Journal of Health and Social Behavior* 43: 359-381

135 Scott M Stanley (2005) 'What is it with men and commitment, anyway' *Threshold* 83: 4-11 . This observation is also consistent with John Gottman's research that shows that where a husband accepts his wife's influence, it has a positive impact on marital relations: John Gottman (1999) *The seven principles for making marriage work* [New York, Three Rivers], 105. See also Steven Nock (1998) *Marriage in men's lives* [New York, Oxford University Press]; and 'US: Healthy marriage' (2005) *Threshold* 83: 29. It is also supported by motivational studies. See 'Nagging is good for you' (2012) *Daily Mail Online*, April 19, citing University of Lincoln research.

136 McAllister (1995) *supra*

137 McAllister (1995) *supra*

138 Eastman (1997) *supra*.

139 J Dominion (1991) *Marital Breakdown and the Health of the Nation* [London, One plus One]

140 Professor Pierre Baume cited in L Slattery (1998) 'The descent of men' *Weekend Australian* 13-14 June.

141 Kate Fairweather-Schmidt *et al* (2010) 'Baseline factors predictive of serious suicidality at follow-up: findings focussing an age and gender from a community-based study' *BioMedCentral Psychiatry* 10: 41

142 Quoted in Augustine J Kposowa (2009) 'Psychiatrist availability, social disintegration, and suicide deaths in US counties, 1990 – 1995' *Journal of Community Psychology* 37.1: 73-87

143 D Ladbrook (1997) *supra*. See also: E Durkheim (1951) *Suicide* [Glencoe Il, The Free Press]

144 Ronald C Kessler, Guilherme Borges and Ellen W Walters (1999) 'Prevalence of and risk factors for lifetime suicide attempts in the National Comorbidity survey' *Archives of General Psychiatry* 56: 617-626

145 K Hegarty and G Roberts (1998) 'How common is domestic violence against women? The definition of partner abuse in prevalence studies' *Australian and New Zealand Journal of Public Health* 22(1): 49-54.

146 See for example Myrna Dawson *et al* (2009) 'National trends in intimate partner homicides: Explaining declines in Canada, 1976-2001' *Violence Against Women* 15.3: 276-306

147 Karen F Parker and Tracy Johns (2002) 'Urban disadvantage and types of race-specific homicides: Assessing the diversity in family structures in the urban context' *Journal of Research in Crime and Delinquency* 39: 277-303

148 John Wooldredge and Amy Thistlewaite (2003) 'Neighbourhood structure and race-specific rates of intimate assault' *Criminology* 41: 393-418

149 Dorothy S Ruiz (2002) 'The increase in incarcerations among women and its impact on the grandmother caregiver: Some racial considerations' *Journal of Sociology and Social Welfare* 29: 179-197

150 Robert J Sampson, John H Laub and Christopher Wimer (2006) 'Does marriage reduce crime? A counterfactual approach to within-individual effects' *Criminology* 44: 465-502

151 Thomas E Hanlon *et al* (2005) 'Incarcerated drug-abusing mothers: Their characteristics and vulnerability' *The American Journal of Drug and Alcohol Abuse* 1: 59-77

152 Christopher J O'Donnell, Angie Smith and Jeanne R Madison (2002) 'Using demographic risk factors to explain variations in the incidence of violence against women' *Journal of Interpersonal Violence* 17: 1239-1262; Judy A Van Wyk *et al* (2003) 'Detangling individual-, partner-, and community-level correlates of partner violence' *Crime and Delinquency* 49: 412-438

153 Greer Litton Fox and Michael L Benson (2006) 'Household and neighbourhood contexts of intimate partner violence' *Public Health Reports* 121: 419-427

154 Laura Ann McCloskey *et al* (2002) 'A comparative study of battered women and their children in Italy and the United States' *Journal of Family Violence* 17.1: 53-74

155 S Sarantakos (1984) *Living Together in Australia* [Melbourne, Longman Cheshire] 138.

156 Sotirios Sarantakos (2001) 'Husband abuse: Fact or fiction' *Threshold* 67: 21 - 23

157 Eric P Baumer (2002) 'Neighbourhood disadvantage and police notification by victims of violence' *Criminology* 40: 579-611

158 McAllister (1995) *supra*

159 Cox, Huppert and Whichelow (1993) *supra*

160 National Center for Health Statistics (1997) *Health and selected socioeconomic characteristics of the family: United States 1988–90* [Washington DC, General Printing Office]

161 Ladbrook *supra*

162 Yael Chatav and Mark W Whisman (2007) 'Marital dissolution and psychiatric disorders: An investigation of risk factors' *Journal of Divorce and Remarriage* 47 (1-2): 1-12

163 Tracie O Afifi, Brian J Cox and Murray W Enns (2006) 'Mental health profiles among married, never-married, and separated/divorced mothers in a nationally representative sample' *Social Psychiatry and Psychiatric Epidemiology* 41: 122-129

164 Adriane Frech and Kristi Willimas (2007) 'Depression and psychological benefits of entering marriage' *Journal of Health and Social Behavior* 48: 149-62

165 Hidehiro Sugiawa *et al* (2002) 'The impact of social ties on depressive symptoms in the US and Japanese elderly' *Journal of Social Issues* 58: 785-804

166 RT Sequares (1985) 'Marital status and psychiatric morbidity in new clinical concepts' in OJWE Bjovksten (ed) *Marital Therapy* [Washington DC, American Psychiatric Press]; and McAllister (1995) *supra*

167 EH Oppenheimer (1984) 'Marital stress and alcoholism' in *Marriage and Health* [London, Marriage Research Centre] There is also an adverse intergenerational impact on children: 'US: Alcoholism effects' (2004) *Threshold* 82: 35

168 Gerard J Molloy *et al* (2009) 'Marital status, gender and cardiovascular mortality: Behavioural distress and metabolic explanations' *Social Science and Medicine* 69.2: 223-228; and Sofia Gerward *et al* (2010) 'Marital status and occupation in relation to short-term case fatality after a first coronary event: A population based cohort' *BioMedCentral Public Health* 10: 235. See also Andrew Steptoe, Karen Lundwall and Mark Cropley (2000) 'Gender, family structure and cardiovascular activity during the working day and evening" *Social Science and Medicine* 50: 531-539 which found "being married and having children has a favourable effect" on blood pressure.

169 Xinguang Chen *et al* (2006) 'Age of smoking onset as a predictor of smoking cessation during pregnancy' *American Journal of Health Behaviors* 30: 247-258

170 Krister Hakansson *et al* (2009) 'Association between mid-life marital status and cognitive function in later life: Population based cohort study' *British Medical Journal* 339: b2462

171 Robert E Mann *et al* (2007) 'Road rage and collision involvement' *American Journal of Health Behavior* 31: 384-91

172 Theodore J Iwashyna and Nicholas A Christakis (2003) 'Marriage, widowhood, and health-care use' *Social Science and Medicine* 57: 2137-2147

173 Corey LM Keyes (2002) 'The mental health continuum: From languishing to flourishing in life' *Journal of Health and Social Behavior* 43: 207-222

174 MDR Evans and Jonathan Kelley (2004) 'Effect of family structure on life satisfaction: Australian evidence' *Social Indicators Research* 69: 303-349

175 Alois Stutzer and Bruno S Frey (2006) 'Does marriage make people happy, or do

happy people get married?' *The Journal of Socio-Economics* 35: 326-347

176 'Marriage reduces risks' (2009) *Threshold* 97: 30

177 Erin Y Cornwell and Linda J Waite (2009) 'Social disconnectedness, perceived isolation, and health among older adults' *Journal of Health and Social Behavior* 50.1: 31-48

178 Anni Skipstein *et al* (2010) 'Trajectories of maternal symptoms of anxiety and depression: A 13-year longitudinal study of a population-based sample' *BMC Public Health* 10: 589

179 Lisa S Segre *et al* (2007) 'The prevalence of postpartum depression: The relative significance of three social status indicators' *Social Psychiatry and Psychiatric Epidemiology* 42: 316-21; Cynthia S Minkovitz *et al* (2005) 'Maternal depressive symptoms and children's receipt of health care in the first 3 years of life' *Pediatrics* 115: 306-314

180 John Cairney *et al* (2004) 'Single mothers and the use of professionals for mental health care reasons' *Social Science and Medicine* 59: 2535-2546

181 SB Campbell *et al* (2009) 'A latent class analysis of maternal depressive symptoms over 12 years and offspring adjustment in adolescence' *Journal of Abnormal Psychology* 118: 479-93

182 SB Campbell *et al* (2007) 'Trajectories of maternal depressive symptoms, maternal sensitivity and children's functioning at school entry' *Developmental Psychology* 43: 1202-15

183 'Impact of divorce on the elderly' (2009) *Threshold* 96: 7, citing research by the Institute for Public Policy Research.

184 Ellen L Lipman *et al* (2002) 'Child well-being in single-mother families' *Journal of the American Academy of Child and Adolescent Psychiatry* 41: 75-82

185 Stephanie Kasen *et al* (2005) 'Dual work and family roles and depressive symptoms in two birth cohorts of women' *Social Psychiatry and Psychiatric Epidemiology* 40: 300-307

186 Valerie King (2003) 'The legacy of a grandparent's divorce: Consequences for ties between grandparents and grandchildren' *Journal of Marriage and Family* 65: 170-183

187 Gunilla Ringback Weitoft, Bo Burstrom and Mans Rosen (2004) 'Premature mortality among lone fathers and childless men' *Social Science and Medicine* 59: 1449-1459

188 Doherty (1997) *supra*

189 RE Emery (1982) *Marriage, divorce and children's adjustment* [Newbury Park CA, Sage Publications]; JM Gottman and LF Katz (1989) 'Effects of marital discord on young children's peer interruption and health' *Developmental Psychology* 25: 373–

381; and JF Kiecolt-Glaser *et al* (1993) 'Negative behavior during marital conflict is associated with immunological regulation' *Psychosomatic Medicine* 55: 395-409.

190 SM Stanley and HJ Markman (1997) *Facts about marital stress and divorce* [Denver, University of Denver] and the studies cited therein.

191 Genevieve Bouchard (2005) 'Transition to motherhood and relationship quality: Does divorce or separation history matter? *Journal of Divorce and Remarriage* 44.: 107-116

192 Avner Ahituv and Robert I Lerman (2007) 'How do marital status, work effort, and wage rates interact?' *Demography* 44: 623-47

193 Thomas A Hirschl, Joyce Altobelli and Mark R Rank (2003) 'Does marriage increase the odds of affluence? Exploring the life course probabilities' *Journal of Marriage and Family* 65: 927-938. See also: 'Marriage increases wealth' (2006) *Threshold* 88: 9

194 'Turns out that marriage does pay off' (2011) *Threshold* 103: 4-5

195 Janet Wilmoth and Gregor Koso (2002) 'Does marital history matter? Marital status and wealth outcomes among preretirement adults' *Journal of Marriage and Family* 64: 254-268

196 Daniel T Lichter, Deborah Roempke and J Brian Brown (2003) 'Is marriage a panacea? Union formation among economically disadvantaged unwed mothers' *Social Problems* 50: 60-86

197 'Canada: Divorce is the most expensive life event' (2004) *Threshold* 82: 37

198 Marcia Carlson, Sara McLanahan and Paula England (2004) 'Union formation in fragile families' *Demography* 41: 237-261

199 Darryl E Getter (2003) 'Contributing to the delinquency of borrowers' *The Journal of Consumer Affairs* 37.1: 86-100

200 'Lose your marriage, lose your home' (2008) *Threshold* 94: 3

201 John Iceland (2003) 'Why poverty remains high: The role of income growth, economic inequality, and changes in family structure, 1949-1999' *Demography* 40: 499-519

202 David Wood (2003) 'Effect of child and family poverty on child health in the United States' *Pediatrics* 112: 707-712

203 Lisa A Keister (2004) 'Race, family structure, and wealth: The effect of childhood family on adult asset ownership' *Sociological Perspectives* 47: 161-187

204 Lenore J Weitzman (1985) *The divorce revolution; The unexpected social and economic consequences for women and children in America* [New York, Free Press]

205 See James B McLindon (1987) 'Separate but unequal: The economic disaster of divorce for women and children' *Family Law Quarterly* 21: 351; Saul D Hoffman

and Greg J Duncan (1988) 'What are the economic consequences of divorce?' *Demography* 25: 641; Hans-Jurgen Andreb *et al* (2006) 'The economic consequences of partnership dissolution – A comparative analysis of panel studies from Belguim, Germany, Great Britain, Italy and Sweden' *European Social Review* 22: 533; Jerry Silvey and Bob Birrell (2004) 'Financial outcomes for parents after separation' *People and Place* 12: 45; Simon Kelly and Ann Harding (2005) *Love can hurt, divorce will cost,* Income and Wealth Report Issue 10 [Canberra, National Centre for Social and Economic Modelling], and David de Vaus *et al* (2012) 'The financial consequences of relationship breakdown and the implications for the Australian social protection system' *Presentation,* Australian Institute of Family Studies conference, Melbourne, July 25-27.

206 See Peter McDonald (ed) (1986) *Settling up: Property and income distribution on divorce in Australia* [Melbourne, Australian Institute of Family Studies]; and Kathleen Funder *et al* (1993) *Settling down: Pathways of parents after divorce* [Melbourne, Australian Institute of Family Studies]

207 Jody Hughes (2000) 'Repartnering after divorce: Marginal mates and unwedded women' *Family Matters* 55: 16

208 Patrick Parkinson (2011) 'Another inconvenient truth: Fragile families and the looming financial crisis for the welfare state' *Family Law Quarterly* 45: 329-352

209 Patricia A McManus and Thomas A DiPrete (2001) 'Losers and winners: The financial consequences of separation and divorce for men' *American Sociological Review* 66: 246-268

210 Paul R Amato *et al* (2009) 'Changes in non-resident father-child contact from 1976 to 2001' *Family Relations* 58: 41

211 Parkinson (2011) *supra.* See also: Patricia A McManus and Thoma A DiPrete (2001) 'Losers and winners: The financial consequences of separation and divorce for men' *American Sociological Review* 66: 246 and de Vaus (2012) *supra*

212 'Divorce hits boomers in the pocket' (2007) *Threshold* 90: 7, citing Australian Institute of Family Studies research. See also Julie Wouters (2003) 'Men and money after marriage breakdown' *Threshold* 78: 27-29

213 'Married bliss add up' (2000) *Threshold* 64: 5; and 'The key to happiness' (2000) *Threshold* 63: 11. See also: 'Why settling down is the best way to save money' (2012) *Daily Mail Online*, July 27); and de Vaus *et al* (2012) *supra*

214 Donald Brice, Karie Barbour and Angela Thacker (2004) 'Welfare program re-entry among post-reform leavers' *Southern Economic Journal* 70: 816-836

215 PL Chase-Lansdale and EM Hetherington (1990) 'The impact of divorce on life-span development: Short and long-term effects' in PB Baltes, DL Featherman and RM Lerner (eds) *Lifespan development and behaviour* (Vol 10: 107-151 [Hillsdale NJ, Erlbaum]; FF Furstenberg and A Cherlin (1991) *Divided families: What happens*

to children when parents part [Cambridge, MA, Harvard University Press]; EM Hetherington (1993) 'An overview of the Virginia Longitudinal study of divorce and remarriage with a focus on early adolescence' *Journal of Family Psychology* 7: 39-56; S McLanahan and G Sandefur (1994) *Growing up with a single parent: What helps, what hurts* [Cambridge MA, Harvard University Press]; JA Seltzer (1994) 'Relationships between fathers and children who live apart: The father's role after separation' *Journal of Marriage and Family* 15: 49-77; N Zill, D Morrison and M Coiro (1993) 'Long-term effects of parental divorce on parent-child relationships, adjustment, and achievement in young adulthood' *Journal of Family Psychology* 7: 91-103; 'Cost to children of marriage break-up' (2003) *Threshold* 75: 35, citing a UK report; and Judith Wallerstein and Sandra Blakeslee (1989) *Second chances: Men, Women and children a decade after divorce* [New York, Ticknor and Fields]. See also the studies cited in *To have and to hold* (1998) *supra*.

216 Robert E Emery (1999) *Marriage, divorce and children's adjustment* (2nd ed.) [Beverly Hills, CA, Sage], and E Mavis Hetherington (2003) *For Better or Worse: Divorce Reconsidered* [New York, WW Norton]

217 Judith Wallerstein and Sandra Blakeslee (1989) *Second chances: Men, women and children a decade after divorce* [New York, Ticknor and Fields]

218 M Rutter, J Kim-Cohen and B Maughan (2006) 'Continuities and discontinuities in psychopathology between childhood and adult life' *Journal of Child Psychology and Psychiatry and Allied Disciplines* 47: 276-295

219 I Bretherton (1992) 'The origins of attachment theory: John Bowlby and Mary Ainsworth' *Developmental Psychology* 28: 759; C Hazen and P R Shaver (1987) 'Romantic love conceptualised as an attachment process' *Journal of Personality and Social Psychology* 52: 511 - 524; and Michael Rutter (1995) 'Clinical implications of attachment concepts: Retrospect and prospect' *Journal of Psychiatry and Psychology* 36: 549-571. Attachment theory does not explain everything about relationships, including what people do once they are in relationships. See Thomas N Bradbury and Benjamin R Karney (2010) *Intimate relationships* [New York, WW Norton and Co], 116

220 Abdul Khaleque and Ronald P Rohner (2012) 'Transnational relations between perceived parental acceptance and personality dispositions of children and adults' *Personality and Social Psychology Review* 16: 103-115; and 'A father's love is one of the greatest influences on personality development' (2012) *Science Blog,* June 12

221 See for example: Susan E Jacquet and Catherine A Surra (2001) 'Parental divorce and premarital couples: Commitment and other relationship characteristics' *Journal of Marriage and Family* 63: 627-638 – Divorce often leads to low trust among children

222 Scott M Stanley (2012) 'Attachment and the perfect storm' *Sliding vs deciding blog*, March 17

223 The early few years of life coincide with the rapid growth of the human brain.

224 See also Michael Marmot (2010) *Fair society, healthy lives.* The report of the Marmot Review into health inequalities [London, HM Government]

225 See: Norval Glenn (1990) 'The social and cultural meaning of contemporary marriage' in Bryce J Christensen (ed) *The retreat from marriage* [Lanham, University of America Press]

226 Prime Minister's Youth Homeless Taskforce (1998) *Putting families in the picture* [Canberra, Department of Family and Community Services]. See also: Joan Smith *et al* (1998) *The family background of homeless young people* [London, Family Policy Studies Centre] for a similar situation in the UK.

227 Department of Health (1997) *National Action Plan for Suicide Prevention* [Canberra, the Department]

228 MPM Richards and M Dyson (1982) *Separation, divorce and the development of children: A review* [London, Department of Health and Social Security]. See also: NR Butling and J Golding (1986) *From birth to five: A study of the health and behaviour of Britain's five year olds* [Oxford, Pergamon Press]

229 E Mavis Hetherington and WG Clingempeel (1992) 'Coping with marital transitions' *Monographs of the Society for Research in Child Development* Series 227 Vol 57 No 2-3, [Chicago, University of Chicago Press]

230 Don Kerr (2004) 'Family transformations and the well-being of children: Recent evidence from Canadian longitudinal data' *Journal of Comparative Family Studies* 35: 73-90

231 Australian Bureau of Statistics, *Marriages and divorces, Australia, 2010*

232 This is an estimate, as the Center for Disease Control ceased collecting the data in 1988 when the number was over 1 million children.

233 Patrick F Fagan and Nicholas Zill (2011) *The second annual index of family belonging and rejection* [Washington DC, Marriage and Religion Research Institute]

234 Royal College of Psychiatrists, *Mental health and growing up* [London, The College]

235 Tim Shipman (2010) 'Broken Britain: Half of all parents split up before their children reach the age of 16' *Daily Mail Online*, December 7, citing a report from the Centre for Social Justice.

236 Department of Justice, Canada, *The effects of divorce on children: A selected literature review* [Ottawa, The Department]

237 Paul Robinson, *Parenting after separation and divorce: A profile of arrangements for spending time with and making decisions for children* [Ottawa, Statistics Canada]

238 McAlister (1995) *supra.*

239 MEJ Wadsworth (1984) 'Early stress and associations with adult health behaviour and parenting' in NR Butler and BD Corner (eds) *Stress and disability in childhood* [Bristol, John Wright and Sons] 100-104.

240 BJ Elliott and MPM Richards (1991) 'Children and divorce: Educational performance and behaviour before and after parental separation' *International Journal of Law and the Family* 5: 258. See also Hetherington and Clingempeel (1992) *supra*.

241 Martijin de Goede *et al* (2000) 'Family problems and youth unemployment' *Adolescence* 35: 595-600

242 Inge Vandervalk *et al* (2004) 'Marital status, marital process, and patrental resources in predicting adolescents' emotional adjustment: A multilevel analysis' *Journal of Family Issues* 25: 291-317

243 Don Kerr and Roderic Beaujot (2003) 'Child poverty and family structure in Canada, 1981-1997' *Journal of Comparative Family Studies* 34: 321-334

244 Frank F Furstenberg and Kathleen E Kiernan (2001) 'Delayed parental divorce: How much do children benefit?' *Journal of Marriage and Family* 63: 452

245 Teresa M Cooney and Jeylan T Mortimer (1999) 'Family structure differences in the timing of leaving home: Exploring mediating factors' *Journal of Research on Adolescence* 9: 367-393

246 Jeanne M Hilton and Karen Kopera-Frye (2007) 'Differences in resources provided by grandparents in single and married-parent families' *Journal of Marriage and Divorce* 47.1/2: 33-54. See also: Rosalie Pattenden (2004) 'Grandparenting in divorced families' *Threshold* 82: 28-29

247 Andrej M Grjibovske *et al* (2005) 'Sociodemographic determinants of initiation and duration of breastfeeding in northwest Russia' *Acta Paediatrica* 94: 588-594

248 Gordon CS Smith and Ian R White (2006) 'Predicting the risk for Sudden Infant Death Syndrome from obstetric characteristics: A retrospective cohort study of 505,011 live births' *Pediatrics* 117: 60-66

249 Charlemagne C Victorino and Anne H Gauthier (2009) 'The social determinants of child health: Variations across health outcomes: A population-based cross-sectional analysis' *BioMed Central Pediatrics* 9.53

250 Z. Tomcikova *et al* (2009) 'Parental divorce and adolescent drunkeness: Role of socioeconomic position, psychological well-being and social support' *European Addiction Research* 15: 202-08; KB Rogers and HA Rose (2002) 'Risk and resiliency factors among adolescents who experience marital transitions' *Journal of Marriage and Family* 64: 1024-1037; WJ Doherty and RH Needle (1991) 'Psychologiccal adjustment and substance use among adolescents before and after a parental divorce' *Child Development* 62: 328-337; and RJ Paxton, RE Valouis and JW Drane (2007) 'Is there a relationship between family structure and substance abuse among public middle school students?' *Journal of Child Family Studies* 16: 593-605

251 Anna Goodman *et al* (2007) 'Child, family, school and community risk factors for poor mental health in Brazilian schoolchildren' *Journal of the American Academy of Child and Adolescent Psychiatry*, 46: 448-456. This study broadly replicated the findings of the British-Child and Adolescent Mental Health Surveys, 1999 and 2004. See: T Ford, R Goodman and H Meltzer (2004) 'The relative importance of child, family, school and neighbourhood correlates of childhood psychiatric disorder' *Social Psychiatry Psychiatric Epidemiology* 29: 487-496; G Canino *et al* (2004) 'The DSM-IV rates of child and adolescent disorders in Puerto Rico: prevalence, correlates, service use, and the effects of impairment' *Archives of General Psychiatry* 61: 85-93. A Scottish study also had similar findings: Helen Sweeting *et al* (2010) 'Can we explain increases in young people's psychological distress over time? *Social Science and Medicine* 71.10:1819-30. See also: Laura Perna *et al* (2010) 'The impact of social environment on children's mental health in a prosperous city: An analysis of data from the city of Munich' *BMC Public Health* 10: 199; and Konstantina Magklara *et al* (2010) 'Socioeconomic inequalities in general and psychological health among adolescents: A cross-sectional study in senior high schools in Greece' *International Journal for Equity in Health* 9: 3

252 Andre Sourander *et al* (2007) 'Who is at greatest risk of adverse long-term outcomes? The Finnish from a boy to a man study' *Journal of the American Academy of Child and Adolescent Psychiatry* 46: 1148-1161. See also Avelardo Valdez *et al* (2007) 'Aggressive crime, alcohol and drug use, and concentrated poverty in 24 US urban areas' *The American Journal of Drug and Alcohol Abuse* 33: 595-603; and Jeannie A Fry (2010) 'Change in family structure and rates of violent juvenile delinquency' *Master's Thesis, Department of Sociology, Virginia Polytechnic Institute and State University*, May 17, 25-40

253 Xiaoming Li *et al* (2002) 'Risk and protective factors associated with gang involvement among urban African-American adolescents' *Youth and Society* 34: 172-194

254 Gina M Wingood *et al* (2002) 'Gang involvement and the health of African American female adolescents' *Pediatrics* 110(5): 57

255 Hyun (Hanna) K Kim *et al* (2007) 'Children's mental health and family functioning in Rhode Island' *Pediatrics 119 Supplement 1*: S23 -28

256 Guang Guo and Yuying Tong (2006) 'Age at first sexual intercourse, genes and social context: evidence from twins and the Dopamine D4 receptor gene' *Demography* 43: 747-769: Teens living in a single-parent family are about a quarter more likely to engage in sexual intercourse than peers from intact two-parent families. Teens growing-up in stepfamilies are more than a third more likely.

257 David W Brown *et al* (2010) Adverse childhood experiences are associated with the risk of lung cancer: A prospective cohort study' *BHC Public Health* 10.20, January 19; James B Kirby (2002) 'The influence of parental separation on smoking initiation

in adolescents' *Journal of Health and Social Behavior* 43: 56-71; and Rebecca L Collins and Phyllis L Ellickson (2004) 'Integrating four theories of adolescent smoking' *Substance Use and Misuse* 39: 179-209

258 Heather S Lonczak *et al* 'Family structure and substance use among American Indian youth: A preliminary study' *Families, Systems and Health* 25.1:10-22; Shanta R Duke *et al* (2003) 'Childhood abuse, neglect, and household dysfunction and the risk of illicit drug use: The adverse childhood experiences study' *Pediatrics* 111: 564-572; Phyllis L Ellickson, Steven C Martino and Rebecca L Collins (2004) 'Marijuana use from adolescence to young adulthood: Multiple development projectories and their associated outcomes' *Health Psychology* 23: 299-307

259 JB Kirby (2006) 'From single-parent families to stepfamilies – is the transition associated with adolescent school initiation?' *Journal of Family Issues* 27: 685-711; and Barbara J Costello, Bradley J Anderson and Michael H Stein (2006) 'Heavy episodic drinking among adolescents: A test of hypotheses derived from control theory' *Journal of Alcohol and Drug Education* 50.1: 35-56

260 Rory C O'Connor, Susan Rasmussen and Keith Hawton (2009) 'Predicting deliberate self-harm in adolescents: A six month prospective study' *Suicide and Life-Threatening Behavior* 39.4: 364-74

261 Andres G Gill, William A Vega and R Jay Turner (2002) 'Early and mid-adolescence risk factors for later substance abuse by African Americans and European Americans' *Public Health Reports* 117.S1: S15-S28

262 David C May (1999) 'Scared kids, unattached kids, or peer pressure: Why do students carry firearms to school?' *Youth and Society* 31: 100-127

263 Carol A Ford, Peter S Bearman and James Moody (1999) 'Forgone health care among adolescents' *Journal of the American Medical Association* 282: 2227-2234.

264 Richard J Petts (2009) 'Family and religious characteristics' influence on delinquency trajectories from adolescence to young adulthood' *American Sociological Review* 74: 465-483

265 S Alexandra Burt (2008) 'Parental divorce and adolescent delinquency: Ruling out the impact of common genes' *Developmental Psychology* 44.6: 1667-1668

266 Anne-Marie Ambert (1999) 'The effects of male delinquency on mothers and fathers: A heuristic study' *Sociological Inquiry* 69(4): 621-640

267 Kennon J Rice and William R Smith (2002) 'Sociological models of automotive theft: Integrating routine activity and social disorganisation approaches' *Journal of Research in Crime and Delinquency* 39: 304-336

268 Lisa A Strohschein (2007) 'Prevalence of Methylphenidate use among Canadian children following parental divorce' *Canadian Medical Association* Journal 176: 1711-1714

269 Fatma G Huffman, Sankarabharan Kanikireddy and Manthan Patel (2010) 'Parenthood: A contributing factor to childhood obesity' *International Journal of Environmental Research and Public Health* 7.7: 2800-2810

270 T Ristkari *et al* (2008) 'Life events, self-reported psychopathology and sense of coherence among young men: A population-based study' *Nordic Journal of Psychiatry* 62.6: 464-471

271 John Hagan and Holly Foster (2003) 'S/He's a rebel: Toward a sequential stress theory of delinquency and gendered pathways to disadvantage in emerging adulthood' *Social Forces* 82: 53-86

272 Anne Mari Undheim and Anne Mari Sund (2010) 'Prevalence of bullying and aggressive behaviours and their relationship to mental health problems among 12- to 15-year old Norwegian adolescents' *European Child and Adolescent Psychiatry* 19.11: 803-11

273 Heather A Turner *et al* (2007) 'Family structure variation in patterns and predictors of child victimisation' *American Journal of Orthopsychiatry* 77: 282-295; and Dana L Hayne and Alex R Piquero (2006) 'Pubertal development and physical victimisation in adolescence' *Journal of Research in Crime and Delinquency* 43: 3-35

274 Donald R Lyman *et al* (2007) 'Longitudinal evidence that psychopathy scores in early adolescence predict adult psychopathy' *Journal of Abnormal Psychology* 116: 155-165

275 Constance R Ahrons (2007) 'Family ties after divorce: long-term implications for children' *Family Process* 46: 53-65

276 Wadsworth (1984) *supra*; and D Kuh and M Maclean (1990) 'Women's childhood experience of parental separation and their subsequent health and socio-economic status in adulthood' *Journal of Biosocial Science* 22: 121.

277 D Kuh and M Maclean (1990) *supra.* See also, RH Needle, SS Su and WJ Doherty (1990) 'Divorce, remarriage and adolescent substance use: A prospective longitudinal study' *Journal of Marriage and the Family* 52: 157-169.

278 Wadsworth (1984) *supra.*

279 Miguel Angel Marinez-Gonzalez *et al* (2003) 'Parental factors, mass media influences, and the onset of eating disorders in a prospective population-based cohort' *Pediatrics* 111: 315-320

280 DA Dawson (1991) 'Family structure and children's health and well-being: data from the 1988 National Survey of Child Health' *Journal of Marriage and the Family* 53: 573-584.

281 Barbara H Bardenheier *et al* (2004) 'Factors associated with underimmunization at 3 months of age in four medically underserved areas' *Public Health Reports* 119: 479-485

282 HS Friedman *et al* (1995) 'Psychological and behavioral predictors of longevity: The ageing and death of the "Termites" ' *American Psychologist* 50(2): 69-78.

283 Bruce J Ellis *et al* (1999) 'Quality of early family relationships and individual differences in the timing of pubertal maturation in girls: A longitudinal test of an evolutionary model' *Journal of Personality and Social Psychology* 77: 387-401

284 Dorothy T Breen and Margaret Crosbie-Burnett (1993) 'Moral dilemmas of early adolescents of divorced and intact families: A qualitative and quantitative analysis' *Journal of Early Adolescence* 13: 168-182

285 Sylvie Drapeau and Camil Bouchard (1993) 'Support networks and adjustment among 6 to 11 year-olds from maritally disrupted and intact families' *Journal of Divorce and Remarriage* 19: 75-97. See also: Kristen M McCabe (1997) 'Sex differences in the long-term effects of divorce on children: Depression and heterosexual relationship difficulties in the young adult years' *Journal of Divorce and Remarriage* 27: 123-134

286 John Guidubaldi, Joseph D Perry and Bonnie K Nastasi (1987) 'Growing up in a divorced family: Initial and long-term perspectives on children's adjustment' *Applied Social Psychology Annual* 7: 202-237

287 Paul Amato and Alan Booth, (1997) *A generation at risk: Growing up in an era of family upheaval* [Cambridge MA, Harvard University Press] at 29-70 and the studies cited therein; and Andrew J Cherlin, Kathleen E Kiernan and P Lindsay Chase-Lonsdale (1995) 'Parental divorce in childhood and democratic outcomes in young adulthood' *Demography* 32: 299-316

288 Frances K Goldscheider and Calvin Goldscheider (1998) 'The effects of childhood family structure on leaving and returning home' *Journal of Marriage and the Family* 60: 745-756

289 Stephen T Mennemeyer and Bisakha Sen (2006) 'Undesirable juvenile behaviour and the quality of parental relationships' *Southern Economic Journal* 73: 437-460

290 Jeanne M Hilton and Stephen Desrochers (2003) 'Children's behaviour problems in single-parent and married-parent families: Development of a Predictive model' *Journal of Divorce and Remarriage* 37: 13-34

291 Larson (1995) *supra*, 121.

292 DA Dawson (1991) *supra*. See also, J Guidubaldi, J Perry and BK Nastasi (1987) 'Assessment and intervention for children of divorce' in JP Vincent (ed) *Advances in family intervention, assessment and theory* V4 [Greenwich CT: JAI Press], 33–69; J Guidubaldi (1987) 'Growing up in a divorced family' in S Oskamp (ed) *Annual review of applied social psychology* [Beverley Hills CA, Sage Publications] 202–237; and J Guidubaldi (1988) 'Differences in children's divorce adjustment across grade level and gender' in S Wochick and P Karoly (eds) *Children of divorce* [Lexington MA, Lexington Books] 185–231.

293 Darlene R Wrights and Kevin M Fitzpatrick (2006) 'Violence and minority youth: The effects of risk and asset factors on flighting among African American children and adolescents' *Adolescence* 41: 251-262

294 DH Demo and AC Acock (1991) 'The impact of divorce on children' in A Booth (ed) *Contemporary families, looking forward, looking back* [Minneapolis MN, National Council on Family Relations]. See also, MEJ Wadsworth (1984) *supra*; BJ Elliott and MPM Richards (1991) *supra*; SM Dornbusch, JM Carlsmith and SJ Bushwall (1985) 'Single parents, extended households and the control of adolescents' *Child Development* 56: 326-342; LD Steinberg (1987) 'Single parents, stepparents, and the susceptibility of adolescents to antisocial peer pressure' *Child Development* 58: 269-275; and DP Farrington (1978) 'The family backgrounds of aggressive youths' in LA Hersov, M Berger and D Shaffer (eds) *Aggressive and antisocial behaviour in childhood and adolescence* [Oxford, Pergamon Press] 73-93.

295 Michelle Crozier Kegler *et al* (2005) 'Relationships among youth assets and neighbourhood and community resources' *Health Education and Behavior* 32: 380.397

296 Shannon E Cavanagh and Aletha C Huston (2006) 'Family instability and children's early problem behavior' *Social Forces* 85: 551-580

297 Julie Messer *et al* (2006) 'Preadolescent conduct problems in girls and boys' *Journal of the American Academy of Child and Adolescent Psychiatry* 45: 184-191. See also: Rex Forehand (1987) 'Family characteristics of adolescents who display overt and covert behaviour problems' *Journal of Behavior Therapy and Experimental Psychiatry* 18: 325-328; Jeffrey J Wood, Rena L Repetti and Scott C Roesch (2004) 'Divorce and children's adjustment problems at home and school: The role of depressive/withdrawn parenting' *Child Psychiatry and Human Development* 35: 131

298 Lisa Strohschein (2007) 'Prevalence of methylphenidate use among Canadian children following parental divorce' *Canadian Medical Association Journal*, 176: 1711-1714.

299 Stephen Demuth and Susan L Brown (2004) 'Family structure, family processes, and adolescent delinquency: The significance of parental absence versus parental gender' *Journal of Research in Crime and Delinquency* 41: 58-81

300 Dilek Sirvanli-Ozen (2005) 'Impacts of divorce on the behaviour and adjustment problems, parenting styles, and attachment styles of children: Literature review including Turkish studies' *Journal of Divorce and Remarriage* 42: 127-146

301 JL Sheline, BJ Skiper and WE Broadhead (1994) 'Risk factors for violent behavior in elementary school boys: Have you hugged your child today?' *American Journal of Public Health* 84: 661–663; P Cohen and J Brook (1987) 'Family factors related to persistence of psychopathology in childhood and adolescence' *Psychiatry* 50: 332–345; and Melinda Yexley, Iris Borowsky and Marjorie Ireland (2002)

'Correlation between different experiences of intrafamilial physical violence and violent adolescent behaviour' *Journal of Interpersonal Violence* 17: 707-720

302 Mary A Kernic *et al* (2002) 'Academic and school health issues among children exposed to maternal intimate partner abuse' *Archives of Pediatric and Adolescent Medicine* 156: 549-555

303 Robert F Valois *et al* (2002) 'Risk factors and behaviours associated with adolescent violence and aggression' *American Journal of Health Behavior* 26: 454-464

304 Janis Hootman, Gail M Houck and Mary Catherine King (2003) 'Increased mental health needs and new roles in school communities' *Journal of Child and Adolescent Psychiatric Nursing* 16.3: 93-101

305 Naomi R Marmorstein and William G Iacono (2005) 'Longitudinal follow-up of adolescents with late-onset antisocial behaviour: A pathological yet overlooked group' *Journal of the American Academy of Child and Adolescent Psychiatry* 44: 1284-1291

306 See also: Frank F Furstenberg Jr and Julien O Teitler (1994) 'Reconsidering the effects of marital disruption: What happens to children of divorce in early adulthood?' *Journal of Family Issues* 15: 179

307 David J Smith and Susan McVee (2003) ' Theory and method in the Edinburgh study of youth transitions and crime' *British Journal of Criminology* 43: 169-186. See also Stephen Collishaw *et al* (2004) 'Time trends in adolescent mental health' *Journal of Child Psychology and Psychiatry* 45: 1352-1362

308 David Fergusson, Nicola Swain-Campbell and John Horwood (2004) 'How does childhood economic disadvantage lead to crime?' *Journal of Child Psychology and Psychiatry* 45: 956-966. See also: H Juby and D P Farrington (2001) 'Disentangling the link between disrupted families and delinquency' *British Journal of Criminology* 41: 22-40

309 Andromachi Tseloni *et al* (2004) 'Burgulary victimisation in England and Wales, the United States and the Netherlands: A cross-national comparative test of routine activities and lifestyle theories' *British Journal of Criminology* 44: 66-91

310 Kathleen Boykin McElhaney and Joseph P Allen (2110) 'Autonomy and adolescent social functioning: The moderating effect of risk' *Child Development* 72: 220-235

311 Thomas D Cook *et al* (2002) 'Some ways in which neighbourhoods, nuclear families, friendships groups, and schools jointly affect changes in early adolescent development' *Child Development* 73: 1283-1309

312 Evidence of Stephen Zubrick and Sven Silburn to the Australian Parliamentary Committee, *Transcript*, pp. 705-727, *To Have and To Hold* (1998) *supra*, 59

313 *To Have and To Hold,* (1998) *supra*, 9.

314 Sven Silburn, *Transcript*, p. 711, *To Have and To Hold* (1998) *supra*, 59-60

315 SR Silburn and SR Zubrick (1996) *The WA Child Health Survey: Methodology and Policy Implications* [Melbourne, Australian Institute of FamilyStudies]

316 James B Kirby (2002) 'The influence of parental separation on smoking initiation in adolescents' *Journal of Health and Social Behavior* 43: 56-71. See also Laura Fingerson (2005) 'Do mothers' opinions matter in teens' sexual activity?' *Journal of Family Issues* 26: 947-974

317 Marielle Kroes *et al* (2002) 'A longitudinal community study: Do psychosocial risk factors and child behavior checklist score a 5 years of age predict psychiatric diagnoses at a later age?' *Journal of the American Academy of Child and Adolescent Psychiatry* 41: 955-963

318 Marieke Zwaanswijk *et al* (2003) 'Factors associated with adolescent mental health service need and utilisation' *Journal of the American Academy of Child and Adolescent Psychiatry* 42: 692-700

319 Andre Sourander *et al* (2004) 'Mental health service use among 18-year-old adolescent boys: A prospective 10-year follow-up study' *Journal of the American Academy of Child and Adolescent Psychiatry* 43: 1250-1258

320 Andre Sourander *et al* (2004) 'Have there been changes in children's psychiatric symptoms and mental health service use? A 10-year comparison from Finland' *Journal of the American Academy of Child and Adolescent Psychiatry* 43: 1134-1145

321 Susan L Brown (2004) 'Family structure and child well-being: The significance of parental cohabitation' *Journal of Marriage and Family* 66: 351-367

322 Ruth N Lopez Turley (2002) 'Are children of young mothers disadvantaged because of their mother's age or family background?' *Child Development* 74: 465-474

323 PL McCall and KC Land (1994) 'Trends in white male adolescent, young-adult, and elderly suicide: Are there common underlying structural factors?' *Social Science Research* 23: 57–81; and JF Robertson and RL Simons (1989) 'Family factors, self-esteem and adolescent depression' *Journal of Marriage and the Family* 51: 125 -138.

324 Fred C Pampei and John R Williamson (2001) 'Age patterns of suicide and homicide mortality rates in high-income nations' *Social Forces* 80: 251-282

325 A Bifulco *et al* (2002) 'Childhood adversity, parental vulnerability and disorder: examining intergenerational transmission of risk' *Journal of Child Psychology and Psychiatry* 43: 1075-1086

326 Mike Stoolmiller, Hyoun K Kim and Deborah M Capaldi (2005) 'The course of depressive symptoms in men from early adolescence to young adulthood: Identifying latent trajectories and early predictors' *Journal of Abnormal Psychology* 114: 331-345

327 Gunilla R Weitoft *et al* (2003) 'Mortality, severe morbidity, and injury in children living with single parents in Sweden: A population based study' *The Lancet* 361 (No. 9354): 289-295; and Margaret Whitehead and Paula Holland (2003) 'What puts children of lone parents at a health disadvantage?' *The Lancet* 361: 271

328 Jeremy Kisch, Victor Leino and Morton M Silverman (2005) 'Aspects of suicidal behaviour, depression, and treatment in college students: Results from the Spring 2000 National College Health Assessment Survey' *Suicide and Life-Threatening Behavior* 35: 3-13

329 Leslie R Martin *et al* (2005) 'Longevity following the experience of parental divorce' *Social Science and Medicine* 61: 2177-2189

330 DP Hogan and EM Kitagawa (1985) 'The impact of social status, family structure, and neighbourhood on the fertility of black adolescents' *American Journal of Sociology* 90: 825-855; BC Miller *et al* (1987) 'Family configuration and adolescent sexual attitudes and behavior' *Population and Environment* 9(2): 111-123; F Mott (1984) 'The patterning of female teenage sexual behavior and its relationship to early fertility' paper presented to the American Public Health Association; and S Newcomer and JR Urdry (1987) 'Parental marital status effects on adolescent sexual behavior' *Journal of Marriage and the Family* 49: 235-240.

331 LB Whitbeck, RL Simons and M Kao (1994) 'The effects of divorced mothers' dating behaviours and sexual attitudes on the sexual attitudes and behaviors of their adolescent children' *Journal of Marriage and the Family* 56: 615-621.

332 SN Seidman, WD Mosher and SO Aral (1994) 'Predictors of high risk behavior in unmarried American women: Adolescent environment as a risk factor' *Journal of Adolescent Health* 15: 126-132.

333 John S Santelli *et al* (2000) 'The association of sexual behaviours with socioeconomic status, family structure, and race/ethnicity among US adolescents' *American Journal of Public Health* 90: 1583-1588

334 Roy F Oman, Sara K Vesely and Cheryl B Aspy (2005) 'Youth assets and sexual risk behavior: The importance of assets for youth residing in one-parent households' *Perspectives on Sexual and Reproductive Health* 37: 25-31. See also Sharon E Lock and Murray L Vincent (1995) 'Sexual decision-making among rural adolescent females' *Health Values* 19: 47-58; Deborah M Capaldi, Lynn Crosby and Mike Stoolmiller (1996) 'Predicting the timing of first sexual intercourse for at-risk adolescent males' *Child Development* 67: 344-359; and Chris Albrecht and Jay D Teachman (2003) 'Childhood living arrangements and the risk of premarital intercourse' *Journal of Family Issues* 24: 867-894

335 Fridrik H Jonsson *et al* (2000) 'Parental divorce: Long-term effects on mental health, family relations, and adult sexual behavior' *Scandanavian Journal of Psychology* 41: 103

336 E Mavis Hetherington, Martha Cox and Roger Cox (1985) 'Long-term effects of divorce and remarriage on the adjustment of children' *Journal of the American Academy of Child Psychiatry* 24: 518-530; and Kathleen E Kiernan (1992) 'The impact of family disruptions in childhood on transitions made in young adult life'

Kevin Andrews

389

Population Studies 46: 213-234. See also: William G Axinn and Arland Thornton (1996) 'The influence of parents' marital dissolution on children's attitudes towards family formation' *Demography* 33: 66-81; and Arland Thornton and Donald Camburn (1987) 'The influence of family on premarital sexual attitudes and behavior' *Demography* 24: 323-340.

337 Bruce J Ellis *et al* (2003) 'Does father absence place daughters at special risk for early sexual activity and teenage pregnancy? *Child Development* 74: 801-821. See also: William H Jeynes (2001) 'The effects of recent parental divorce on their children's sexual attitudes and behavior' *Journal of Divorce and Remarriage* 35: 125-133

338 See also: Jenifer K McGuire and Bonnie L Barber (2010) 'A person-centered approach to the multifaceted nature of young adult sexual behavior' *Journal of Sex Research* 47: 308, 310, and the studies cited therein.

339 Frank F Furstenberg Jr and Julien O Teitler (1994) 'Reconsidering the effects of marital disruption: What happens to children of divorce in early adulthood?' *Journal of Family Issues* 15: 173-190; Ed Spruijt and Vincent Duindam (2005) 'Problem behaviour of boys and young men after parental divorce in the Netherlands' *Journal of Divorce and Remarriage* 34: 150; and Robert F Anda *et al* (2002) 'Adverse childhood experiences and risk of paternity in teen pregnancy' *Obstetrics and Gynecology* 100; 37-45

340 Kathleen M Harris, Greg J Duncan and Johanne Boisjoly (2002) 'Evaluating the role of 'nothing to lose' attitudes on risky behaviour in adolescence' *Social Forces* 80: 1005-1039

341 Judith Landau *et al* (2000) 'Family connectedness and women's sexual risk behaviours: Implications for the prevention/intervention of STD/HIV infection' *Family Process* 39(4): 461-475

342 Susan E Jacquet and Catherine A Surra (2001) 'Parental divorce and premarital couples: Commitment and other relationship characteristics' *Journal of Marriage and Family* 63: 627

343 Stacy G Johnston and Amanda Thomas (1996) 'Divorce versus intact parental marriage and perceived risk and dyadic trust in present heterosexual relationships' *Psychological Reports* 78: 387-390

344 Daniel J Weigel (2007) 'Parental divorce and the types of commitment-related messages people gain from their families of origin' *Journal of Divorce and Remarriage* 47: 23

345 Wendy D Manning, Monica A Longmore and Peggy C Giordana (2007) 'The changing institution of marriage: Adolescents' expectataions to cohabit and to marry' *Journal of Marriage and Family* 69: 559-575.

346 Ming Cui and Frank D Fincham (2010) 'The differential effects of parental divorce and marital conflict on young adult romantic relationships' *Personal Relationships*

17: 340. See also: Fridrik H Jonsson *et al* (2000) 'Parental divorce: Long-term effects on mental health, family relations, and adult sexual behaviour' *Scandanavian Journal of Psychology* 41: 103; Susan E Jacquet and Catherine Surra (2001) 'Parental *divorce and premarital couples: Commitment and other relationship characteristics' Journal of Marriage and Family* 63: 627-638; and Stephanie Schamess (1993) 'The search for love: Unmarried adolescent mothers' views of and about relationships with men' *Adolescence* 28: 306-322

347 Sharon C Risch, Kathleen M Jodl and Jacquelynne S Eccles (2004) 'Role of the father-adolescents relationship in shaping adolescents' attitudes towards divorce' *Journal of Marriage and the Family* 66: 55

348 Daniel J Weigel (2007) 'Parental divorce and the types of commitment-related messages people gain from their families of origin' *Journal of Divorce and Remarriage* 47: 23

349 Kristen A Moore and Thomas M Stief (1989) *Changes in marriage and fertility behavior: Behavior versus attitudes of young adults* [Washington DC, Child Trends, July 1989]

350 Jennifer Langhinrichsen-Rohling and Colleen Dostal (1996) 'Retrospective reports of family-of-origin divorce and abuse and college students' pre-parenthood cognitions; *Journal of Family Violence* 11: 331-348

351 Renee P Dennison and Susan S Koerner (2008) 'A look at hopes and worries about marriage: The views of adolescents following parental divorce' *Journal of Divorce and Remarriage* 48: 98; Renee P Dennison and Susan S Koerner (2006) 'Post-divorce interparental conflict and adolescents' attitudes about marriage' *Journal of Divorce and Remarriage* 45: 40. See also: Heidi R Riggio and Dana A Weiser (2008) 'Attitudes toward marriage: Embeddedness and outcomes in personal relationships' *Personal Relationships* 15: 134

352 Patrick F Fagan and Aaron Churchill (2012) *The effects of divorce on children* [Washington DC, MARRI, Family Research Council], 23-25 and the studies cited therein.

353 Fagan and Churchill (2012) *supra*, 25

354 A Marlene Jennings, Connie J Salts and Thomas A Smith Jr (1992) 'Attitudes toward marriage: Effects of parental conflict, family structure, and gender' *Journal of Divorce and Remarriage* 17: 67 - 78

355 Paul R Amato and Alan Booth (1991) 'The consequences of divorce for attitudes towards divorce and gender roles' *Journal of Family Issues* 12: 306 - 322

356 JS Coleman *et al* (1966) *Equality of Educational Opportunity*, [Washington DC, US Department of Health, Education and Welfare] 22

357 See for example: Vincent J Roscigno (1999) 'The black-white achievement gap, family-school links, and the importance of place' *Sociological Inquiry* 69(2): 159-86

358 Kathryn Harker Tillman (2007) 'Family structure pathways and academic disadvantage among adolescents in stepfamilies' *Sociological Inquiry* 77:383-424. See also: GR Weitoft, A Hjern and M Rosen (2004) 'School's out! Why earlier among children of lone parents?' *International Journal of Social Welfare* 13.2: 134-144

359 Gordon E Finley and Seth J Schwartz (2010) 'The divided world of the child: Divorce and long-term psychological adjustment' *Family Court Review* 48.3: 516-27

360 Lisa Stroschein *et al* (2009) 'Family structure histories and high school completion: Evidence from a population-based registry' *Canadian Journal of Sociology* 34.1:83-103

361 Kyle Crowder and Jay Teachman (2004) 'Do residential conditions explain the relationship between living arrangements and adolescent behaviour?' *Journal of Marriage and Family* 66: 721-738

362 Du Feng *et al* (1999) 'Intergenerational transmission of marital quality and marital instability' *Journal of Marriage and Family* 61: 451-63; RA Wojkiewicz (1993) 'Simplicity and complexity in the effects of parental structure on high school graduation' *Demography* 30(4): 701–717; and N Zill, DR Morrison and MJ Coiro (1993) 'Long term effects of parental divorce on parent-child relationships, adjustment, and achievement in young adulthood' *Journal of Family Psychology* 7(1): 91–103.

363 Sarah McCue Horwitz *et al* (2003) 'Language delay in a community cohort of young children' *Journal of the American Academy of Child and Adolescent Psychiatry* 42: 932-940

364 Barry D Ham (2003) 'The effects of divorce on the academic achievement of high school seniors' *Journal of Divorce and Remarriage* 38: 167-185

365 MDR Evans, Jonathan Kelley and Richard A Wanner (2001) 'Educational attainment of the children of divorce: Australia, 1940-1990' *Journal of Sociology* 37: 285-287

366 John Guidubaldi, Joseph D Perry and Bonnie K Nastasi (1987) 'Growing up in a divorced family: Initial and long-term perspectives on children's adjustment' *Applied Social Psychology Annual* 7: 202-237; Kimberly A Shaff *et al* (2008) 'Family structure transitions and child achievement' *Sociological Spectrum* 28: 691-694; Jim Stevenson and Glenda Fredman (1990) 'The social environmental correlates of reading ability' *Journal of Child Psychology and Psychiatry* 31: 689-690; Barry D Ham (2003) 'The effects of divorce on the academic achievement of high school seniors' *Journal of Divorce and Remarriage* 38: 176; William H Jeynes (2000) 'The effects of several of the most common family structures on the academic achievement of eighth graders' *Marriage and Family Review* 30: 88; Yongman Sun and Yuanzhang Li (2002) 'Children's well-being during parents' marital disruption process: A pooled time-series analysis' *Journal of Marriage and Family* 64: 479; and Jonathan Gruber

(2004) 'Is making divorce easier bad for children? The long-run implications of unilateral divorce' *Journal of Labor Economics* 22: 830

367 KAS Wickrama *et al* (2003) 'Linking early social risks to impaired physical health during the transmission to adulthood' *Journal of Health and Social Behavior* 44: 61-74

368 M MacLean and MEJ Wadsworth (1988) 'The interests of children after parental divorce: A long term perspective' *International Journal of Law and the Family* 2:155; J Guidubaldi (1987) *supra*; FF Furstenberg, SP Morgan and PD Allison (1987) 'Parental participation and children's well being after marital dissolution' *American Sociological Review* 52: 695; PD Alison and FF Furstenberg (1989) 'How marital dissolution affects children' *Developmental Psychology* 25: 540; E Milling Kinard and Helen Reinherz (1986) 'Effects of marital disruption on children's school aptitude and achievement' *Journal of Marriage and the Family* 48: 289-290; Daniel Potter (2010) 'Psychosocial well-being and the relationship between divorce and children's academic achievement' *Journal of Marriage and the Family* 72: 941; and D Dawson (1991) *supra*

369 Allison and Furstenberg (1989) *supra*

370 MacLean and Wadsworth (1988) *supra*

371 MacLean and Wadsworth (1988) *supra;* Elliott and Richards (1991) *supra*; and HM Aro and UK Palosaari (1992) 'Parental divorce, adolescence and the transition to young adulthood: a follow-up study *American Journal of Orthopsychiatry* 62(3): 412-428

372 Toby L Parcel and Mikaela J Dufur (2001) 'Capital at home and at school: Effects on student achievement' *Social Forces* 79: 881-912. By contrast, higher maternal working hours were negatively associated with math and reading achievement.

373 Jacqueline Scott (2004) 'Family, gender, and educational attainment in Britain: A longitudinal study' *Journal of Comparative Family Studies* 35: 565-589

374 Alison L Bryant and Marc A Zimmerman (2003) 'Role models and psychosocial outcomes among African-American adolescents' *Journal of Adolescent Research* 18.1: 36-67

375 Australian Bureau of Statistics (2010) 'Parental divorce or death during childhood' *Australian Social Trends* (Cat 4202.0)

376 Fiona Steele, Wendy Sigle-Rushton and Oystein Kravdal (2009) 'Consequences of family disruption on children's educational outcomes in Norway' *Demography* 46.3: 553-574

377 Paul R Amato and B Keith (1991) 'Parental divorce and adult well-being: A meta-analysis' *Journal of Marriage and the Family* 53: 43-58; Sara McLanahan and Gary Sandefur (1994) *Growing up with a single parent: What hurts? What helps?* [Cambridge MA, Harvard University Press]; B Rogers and J Pryor (1998) *Divorce*

and separation: The outcomes for children [York UK, Joseph Rowntree Foundation], and W Sigle-Rushton and Sara McLanahan (2004) 'Father absence and child well-being: A critical review' in DP Moynihan, T Smeeding and L Rainwater (eds) (2006) *The future of the family* [New York, Russell Sage Foundation]

378 Du Feng, *supra*

379 Justine Ferrari (2012) 'Income shaping children's progress at school' *The Australian,* January 4, 2012

380 OS Dalgard *et al* (2007) 'Education, sense of mastery and mental health: Results from a nationwide health monitoring study in Norway' *BioMed Central Psychiatry* 7:20 and S Krokstad, A E Kunst and S Westin (2002) 'Trends in health inequalities by educational level in a Norwegian total population study' *Journal of Epidemiology and Community Health* 56: 375-80

381 TH Lyngstad (2004) 'The impact of parents' and spouses' education on divorce rates in Norway' *Demographic Research* 10 (article 5): 121-42

382 Statistics Norway (2005) *Wage Statistics. All employees.*

383 Nazmiya Civitci, Asim Civitci and N Ceren Fiyakali (200) 'Loneliness and life satisfaction in adolescents with divorced and now-divorced parents' *Education Sciences: Theory and Practice* 9.2: 513-25

384 Edward Scanlon and Kevin Devine (2001) 'Residential mobility and youth well-being: Research, policy and practice issues' *Journal of Sociology and Social Welfare* 35(1): 119-136

385 Paul R Amato and Jacob Cheadle (2005) 'The long reach of divorce: Divorce and child well-being across three generations' *Journal of Marriage and Family* 67: 191-206

386 Catherine E Ross and John Mirosky (1999) 'Parental divorce, life-course disruption, and adult depression' *Journal of Marriage and Family* 61: 1034-1045

387 Frank F Furstenberg and Kathleen E Kiernan (2001) 'Delayed parental divorce: How much do children benefit?' *Journal of Marriage and Family* 63: 452

388 Kathleen Kiernan (1997) *The legacy of parental divorce: Social, economic and demographic experiences in childhood* [London, Centre for the Analysis of Social Exclusion]

389 Lisa A Keister (2004) 'Race, family structure, and wealth: The effect of childhood family on adult asset ownership' *Sociological Perspectives* 47: 179

390 Greg J Duncan, Martha s Hill and Saul D Hoffman (1988) 'Welfare dependence within and across generations' *Science* 239: 468

391 Patrick Fagan (1999) 'How broken families rob children of their chances for future prosperity' *Backgrounder* [Washington DC, Heritage Foundation], 3, citing OECD data.

392 Julia A Heath (1992) 'Determinants of spells of poverty following divorce' *Review of Social Economy* 50: 305-315. See also: Thomas L Hanson, Sara S McLanahan and Elizabeth Thomson (1998) 'Windows on divorce: Before and after' *Social Science Research* 27: 337

393 Matthew Gray and Bruce Chapman (2008) *Relationship breakdown and the economic welfare of Australian mothers and their children* [Canberra, Crawford School of Economics and Government, Australian National University], 28

394 Sue King *et al* (2012) *What will I be when I grow up?* [Sydney, Anglicare], 4

395 McAllister (1995) *supra.*

396 Anne N McMunn *et al* (2001) 'Children's emotional and behavioural well-being and the family environment: findings from the Health Survey for England' *Social Science and Medicine* 53: 423-440

397 Susan Silverberg Koerner *et al* (2004) 'Mothers re-partnering after divorce: Diverging perceptions of mothers and adolescents' *Journal of Divorce and Remarriage* 41.1/2: 25-38

398 Stephen Claxton-Oldfield, Tracey Garber and Kimberly Gillcrist (2006) 'Young adults' perceptions of their relationships with their stepfathers and biological fathers' *Journal of Divorce and Remarriage* 45.1/2: 51-61

399 Tamara D Afifi and Stacia Keith (2004) 'A risk and resiliency model of ambiguous loss in postdivorce stepfamilies' *The Journal of Family Communication* 4: 65-98

400 Susan L Brown (2006) 'Family structure transitions and adolescent well-being' *Demography* 43: 447-461

401 Rubab G Arim *et al* (2007) 'Patterns and correlates of pubertal development in Canadian youth: effects of family context' *Canadian Journal of Public Health* 98.2: 91-95

402 Heather A Turner, David Finkelhor and Richard Ormrod (2007) 'Family structure variations in patterns and predictors of child victimisation' *American Journal of Orthopsychiatry* 77: 282-295; Daniel H Freeman Jr and Jeff R Temple (2010) 'Social factors associated with history of sexual assault among ethnically diverse adolescents' *Journal of Family Violence* 25.3: 349-56

403 Andrew J Sedlak *et al* (2010) *Fourth National Incidence Study of Child Abuse and Neglect, Report to Congress* [Washington DC, US Department of Health and Human Services, Administration for Children and Families]

404 Frank W Putman (2003) 'Ten-year research update review: Child sexual abuse' *Journal of the American Academy of Child and Adolescent Psychiatry* 42: 269-278

405 Barry D Ham (2004) 'The effects of divorce and remarriage on the academic achievement of high school seniors' *Journal of Divorce and Remarriage* 42.1/2: 159-178

406 Kathryn H Tillman (2007) 'Family structure pathways and academic disadvantage among adolescents in stepfamilies' *Sociological Inquiry* 77: 408

407 Scott Talkington, 'Ever received a Bachelor's degree by structure of family of origin' in Fagan and Churchill (2012) *supra*, p 31

408 Ming Wen (2008) 'Family structure and children's health and behaviour: Data from the 1999 National Survey of America's Families' *Journal of Family Issues* 29: 1492-1519.

409 Amanda M White and Constance T Gager (2007) 'Idle hands and empty pockets? Youth involvement in extracurricular activities, school capital, and economic status' *Youth and Society* 39: 75-111; LaJeana D Howie *et al* (2010) 'Participation in activities outside of school hours in relation to problem behaviour and social skills in middle childhood' *Journal of School Health* 80.3: 119-25

410 Shelley Clark and Catherine Kenney (2010) 'Is the United States experiencing a 'matrimonial tilt?' Gender, family structure, and financial transfers to adult children' *Social Forces* 88.4: 1753-76

411 Wendy D Manning and Kathleen A Lamb (2003) 'Adolescent well-being in cohabiting, married, and single-parent families' *Journal of Marriage and Family* 65: 876-893

412 Nan M Astone and Sara S McLanahan (1994) 'Family structure, residential mobility, and school dropout: A research note' *Demography* 31: 582

413 S Sarantakos (1996) 'Children in three contexts: family, education and social development' *Children Australia* 21: 23-31

414 Loren Marks (2012) 'Same-sex parenting and children's outcomes: A closer examination of the American psychological association's brief on lesbian and gay parenting' *Social Science Research* 41: 735-751

415 Mark Regnerus (2012) 'How different are the adult children of parents who have same-sex relationships? Findings from the New Family Structures Study' *Social Science Research* 41: 752-770

416 J Wallerstein (1989) 'Daughters of divorce' *American Journal of Orthopsychiatry* 59: 593; J Wallerstein and S Blakeslee (1989) *Second chances: Men, women and children a decade after divorce* [New York, Ticknor and Fields]; and J Wallerstein 'The long-term effects of divorce upon children: a review' *Journal of the American Academy of Child Adolescent Psychiatry* 30(3): 349-360.

417 B Vobejda (1997) 'Children of divorce heal slowly study finds' *The Washington Post,* June 3, E1.

418 J Wallerstein 1989 'Children after divorce: Wounds that don't heal' *New York Times Magazine,* January 22 ,20.

419 KE Kiernan (1986) 'Teenage marriage and marital breakdown: A longitudinal

study' *Population Studies* 40: 35.

420 Kuh and MacLean (1990) *supra*

421 MN Brohlchain, R Chappell and I Diamond (1994) 'Educational and socio-demographic outcomes among children of disrupted and intact marriages' *Population* 49(6): 1585–1612. See also Kyle Crowder and Jay Teachman (2004) 'Do residential conditions explain the relationship between living arrangements and adolescent behaviour?' *Journal of Marriage and Family* 66: 721-738

422 Wadsworth (1994) *supra.*

423 Robert Bolgar, Hallie Sweig-Frank and Joel Paris (1995) 'Childhood antecedents of interpersonal problems in young adult children of divorce' *Journal of the American Academy of Child and Adolescent Psychiatry* 34: 143-150

424 LB Story, BR Karney, E Lawrence and TN Bradbury (2004) 'Interpersonal mediators in the intergenerational transmission of marital dysfunction' *Journal of Family Psychology* 18: 519-529

425 Zeng-Yin Chen and Howard B Kaplan (2001) 'Intergenerational transmission of constructive parenting' *Journal of Marriage and the Family* 62: 17-31

426 Australian Bureau of Statistics (2010) 'Parental divorce or death during childhood' *Australian Social Trends* Cat. 4102.0

427 PR Amato and B Keith (1991) 'Parental divorce and adult well-being: A meta-analysis' *Journal of Marriage and the Family* 53: 43.

428 PR Amato (1996) 'Explaining the intergenerational transmission of divorce' *Journal of Marriage and the Family* 58: 628-640; and (1997) *Threshold* 54: 15-27.

429 William S Aquilino (1994) 'Later life parental divorce and widowhood: Impact on young adults' assessment of parent-child relations' *Journal of Marriage and the Family* 56: 908-922

430 AJ Cherlin, PL Chase-Lansdale and C McRae (1998) 'Effects of parental divorce on mental health throughout the life course' *American Sociological Review* 63: 239–249.

431 AJ Cherlin *et al* (1991) 'Longitudinal studies of the effects of divorce on children in Great Britain and the United States' *Science* 252: 1386-1389.

432 Cherlin, Chase-Lansdale and McRae (1998)*supra.*

433 Sandra L Hofferth and Frances Goldscheider (2010) 'Family structure and the transition to early parenthood' *Demography* 47.2: 415-37

434 Susan E Jacquet and Catherine A Surra (2001) 'Parental divorce and premarital couples: Commitment and other relationship characteristics' *Journal of Marriage and Family* 63: 627-638

435 *Ibid.*

436 Wallerstein and Blakeslee, *supra*, 297-307. See also Jacquet and Surra, *supra*; and Sarah W Whitton, Galena K Rhoades, Scott M Stanley and Howard J Markman (2008) 'Effects of parental divorce on marital commitment and confidence' *Journal of Marriage and the Family* 22: 791

437 Robert Bolgar, Hallie Zwuig-Frank and Joel Paris (1995) 'Childhood antecedents of interpersonal problems in young adult children of divorce' *Journal of the American Academy of Child and Adolescent Psychiatry* 34: 143-150

438 Silvio Silvestri (1992) 'Marital instability in men from intact and divorced families: Interpersonal behaviour, cognitions and intimacy' *Journal of Divorce and Remarriage* 18: 79-106

439 Robert E Billingham and Nicole Notebaert (1993) 'Divorce and dating violence revisited: Multivariate analyses using Straus's conflict tactics subscores' *Psychological Reports* 73: 679-684 and Pamela S Webster, Terru L Orbuch and James S House (1995) 'Effects of childhood family background on adult marital quality and perceived stability' *American Journal of Sociology* 101: 404-432

440 Jay D Teachman (2002) 'Childhood living arrangements and the intergenerational transmission of divorce' *Journal of Marriage and the Family* 64: 717-729. See also Australian Bureau of Statistics (2010), *supra*, for Australian data showing similar trends; and Susan E Jacquet and Catherine A Surra (2001) 'Parental divorce and premarital couples: Commitment and other relationship characteristics' *Journal of Marriage and Family* 63: 636

441 Nicholas H Wolfinger (2003) 'Parental divorce and offspring marriage: Early or late?' *Social Forces* 82: 337-353. For the effects of cohabitation, see chapter 8

442 Carolyn A Kapinus (2004) 'The effects of parents' attitudes towards divorce on offspring's attitudes: Gender and parental divorce as mediating factors' *Journal of Family Issues* 25: 112-135

443 Nicholas H Wolfinger (2003) 'Parental divorce and offspring marriage: Early or late?' *Social Forces* 82: 337-353

444 Jay D Teachman (2004) 'The childhood living arrangements of children and the characteristics of their marriages' *Journal of Family Issues* 25: 86-111

445 Australian Bureau of Statistics (2010), *supra*

446 Lisa Strohschein (2005) 'Parental divorce and child mental health trajectories' *Journal of Marriage and Family* 67 : 1286-1297. See also: Hetherington (2003) *supra*

447 Inge Vander Valk *et al* (2005) 'Family structure and problem behaviour of adolescents and young adults: A growth-curve study' *Journal of Youth and Adolescence* 34: 533-546

448 Kathlen B Rogers and Hillary A Rose (2002) 'Risk and resiliency factors among adolescents who experience marital transitions' *Journal of Marriage and the Family*

64: 1024-1037

449 Lisa Laumann-Billings and Robert E Emery (2000) 'Distress among young adults from divorced families' *Journal of Family Psychology* 14: 671-687

450 George J Cohen *et al* (2002) 'Helping children and families deal with divorce and separation' *Pediatrics* 110: 1019-1022

451 American Academy of Pediatrics Taskforce on the Family (2003) 'Family pediatrics' *Pediatrics* 111: 1541-1553 (Supplement).

452 Demo and Acock (1991) *supra*

453 McAllister *et al* (1995) *supra*

454 M Crockett and J Tripp (1994) *The Exeter family study: Family breakdown and its impact on children* [Exeter, University of Exeter Press]

455 LA Kurdek (1991) 'The relationship between reported well-being and divorce history, availability of proximate adult and gender' *Journal of Marriage and the Family* 53: 71. See also LA Kurdek (1993) 'Issues in proposing a general model of effects of divorce on children' *Journal of Marriage and the Family* 55(1): 39; S Gable, K Crnic and J Belsky (1994) 'Co-parenting within the family system: Influences on children's development' *Family Relations* 43(4): 380; and JH Grych and FD Fincham (1990) 'Marital conflict and children's adjustment: A cognitive contextual framework' *Psychological Bulletin* 108: 215-230.

456 PL Chase-Lansdale, AJ Cherlin and KE Kiernan (1995) 'The long-term effect of parental divorce on the mental health of young adults: A developmental perspective' *Child Development* 66: 1614-1634.

457 PR Amato and A Booth (1997) *A generation at risk: Growing up in an era of family upheaval* [Cambridge MA, Harvard University Press]

458 PR Amato cited in K Peterson (1998) *USA Today,* February 19

459 Lisa Strohschein (2005) 'Parental divorce and child mental health trajectories' *Journal of Marriage and Family* 67: 1286

460 Dona R Morrison (1999) 'Parental conflict and marital disruption: Do children benefit when high-conflict marriages are dissolved?' *Journal of Marriage and Family* 61: 626-637

461 Amato and Booth (1997) *supra*

462 R Stewart (2001) *The early identification and streaming of cases of high conflict separation and divorce: A review* [Ottawa, Family Children and Youth Section, Department of Justice], cited in Andrea Mrozek (2012) *Finding fault with no-fault divorce* [Ottawa, Institute of Marriage and Family, Canada]

463 *ibid.*

464 *ibid.*

465 Fiona McAllister *et al* (1995) *supra* 30

466 See the data in chapter seven

467 The issue of cohabitation is discussed more generally in chapter 8

468 Alexandra Frean (2005) 'Unmarried families are more likely to fall apart' *The London Times*, February 5

469 Cynthia Osborne *et al* (2007) 'Married and cohabiting parents' relationship stability: A focus on race and ethnicity' *Journal of Marriage and Family* 69: 1345. See also: Kathleen Kiernan (1999) 'Childbearing outside marriage in Western Europe' *Population Trends* 98: 11; Ann Berrington (2001) 'Entry in parenthood and the outcome of cohabiting partnerships in Britain' *Journal of Marriage and Family* 63: 80; and Ruth Weston and Lixia Qu (2007) 'Family statistics and trends: Trends in couple dissolution' *Family Relationships Quarterly* 2: 9

470 The fragile families and child well-being study (2011) *About fragile families* [Princeton NJ, Princeton University]

471 Pamela Smock and Fiona R Greenland (2010) 'Diversity in pathways to parenthood: Patterns, implications and emerging research directions' *Journal of Marriage and Family* 72: 576-593

472 Larry Bumpass and Hsien-Hen Lu (1998) 'Trends in cohabitation and implications for children's family context' *Unpublished manuscript* [Madison WA, Center for Demography, University of Wisconsin] cited in Popenoe and Whitehead, *supra*

473 Cynthia Osborne, Wendy D Manning and Pamela J Smock (2007) *Married and cohabiting parents' relationship stability: A focus on race and ethnicity* [Austin TX, LBJ School of Public Affairs and Population Research Center]

474 Peter Butterworth *et al* (2008) 'Factors associated with relationship dissolution of Australian families with children' *Social Policy Research Paper* No 37, 22, 29

475 S Sarantakos (1996) 'The virtues of liberation' *Threshold* 53: 9-11. See also: Susan L Brown (2004) 'Family structure and child well-being: The significance of parental cohabitation' *Journal of Marriage and Family* 66: 351-367; Julie E Artis (2007) 'Maternal cohabitation and child well-being among kindergarten children' *Journal of Marriage and Family* 69: 222-236;

476 See also: Sandra L Hofferth (2006) 'Residential father family type and child well-being: Investment versus selection' *Demography* 43: 53-77

477 S Sarantakos (1996) 'Children in three contexts' *Children Australia* 21(3) 23–31. See also R Kelly Raley, Michelle L Frisco and Elizabeth Wildsmith (2005) 'Maternal cohabitation and educational success' *Sociology of Education* 78: 144-164, showing children living with cohabiting mothers fare exceptionally poorly in school.

478 S Sarantakos 'Children of cohabiting couples' cited in *To have and to hold* (1998) *supra*

479 S Sarantakos (1997) 'Cohabitation, marriage and delinquency: The significance of family environment' *Australian and New Zealand Journal of Criminology* 30(2): 187-199.

480 Gunilla Ringback Weitoft *et al* (2003) "Mortality, severe morbidity, and injury in children living with single parents in Sweden: A population-based study' *The Lancet* 361: 289-295

481 An-Magritt Jensen and Sten-Erik Clauseb (2003) 'Children and family dissolution in Norway: The impact of consensual unions' *Childhood* 65-81

482 The Social Policy Justice Group (2006) *Fractured families,* The state of the nation report [London, Social Policy Justice Group]. See also: Anna Sarkadi *et al* (2008) ' Fathers' involvement and children's developmental outcomes: A systematic review of longitudinal studies' *Acta Paediatrica* 92: 153-158

483 Jay Fagan (2011) *Effects of divorce and cohabitation dissolution on preschoolers' literacy* [Philadelphia, College of Health Professions and Social Work, Temple University]

484 Lixia Qu and Ruth Weston (2011) 'Parental social marital status and children's wellbeing' *Presentation to the Growing Up in Australia and Footprints in Time conference* [Melbourne, Australian Institute of Family Studies]. See also 'Couples who tie the knot may give children a more tangle-free life' (2008) *Threshold* 93: 27

485 Robert Whelan (1993) *Broken homes and battered children: A study of the relationship between child abuse and family type* [London, Family Education Trust] See also Patrick F Fagan and Dorothy B Hanks (1997) *The child abuse crisis: The disintegration of marriage, family and the American community* [Washington DC, Heritage Foundation]

486 Patrick Parkinson with Antoine Kazzi (2011) *For Kid's Sake – Repairing the social environment for Australian children and young people* [Vos Foundation]

487 For a summary of the report, see Adele Horin (2011) 'Falling marriage rates hurting children: report', *Sydney Morning Herald*, September 6. See also Kevin Andrews (2011) 'Stable families, stable society. Its that simple', *The Punch*, September 6. [www.thepunch.com.au]

488 Australian Institute of Health and Welfare (2012) *Child Protection, Australia 2010-11*; and correspondence with the Australian Institute of Criminology, June 19, 2012.

489 National Association for the Prevention of Child Abuse and Neglect (2009), cited in *Media Release* '$30 billion spent on child abuse' [South Melbourne, Childwise]

490 Leah Ward Sears (2006) 'A case for strengthening marriage' *Threshold* 88: 35

491 Laura Clark (2012) '10,000 children taken into care: Numbers have doubled in the past four years' *Daily Mail Online*, April 11

492 *Ibid*

493 Jack Doyle (2012) 'Poor parenting get the blame for riots: Clegg's panel of experts highlights "forgotten families"' *Daily Mail Online* March 28 . See also: Riots Communities and Victims Panel (2012) *Final Report* [London, The Panel]

494 'It's official: Most of Britain's 72,000 dysfunctional families have no father at home' *Daily Mail Online*, March 11

495 Andrew J Sedlak *et al* (2010) *Fourth National Incidence Study of Child Abuse and Neglect* [NIS-4] Report to Congress [Washington DC, US Department of Health and Human Services, Administration for Families and Children]

496 See Jocelyn Brown *et al* (1998) 'A longitudinal analysis of risk factors for child maltreatment: Findings of a 17-year prospective study of officially recorded and self-reported child abuse and neglect' *Child Abuse and Neglect* 22: 1065-78; Maxia Dong *et al* (2003) 'The relationship of exposure to child sexual abuse to other forms of abuse, neglect, and household dysfunction during childhood' *Child Abuse and Neglect* 27:632; and Yuriko Egami (1996) 'Psychiatric profile and sociodemographic characteristics of adults who report physically abusing or neglecting children' *American Journal of Psychiatry* 153: 925

497 SN Padu and K Peltzer (2000) 'Risk factors and child sexual abuse among secondary school students in the Northern Province (South Africa)' *Child Abuse and Neglect* 24(2): 259-268

498 Gisle C Alexandre *et al* (2010) 'The presence of a stepfather and child physical abuse, as reported by a sample of Brazilian mothers in Rio de Janeiro' *Child Abuse and Neglect* 34: 963

499 Margo Wilson and Marin Daly 'The risk of maltreatment of children living with stepparents' in Richard J Gelles and Jane B Lancaster, eds (1987) *Child abuse and neglect: Biosocial dimensions, Foundations of human behaviour* [New York, Aldine de Gruyter], 215 – 232. See also: Kate Cavanagh *et al* (2007) 'The murder of children by fathers in the context of child abuse' *Child Abuse and Neglect* 31: 736; and Patricia G Schnitzer and Bernard G Ewigman (2005) 'Child deaths resulting from inflicted injuries: Household risk factors and perpetrator characteristics' *Pediatrics* 116: e690

500 Miriam K Ehrensaft, Terrie E Moffitt and Avshalom Caspi (2004) 'Clinically abusive relationships in an unelected birth cohort: Men's and women's participation and developmental antecedents' *Journal of Abnormal Psychology* 113: 258-270

501 Human Rights and Equal Opportunity Commission (1989) *National Inquiry into Youth Homelessness.*

502 Steve Doughty (2011) 'Less than fifth of child runaways reported missing by parents and guardians' *Daily Mail*, November 15, citing a Children's Society report.

503 Daniel Patrick Moynihan (1965) *The negro family: The case for national action* [Washington DC, US Department of Labor]

504 Daniel Patrick Moynihan (1965) *supra*. The historian, Jacques Barzun, made similar observations in *From dawn to decadence: 500 years of Western cultural life* [New York, Harper Collins, 2000] 780-790.

505 See: Frank F Furstenberg Jr (2009) 'If Moynihan had only known: Race, class, and family change in the late twentieth century' *The Annals of the American Academy of Political and Social Science* 621: 94-110

506 Eric Dearing, Kathleen McCartney and Beck A Taylor (2001) 'Change in family income-to-needs matters more for children with less' *Child Development* 72: 1779-1793

507 Centre for Social Justice (2006) *Breakdown Britain* [London, the Centre]

508 Sanjiv Gupta, Pamela J Smock and Wendy D Manning (2004) 'Moving out: Transition to nonresidence among resident fathers in the United States, 1968 – 1997' *Journal of Marriage and Family* 66: 627-638

509 See for example, David Blankenhorn (1995) *Fatherless America* [New York, Basic Books]

510 See for example, Susan K Williams and F Donald Kelly (2005) 'Relationships among involvement, attachment, and behavioural problems in adolescence: Examining father's influence' *Journal of Early Adolescence* 25: 168-196

511 Nicole J Cronk *et al* (2004) 'Risk separation anxiety disorder among girls: Paternal absence, socioecomonic disadvantage, and genetic vulnerability' *Journal of Abnormal Psychology* 113: 237-247

512 Charles E Kubrin and Ronald Weitzer (2003) 'Retaliatory homicide: Concentrated disadvantage and neighbourhood culture' *Social Problems* 50: 157-180

513 Judith S Wallerstein and Joan Berlin Kelly (1996) *Surviving the breakup: How children and parents cope with divorce* [New York, Basic Books] 224-225. See also: Paul R Amato and Tamara D Afifi (2006) 'Feeling caught between parents: Adult children's relations with parents and subjective well-being' *Journal of Marriage and Family* 68: 231

514 S McLanahan and G Sandefurs (1994*) Growing up with a single parent; What hurts, What helps* [Cambridge MA, Harvard University Press]

515 Catherine E Ross and John Mirowsky (2001) 'Neighbourhood disadvantages, disorder, and health' *Journal of Health and Social Behavior* 42: 258-276

516 Council on Families in America (1995) *Marriage in America: A report to the nation* [New York, Institute for American Values] 6-7

517 Urie Bronfenbrenner (1994) Address to Australian Institute of Family Studies seminar Melbourne University: July. See also: Urie Bronfenbrenner (1991) 'What do families do?' *Family Affairs*, Winter/Spring.

518 For example, National Commission on Children (1991*) Beyond Rhetoric: A new American agenda for children and families* [Washington DC, The Commission];

National Commission on America's Urban Families (1993) *Families First* [Washington DC, The Commission]; D Popenoe (1988) *Disturbing the Nest* [New York, Walter de Gruyter]

519 D Edgar (1997) *Men, Mateship, Marriage* [Sydney, Harper Collins] 313.

520 Andrew J Cherlin (2009) *The marriage-go-round* [New York, Vintage Books] 23

521 *Ibid*

522 *Ibid*

523 See for example: Sara McLanahan and Gary Sandefur (1994) *Growing up with a single parent: What hurts, what helps* [Cambridge MA, Harvard University Press]

524 Quoted by Scott M Stanley (2012) 'Is marriage irrelevant?' *Sliding vs deciding blog* (February 20) from Sara McLanahan and Irving Garfinkel (2012) 'Fragile families: Debates, facts and solutions' in Elizabeth Scott (ed) *Marriage at a crossroads* (forthcoming)

525 Patrick F Fagan and Aaron Churchill (2012) *The effects of divorce on children* [Washington DC, Marriage and Religion Research Institute], 2

526 Marjorie A Pett *et al* (1999) 'Paths of influence of divorce on preschool children's psychosocial adjustment' *Journal of Family Psychology* 13(2): 145-164. See also: Jeanne M Hilton and Ester L Devall (1998) 'Comparison of parenting and children's behaviour in single-mother, single-father, and intact families' *Journal of Divorce and Remarriage* 29(3/4): 23-50

527 Research indicates that spending time away from both parents, no matter the reason, is associated with an increased risk of subsequent divorce for the child: Jay D Teachman (2002) 'Childhood living arrangements and the intergenerational transmission of divorce' *Journal of Marriage and the Family* 64: 717-729

528 National Council for the Single Mother and her Child, *Submissions to the Australian Parliamentary Inquiry*, p. S257, *To Have and To Hold* (1998) *supra*, 49

529 Cited by Relationships Australia (Western Australia) at< www.relationships.com.au> in *To Have and To Hold* (1998) supra, 9

530 Paul Amato and Alan Booth (2000) *A generation at risk: Growing up in an era of family upheaval* [Cambridge MA, Harvard University Press]

531 Linda J Waite *et al* (2002) *Does divorce make people happy? Findings from a study of unhappy marriages* [New York, Institute for American Values]

532 I am indebted to Scott Stanley and Sara McLanahan for this idea. See Stanley (2012) *supra*

533 Jonathan Sacks (2000) *The politics of hope* [London, Vintage] 193

534 John Stuart Mill, *Utilitarianism, On Liberty and Considerations on Representative Government*, 177

535 John Paul II, *Message* to the 'Family: Dare to Dream' conference, Melbourne 2000

536 Mary Ann Glendon (1993) *Rights talk: The impoverishment of political discourse* [New York, Free Press]. See also: Mary Ann Glendon and David Blankenhorn (1995) *Seedbeds of virtue: Sources of competence, character and citizenship in American society* [Madison Books]

537 DH Lawrence (1961) *Apropos of Lady Chatterley's Lover* [London, Phoenix], 27

538 John Paul II (1998) *Homily* at Santa Clara, Cuba, January 22

539 Judith Wallerstein and Sandra Blakeslee (1995) *The good marriage: How and why love lasts* [New York, Houghton Mifflin]

540 See Council on Families in America (1995) *Marriage in America* [New York, Institute for American Values], 12-13

541 William J Goode (2003) 'Family changes over the long term: A sociological commentary' *Journal of Family History* 28: 15-30

542 Martin Luther King (1965) *Speech* at Westchester County, New York

543 Nicholas H Wolfinger and Raymond E Wolfinger (2008) 'Family structure and voter turnout' *Social Forces* 86.4: 1513-28

544 Corey LM Keyes (2002) 'Social civility in the United States' *Sociological Inquiry* 72: 393-408

545 Carol L Bankston III and Min Zhou (2002) 'Social capital as process: The meanings and problems of a theoretical metaphor' *Sociological Inquiry* 72: 285-317

546 Charis E Kubrin (2003) 'Structural covariates of homicide rates: Does type of homicide matter?' *Journal of Research in Crime and Delinquency* 40: 139-170

547 Christopher T Lowenkamp, Francis T Cullen and Travis C Pratt (2003) 'Replicating Sampson and Grove's test of social disorganisation theory: Revisiting a criminological classic' *Journal of Research in Crime and Delinquency* 40: 351-373

548 Anna M Ziersch (2005) 'Health implications of access to social capital: finds from an Australian study' *Social Science and Medicine* 61: 2119-2131

549 Janet Wilmoth and Gregor Koso (2002) 'Does marital history matter? Marital status and wealth outcomes among preretirement adults' *Journal of Marriage and the Family* 64: 254-268

550 David Popenoe and Barbara Dafoe Whitehead, 'The surprising economic benefits of marriage' in Popenoe and Whitehead (2005) *The state of our unions* [Rutgers, National Marriage Projecvt], 17. See also W Bradford Wilcox (2009) *The state of our unions – Marriage and money* [Charlottesville VA, National Marriage Project]

551 Thomas A Hirschl, Joyce Altobelli and Mark R Rank (2003) 'Does marriage increase the odds of affluence? Exploring the life course probabilities' *Journal of*

Marriage and the Family 65: 927-938; Joseph Lupton and James P Smith (2003) 'Marriage, assets and savings' in Shoshana A Grossbard-Schectman (ed) *Marriage and the economy* [Cambridge, Cambridge University Press], 129-152

552 Hyunbae Chun and Injae Lee (2001) 'Why do married men earn more: Productivity or marriage selection? *Economic Inquiry* 39: 307-319; S Korenman and D Neumark (1991) 'Does marriage really make men more productive?' *Journal of Human Resources* 26: 282-307; K Daniel (1995) 'The marriage premium' in M Tomassi and K Ierulli (eds) *The new economics of human behaviour* [Cambridge, Cambridge University Press], 113-125

553 Gary S Becker (1991) *A treatise on the family* [Cambridge MA, Harvard University Press]

554 See also: Martha S Hill (1979) 'The wage effects of marital status and children' *Journal of Human Resources* 14: 579-594; and Sanders Korenman and David Neumark (1991) 'Does marriage really make men more productive?' *Journal of Human Resources* 26: 283-307

555 BV Brown (2000) 'The single-father family: Demographic, economic, and public transfer use characteristics' *Marriage and Family Review* 29: 203-220.

556 Avner Ahituv and Robert Lerman (2007) 'How do marital status, labour supply, and wage rates interact? *Demography* 44: 623-647

557 Pamela J Smock, Wendy D Manning and Sanjiv Gupta (1999) 'The effect of marriage and divorce on women's economic well-being' *American Sociological Review* 64: 803

558 Ryan C MacPherson (2012) 'Marital Parenthood and American prosperity: As goes the middle-class family, so goes the nation' *The Family in America* Online

559 Robert I Lerman (1996) 'The impact of the changing US family structure on child poverty and income inequality' *Economica* 63: S119-139, S137

560 George A Akerlof (1998) 'Men without children' *The Economic Journal* 108: 287-309

561 Daniela Casale (2010) 'The male marital earnings premium in the context of bride wealth payments: Evidence from South Africa' *Economic Development and Cultural Change* 58: 219

562 Robert F Schoeni (1995) 'Marital status and earnings in developed countries' *Journal of Population Economics* 8: 357

563 Naoko Akashi-Ronquest (2009) 'The impact of biological preferences on parental investments in children and step-children' *Review of Economics of the Household* 7: 73. According to this study, men in stepfamilies earned 15 per cent less per hour than fathers in intact families.

564 T Edwards *et al* (2007) 'Parenting program for parents of children at risk of

developing conduct disorder: cost effectiveness analysis' *British Medical Journal* 334: 682

565 Patrick Parkinson (2011) 'Another inconvenient truth: Fragile families and the looming financial crisis for the welfare state' *Family Law Quarterly* 45: 329-352

566 Loretta Brewer (2001) 'Gender socialisation and the cultural construction of elder caregivers' *Journal of Aging Studies* 15: 217

567 See for example, David de Vaus (2007) *The consequences of divorce for financial living standards in later life* [Melbourne, Australian Institute of Family Studies]

568 Parkinson (2011) *supra*

569 W Bradford Wilcox (2009) *supra*. According to one study, the majority of children who grow up outside of married families have experienced at least one year of dire poverty: Mark R Rank and Thomas A Hirschl (1999) 'The economic risk of childhood in America: Estimating the probability of poverty across the formative years' *Journal of Marriage and the Family* 61: 1058-1067

570 Adam Thomas and Isabel Sawhill (2001) 'For richer or for poorer: Marriage as an antipoverty strategy' *Journal of Policy Analysis and Management* 21: 587-599

571 See: Kevin Andrews (2009) 'Our congested cities' *Australian Polity* 3: 17-18. See also: Pamela Symes (1985) 'Indissolubility and the clean break' *Modern Law Review* 48: 44

572 Henry Potrykus, Patrick Fagan and Robert Schwarzwalder (2011) *Our fiscal crisis: We cannot tax, spend, and borrow enough to substitute for marriage* [Washington DC, Marriage and Religion Research Institute] using US Bureau of Economic Analysis data.

573 *Ibid*. It has been estimated for the UK that the productivity loss to the state as a result of youth unemployment is £10 million every day: The Prince's Trust (2007) *The cost of exclusion: Counting the cost of youth disadvantage in the UK*. The average cost of an individual spending a lifetime on benefits is £430,000, not including the tax revenue: Graham Allen and Iain Duncan Smith (2008) *Early intervention: Good parents, great kids, better citizens* [London, Centre for Social Justice], 33

574 Popenoe and Whitehead (2005) *supra*

575 John Iceland (2003) 'Why poverty remains high: The role of income growth, economic inequality, and changes in family structure' *Demography* 40: 499-519

576 Joseph Lupton and James P Smith (1999) 'Marriage, assets and savings' *Labor and Population Program* Working Paper Series 99-12: 16-17

577 'Divorce bad for the environment: Study' (2008) *Threshold* 93: 3

578 Parkinson (2011) *supra*. See also: de Vaus *et al* (2012) *supra*

579 D Edgar (1988) 'The new marriage: Changing rules for changing times' *Threshold*

22: 9. See also: Martha J Bailey (2010) 'Momma's got the pill: How Anthony Comstock and Griswold v. Connecticut shaped US childbearing' *Economic Review* 100.1: 98 – 129 (on the impact of contraception on fertility rates).

580 See also: Lawrence B Finer (2007) 'Trends in premarital sex in the United States, 1954-2003' *Public Health Reports* 122: 73-78

581 Mary Ann Glendon (2001) *A world made new* [New York, Random House]

582 A Tapper (1990) *The Family in the Welfare State* [Sydney, Allen and Unwin]; A Carlson (1988) *The Family Wage* [Rockford, The Rockford Institute]

583 D Yankelovich (1994) 'How changes in the economy are reshaping American values' in HJ Aaron, TE Mann and T Taylor (eds) *Values and Public Policy* [Washington DC, The Brookings Institution]

584 H McKay (1997) *Generations–Baby boomers, their parents and their children* [Sydney, McMillan] 118-119.

585 *Ibid.* 136. James Q Wilson reaches similar conclusions in *The marriage problem: How our culture has weakened families* [New York, Harper Collins, 2002]. See also: Ron Lesthaeghe (2010) 'The unfolding story of the second demographic transition' *Whither the child? Meeting Paper* [Barcelona, Social Trends Institute]

586 Michel Foucault (1997) *Ethics, subjectivity and truth* [New York, New Press] 163

587 Jacques Derrida, *Glas*, in Peggy Kamuf (ed) (1991) *A Derrida reader; Between the blinds* [New York, Columbia University Press] 382

588 *Ibid.*, 387-388

589 Daniel R Heimbach (2005) 'Deconstructing the family' *The Religion and Society Report* 22(7): 10. I am indebted to Professor Heimbach for this discussion of Foucault, Derrida and Freud.

590 Joseph D Unwin (1935) *Sexual regulations and cultural behaviour* [London, Oxford University Press] 31; and Joseph D Unwin (1934) *Sex and culture* [London, Oxford University Press] 326

591 Joseph D Unwin (1940) *Hopousia: Or the sexual and economic foundations of a new society* [London, George Allen and Unwin] 84-85

592 See for example, Anthony Giddens (1992) *The transformation of intimacy* [Stanford CA, Stanford University Press]

593 Edmund Leach (1967) *A runaway world?* [London, BBC]

594 Rebecca Probert and Samantha Callan (2011) *History and family: Setting the records straight* [London, Centre for Social Justice]

595 David Cooper (1971) *The Death of the Family* [London, Allen Lane,]

596 RD Laing (1967) *The Politics of Experience* [London, Penguin Books]

597 Anthony Giddens (1999) *Runaway World* [London, BBC]

598 Steve Duck (1998) *Understanding relationships* [Thousand Oaks CA, Sage Publications] 109

599 Hal Stone and Sidra Stone (2000) *Partnering: A new kind of relationship* [Albion CA, Delos]

600 Dan Cere (2000) *The experts' story of marriage* [New York, Institute for American Values] 19. The major approaches identified by Cere are John Bowlby's 'Attachment theory', Robert J Sternberg's 'Triangular theory of love' and John Alan Lee's 'Love styles'.

601 *Ibid.*, 28-29

602 Council on Families in America (1995) *Marriage in America* [New York, Council on Families in America] 3.

603 JL Rogers, PA Nakonezny and RD Shull (1997) 'The effect of no-fault divorce legislation on divorce: A response to a reconsideration' *Journal of Marriage and the Family* 59: 1026-1030.

604 N Glenn (1990) 'The social and cultural meaning of contemporary marriage' in BJ Christensen (ed) *The retreat from marriage* [Lanham, University Press of America] 50.

605 'How divorce spreads' (2010) *Threshold* 99: 4

606 ND Glenn (1991) 'The recent trend in marital success in the United States' *Journal of Marriage and the Family* 53: 261-270.

607 *Ibid.* 268.

608 SJ Rogers and PR Amato (1997) 'Is marital quality declining: The evidence from two generations' *Social Forces* 75: 1089-1100.

609 Glenn (1991) *supra* 268

610 Paul R Amato and Bryndl Hohmann-Marriott (2007) 'A comparison of high- and low-distress marriages that end in divorce' *Journal of Marriage and Family* 69: 621-38

611 Joseph L Rodgers, Paul A Nakonezny and Robert D Shall (1999) 'Did no-fault divorce legislation matter?' *Journal of Marriage and the Family* 61: 803-809

612 Rogers and Amato (1997) *supra* 1098.

613 *Ibid.*, 1099

614 Allen M Parkman (2004) 'The importance of gifts in marriage' *Economic Inquiry* 42: 483-495

615 Paul R Amato and Danelle D DeBoer (2001) 'The transmission of marital instability across generations: Relationships skills or commitment to marriage?' *Journal of Marriage and Family* 63: 1038-1051

616 Barbara Baker (2011) 'Break the habit: Why you should cherish Mr All-Right'

Daily Mail Online, April 28; and (2008) 'Why divorce lawyers will rub their hands today' *Daily Mail Online*, January 6.

617 In Australia for example, the government's support for 'Marriage Education' is now referred to as support for 'Family Relationships Education.' The organisation formerly known as the 'Marriage Guidance Council' is now 'Relationships Australia.'

618 Family Impact Seminar (1997) 'Reasons for avoiding the 'M' word' *Threshold* 57: 8.

619 *Ibid.*

620 US Bureau of Statistics (1994) *Statistical Abstract of the United States.*

621 'Tomorrow's second sex' (1996) *The Economist* September 28, 23-24.

622 See AR Hochschild (1989) *The Second Shift* [New York, Viking]

623 Paula England, Carmen Carcia-Beaulieu and Mary Ross (2004) 'Women's employment among Blacks, Whites, and three groups of Latinas: Do more privileged women have higher employment?' *Gender and Society* 18: 494-509 which revealed that the there is a higher proportion of mothers in the workforce amongst the wives of high earner males.

624 J Strachan (1992) 'Women and changing attitudes' *Presentation*, National Women's Convention Sydney.

625 Liz Hull (2012) 'Majority of British mothers feel guilty about going to work and not spending enough time with their children' *Daily Mail*, March 8, citing a report 'Changing face of motherhood' by the Social Issues Research Centre, Oxford.

626 Catherine Hakim (2000) *Work-Lifestyle choices in the 21ˢᵗ century* [Oxford, Oxford University Press]. See also Catherine Hakim (2004) *Key issues in women's work* [London, Glasshouse Press]

627 Catherine Hakim (2003) *Models of the family in modern societies* [London, Ashgate]

628 Australian Bureau of Statistics (2011) *Labour Force, Australia: Labour Force Status and other characteristics of Families,* June 2011, Cat 6223.0.55.001

629 *Ibid.*

630 Australian Bureau of Statistics, *Australian Social Trends, 2008*, Cat. 4102.0; and *Australian Social Trends, Dec 2011*, Cat 4102.0. See also Mariah Evans (1995) 'Norms on women's employment over the life course, Australia, 1989-1993' *International Social Science Survey* [Canberra, Australian National University]

631 See for example Catherine Carroll and April Brayfield (2007) 'Lingering nuances: Gender career motivations and aspirations of first-year law students' *Sociological Spectrum* 27: 225-55 for a discussion of different aspirations.

632 Pew Research Center (2007) 'From 1997-2007: Fewer mothers prefer full-time

work' *A social and demographic trends report.*

633 June O'Neill (2003) 'Catching up: The gender gap in wages circa 2000' *The American Economic Review* 93: 309-314

634 James M White (1999) 'Work-family stage and satisfaction with work-family balance' *Journal of Comparative Family Studies* 30(2): 163-75

635 Chinhui Juhn and Simon Potter (2006) 'Changes in labor force participation in the United States' *Journal of Economic Perspectives* 20: 27-46

636 Studies consistently reveal that married women do more work in the home than their husbands: See, for example: Janeen Baxter (2005) 'To marry or not to marry: Marital status and the household division of labor' *Journal of Family Issues* 26: 300-321

637 Julie Brines (1994) 'Economic dependency, gender, and the division of labor at home' *American Journal of Sociology* 100: 652-688; Laura Sanchez (1994) 'Gender, labor allocations, and the psychology of entitlement within the home' *Social Forces* 73: 533-553. See also Lyn Craig (2006) 'Does father care mean fathers share? A comparison of how mothers and fathers in intact families spend time with children' *Gender and Society* 20: 259-281; and Janine Baxter (2006) 'Gender, work and families' *Threshold* 87: 25-29

638 Kei M Nomaguchi and Melissa A Milkie (2006) 'Maternal employment in childhood and adults' retrospective reports of parenting practices' *Journal of Marriage and Family* 68: 573-594

639 Stacey J Rogers and Paul R Amato (2000) 'Have changes in gender relations affected marital quality?' *Social Forces* 79: 731-753

640 Mattias Strandh and Mikael Nordenmark (2006) 'The interference of paid work with household demands in different social policy contexts: Perceived work-household conflict in Sweden, the UK, the Netherlands, Hungary, and the Czech Republic' *The British Journal of Sociology* 57: 597-617. By contrast, Amato and colleagues found little evidence that increases in wives' hours of employment and work demands had generally negative consequences for marital quality: Paul R Amato, Alan Booth, David R Johnson and Stacy J Rogers (2007) *Alone together* [Cambridge MA, Harvard University Press], 136

641 Shirley Glass (2003) *Not 'just friends'* [New York, The Free Press]

642 Scott J South (2001) 'Time-dependent effects of wives' employment on marital dissolution' *American Sociological Review* 66: 226-245. Behavioural problems amongst children where parents, especially mothers, work non-standard hours have also been observed: Lyndall Strazdins *et al* (2004) 'Around-the-clock: parent work schedules and children's well-being in a 24-h economy' *Social Science and Medicine* 59: 1517-1537. A study from the Netherlands concludes that divorce is significantly more likely to occur within ten years of a marriage when a couple reverse traditional

sex-roles in the first five years after the wedding: Anne-Rigt Poortman (2005) 'How work affects divorce: The mediating role of financial and time pressures' *Journal of Family Issues* 26: 168-195. See also; Scott J South and Kim M Lloyd (1995) 'Spousal alternatives and marriage dissolution' *American Sociological Review* 60: 21-35 – linking the prevalence of divorce to the proportion of unmarried women in the labor force.

643 J Strachan (1995) 'What young couples want in the nineties' *Threshold* 49: 13–15.

644 Matthus Kalmijn, Paul M De Graaf, and Anne-Rigt Poortman (2004) 'Interactions between cultural and economic determinants of divorce in the Netherlands' *Journal of Marriage and Family* 66: 75-89

645 Stacey J Rogers (2004) 'Dollars, dependency and divorce: Four perspectives on the role of wives' income' *Journal of Marriage and the Family* 66: 59-74. This also reflects the theory of the American economist, Gary Becker, that wedlock makes the most economic sense when husbands and wives specialise in complementary work: Gary S Becker (1991) *A treatise on the family* [Cambridge MA, Harvard University Press]

646 Amato, Booth, Johnson and Rogers (2007) *supra*, 138. See also Belinda Hewitt, Janeen Baxter and Mark Western (2006) 'Family, work, and health: The impact of marriage, parenthood, and employment on self-reported health of Australian men and women' *Journal of Sociology* 21: 61-78 on the impact of work and family commitments on health.

647 'Work and marital quality' (2011) *Threshold* 103: 6

648 AR Hochschild (1997) *The Time Bind: When work becomes home and home becomes work* [New York, Metropolitan Books] See also, *New York Times Magazine* April 20, 1997; and 'Resource Notes' No 23: 85, in Supplement to (1998) *Threshold* 58

649 Scott J South, Katherine Trent, and Yang Shen (2001) 'Changing partners: Toward a macrostructural-opportunity theory of marital dissolution' *Journal of Marriage and the Family* 63: 743-754. In contrast, the researchers could find "no evidence that couples are more apt to divorce when husbands work with a larger than average number of women." See also: 'Is divorce contagious?' (2002) *Threshold* 74: 3, citing a Swedish report that exposure to divorced co-workers increased the likelihood of divorce.

650 K Jill Kiecolt (2003) 'Satisfaction with work and family life: No evidence of a cultural reversal' *Journal of Marriage and the Family* 65: 23-25

651 D Ladbrook (1991) 'Building our relationship assets' *Threshold* 46: 6.

652 J Bernard (1972) *The Future of Marriage* [New York, World Publishing] 51.

653 *Ibid.*, 294

654 *Ibid.*, 272-273

655 *Ibid.*, 288.

656   Barbara Dafoe Whitehead (1992) *The Experts' Story of Marriage* [New York, Council on Families]

657 James Q Wilson (1993) 'The Family Values Debate' *Commentary* April: 24-25.

658 Moira Eastman (1996) 'Myths of Marriage and Family' in D Popenoe, JB Elshtain and D Blankenhorn (eds) *Promises to Keep* [Lanham MD, Rowman and Littlefield]

659 Hilary R Clinton (1996) *It Takes a Village* [New York, Simon and Schuster] 39.

660 Michael Duffy (1995) 'Is childcare bad for kids?' *The Independent Monthly* October, 36-42.

661 National Commission on America's Urban Families (1993) *Families First* [Washington DC, The Commission] 31.

662 See for example: Edmund Leach in Nicholas Pole (ed) (1972) *Environmental Solutions* [Cambridge, Cambridge University Press], 105; and Germaine Greer (1971) *The female eunuch* [London, Granada], 221

663 Ferdinand Mount (1982) *The subversive family* [London, Jonathan Cape], 9-10

664 Pat Thane (2010) *Happy families? History and family policy* [London, British Academy]

665 Rebecca Probert and Samantha Callan (2011) *History and family: Setting the records straight* [London, The Centre for Social Justice]

666 See for example, Anthony Elliott (1998) 'Families evolve from the ashes' *Sunday Age*, March 15

667 Paul Amato (2004) 'Tension Between institutional and individual views of marriage' *Journal of Marriage and Family*, 66: 959-965; and Paul Amato (2007) 'Strengthening marriage is an appropriate social policy goal' *Journal of Policy Analysis and Management*, 16: 952-956

668 Stephanie Coontz (2004) 'The world historical transformation of marriage' *Journal of Marriage and Family* 66: 974-979. See also: Stephanie Coontz (2000) *The way we never were: American families and the nostalgia trap* [New York, Basic Books]

669 Judith Stacey (1996) *In the name of the family: Rethinking family values in the postmodern age* [Boston, Beacon Press] 11

670 Betsey Stevenson and Justin Wolfers (2009) 'The paradox of declining female happiness' National Bureau of Economic Research, *Working Papers Series* No. 14969

671 Jonathan Sacks (2007) *The home we build together* [London, Continuum] 213

672 House of Representatives Legal and Constitutional Affairs Committee (1998) *To have and to hold* [Canberra, Parliament of Australia] 72

673 Anthony Giddens (2007) *Over to you, Mr Brown* [London, Policy Network] 21

674 David Blankenhorn (2007) *The future of marriage* [New York, Encounter], 91

675 Plato, *The Republic*, V, 464

676 Aristotle, *Politics*, Jowett (trans) [Oxford, Oxford University Press, 1921] II, 4

677 David Blankenhorn, 'Introduction' in David Blankenhorn, Steven Bayne and Jean Bethke Elstain (1990) *Rebuilding the nest* [Milwaukee, Family Service America]

678 Plato, *The Republic*, V, 464

679 Karl Marx and Friedrich Engels, *Communist manifesto*, [Pelican edition, 1967], 100-101

680 Adolf Hitler, (1929) *Mein Kampf* [Munich], 276. See also, Ferdinand Mount (1982) *The subversive family* [London, Jonathan Cape], 30-32

681 John Locke (1690) *Second treatise on government*

682 See for example: C Owen Lovejoy (1981) 'The origin of man' *Science* 211: 341-356, and (1982) 'Models of human evolution' *Science* 217: 304-306

683 Richard Stith 'On the legal validation of sexual relationships' in Scott Fitzgibbon, Lynn D Wardle and A Scott Loveless (2010) *The jurisprudence of marriage and other intimate relationships* [Buffalo, NY, William S Hein]

684 W Kent Geiger (1968) *The family in Soviet Russia* [Cambridge MA, Harvard University Press], 22. See also Freidrich Engels (1884) *The origin of the family, private property and the state*

685 Patrick Parkinsion (2011) *Family Law and the Indissolubility of Parenthood* [Cambridge, Cambridge University Press] 270. I am indebted to Professor Parkinson's work for the discussion in this section.

686 Mary Ann Glendon (1977) *State, law, and family: Family Law in transition in the United States and Western Europe* [Elsevier North Holland]; Mary Ann Glendon (1987) *Abortion and divorce in western law* [Cambridge MA, Harvard University Press]

687 Jan Gorecki, (1972) 'Communist Family Pattern: Law as an implement of change' 1 *University of Illinois Law Forum*, 121, 124.

688 Parkinson, *supra*, 271, citing the *Russian Socialist Federative Soviet Republic Code* (1926)

689 Jacob Sundberg (1975) 'Recent changes in Swedish family law: Experiment repeated', 23 *American Journal of Comparative Law* 34, 44

690 John Hazard (1939) 'Law and the Soviet Family', *Wisconsin Law Review* 224, 246

691 Lynn Wardle (2004) 'The "withering away" of marriage: Some lessons from the Bolshevik family law reforms in Russia, 1917-1926', 2 *Georgetown Journal of Law*

and Public Policy, 469, 490-496

692 Geiger, *supra*, 95-98 and 255-58

693 Parkinson, *supra*, 277

694 This includes the Christian view of marriage. See for example: Kathleen M Walters (2011) 'The purposes of marriage' *Threshold* 102: 36; Peter Elliott (1990) *What God has joined* [Homebush, NSW, St Paul]

695 "Marriage . . . is a means of facilitating in an orderly fashion the voluntary assumption of mutual rights and obligations by adults committed to each other's well-being" – Law Commission of Canada (2001) *The legal organisation of personal relationships* [Ottawa, the Commission]

696 Andrew Rugg (2012) 'Obama's gay marriage gamble' *The Enterprise Blog* [Washington DC, American Enterprise Institute], May 10. Four states – Maine, Minnesota, Maryland and Washington – were scheduled to consider marriage proposals in November 2012.

697 Although in the most recent case, the courts of Hawaii upheld the traditional definition: *Jackson v. Abercrombie* (2012) August 8

698 See John Locke (1690) *Second Treatise of Government*

699 Seana Sugrue (2006) *Canadian marriage policy: A tragedy for children* [Ottawa, Institute of Marriage and Family Canada]

700 Don S Browning (2004) 'The liberal case against same-sex marriage' *The New York Times*, March 9

701 Law Commission of Canada (2001) *Beyond conjugality – Recognising and supporting close personal adult relationships* [Ottawa, The Commission], xviii. See also: *Goodridge* v. *Department of Public Health*, Massachusetts Supreme Court, November 18, 2003, for a similar proposition.

702 Stephen J Heaney (2012) 'Two steps from reasonable about marriage' *The Public Discourse*, May 7

703 Research also indicates that same-sex unions are far less stable than heterosexual marriages, and subject to greater promiscuity: See David McWhirter and Andrew Mattison (1985) *The male couple* [New York, Prentice Hall] and Andrew Sullivan (1996) *Virtually normal* [New York, Vintage].

704 Sherif Girgis, Robert P George and Ryan T Anderson (2011) 'What is marriage?' *Harvard Journal of Law and Public Policy* 34: 245-260.

705 Brendan O'Neill (2012) ' "I now pronounce you partner 1 and partner 2": Why gay marriage is bad for us all' *The Australian*, Inquirer Section, April 7-8, 22

706 Christopher Caldwell (2009) *Reflections on the revolution in Europe* [London, Allen Lane], 182. There are campaigns for legal recognition of 'marriages' involving

more than two people. See, for example, Ean Higgins (2012) 'Menage a quatre in Senate sex push' *The Australian*, May 21, 3. Many Muslim leaders also advocate legalising polygamy.

707 Editorial (2011) 'Gay marriage: A milestone' *New York Times*, June 26

708 Canadian provincial legislation replaces 'mother' and 'father' with 'parent 1' and 'parent 2'. See also: *AA* v. *BB and CC* in which the Ontario Court of Appeal ruled that a child can have three parents.

709 *Same-Sex Relationships (Equal Treatment in Commonwealth Laws) Act* 2008

710 *Gas and Dubois* v. *France*, (2012) Case 25951/07; and *Shalk and Kopf* v *Austria*, (2010) Case 30241/04. See also: *Joslin et al* v. *New Zealand* (2002) United Nations Human Rights Committee.

711 James Q Wilson (1996) 'Against homosexual marriage' *Commentary* (March)

712 For a contrary view, see David Blankenhorn (2012) 'How my view on gay marriage changed' *New York Times* Online, June 22. For a response, see Maggie Gallagher (2012) 'Bigotry, David Blankenhorn, and the future of marriage' *Public Discourse*, June 25

713 John Witte, Jr (1997) *From Sacrament to contract – marriage, religion and law in the western tradition.* [Louisville, Kentucky, Westminster John Knox Press]

714 For a discussion of views about marriage from John Locke onwards, see Scott Yenor (2011) *Family politics – The idea of marriage in modern political thought* [Waco TX, Baylor University Press]

715 This had already occurred in many jurisdictions for couples in *de facto* unions. In the Australian states of New South Wales, under the *De Facto Relationships Act,* and Victoria, under the *Property Law Act,* couples have been able to enter legally binding agreements about property settlements for many years.

716 Tamara Metz (2010) *Untying the knot: Marriage, the state, and the case for their divorce* [Princeton, Princeton University Press]

717 Law Commission of Canada (2001) *supra*

718 The Commission proposed a system of registration. *Ibid.*, 118

719 Renata Alexander (1999) 'Family law in the future' *Alternative Law Journal*, 24: 112-116. See also: Nicola Berkovic (2012) 'Sharia blend "bad for women" *The Australian,* June 28, 6

720 *Ibid.*

721 *Family Law Act* 1975, Part VIIAB

722 *Family Proceedings Act* 1980, s. 79

723 See for example the comment of the Archbishop of Canterbury, Dr Rowan Williams (2008) 'Civil and religious law in England: A religious perspective' *The*

Guardian, February 7. It is estimated that between 200,000 and 400,000 people in France alone live in polygamous families: Stanley Kurtz (2006) 'Polygamy versus democracy' *Weekly Standard* (June 5), 23. Other estimates put the number much lower at 10,000 – 20,000 families: Axel Veiel (2005) 'Atemberaubende krawalltheorien' *Neue Zurcher Zeitung* (November 20). For a discussion of marriage and sharia in Europe see Christopher Caldwell (2009) *Reflections on the revolution in Europe* [London, Allen Lane], 172-199

724 The Home Office (1998) *Supporting families – a consultation document.* [London, The Home Office] See also 'Struggling with the 'M' word' (2000) *Marriage, Family and Society Issues*, 4: 41-42.

725 Irish Commission on the Family (1998) *Strengthening Families for Life.* [Dublin, The Stationary Office]

726 Centre for Social Justice (2009) *Every family matters* [London, The Centre for Social Justice] 20

727 Walter Olson (1997) 'Free to commit' *Reason*, October, 60-62

728 See: 'Polygamous and underage marriages in Australia' (2010) *Threshold* 102: 25

729 Tony Kerin (2011) 'The history of marriage consent' *Threshold* 102: 8-9

730 See for example: Lawrie Molony (2011) 'The decision to marry: Freedoms, constraints and individual rights' *Threshold* 102: 10-14

731 Norval D Glenn (2008) 'Against family fatalism' *Cato Unbound*. January 21

732 I am indebted to the Australian Parliamentary Library for the demographic data upon which the tables in this chapter are based.

733 For a previous comparison, see: Kevin and Margaret Andrews (1999) 'Family composition and social change' *Marriage, Family and Society Issues* 1: 10-14

734 2007 Census data revealed that for the first time in more than 90 years, the number of adults who had not married had risen above 50 per cent: 'Fewer marriages but babies boom' (2007) *Threshold* 90: 3

735 'Canada: Fewer legal marriages' (2005) *Threshold* 83: 28, citing the Vanier Institute report, *Profiling Canada's Families III*

736 See also: 'Two-thirds of Czech marriages divorce' (2007) *Threshold* 90: 5; 'Spanish divorce rates' (2007) *Threshold* 90: 5

737 Imran Rasul (2006) 'The impact of divorce laws on marriage' *Unpublished paper* [London, University College] cited in Betsey Stevenson and Justin Wolfers (2007) 'Marriage and divorce: Changes and their driving forces' *Journal of Economic Perspectives* 21: 27-52

738 Betsey Stevenson (2007) 'The impact of divorce laws on investment in marriage-specific capital' *Journal of Labor Economics* 25: 75-94

739 See for example: 'Europe: Marriage on the increase' (2002) *Threshold* 73: 5

740 Lixia Qu and Grace Soriano (2004) 'Forming couple relationships' *Family Matters* 68: 43-49

741 Claudia Goldin (2006) 'The quiet revolution that transformed women's employment, education, and family' *The American Economic Review* 96: 1-21

742 Cheryl Wetzstein (2012) 'US marriage rate continues to decline; men tie knot later' *The Washington Times* (February 5)

743 Pew Research Center (2010) *The decline of marriage and rise of new families* [Washington DC, The Center]

744 Melinda J Messineo and Roger A Wojtkiewicz (2004) 'Coresidence of adult children with parents from 1960 to 1990: Is the propensity to live at home really increasing?' *Journal of Family History* 29: 71-83

745 Frank F Furstenberg Jr *et al* (2004) 'Growing up is hard to do' *Contexts* 3. See also: Ruth Weston *et al* (2007) 'Leaving home trends' *Threshold* 91: 24-25 for a discussion of Australian trends.

746 TW Smith (1999) *The emerging 21ˢᵗ century family*, GSS Social Change Report No 42 [Chicago, National Opinion Research Center, University of Chicago] 23; Chandra A Martinez *et al* (2005) 'Fertility, family planning, and reproductive health of US women: Data from the 2002 National Survey of Family Growth' *Vital Health Statistics* 23 (25)

747 Ben Wilson (2009) *Estimating the cohabiting population* [London, Office for National Statistics], Table 3

748 John Hayward and Guy Brandon (2011) *Cohabitation: An alternative to marriage?* [Cambridge UK, The Jubilee Centre] 5

749 Larry Bumpass and Hsien-Hen Lu (1998) 'Trends in cohabitation and implications for children's Family contexts' *Unpublished manuscript* [Madison WI, Center for Demography, University of Wisconsin]

750 Elizabeth Wildsmith, Nicole R Steward-Streng and Jennifer Manlove (2011) *Childbearing outside marriage: Estimates and trends in the United States* [Washington DC, Child Trends], 4. The proportion of nonmarital births in cohabiting unions varied by race: for white women (61 per cent) Hispanics (65 per cent) and black women (30 per cent).

751 Sara McLanahan (2011) 'Family instability and complexity after a nonmarital birth: Outcomes for children in fragile families' in MJ Carlson and P England (eds) *Social class and changing families in an unequal America* [Stanford, Stanford University Press]

752 Elizabeth Wildsmith *et al* (2011), *supra*, at 5

753 Anna Reimondas, Ann Evans and Edith Gray (2011) 'Living-apart-together

(LAT) relationships in Australia' *Family Matters* 87: 43-55

754 William Galston (1994) *Beyond the Murphy Brown debate* [New York, Institute for American Values]

755 'The flight from marriage' (2010) *The Economist*, August 20, 18

756 'Russia: Marriage and divorce' (2005) *Threshold* 83: 27, citing the *Moscow Times*, December 8, 2004

757 See: *To have and to hold* (1998) *supra*, 16

758 'The three year glitch' (2011) *Threshold* 102: 3; and 'Seven year itch has become the three year ditch' (2012) *Daily Mail Online*, April 18

759 *To have and to hold* (1998) *supra*, 16

760 Helen Glezer (1994) 'Family backgrounds and marital breakdown' *Threshold* 43: 16-19

761 'More children experience separation' (2004) *Threshold* 81: 3-4

762 Australian Bureau of Statistics (2010) 'Parental divorce or death during childhood' *Australian Social Trends* (Cat 4102.0)

763 Australian Bureau of Statistics, *Marriages and Divorces, Australian 2009* (Cat No 3310.0)

764 Australian Bureau of Statistics, *Marriages and divorces, Australia, 2010*

765 John Hayward and Guy Brandon (2011) *Cohabitation: An alternative to marriage?* [Cambridge UK, The Jubilee Centre]

766 'Mothers and children post separation' (2011) *Threshold* 101: 6, reporting Australian Institute of Family Studies research that one-third of children never stayed with their father post-separation, with 11 per cent never seeing their father and 23 per cent seeing their father only during the daytime.

767 This is an estimate, as the Center for Disease Control ceased collecting the data in 1988 when the number was over 1 million children.

768 Patrick F Fagan and Nicholas Zill (2011) *The second annual index of family belonging and rejection* [Washington DC, Marriage and Religion Research Institute]

769 Royal College of Psychiatrists, *Mental health and growing up* [London, The College]

770 Tim Shipman (2010) 'Broken Britain: Half of all parents split up before their children reach the age of 16' *Daily Mail Online*, December 7, citing a report from the Centre for Social Justice.

771 Department of Justice, Canada, *The effects of divorce on children: A selected literature review* [Ottawa, The Department]

772 Paul Robinson, *Parenting after separation and divorce: A profile of arrangements*

for spending time with and making decisions for children [Ottawa, Statistics Canada]

773 Paul R Amato (2000) 'The consequences of divorce for adults and children' *Journal of Marriage and Family* 62: 1269

774 'Divorce rates down' (2008) *Threshold* 94: 4

775 Stephanie Coontz (2005) *Marriage, a history: From obedience to intimacy, or how love conquered marriage* [New York, Viking]; Betsey Stevenson and Justin Wolfers (2007) 'Marriage and divorce: Changes and their driving forces' *Journal of Economic Perspectives* 21: 27-52

776 Stevenson and Wolfers, *supra*, 38

777 David Popenoe (2008) 'Cohabitation, marriage and child wellbeing' *Threshold* 93: 20-23, and 25.

778 Social Policy Justice Group (2006) *Fractured families*, The State of the nation report [London, the Social Policy Justice Group] 9-13

779 See Ruth Weston and Lixia Qu (2006) 'Family statistics and trends: Trends in couple dissolution' *Family Relationships Quarterly* 2: 9 (Australia); Sheela Kennedy and Elizabeth Thomson (2010) 'Children's experiences of family disruption in Sweden: Differentials by parent education over three decades' *Demographic Res* 23: 479, 481 ; Office of National Statistics (2011) *Divorces in England and Wales*; Andrew J Cherlin (2010) 'Demographic trends in the United States: A review of research in the 2000s' *Journal of Marriage and Family* 72: 403; Anne-Marie Ambert (2009) *Divorce: Facts, causes and consequences* (3rd ed) [Ottawa, Vanier Institute of the Family]; and 'Divorce rate hits 40 year low as couples marry later in life, and figure looks set to drop further' (2012) *Daily Mail Online*, June 30

780 Elissa Doherty (2012) 'Love me do, but just for nine years it seems' *Herald Sun*, March 29, citing the Australian Bureau of Statistics report, *Love me do*

781 'Divorce rates fall' (2006) *Threshold* 88: 3-4; ABS, *Divorces, Australia, 2005* Cat 3307.9.55.00; 'The 27-year itch' (2007) *Threshold* 91: 3; Ruth Weston (2007) 'Later life divorces' *Threshold* 91: 12-13; and Daniel Martin and Tom Kelly (2011) 'Rise of the "silver separations": Divorce rate for the over 60s surges' *Daily Mail*, November 18

782 Tara Parker-Pope (2010) *For better: The science of a good marriage* [New York, Dutton], 13, citing research by Adam Isen and Betsey Stevenson from the University of Pennsylvania.

783 See: 'Global marriage crisis' (2009) *Threshold* 96: 4; and 'Irish recession strains marriages' (2009) *Threshold* 96: 6

784 Jason Fields (2000) *America's families and living arrangements: Population characteristics, 2000,* Current Population Reports P20-537 [Washington DC, US Bureau of Census] 9. See also: 'US: More putting off marriage' (2005) *Threshold*

83: 27-28

785 *Ibid.*, 11

786 Stephanie Coontz (2004) 'The world historical transformation of marriage' *Journal of Marriage and Family* 66: 974-979

787 'The flight from marriage' (2010) *The Economist* (August 20), 18

788 Denis Ladbrook (1995) *Social contexts of marriage and family in Australia in the mid to late 1990s* [Kenmore Qld, Prepare-Enrich Australia], cited in Andrews and Curtis (1998) *supra*, 44

789 *Ibid.*

790 Pascale Beaupre (2008) *I do ... take two? Changes in intentions to remarry among divorced Canadians during the past 20 years* [Ottawa, Statistics Canada]

791 Norval D Glenn (2005) *With this ring ... A national survey on marriage in America* [Washington DC, National Fatherhood Initiative], 11

792 US Census Bureau (2006) 'Remarriage in the US' *Slideshow*, using National Center of Health Statistics and the Survey of Income and Program Participation data.

793 Office of National Statistics (2007) *UK – Marriage, Divorce and Adoption Statistics, England and Wales* (Series FM2), No 35, 2007 (table 2.2 and 2.1)

794 New Zealand Statistics, *Marriages, civil unions, and divorces*, Year ended Dec 2005 and 2010

795 Linda Kelsy (2010) 'The lonely truth about middle-aged divorce: How finding a new partner mid-life can be soul destroying' *Daily Mail Online*, February 8; Haya El Nasser (2012) 'Americans putting off having babies amid poor economy', *USA Today*, July 25

796 See: John C Caldwell (1999) 'The delayed western fertility decline: An examination of English-speaking countries' *Population and Development Review* 25(3): 479-513

797 Cited in Kevin Andrews (2009) 'Population, immigration and Australia's future' *Australian Polity* 3: 12-16

798 'Baby gap' (2006) *Threshold* 87: 5 (See also *The Times*, February 20, 2006)

799 Steve Doughty (2011) 'A generation of childless women: How a fifth of 45 year olds have not started a family' *Daily Mail Online* December 17.

800 Ruth Weston *et al* (2005) 'It's not for lack of wanting kids ...' *Threshold* 83: 24-25

801 'Australian birth rates climb' (2006) *Threshold* 88:3; ABS, *Births, Australian 2005* Cat 3301.0

802 Donald T Rowland (2007) 'Historical trends in childlessness' *Journal of Family Issues* 28: 1311-37

803 Tanya Koropeckyj-Cox and Vaughn RA Call (2007) 'Characteristics of childless persons and parents' *Journal of Family Issues* 28: 1362-1414

804 Zheng Wu (2000) *Cohabitation: An alternative form of family living* [New York, Oxford University Press] 152

805 David Popenoe (2008) *supra*, citing Marta Dominguez *et al* (2007) 'European latecomers: Cohabitation in Italy and Spain' *Paper* delivered at the Population Association of America annual meeting.

806 Australian Bureau of Statistics (2012) *Quick stats*, from the 2011 census.

807 Barbara Dafoe Whitehead (2008) 'Life without children: The social retreat from children and how it's changing America' *The State of Our Unions* [Rutgers NJ, National Marriage Project]. The 2010 US Census data revealed that only 48 per cent of households included a married husband and wife, down from 78 per cent in 1950: 'The end of marriage? Husband and wife households at record lows' (2012) *ABC News* (April 25)

808 See: Jo Anna Gray, Jean Stockard and Joe Stone (2006) 'The rising share of nonmarital births: Fertility choice or marriage behavior' *Demography* 43: 241-253

809 Australian Bureau of Statistics, *Ex-nuptial births, Australia*, (on age of mother, selected years 1976-2006) reproduced in 'Ex-nuptial birth trends in Australia' (2008) *Threshold* 93: 26

810 Bryan Rogers *et al* (2011) 'Parental divorce and adult family, social and psychological outcomes: The contribution of childhood family adversity' *Social Policy Research Paper* No 42, 9

811 Jason DeParle and Sabrina Tavarnise (2010) 'Unwed mothers now a majority before age 30' *New York Times*, A1, (February 18). There is also a significant racial divide: 73 per cent of black children are born outside marriage, compared to 53 per cent of Latinos and 29 per cent of whites.

812 JA Martin *et al* (2011) *Births, Final data for 2009*. National Vital Statistics Reports 60(1) [Hyattsville MD, National Center for Health Statistics], SJ Ventura and CA Bachrack (2000) *Nonmarital childbearing in the United States, 1940-1999*. National Vital Health Statistics 48(16) [Hyattsville MD, National Center for Health Statistics]. See also: 'Vital signs: Teen pregnancy – United States, 1991-2009' (2011) *Morbidity and Mortality Weekly Report* 60 (13): 414-420 (April 8)

813 Rose M Kreider and Renee Ellis (2011) *Living arrangements of children* [Washington DC, US Census Bureau]

814 'Marriage decline?' (2006) *Threshold* 87: 4-5 (See also *Telegraph*, February 22, 2006)

815 See: David Popenoe (2008) 'Cohabitation, marriage and child wellbeing' *Threshold* 93: 23

816 Kathryn Edin and Maria Kefalas (2005) *Promises I can keep: Why poor women put motherhood before marriage* [Berkeley CA, University of California Press]

817 Zhenchao Qian, Daniel T Lichter and Leanna M Mellot (2005) 'Out-of-wedlock childbearing, marital prospects and mate selection' *Social Forces* 84: 473-491

818 Patrick Heuveline, JM Timberlake and FF Furstenberg Jr (2003) 'Shifting childrearing to single mothers: Results from 17 western countries' *Population and Development Review* 29: 47-71

819 See for example, Kevin Kinsella and David R Phillips (2005) 'Global aging: The challenge of success' *Population Bulletin* 60.1: 3-39; Richard Jackson and Neil Howe (2008) *The graying of the great powers* [Washington DC: Center for Strategic and International Studies]

820 'Home alone: the nation's future' (2004) *Threshold* 82: 27

821 By contrast, in South Asia and China, 98 per cent of men and women marry, very few cohabit, and only 2 per cent of births are outside wedlock: 'The flight from marriage' (2011) *The Economist* (August 20), 17

822 Andrew J Cherlin (2009) *The marriage-go-round* [New York, Vintage Books] 3 and 16-19

823 David Willetts argues that the increasing fragility of marriage is a result, at least in part, of the fact that many more people decided to marry in the 1960s. See Willetts (2010) *supra*

824 David Blankenhorn *et al* (2009) *The Marriage Index* [New York, Institute for American Values; and Hampton VA, National Center of African American Marriages and Parenting]

825 'Australia's marriage index falls' (2010) *Australian Polity* 4: 23. See also David Blankenhorn *et al* (2010) 'We need a marriage index' *Australian Polity* 4: 20-24; and 'Australia's marriage index falls' (2010) *Threshold* 98: 36

826 See: *Threshold*, (2009) 97: 10-13

827 Jonathan Kelley *et al* (1984-1995/96) *National Social Science Survey* [Canberra, Australian National University]

828 Glezer (1994) *supra*. See also: Gordon Dahl (2005) 'Myopic matrimony and dropout decisions? Evidence using state laws for marriage, schooling and work' *Working Paper 11328* [National Bureau of Economic Research]

829 Ariel Kalil and James Kunz (2002) 'Teenage childbearing, marital status, and depressive symptoms in later life' *Child Development* 73: 1748-1760

830 Greg Pogarsky, Alan J Lizotte and Terrance P Thornberry (2003) 'The delinquency of children born to young mothers: Results from the Rochester Youth Development Study' *Criminology* 41: 1249-1281

831 E Madur (1993) 'Developmental differences in children's understanding of marriage, divorce and remarriage' *Journal of Applied Developmental Psychology* 14: 191-212; PR Amato (1988) 'Parental divorce and attitudes towards marriage and family life' *Journal of Marriage and the Family* 50: 453-461; PR Amato (1997) 'Explaining the intergenerational transmission of divorce' *Threshold* 54: 15-27; and DB Larson *et al* (1996) *The costly consequences of divorce* [Rockville MD, National Institute for Healthcare Research] and the studies cited therein.

832 DB Larson (1996) *supra*, and the studies cited therein

833 TC Marton and LL Bumpass (1989) 'Recent trends in marital disruption' *Demography* 26: 37-51; AJ Norton and PC Glick (1979) 'Marital instability in America: Past, present and future' in G Levinger and OC Moles (eds) *Divorce and separation: Context, causes, and consequences* [New York, Basic Books]; and SL Nock (1987) *The sociology of the family* [Englwood Cliffs NJ, Prentice Hall]

834 Mark Regnerus (2009) 'Say yes. What are you waiting for?' *Washington Post*, April 26

835 'Early living together, marriage, parenting benefits some young adults' (2008) *News Release*, Pennsylvania State University, (March 28) See also Kevin Andrews (1996) 'The age for marriage' *Threshold* 54: 10-11

836 Deborah Roempke Graefe and Daniel T Lichter (2007) 'When unwed mothers marry: The marital and cohabitating partners of midlife women', *Journal of Family Issues* 28: 595-622

837 Daniel T Lichter and Deborah Roempke (2007) 'Men and marriage promotion: Who marries unwed mothers?', *Social Services Review* 81: 397-420

838 Ilene Wolcott and Jody Hughes (1999) *Towards understanding the reasons for divorce* [Melbourne, Australian Institute for Family Studies], 21

839 Scott J South and Kim M Lloyd (1995) 'Spousal alternatives and marriage dissolution' *American Sociological Review* 60: 21-35. See also: Tammy Nelson (2011) 'Affair proof your marriage' *Huffington Post* (November 15) citing Peggy Vaughan, author of *The Monogamy Myth*, that as many as 60 per cent of men and 40 per cent of women have an affair, and Janis Abrahms Spring, author of *After the Affair*, that infidelity affects one out of every 2.7 couples in the US.

840 W Bradford Wilcox (ed) (2011) 'When baby makes three', *The State of our Unions,* [Charlottesville, VA, The National Marriage Project]. See also chapter 11.

841 'Children make married parents happier' (2009) *Threshold* 97: 3

842 See: 'Do daughters cause divorce?' (2011) *Threshold* 103: 6 and the studies cited therein.

843 Wilcox (2011), *supra*

844 Jeffry H Larson (2000) *Should we stay together?* [San Francisco, Jossey-Bass].

See also 'Happily ever after ... maybe' (2000) *Threshold* 65: 6-7

845 There is some evidence that sexual desire differs between genders, with women experiencing different levels to men. See for example: 'Sex? I'd rather have a pet hamster' (2011) *Threshold* 103: 6-7. See generally: Bettina Arndt (2009) *The sex diaries* [Melbourne, Melbourne University Press]; Michele Weiner-Davis (2003) *The sex starved marriage* [New York, Simon and Shuster]; and Steven E Rhoads (2004) *Taking sex differences seriously* [San Francisco, Encounter]

846 This accords with other studies of successful marriage, for example, the work of John Gottman (1999) *The seven principles for making marriage work* [New York, Three Rivers Press]. See also: 'Gratitude boosts romantic relationships' (2010) *Threshold* 99: 3-4

847 Scott M Stanley *et al* (2006) 'Sacrifice as a predictor of marital outcomes' *Family Process* 45: 289-303. See also: Steven Stosny (2010) 'The best marriage therapy tool' *Psychology Today* (June 13)

848 Wilcox, *supra*. See also: K Daniel O'Leary *et al* (2011) 'Is long-term love more than a rare phenomenon? If so, what are its correlates?' *Social Psychology and Personality Science* (August 5): correlates of long-term intense love were shown to be thinking positively about the partner, thinking about the partner when apart, affectionate behaviours and sexual intercourse, shared novel and challenging activities, and general life happiness.

849 See also: Scott M Stanley (1998) *The heart of commitment* [Nashville, Thomas Nelson]

850 Jason S Carroll *et al* (2011) 'Materialism and marriage: Couple profile on congruent and incongruent spouses' *Journal of Couple and Relationship Therapy* 10: 287-308

851 Paul R Amato, Alan Booth, David R Johnson and Stacy J Rogers (2007) *Alone together* [Cambridge MA, Harvard University Press], 263

852 'Optimising the marriage market' (2009) *Threshold* 97: 3

853 See: *To have and to hold* (1998) *supra*, at 91-92; Kathleen M Walters (2005) 'Do couples who pray together, stay together?' *Threshold* 84: 25-27, and the studies cited therein; 'Praying for your partner stops you straying' (2011) *Threshold* 101: 7; and 'Couples that pray together are happier' (2011) *Threshold* 102: 4-5

854 'Modern marriage' (2007) *Pew Social and Demographic Trends* [Washington DC, Pew Research Center]

855 MDR Evans and Jonathan Kelley (2004) 'Effect of family structure on life satisfactions: Australian evidence' *Social Indicators Research* 69: 303-349

856 Bruce Headey *et al* (1991) *supra*, 90

857 Barbara Dafoe Whitehead and David Popenoe (2001) 'Who wants to marry a soul

mate' *The State of our Unions*, [Rutgers NJ, The National Marriage Project], 6

858 *Ibid*, 10

859 This discussion on cohabitation is updated from the report, *To have and to hold* (1998) [Canberra, Legal and Constitutional Affairs Committee, Australian House of Representatives], of which I was the chair and principal author.

860 See chapter seven . See also: Ann-Zofie E Duvander (1999) 'The transition from cohabitation to marriage: A longitudinal study of the propensity to marry in Sweden in the early 1990s' *Journal of Family Issues* 20(5): 698-717

861 W Bradford Wilcox (ed) (2010) 'When marriage disappears' *The State of our Unions 2010* [Charlottesville, VA, The National Marriage Project]. See also: Sheila Kennedy and Larry Bumpass (2008) 'Cohabitation and children's living arrangements: New estimates from the United States' *Demographic Research* 19: 1663-1692

862 In Australia, for example, the proportion of cohabiting couples increased from six per cent of all couples in 1986 to 15 per cent in 2006. Most ex-nuptial births are to cohabiting couples.

863 ED Macklin 1983 'Nonmarital Heterosexual Cohabitation: An Overview' in *Contemporary Families and Alternative Lifestyles* ED Macklin and RH Rubin (eds) [Beverley Hills, California, Sage Publications] cited in H Anderson and R Cotton Fite 1993 *Becoming Married* [Louisville KY, John Knox Westminster Press] See also: Sotirios Sarantakos (1984) *Living Together in Australia* [Melbourne, Longman Cheshire]; and Sandra Buchler *et al* (2009) 'The social and demographic characteristics of cohabiters in Australia: Towards a typology of cohabiting couples' *Family Matters* 82: 22; and 'The family in Europe' (1999) *Bulletin Plus* [London, One plus One], describing different cohabitation patterns across the continent.

864 According to the Australian Bureau of Statistics, 42 per cent of those in a *de facto* relationship in 2006-07 expected to marry their current partner: ABS (2011) *Family characteristics and transitions, Australia 2006-07*

865 R Hawes and J Cribb (1993) 'Two-parent families rule the roost' *The Australian* November 24

866 LL Bumpass (1994) 'The Declining Significance of Marriage: Changing Family Life in the United States' Working Paper No 66 *A National Survey of Families and Households* [Centre for Demography and Ecology, University of Wisconsin]

867 SM Stanley, SW Whitton and HJ Markman (2004) 'Maybe I do: Interpersonal commitment and premarital or nonmarital cohabitation' *Journal of Family Issues* 25: 496-519

868 Linda J Waite (2003) 'Uncommitted cohabitation versus marriage' *Threshold* 76: 17-20

869 MD Bramlett and WD Mosher (2002) 'Cohabitation, marriage, divorce, and

remarriage in the United States' National Center for Health Statistics, *Vital Health Statistics* 23(22). See also: Hara Estroff Marano and Carlin Flora (2004) 'The truth about compatibility' *Psychology Today*, September 1.

870 Pamela Smock *et al* (2006) *Heterosexual cohabitation in the United States: Motives for living together among men and women* [Ann Arbor MI, University of Michigan Population Studies Center]; 'US: Couples live together for convenience' (2004) *Threshold* 82: 36-37

871 S Sarantakos (1991) 'Cohabitation Revisited: Paths of Change Along Cohabiting and Noncohabiting Couples' *Australian Journal of Marriage and Family* 12: 3 144-155.

872 S Sarantakos (1991) 'Unmarried Cohabitation: Perceptions of a Lifestyle' *Australian Social Work* 44: 4 23-32.

873 S Sarantakos (1984) *Living Together in Australia* [Melbourne, Longman Cheshire] 142.

874 See CM Dash Bush, CL Cohan and PR Amato (2003) 'The relationship between cohabitation and marital quality and stability: Change across cohorts?' *Journal of Marriage and Family* 65: 539-549; GK Rhoades, SM Stanley and HJ Markman (2009) 'The pre-engagement cohabitation effect: A replication and extension of previous findings' *Journal of Family Psychology* 23: 107-111

875 Ruth Weston, Lixia Qu and David de Vaus (2008) 'Cohabitation: Level of stability and post-cohabitation pathway' *Threshold* 92: 18-20

876 John Hayward and Guy Brandon (2011) *Cohabitation: An alternative to marriage?* [Cambridge UK, the Jubilee Centre],

877 Paul Taylor, Cary Funk and April Clark (2007) *As marriage and parenthood drift apart, public is concerned about social impact* [Washington DC, Pew Research Center], 34

878 H Glezer (1991) 'Cohabitation' *Family Matters* 30: 24-27.

879 S Sarantakos (1996) 'The virtues of liberation: A sequel to Kevin Andrews' *Threshold* 53: 9-11.

880 Georgina Binstock and Arland Thornton (2003) 'Separations, reconciliations and living apart in cohabiting and marital unions' *Journal of Marriage and Family* 65: 432-443

881 CM Kamp Dush, CM Cohan and PR Amato (2003) 'The relationship between cohabitation and marital quality and stability: Change across cohorts?' *Journal of Marriage and the Family* 65: 539

882 JD Teachman (2003) 'Premarital sex, premarital cohabitation, and the risk of subsequent marital dissolution among women' *Journal of Marriage and Family* 65: 444-455

883 John Hayward and Guy Brandon (2011) *Cohabitation: An alternative to marriage?* [Cambridge UK, The Jubilee Centre]

884 Martin Beckford (2010) 'Marriage more stable than living together, Office for National Statistics finds' *The Telegraph*, March 26, citing the ONS report, *Population Trends*.

885 Karen Benjamin Guzzo *The changing nature of cohabitation*, PowerPoint presentation [Center for Family and Demographic Research, Bowling Green State University]

886 Mark Regnerus and Jeremy Uecker (2011) *Premarital sex in America* [New York, Oxford University Press], 100

887 Mindy E Scott *et al* (2011) *Characteristics of young adult sexual relationships: Diverse, sometimes violent, often loving* [Washington DC, Child Trends], 3

888 See: Mayrav Saar (2011) 'Cheap dates' *New York Post*, September 24

889 'One in three single girls has used a male "friend with benefits" for sex' (2011) *Daily Mail Online,* November 8, citing a poll of 2,168 women.

890 Norval Glenn and Elizabeth Marquardt (2001) *Hooking up, hanging out, and hoping for Mr Right: College women on mating and dating today* [New York, Institute for American Values]

891 Christian Smith, Kari Christofferson, Hilary Davidson and Patricia Snell Herzog (2011*) Lost in transition – The dark side of emerging adulthood* [New York, Oxford University Press], 176. Young adult relationships have also been found to have relatively high levels of violence: Mindy E Scott, Nicole R Steward-Streng and Jennifer Manlove (2011) *Characteristics of young adult sexual relationships: Diverse, sometimes violent, often loving* [Washington DC, Child Trends], 4

892 Kate Bolick (2011) 'All single ladies' *The Atlantic*, (November) 116-136. See also: Bernard Salt (2006) *The big picture* [Prahan, Australia, Hardie Grant Books] about changing demographic patterns.

893 Sophie Borland (2011) 'Men have twice as many sexual partners as women, notching up 10 during their lives' *Daily Mail Online,* December 17

894 Robert Schoen, Nancy S Landale and Kimberly Daniels (2007) 'Family transitions in young adulthood' *Demography* 44: 807-20

895 Regerus and Uecker (2011) *supra*, 199

896 Smith, Christofferson, Davidson and Herzog (2011*) supra,* 11-12

897 Norval D Glenn (2005) *With this ring: A national survey of marriage in America* [Gaithersberg MD, National Fatherhood Initiative], 18

898 1995 Monitoring the Future Survey, Survey Research Center, University of Michigan, cited in David Popenoe and Barbara Defoe Whitehead (1999) *Should we live together?* [Rutgers NJ, The National Marriage Project]

899 Mindy E Scott et al (2009) *Young adult attitudes about relationships and marriage: Times may have changed, but expectations remain high* [Washington DC, Child Trends], 3

900 M Evans (1991) 'Alternative to Marriage' *National Social Survey Report* Vol. 2 No. 5 7–8.

901 AGB McNair Anderson survey (1995) 'Love, Sex and Marriage in Australia' *A Current Affair* [Sydney, Channel 9] February 13.

902 Helen Glezer (1991) 'Cohabitation' *Family Matters* 30: 24-27.

903 David de Vaus (1997) 'Family values in the nineties' *Family Matters* 48: 4-10.

904 Whitehead and Popenoe, *supra*, 10. See also: SM Stanley, GK Rhoades and HJ Markman (2008) 'Major findings related to the cohabitation effect' *Threshold* 92: 7

905 JP Montgomery 'Towards an understanding of cohabitation' quoted in C Danziger (1978) *Unmarried Heterosexual Cohabitation* [San Francisco, RE.] See also: J Trost (1975) 'Married and unmarried cohabitation: The case of Sweden, with some comparisons' *Journal of Marriage and the Family* 37: 677-682.

906 Scott M Stanley and Galena Rhoades (2009) ' "Sliding vs deciding": understanding a mystery' *NCFR Report* (Summer 2009 Issue) [Minneapolis MN, National Council on Family Relations]

907 See also: Wendy D Manning and Jessica Cohen (2012) 'Premarital cohabitation and marital dissolution: An examination of recent marriages' *Journal of Marriage and Family* 74: 377-387 at 384: "To date, no study has found a protective influence of cohabitation on marital instability."

908 A Crawford (1992) 'Living together: a key to unhappy marriage' *The Sunday Age* Melbourne, June 21, reporting the *Family Formation Survey* (1991) [Melbourne, Australian Institute of Family Studies]

909 Belinda Hewitt, Janeen Baxter and Mark Western (2005) 'Marriage breakdown in Australia: The social correlates of separation and divorce' *Journal of Sociology* 41: 163-183. See also: 'Cohabitation more unstable' (2007) *Threshold* 89: 9, reporting a study by the Australian Institute of Family Studies

910 See for example: Helen Glezer (1997) 'Cohabitation and marriage relationships in the 1990s' *Family Matters* 47: 5; and Steven L Nock (1995) 'A comparison of marriages and cohabiting relationships' *Journal of Family Studies* 16: 53

911 DR Hall and J Zhao (1995) 'Cohabitation and Divorce in Canada' *Journal of Marriage and the Family* 57: 421-427.

912 Social Policy Justice Group (2006) *Fractured families*, The State of the nation report [London, the Social Policy Justice Group] 9-13

913 'UK studies on cohabitation' (2010) *Threshold* 98: 34-35, citing the report *Cohabitation in the 21st century* [Cambridge UK, The Jubilee Centre]. See also:

'Cohabitation and divorce' (2011) *Threshold* 103: 3

914 John Hayward and Guy Brandon (2010) *Cohabitation in the 21ˢᵗ century* [Cambridge UK, The Jubilee Centre] , 5

915 J Hadkey (1992)'Pre-Marital Cohabitation and the Probability of Subsequent Divorce, Office of Population Censuses and Surveys *Population Trends* 68 Summer.

916 L Bumpass and J Sweet (1994) *National Survey of Families and Households* [University of Wisconsin]

917 Georgina Binstock and A Thornton (2003) 'Separations, reconciliations and living apart in cohabiting and marital unions;' *Journal of Marriage and Family* 65: 432-443

918 TR Balakrishnan, KV Rao, E Lapierre-Adamcyk and KJ Krotki (1987) 'A hazard model analysis of the covariates of marital dissolution in Canada' *Demography* 24: 395-406; NG Bennett, AK Blanc and DE Bloom 'Commitment and the modern union: Assessing the link between premarital cohabitation and subsequent marital stability' *American Sociological Review* 53: 127-138; and A Booth and D Johnson (1988) 'Premarital cohabitation and marital success' *Journal of Family Issues* 9: 255-272.

919 NG Bennett, AK Blane and DE Bloom (1988) 'Commitment and the modern union: Assessing the link between premarital cohabitation and subsequent marital stability' *American Sociological Review* 53: 127-138.

920 JD Teachman and KA Polonko (1990) 'Cohabitation and marital stability in the United States' *Social Forces* 69: 207-220.

921 A DeMaris and KV Rao (1992) 'Premarital cohabitation and subsequent marital stability in the United States: A Reassessment' *Journal of Marriage and the Family* 54: 178-190.

922 See CM Dash Bush, CL Cohan and PR Amato (2003) 'The relationship between cohabitation and marital quality and stability: Change across cohorts?' *Journal of Marriage and Family* 65: 539-549; GK Rhoades, SM Stanley and HJ Markman (2009) 'The pre-engagement cohabitation effect: A replication and extension of previous findings' *Journal of Family Psychology* 23: 107-111

923 Matthis Kalmijn and Paul M De Graaf and Anne-Rigt Poortman (2004) 'Interactions between cultural and economic determinants of divorce in The Netherlands' *Journal of Marriage and Family* 66: 75-89

924 An-Magritt Jensen and Sten-Erik Clausen (2003) 'Children and family dissolution in Norway: The impact of consensual unions' *Childhood* 65-81

925 Sheela Kennedy and Elizabeth Thomson (2010) 'Children's experiences of family disruption in Sweden: Differentials by parent education over here decades' *Demographic Research* 23: 479-508

926 David Popenoe (2008) 'Cohabitation, marriage and child wellbeing' *Threshold* 93: 20

927 S Reinhold (2010) 'Reassessing the link between premarital cohabitation and marital instability' *Demography* 47: 719-733; B Hewitt and D De Vaus (2009) 'Change in the association between premarital cohabitation and separation, Australia 1945 – 2000' *Journal of Marriage and Family* 71: 353-361; and Wendy D Manning and Jessica Cohen (2012) 'Premarital cohabitation and marital dissolution: An examination of recent marriages' *Journal of Marriage and Family* 74: 377-387

928 See LA Lillard, MJ Brien and LJ Waite (1995) 'Premarital cohabitation and subsequent marital dissolution: A matter of self-selection?' *Demography* 32: 437-457

929 Celine Le Bourdais and Evelyne Lapierre-Adamcyk (2004) 'Conjugal changes in Canada: Is cohabitation progressively replacing marriage?' *Journal of Marriage and Family* 66: 929-942

930 Manning and Cohen (2012) *supra*, 384. See also: Scott M Stanley (2012) 'Is marriage irrelevant?' *Sliding vs Deciding blog* (February 20)

931 MD Newcombe and P Bentler (1980) 'Assessment of personality and demographic aspects of cohabitation and marital success' *Journal of Personality Assessment* 44: 11-24

932 Casey E Copen *et al* (2012) 'First marriages in the United States: Data from the 2006-2010 National Survey of Family Growth' *National Health Statistics Reports* 49 (March 22). At years 5, 10 and 15, there was not a significant difference in the probability of marital duration.

933 Norval D Glenn (2005) *With this ring. . . A national survey on marriage in America* [Washington DC, National Fatherhood Initiative], 18-19

934 A Booth and D Johnson (1988) 'Premarital cohabitation and marital success' *Journal of Family Issues* 9: 255-272; A DeMaris and GR Leslie (1984) 'Cohabitation with the future spouse: Its influence upon marital satisfaction and communication' *Journal of Marriage and the Family* 46: 77-84; and REL Watson (1983) 'Premarital cohabitation vs. traditional courtship' *Family Relations* 32: 139-147. See also, P Yelsma (1986) 'Marriage vs cohabitation: Couples' communication practices and satisfaction' *Journal of Communication* Autumn 94-107.

935 DeMaris and Leslie (1984) *supra*

936 CL Cohan and S Kleinbaum (2002) 'Toward a greater understanding of the cohabitation effect: Premarital cohabitation and marital communication *Journal of Marriage and Family* 64: 180-192; Kline *et al* (2004) 'Timing is everything: Pre-engagement cohabitation and the increased risk for poor marital outcomes' *Journal of Family Psychology* 18: 311-318; SM Stanley, SW Whitton and HJ Markman (2004) 'Maybe I do: Interpersonal commitment levels and premarital and non-marital cohabitation' *Journal of Family Issues* 25: 496-519; E Thomson and U Colella (1992) 'Cohabitation and marital stability: Quality or commitment?' *Journal of Marriage and Family* 54: 259-267

937 SL Brown (2004) 'Moving from cohabitation to marriage: Effects on relationship quality' *Social Science Research* 33: 1-20; SL Brown and A Booth (1996) 'Cohabitation versus marriage: A comparison of relationship quality' *Journal of Marriage and Family* 58: 668-678; SL Nock (1995) 'A comparison of marriages and cohabiting relationships' *Journal of Family Issues* 16: 53-76; L Stafford, SL Kline and C Rankin (2004) 'Married individuals, cohabiters, and cohabiters who marry: A longitudinal study of relational and individual well-being' *Journal of Social and Personal Relationships* 21: 231-248; and Stanley *et al* (2004), *supra*

938 Steven Stack and J Ross Eshleman (1998) 'Marital status and happiness: A 17-nation study' *Journal of Marriage and Family* 60: 527-536

939 CM Kamp Dash, CL Cohan and PR Amato (2003) 'The relationship between cohabitation and marital quality and stability: Change across cohorts?' *Journal of Marriage and the Family* 65: 539; L Stafford *et al* (2004) *supra*; E Thompson and U Colella (1992) *supra*; PY Goodwin, WD Mosher and A Chanfra (2010) 'Marriage and cohabitation in the United States: A statistical portrait based on cycle 6 (2002) of the National Survey of Family Growth' *Vital Health Statistics* 23: 1-55

940 Kelley Musick and Larry Bumpass (2012) 'Reexamining the case for marriage: Union formation and changes in well-being' *Journal of Marriage and Family* 74: 1 -18

941 Cited in *To Have and To Hold* (1998) *supra*, 82

942 K Yllo and MA Straus (1981) 'Interpersonal violence among married and cohabiting couples' *Family Relations* 30: 339-347; Maria Testa, Jennifer A Livingston and Kenneth E Leonard (2003) 'Women's substance use and experiences of intimate partner violence: A longitudinal investigation among a community sample' *Addictive Behaviors* 28: 1649-1664; GH Kline *et al* (2004), *supra*, note 633; and Scott M Stanley, Sarah W Whitton and Howard J Markman (2004) 'Maybe I do: Interpersonal commitment and premarital or nonmarital cohabitation' *Journal of Family Issues* 25: 496-519.

943 SM Stanley *et al* (2004), *supra*. See also: Scott M Stanley, Galena K Rhoades and Howard J Markman (2008) 'Commitment and cohabitation' *Threshold* 92: 8

944 Manning and Cohen (2012) *supra*, 384

945 Eva Bernhardt, T Noack and KA Wiik *Cohabitation and commitment: Is cohabitation really indistinguishable from marriage in Norway and Sweden?* [Stockholm, Center for Gender Studies]

946 Carolyn Vogler (2005) 'Cohabiting couples: Rethinking money in the household at the beginning of the twenty-first century' *The Sociological Review* 53: 1-29

947 Anne-Rigt Poortman and Melinda Mills (2012) 'Investments in marriage and cohabitation: The role of legal and interpersonal commitment' *Journal of Marriage and Family* 74: 357-376

948 Julie Pulerwitz Jose-Antonio Izazola-Licea and Steven L Gortmaker (2001) 'Extrarelational sex among Mexican men and their partners' risk of HIV and other sexually transmitted diseases' *American Journal of Public Health* 91: 1650-1652

949 Scott M Stanley, Galena K Rhoades and Howard J Markman (2008) 'Relationship inertia' *Threshold* 92: 9-11. For a discussion of the role of commitment, see Scott M Stanley (1998) *The heart of commitment* [Nashville, Thomas Nelson]; and Scott M Stanley, Galena K Rhoades and Sarah W Whitton (2010) 'Commitment: Functions, formation and the security of romantic attachment' *Journal of Family Theory and Review* 2: 243-257

950 Barbara Dafoe Whitehead and David Popenoe (2002) 'Why men won't commit' *The State of our Unions* [Rutgers NJ, The National Marriage Project]

951 Ted L Huston (2009) 'What's love got to do with it? Why some marriages succeed and others fail' *Personal Relationships* 16: 301-327

952 Scott M Stanley (2010) 'Relationship development and oxytocin' *Threshold* 98: 15-16

953 Stanley (2010) *supra*, 16.

954 Manning and Cohen (2012) *supra*. See also: Poortman and Mills (2012) *supra*; and J A Seltzer (2004) 'Cohabitation in the United States and Britain: Demography, kinship and the future' *Journal of Marriage and Family* 66: 921-928

955 Wendy D Manning and Jessica Cohen (2012) *supra*, 384

956 Scott M Stanley (2008) *supra*. See also: Penelope Huang *et al* (2011) 'He says, she says: Gender and cohabitation' *Journal of Family Issues* 32: 876; Susan L Brown (2000) 'Union transitions among cohabiters: The significance of relationship assessments and expectations' *Journal of Marriage and Family* 62: 833

957 Whitehead and Popenoe (2002) *supra*

958 Stanley (2010) *supra*, 15

959 SL Brown and A Booth (1996) 'Cohabitation versus marriage: A comparison of relationship quality' *Journal of Marriage and the Family* 58(3): 668-678.

960 SL Nock (1995) 'A comparison of marriages and cohabiting relationships' *Journal of Family Issues* 16: 53-76.

961 S Sarantakos (1994) 'Trial cohabitation on trial' *Australian Social Work* 47(3): 13-25.

962 S Sarantakos (1996) 'The virtues of liberation' *Threshold* 53: 9–11.

963 A Booth and DR Johnson (1988) 'Premarital cohabitation and marital success' *Journal of Family Issues* 9: 255-272.

964 WG Axinn and A Thornton (1992) 'The relationship between cohabitation and divorce: Selectivity or casual influence?' *Demography* 29: 357–374.

965 See: CM Dash Bush, CL Cohan and PR Amato (2003) 'The relationship between cohabitation and marital quality and stability: Change across cohorts?' *Journal of Marriage and Family* 65: 539-549; GK Rhoades, SM Stanley and HJ Markman (2009) 'The pre-engagement cohabitation effect: A replication and extension of previous findings' *Journal of Family Psychology* 23: 107-111

966 Catherine L Cohan and Stacey Kleinbaum (2002) 'Toward a greater understanding of the cohabitation effect: Premarital cohabitation and marital communication' *Journal of Marriage and the Family* 64: 180-192

967 K James (1994) *The Midday Show* [Sydney, Channel 9] June 14

968 H Glezer (1991) 'Cohabitation' *Family Matters* 30: 24–27

969 Quoted in A Crawford *supra*.

970 Scott M Stanley, Galena K Rhoades and Howard J Markman (2006) 'Sliding vs deciding: Inertia and the premarital cohabitation effect' *Family Relations* 55: 499-509 and the studies cited therein.

971 See for example: David de Vaus, Lixia Qu and Ruth Weston (2003) 'Does premarital cohabitation affect the chances of marriage lasting?' *Paper* [Melbourne, Australian Institute of Family Studies]; and 'Cohabitation a risk factor' (2003) *Threshold* 76: 30

972 Stanley and Rhoades (2009) *supra*

973 Galena K Rhoades, Scott M Stanley and Howard J Markman (2008) 'The pre-engagement cohabitation effect: A replication and extension of previous findings' *Journal of Family Psychology* 23: 107-111

974 Paul Amato, Alan Booth, David R Johnson and Stacy J Rogers (2007) *Alone together – How marriage in America is changing* [Cambridge MA, Harvard University Press], 21

975 *Ibid.*, 22

976 Andrew J Cherlin (2009) *The marriage-go-round* [New York, Vintage Books] 138

977 H Glezer (1994) 'Family backgrounds and marital breakdown' *Threshold* 43: 16-19.

978 SM Stanley, GK Rhoades and HJ Markman (2006) 'Sliding vs deciding: Inertia and the premarital cohabitation effect' *Family Relations* 55: 659-675.

979 Stanley and Rhoades (2009) *supra*

980 Scott M Stanley *et al* (2011) 'Understanding romantic relationships among emerging adults: The significant roles of cohabitation and ambiguity' in FD Fincham and M Cui (eds) *Romantic relationships in emerging adulthood* [New York, Cambridge University Press], 234-251

981 SM Stanley *et al* (2008), *supra*

982 Scott Stanley (2005) 'What is it with men and commitment, anyway?' *Threshold* 83: 4-11

983 Judith E Owen Blakemore *et al* (2005) 'I can't wait to get married: Gender differences in drive to marry' *Sex Roles* 53: 327-335 – indicating that women are more motivated to marry. There may also be hormonal factors at play: See Scott Stanley (2009) 'Relationship development and oxytocin' *Threshold* 98: 15 – 16. See also Mindy E Scott et al (2009) *Young adult attitudes about relationships and marriage: Times may have changed, but expectations remain high* [Washington DC, Child Trends], 5 which indicates that 44 per cent of 20 – 24 year olds in cohabiting relationships reported that currently they would like to be married; and Joelle Caputa (2012) 'Why women in their 20s get hitched when they should've ditched' *Huffington Post*, November 7

984 Norval D Glenn (2005) *With this ring ... A national survey on marriage in America* [Washington DC, National Fatherhood Initiative], 18

985 Galena K Rhoades, Scott M Stanley and Howard J Markman (2012) 'A longitudinal investigation of commitment dynamics in cohabiting relationships' *Journal of Family Issues* 33: 369-390

986 Barbara Dafoe Whitehead (2004) *Why there are no good men left* [New York, Broadway Books] 12

987 *Ibid.*, 140

988 Norval D Glenn (2005) *With this ring. . . A national survey on marriage in America* [Washington DC, National Fatherhood Initiative], 20

989 Galena K Rhoades, Scott M Stanley and Howard J Markman (2009) 'The pre-engagement cohabitation effect: A replication and extension of previous findings' *Journal of Family Psychology* 23: 107-111

990 Cited by Stevenson and Wolfers, *supra*, 37

991 Copen *et al* (2012), *supra*

992 John Hayward and Guy Brandon (2011) *Cohabitation: An alternative to marriage?* [Cambridge UK, The Jubilee Centre], 16

993 Scott M Stanley (2010) 'The pre-engagement cohabitation effect' *Threshold* 98: 21-33, reporting US Centers for Disease Control – National Centers for Statistics – data. See also: Sandra Buchler *et al* (2009) 'Cohabitation outcomes: The effect of fertility intentions, relationship satisfaction and union length on cohabitation transitions' *Paper*, Household Income and Labour Dynamics in Australia Survey Research Conference [Melbourne, Melbourne Institute for Applied Economic and Social Research]

994 Copen *et al* (2012) *supra*

995 Judith Wallerstein and Sandra Blakeslee (1995) *The good marriage: How and why love lasts* [New York, Houghton Mifflin]

996 Paul Amato, Alan Booth, David R Johnson and Stacy J Rogers (2007) *Alone together – How marriage in America is changing* [Cambridge MA, Harvard University Press], 12-15

997 *Ibid.*, 14

998 Yenor (2011) *supra.*

999 Andrew Cherlin (2004) 'The deinstitutionalisation of American marriage' *Journal of Marriage and Family* 66: 848-861

1000 Amato *et al* (2007), *supra*, 16

1001 For a discussion of paradox, see: Herbert Anderson and Robert Cotton Fite (1993) *Becoming married* [Louisville KY, Westminster/John Knox Press]

1002 Scott Yenor (2011) *supra*, 270

1003 Bob Birrell and Virginia Rapson (1999) *A not so perfect match* [Melbourne, Centre for Population and Urban Research, Monash University]. For a summary, see Bob Birrell and Virginia Rapson (1999) 'A not so perfect match' *Marriage, Family and Society Issues* 2: 16-21

1004 Karen Rowlinson and Stephen McKay (1998) *The growth of lone parenthood* [London, Policy Studies Institute], 82

1005 Bob Birrell and Virginia Rapson (1999) 'A not so perfect match' *Marriage, Family and Society Issues* 2: 16-21, 21

1006 Bob Birrell, Virginia Rapson and Clare Hourigan (2004) *Men + women apart: Partnering in Australia* [Melbourne, Centre for Population and Urban Research, Monash University],vii

1007 This pattern was confirmed in subsequent research: See Geneveive Heard (2008) 'Partnerships at the 2006 census: Preliminary findings' *People and Place* 16: 31-39. For an emerging divide in Canada: 'Education and marriage' (2003) *Threshold* 75: 35

1008 Wendy Wang and Kim Parker (2011) *Women see value and benefits of college; Men lag on both fronts, survey finds* [Washington DC, Pew Research Center]

1009 'Why more and more intelligent women are being forced to "marry down" and find a less-educated man as females win out at work and school' (2011) *Daily Mail Online*, November 7

1010 Barbara Dafoe Whitehead (2003) *Why there are no good men left* [New York, Broadway Books]. See also Kathleen M Walters (2004) 'There are no good men left' *Threshold* 81: 8-11

1011 By contrast, there is a massive over-supply of men in China and India, largely as a consequence of the policy of sex-selective abortion: 'The flight from marriage' (2010) *The Economist* (August 20), 20. It would also appear that some immigrant populations have taken their preferences for boys to their new home countries. See: 'Gendercide in Canada' (2012) *The Economist*, May 5, 44 and Bernard Salt (2012) 'No change in singles market: man drought still as bad as ever' *The Australian*, 16 August, 29

1012 Bernard Salt (2006) *The big picture* [Prahran, Australia, Hardie Grant Books], 244. See also: Wu Ching-chun and Jamie Wang (2012) '70% of wage earners lack finances for marriage: poll' *Focus Taiwan News Channel*, August 18, for similar trends in Taiwan.

1013 Carrie A Bredow, Ted L Huston and Norval D Glenn (2011) 'Market value, quality of the pool of potential mates, and singles' confidence about marrying' *Personal Relationships* 18: 39-57

1014 See also: 'Educated women more likely to marry' (2004) *Threshold* 81: 16

1015 Birrell, Rapson and Hourigan (2004) *supra*, ix

1016 Jason DeParle and Sabrina Tavernise (2012) 'Unwed mothers now a majority before age 30' *New York Times*, A1, February 18, citing Child Trends analysis of National Vital Statistics data.

1017 Elizabeth Wildsmith, Nicole R Steward-Streng and Jennifer Manlove (2011) *Childbearing outside of marriage: Estimates and trends in the United States* [Washington DC, Child Trends]

1018 W Bradford Wilcox (2010) 'When marriage disappears: The retreat from marriage in middle America' *State of our unions 2010* [Charlottesville VA, The National Marriage Project], 14

1019 Michael Greenstone and Adam Looney (2012) 'The marriage gap: The impact of economic and technological change on marriage rates' *Up Front Blog* [Washington DC, Brookings Institution, February 7]

1020 Pew Research Center (2010) *The decline of marriage and rise of new families* [Washington DC, The Center]

1021 Richard Fry and D'Vera Cohn (2011) *Living together: The economics of cohabitation* [Washington DC, Pew Research Center]

1022 Nancy Cook (2012) 'For richer (not for poorer): The inequality crisis of marriage' *The Atlantic*, March 14

1023 Quoted in Peter Wehner and Robert P Beschel (2012) 'How to think about inequality' *National Affairs* 11 (Spring). UK research reveals a similar trend: Richard Darlington (2012) *Modern women marrying men of the same or lower social class* [London, Institute for Public Policy Research]

1024 K Edin, MJ Kefalas and JM Reed (2004) 'A peek inside the black box: What marriage means for poor unmarried parents' *Journal of Marriage and Family* 66: 1007-1014

1025 Andrew J Cherlin and W Bradford Wilcox (2010) 'The generation that can't move on up' *The Wall Street Journal* September 2

1026 William Julius Wilson (1997) *When work disappears: The world of the new urban poor* [New York, Alfred A Knopf]

1027 Stevenson and Wolfers (2007) *supra*

1028 W Bradford Wilcox (2011) 'When baby makes three: How parenthood makes life meaningful and how marriage makes parenthood bearable' *State of our unions 2011* [Charlottesville VA, The National Marriage Project], 18

1029 Kay Hymowitz (2006) *Marriage and caste in America: Separate and unequal families in a post-marital age* [Chicago, Ivan Dee]

1030 Bhashkar Mazumder and David I Levine (2004) *The growing importance of family and community: An analysis of changes in the sibling correlation in earnings* [Chicago, Federal Reserve Bank of Chicago]

1031 Henry Benson, Bristol Community Family Trust, cited in David Willetts (2010) *The pinch – How the baby boomers took their children's future – and why they should give it back* [London, Atlantic Books]

1032 Kathleen Kiernan (1999) 'Childbearing outside marriage in Western Europe' *Population Trends*, vol 98 [London, Office of National Statistics]

1033 Charles Murray (2012) *Coming apart: The state of white America, 1960-2010* [New York, Crown Forum]

1034 Ralph Richard Banks (2011) *Is marriage for white people?* [New York, Dutton]

1035 'Black women should look outside their race for a successful man, says Stanford law professor' (2011) *Daily Mail Online*, October 20

1036 'Working hours' (2007) *Threshold* 90: 6

1037 Francis Fukuyama (2012) 'The future of history: Can liberal democracy survive the decline of the middle class?' *Foreign Affairs* (Jan/Feb 2012)

1038 Murray (2012) *supra*

1039 See for example, William Julius Wilson (1990) *The truly disadvantaged: The inner city, the underclass, and public policy* [Chicago, University of Chicago Press]

1040 See also: Kay S Hymowitz (2006) *Marriage and caste in America: Separate and unequal families in a post-marital age* [Chicago, Ivan R Dee]

1041 W Bradford Wilcox, *supra*, 16

1042 Martha J Bailey and Susan M Dynarski (2011) 'Gains and gaps: Changing inequality in US college entry and completion' *Working Paper* [Cambridge MA, National Bureau of Economic Research]

1043 Ted Boscia (2012) 'Among disadvantaged, college reduces odds for marriage' *Chronicle Online* [New York, Cornell University] (January 24) citing research by Kelley Musick *et al* (2012) 'Variation in the relationship between education and marriage: Marriage market mismatch' *Journal of Marriage and Family* 74: 53-69

1044 Michael Greenstone and Adam Looney (2011) *What is happening to America's children? A look at the widening opportunity gap for today's youth* [Washington DC, The Brookings Institution]

1045 *Ibid.*

1046 Stephen L Nock (2006) 'Illustrations of family scholarship: Introduction to the special issue' *Social Science Research* 35: 322-331

1047 Benjamin Disraeli (1845) *Sybil – or the two nations*

1048 Urie Bronfenbrenner (1994) *Address* to an Australian Institute of Family Studies workshop, Melbourne, July 1994.

1049 David Popenoe (1988) *Disturbing the nest* [New York, Aldine de Gruyter] 7.

1050 See for example, David Blankenhorn, 'American family dilemmas' in David Popenoe, Steven Bayne and Jean Bethke Elshtain (1990) *Rebuilding the nest* [Milwaukee, Family Service America]

1051 Popenoe (1988) *supra*, 34

1052 See: See Kevin Andrews (2000) 'Family policies that work,' *Marriage, Family and Society Issues* 4: 31-35 for a previous discussion of policy responses.

1053 See: Nicholas Eberstadt (2000) 'Last one turn out the lights?' *Marriage, Family and Society Issues*

1054 See: Alan Tapper(1990) *The family in the welfare state* [Sydney, Allen and Unwin]; Alan Jordan (1987) *The common treasury: The distribution of income to families and households* [Canberra, Social Security Review]; Alan Tapper and David Thomson (1993) 'The way we are' *Independent Monthly*, April 20-23; and David Willetts (2010) *The pinch – How the baby boomers took their children's future – and why they should give it back* [London, Atlantic Books] . In the US, Social Security has began paying out more to the elderly than it is taking from current workers: Social Security and Medicare Boards of Trustees (2011) *A summary of the 2011 annual reports* [Washington DC, Social Security Administration]

1055 Sanghan Yea (2004) 'Are we prepared for world population implosion?' *Futures* 36: 583-601

1056 Barbara Beck (2009) 'A slow burning fuse' *The Economist* (Special Report) June 27, 3. See also: National Institute on Ageing (2007) *Why population ageing matters: A global perspective* [Washington DC, US Department of Health and Human Services]

1057 Nicholas Eberstadt (2007) *Too many people?* [London, International Policy Network]

1058 'Too many or too few' (1999) *The Economist* September 23. Even the US birthrate has fallen below replacement levels: Haya El Nasser (2012) 'Americans put off having babies amid poor economy' *USA Today*, July 25

1059 See: United Nations Population Division (2011) *World population prospects , the 2010 revision* [New York, United Nations]

1060 See: Peter MacDonald (2000) 'Low fertility in Australia: Evidence, causes and policy responses' *People and Places* 8: 6-21; and Peter MacDonald and Rebecca Kippen (2000) 'Population projections for Australia' *BCA Papers*, September, 96-104, cited in Kevin Andrews (2009) 'Population, immigration and Australia's future' *Australian Polity* 3: 12-16

1061 For example: Robert Kunzig (2011) 'Population 7 billion' *National Geographic* 219.1: 32-69

1062 See for example: Richard Ottaway and Geneveive Hutchinson (2011) *Sex, ideology, religion* [London, The authors]. Earlier works include Paul Ehrlich (1968) *The population bomb*

1063 John C Caldwell and Thomas Schindlmayr (2003) 'Explanations of the fertility crisis in modern societies: A search for commonalities' *Population Studies* 57: 241-263

1064 www.ipss.go.jp/index-e.asp

1065 'Population shrinking' *The Age*, Melbourne, January 31, 2012, 9

1066 Nicholas Eberstadt (2012) 'Japan shrinks' *The Wilson Quarterly* (Spring) 30-37

1067 *CNA Daily News Digest*, May 7, 2012

1068 Nicholas Eberstadt (2011) 'Demographic trends cloud China's long term economic outlook' *Japan Spotlight* March/April 26-29

1069 Nicholas Eberstadt (2011) 'The dying bear' *Foreign Affairs* 90: 95-108. See also: Marcus Roberts (2012) 'Putin wants more babies' *MercatorNet.com*, February 15

1070 Nicholas Eberstadt (2012) 'Fertility decline in the Muslim world' *Policy Review*, No 173, [Hoover Institution]. See also: Youssef Courbage and Emmanuel Todd (2011) *A convergence of civilisations: The transformation of Muslim societies around the world* [New York, Columbia University Press], David P Goldman (2011) *How civilisations die (and why Islam is dying too)* [Washington DC, Regnery] and Lant H Pritchett (1994) 'Desired fertility and the impact of population policies' *Population and Development Review* 20: 1-55

1071 Ralph Lattimore and Clinton Pobke (2008) *Recent trends in Australia's fertility* [Canberra, Productivity Commission] 70-71. The impact includes the social development of children: Douglas B Downey and Dennis J Condron (2004) 'Playing well with others in kindergarten: The benefit of siblings at home' *Journal of Marriage and Family* 66: 333-350

1072 Chenying Liu, Tsunetsugu Munakata and Francis N Onuoha (2005) 'Mental health conditions of the only-child: A study of urban and rural high school students in China' *Adolescence* 40: 831-845

1073 Sanghan Yea (2004) *supra*

1074 Nicholas Eberstadt (2011) 'World population prospects and the global economic outlook: The shape of things to come' *Working Series Paper on Development Policy* 5 [Washington DC, American Enterprise Institute]

1075 US Census Bureau, *International Data Base*. www.census.gov

1076 Linda G Martin *et al* (2010) 'Trends in disability and related chronic conditions among people ages fifty to sixty-four' *Health Affairs* 29: 725-731. It has been estimated, for example, that obesity could affect 42 per cent of Americans by 2030: Nanci Hellmich (2012) 'Obesity could affect 42% of Americans by 2030' *USA Today*, May 8, citing a study by health economists.

1077 Richard Jackson, Neil Howe and Keisuke Nakashima (2010) *The global aging preparedness index* [Washington DC, Center for Strategic and International Studies]

1078 David E Bloom *et al* (2003) *The demographic dividend: A new perspective on the economic consequences of population change* [Santa Monica CA, The Rand Corporation]

1079 See for example, Richard Jackson and Neil Howe (2008) *The graying of the great powers* [Washington DC, Center for Strategic and International Studies]

1080 Andrews (2009) *supra*, 14

1081 Cited in K Andrews (2009) 'Population, immigration and Australia's future' *The Australian Polity* 3: 12-16

1082 *Ibid*

1083 *Ibid*

1084 Nicholas Eberstadt (2007) 'Global demographic outlook to 2025' *Speech*, Economic Conference on Demography, Growth and Wellbeing , Zurich [Washington DC, American Enterprise Institute]

1085 See for example: 'China: Changes to marriage' (2005) *Threshold* 83:28

1086 See: John P Martin (2008) *International Migration Outlook* [Paris, OECD]

1087 R Lesthaeghe, H Page and J Surkyn (1988) *Are immigrants substitutes for birth?* Inter-university program in demography, working paper 1988-3 [Brussels, Inter-university]

1088 United Nations (2000) *Replacement migration: is it a solution to declining and ageing populations?* [Geneva and New York, Department of Economic and Social Affairs, Population Division]

1089 Jonathan Grant *et al* (2004) *Low fertility and population ageing* [Leiden, The Netherlands, Rand Europe] 135

1090 See for example, Samuel P Huntington (2004) *Who are we?* [New York, Simon and Schuster]; and Jonathan Sacks (2007) *The home we build together* [London, Continuum]

1091 Graeme Hugo (2000) 'Declining fertility and policy intervention in Europe: some lessons for Australia' *Journal of Population Research*, November 2000.

1092 One of the most recent nations to offer pronatalist inducements is Russia, where Prime Minister Putin announced special allowances for women who have more than two children, as well as housing priority, special benefits and childcare support: Marcus Roberts (2012) 'Putin wants more babies' *MercatorNet.com*, February 15

1093 M Murphy (1993) 'The contraceptive pill and women's employment as factors in fertility change in Britain 1963-1980: A challenge to the conventional view,' *Population Studies*, 47: 221-243

1094 Grant *et al* (2004),supra, 31

1095 Hugo (2000) *supra*

1096 Saw Swee-Hock (1990) 'Changes in the fertility policy of Singapore,' *Institute of Policy Studies Occasional Paper No 2* [Singapore, Times Academic Press]

1097 Hugo (2000) *supra*

1098 'Singapore, Hoping for a Baby boom, Makes Sex a Civic Duty' (2001) *New York Times*, April 21

1099 'Marriage Central Singapore' (2007) *Threshold* 90: 4. See also 'Promoting marriage' (2003) *Threshold* 75: 35

1100 Lovebyte.org.sg See: 'The flight from marriage' (2010) *The Economist*, August 20, 20

1101 Singapore Department of Statistics (2008) 'Key demographic Indicators, 1970 – 2007,' *Population Trends 2008*

1102 There is evidence that children have better health outcomes when their mothers have more time with them following birth: Rajeev Dehejia and Adriana Lleras-Muney (2004) 'Booms, busts, and babies' health' *Quarterly Journal of Economics* 119: 1091-1130

1103 Australian Bureau of Statistics (2010) *Births, Australia* Cat 3301

1104 Ralph Lattimore and Clinton Pobke (2008) *Recent trends in Australia's fertility* [Productivity Commission: Canberra] 70-71. See also: Robert Drago *et al* (2010) *Did Australia's baby bonus increase the fertility rate?* [Melbourne, Melbourne Institute for Applied Economic and Social Research] Working Paper 1/09

1105 Rodolfo E Manuelli and Ananth Seshadri (2009) 'Explaining international fertility differences' *The Quarterly Journal of Economics* 124: 771-807

1106 Grant *et al* (2004), *supra* 75

1107 Grant *et al* (2004) *supra* 77-78

1108 Hugo (2000) *supra.*

1109 See for example, P McDonald and R Kippen (2000) *Population futures for Australia: The policy alternatives*, Research Paper No 5 [Canberra, Parliamentary Library] 4-5

1110 A Myrdal (1941) *Nation and Family* [New York, Harper] See: David Popenoe (1988) *Disturbing the nest* [New York, Aldine de Gruyter] for a discussion of Swedish policy

1111 JM Hoem (1990) 'Social policy and recent fertility change in Sweden,' *Population and Development Review* 16(4): 735-748 at 740-741

1112 HP Kohler (1999) *The Swedish baby bomb and bust of 1985-1996. Revisited: the role of tempo, quantum and variance effects.* [Max Planck Institute for Demographic Research]

1113 Swedish Institute (2003) *Factsheets on Sweden – the Swedish population*

1114 L Jonsson (2003) 'Fertiilty changes and family policy in Sweden,' in MT Letablier and S Pennec (eds) *Changing family structure in Europe: new challenges for public policy* [Loughborough, European Research Centre]

1115 Jaane Haarland-Matlary, (1997) *Address* to the Pastoral and Theological Congress, Rio de Janeiro, Brazil

1116 Ontario Government (2003) *Early year's plan: A report to Ontario families* [Toronto, Ontario Government]

1117 Centre for Social Justice (2009) *Every Family Matters* [London, The Centre for Social Justice] 20

1118 Tim Shipman (2009) 'Only marriage can mend broken Britain, says top judge in attack on 'pass the partner' society' *Daily Mail Online*, June 6

1119 Steve Doughy (2008) 'Family life is in 'meltdown': Judge launches devastating attack on our fractured society' *Daily Mail Online* April 4

1120 Quoted in Kathleen M Walters (1997) 'Marriage southern style' *Threshold* 57: 13-15

1121 *To have and to hold* (1998) *supra*, 50-51

1122 Institute of Marriage and Family Canada (2009) *Private choices, Public costs: How failing families cost us all* [Ottawa, The Institute]

1123 Relationships Foundation (2008) When *relationships go wrong: Counting the cost of family failure* [Cambridge UK, Relationships Foundation]

1124 Centre for Social Justice (2009) *Every family matters* [London, The Centre]

1125 Alan J Hawkins (1999) 'Perspectives on Covenant Marriage' *Marriage, Family and Society Issues*, 3:14-20. See also: Steven L Nock, Laura A Sanchez and James D Wright (2008) *Covenant marriages: The movement to reclaim tradition in America*

[New Brunswick NJ, Rutgers University Press]; and Kathleen M Walters (1997) 'Marriage southern style' *Threshold* 57: 13-15

1126 Don Monkerud (2006) 'Covenant marriage on the rocks' <www.opednews.com>

1127 Kim Leon (2009) 'Covenant marriage: What is it and does it work?' <www. missourifamilies.org>

1128 Steven L Nock, Laura A Sanchez and James D Wright (2008) *Covenant marriages: The movement to reclaim tradition in America* [New Brunswick NJ: Rutgers University Press]. See also: AJ Hawkins, SL Nock, JC Wilson L Sanchez and JD Wright (2002) 'Attitudes about covenant marriage and divorce: Policy implications from a three-state comparison' *Family Relations*, 51: 166-175

1129 Amy Kirk (2007) 'Committed to constraints: A preliminary look at ten years of covenant marriage rhetoric' *Paper*, American Sociological Association, New York.

1130 Quoted in Monkerud (2006) *supra.*

1131 Lawrie Maloney and Bruce Smyth (2004) 'Family relationship centres in Australia' *Family Matters* 69: 64-70

1132 House of Representatives Standing Committee on Family and Community Affairs (2003) *Every picture tells a story* [Canberra, Parliament of Australia]. Child support, access and custody have been the subject of a series of Parliamentary reports since the introduction of *the Family Law Act* 1975.

1133 John Howard (Prime Minister of Australia) (2004) 'Announcement of Family Law Package' *Transcript of Speech* delivered at Anglicare Western Australia, Perth, July 29, quoted in Elizabeth van Acker (2008) *Governments and marriage education policy* [Basingstoke, Hampshire, Palgrave Macmillan] 104

1134 '$15 million boost to family services' (2004) *Threshold* 82:3

1135 Kevin and Margaret Andrews (1997) *With this ring: Rebuilding a culture of marriage* [Melbourne, Threshold Publishing] 42

1136 J Crawley (1986) 'The Attorney-General's stable door: Marriage counselling services in Australia' cited in K Andrews (1993) *The provision of family services* [Canberra, Liberal and National Parties]

1137 Working Party on Marriage Guidance (1979) *Marriage Matters* [London, HMSO] 3

1138 Committee on Procedure in Matrimonial Causes (Denning Committee) (1947) Final Report, *Cmnd* 7024 [London, HMSO]

1139 Prior to this, state laws prevailed, although the Australian Constitution gave the national Parliament powers to enact laws pertaining to divorce and matrimonial causes.

1140 Garfield Barwick (1959) *Hansard* [Canberra, House of Representatives] 2225

1141 *Marriage Act* 1961

1142 Departmental Committee on Grants for the Development of Marriage Guidance (Haris Committee) Report, (1948) *Cmnd* 7566 [London, HMSO]

1143 See *Matrimonial Causes Act* 1959; *Family Law Act* 1975, ss 4(1) and 12

1144 Barwick (1959) *supra*.

1145 Kevin and Margaret Andrews (1997) 'Strategies to strengthen marriage: The Australian experience' in Theodora Ooms (ed), *Strategies to strengthen marriage: What do we know? What do we need to know?* [Washington DC, Family Impact Seminar]. See also see Elizabeth van Acker (2008) *Governments and marriage education policy* [Basingstoke, Hampshire, Palgrave Macmillan]

1146 Joint Select Committee on Certain Aspects of the Operation and Interpretation of the Family Law Act (1992) *Certain Aspects of the Operation and Interpretation of the Family Law Act* [Canberra, Australian Parliament] para 4.97

1147 For an overview of these developments, see Elizabeth van Acker (2008) *supra*

1148 *To have and to hold* (1998) *supra*, 111-207. See also 'National families strategy launched' (1999) *Threshold* 62: 3 for the Australian government's response to the Parliamentary report.

1149 By 2007, 62.9 per cent of marriages were performed by a civil celebrant. This figure included second and subsequent weddings which are largely performed by civil celebrants. Approximately 22 per cent of weddings involved at least one person who had married before : 'Marriages, civil weddings up' (2008) *Threshold* 94: 18.

1150 Kevin Andrews (2009) 'The heart and soul of celebrancy' *Threshold* 96: 29

1151 Brian D Doss, Galena K Rhoades, Scott M Stanley, Howard J Markman and Christine A Johnson (2009) 'Differential use of premarital education in first and second marriages' *Journal of Family Psychology* 23(2): 268-273

1152 Kevin Andrews (2008) 'Governments and marriage education policy' *Threshold* 94: 28-29. See also Elizabeth van Acker (2008) *supra*, 202

1153 For example: Daniel Patrick Moynihan (1965) *The negro family: The case for national action* [Washington DC, Office of Policy and Planning Research, US Department of Labor]; National Commission on America's Urban Families (1983) *Families First* [Washington DC, US Government Printing Office]; US National Commission on Children (1991) *Beyond Rhetoric* [Washington DC, US Government Printing Office]

1154 For example: Daniel Patrick Moynihan (1986) *Family and nation* [San Diego, Harcourt Brace]; Council on Families in America (1995) *Marriage in America* [New York, Council on Families]; David Blankenhorn (1995) *Fatherless America* [New York, Basic Books]; David Blankenhorn, Jean Bethke Elstain and Steven Bayne (eds) (1990) *Rebuilding the nest: A new commitment to the American family* [Milwaukee

WI, Family Service America]; David Popenoe (annually*) The state of our unions* [Piscataway NJ, The National Marriage Project, Rutgers University]; Don S Browing *et al* (1997) *From culture wars to common ground* [Louisville, KY, Westminster John Knox Press]; Allan C Carlson (1990) *Family questions: Reflections on the American social crisis* [New Brunswick, Transaction Books]; Theodore Ooms (ed) (1997) *Strategies to strengthen marriage* [Washington DC, Family Impact Seminar]; Institute for American Values (2000) *The marriage movement: A statement of principles* [New York, IAV]; Institute for American Values (2002) *Why marriage matters: Twenty-one conclusions from the social sciences* [New York, IAV]

1155 Hilary Clinton (1996) *It takes a village* [New York, Simon and Schuster]

1156 William Galston (1996) *Divorce American-style*, Council on Families in American Working Paper No 49 [New York, Institute for American Values]

1157 *Temporary Assistance for Needy Families Act* [TANF]

1158 MR Dion *et al* (2008) *Implementation of the building strong families program: Executive summary* 8935-134

1159 Elizabeth van Acker(2008) *supra*, chapter 5

1160 For example, Diane Sollee, the founder and director of the grassroots Coalition for Marriage, Family and Couples Education and Smart Marriages which acted as a daily clearing house for information about marriage, and conducted the annual Smartmarriages conference. <www.smartmarriages.com>

1161 For example, Allan Carlson, David Popenoe, David Blankenhorn, Don Browning, Paul Amato, Barbara Dafoe Whitehead, and Linda Waite.

1162 Including John Gottman at the Seattle Marital and Family Institute and author of a series of books including *The seven principles for making marriage* work [New York, Crown, 1999], Howard Markman and Scott Stanley at the University of Denver, authors of a series of books including *Fighting for your marriage* [San Francisco, Jossey-Bass, 1994] and the PREP marital education program, and Thomas Bradbury and Benjamin Karney at the University of California, Los Angeles, authors of *Intimate relationships* [New York, WW Norton]

1163 Including the Institute for American Values, the Family Research Council, the Heritage Foundation and the Family, Religion and Culture Project at the University of Chicago

1164 For example: M Scott Peck (1978) *The road less travelled* [New York, Random House]; Harville Hendrix (1988) *Getting the love you want* [New York, Simon and Schuster]; John Gray (2004) *Men are from Mars and Women are from Venus* [New York, Harper]; and Michele Weiner-Davis (1992) *Divorce busting* [New York, Summit Books]

1165 'Death of a marriage education pioneer' (2008) *Threshold* 94: 32. The Maces were active in establishing the National Marriage Guidance Council in the UK before moving to the US where they founded the Association for Couples in Marriage Enrichment [ACME]. They also advised the Australian government in the 1950s about marriage support programs.

1166 David and Vera Mace became joint Executive Directors of the American Association of Marriage Counselors (now AAMFT) and provided training in many countries for various organisations, including the UN Institute for the Family. They published numerous articles. Their best known book is *How to have a happy marriage* [Nashville, Abington Press, 1977]

1167 There are many examples. The US Catholic Bishops' Conference has initiated a 'For your marriage' program comprising a website, billboards, media spots across the country. www.foryourmarriage.com David and Claudia Arp, founders of Marriage Alive conduct seminars and conferences throughout the US and internationally. < www.marriagealive.org > Bill Doherty, a past president of the National Council on Family Relations, has promoted community family initiatives.

1168 For example, dioceses of the Catholic Church adopted a 'Common Marriage Policy': National Conference of Catholic Bishops (1988) *Faithful to each other forever* [Washington DC, NCCB]; and many churches offered marriage preparation programs, including the use of the pre-marital inventories PREPARE, FOCCUS and RELATE.

1169 Michael J McManus (1993) *Marriage savers: Helping your friends and family avoid divorce* [Grand Rapids MI, Zondervan] 302-306

1170 Personal communication with Mike McManus, July 2009.

1171 PJ Birch, SE Weed and J Olsen (2004) 'Assessing the impact of community marriage policies on county divorce rates' *Family Relations* 53(5): 495-503

1172 *Ibid.*

1173 Personal communication with Mike McManus, July 2009

1174 Birch *et al* (2004) *supra*, 501

1175 Other community initiatives include First Things First – W Doherty and J Anderson (2004) 'Community marriage initiatives' *Family Relations* 53: 425-432, and the Oklahoma Marriage Initiative – Elizabeth van Acker (2008) *supra*, 143

1176 Norval D Glenn (2005) *With this ring: A national survey of marriage in America* [Washington DC, National Fatherhood Initiative], 24

1177 I am indebted to my late friend, Don Browning, for this title. It is taken from one of the books in the Family, Religion and Culture series: Don S Browning *et al* (1997) *From culture wars to common ground* [Lousiville KY, Westminster John Knox Press]

1178 James Davidson Hunter (1990) *Culture wars* [New York, Basic Books] See also: B and P Berger (1983) *The war over the family* [San Diego, Harcourt Brace Javanovich]

1179 See: for example: Bettina Cass and David Cappo (1993) 'Dismissive approach to IYF' *The Australian* (November 15); Kevin Andrews (1993) 'Marriage: the aspect of family Keating forgot' *The Age* (Melbourne, December 7); David Cappo (1993) 'Support the key focus for families' *Canberra Times* (December); Kevin Andrews and John Herron (1993) 'Public policy failing to recognise the 'ideal' family' *Canberra Times*, (December 28); Kevin Andrews (1993) 'Why families are in crisis' *The Age* (Melbourne) November 4; and Kevin Andrews (1993) 'Keating fails our families' *Herald Sun* (Melbourne) December 7

1180 Kingsley Davis (1985) 'The meaning and significance of marriage in contemporary society' in Kingsley Davis (ed) *Contemporary marriage* [New York, Russell Sage Foundation], 21

1181 See: Norval Glenn and Thomas Sylvester (2006) *The shift: Scholarly views on family structure effects on children, 1977-2002* [New York, Institute for American Values]

1182 National Commission on Children (1991) *Beyond rhetoric: A new American agenda for children and families* [Washington DC, The Commission], 37

1183 National Commission on America's Urban Families (1993) *Families first* [Washington DC, The Commission]

1184 Linda J Waite and Maggie Gallagher (2000) *The case for marriage: Why married people are happier, healthier, and better off financially* [New York, Doubleday]

1185 Barbara Dafoe Whitehead (1993) 'Dan Quayle was right' *Atlantic Monthly*, (April) 47-84

1186 Paul Amato (1987) *Children in Australian families: The growth of competence* [Melbourne, Australian Institute of Family Studies]

1187 Paul Amato and Allan Booth (1997) *A generation at risk: Growing up in an era of family upheaval* [Cambridge MA, Harvard University Press]

1188 Penelope Gibb (1999) 'Supporting families' *Marriage, Family and Society Issues* 1: 15-16

1189 Edgar, *supra*,

1190 William Galston (1994) *Beyond the Murphy Brown debate* [New York, Institute for American Values]

1191 Blankenhorn founded the Council on Families in America which has published a series of influential reports. He also authored and edited a series of books including *The future of marriage* [New York, Encounter Books, 2007]

1192 See for example: Don S Browning *et al* (1997) *From culture wars to common ground* [Louisville KY, Westminster John Knox Press]; Katherine Anderson, Don Browning and Brian Boyer (eds) (2002) *Marriage – Just a piece of paper?* [Grand Rapids MI, William B Eerdmans]; and Don S Browning and David A Clairmont (eds)

(2007) *American religions and the family* [New York, Columbia University Press]

1193 Doherty was president of America's oldest scholarly and professional therapists' organisation, the National Council on Family Relations. Sollee is the founding director of the Coalition for Marriage, Families and Couples Education and was founder of the US National Marriage Education conference, 'Smartmarriages'.

1194 Amitai Etzioni (1993) *The spirit of community* [New York, Crown Publishers]

1195 Glendon has authored and edited a series of books on marriage and family, including *Seedbeds of virtue* [Madison Books, 1995]

1196 Elshtain authored and co-edited a series of books including *Promises to keep* [Rowman and Littlefield, 1996], *Rebuilding the nest* [Manticore, 1991], *Family in political thought* [Prentice Hall/Harvester Wheatsheet, 1984] and *The meaning of marriage* [Dallas, Spence Publishing, 2006]

1197 Carlson is the Director of the Howard Center, founder of the World Congress of Families, and author of numerous books on the family, including *Family questions* [New Brunswick, Transaction Books, 1990] and *Fractured generations* [New Brunswick, Transaction Books, 2005]

1198 Fagan was a senior official in the US Department of Health and Human Services before joining the Heritage Foundation, and subsequently the Family Research Council.

1199 See, for example, Charles Murray (2012) *Coming apart* [New York, Crown Forum]

1200 See for example: Jill Kirby (2002) *Broken hearts – family decline and the consequences for society* [London, the Centre for Policy Studies]; Kieran McKeown and John Sweeney (2001) *Family well-being and family policy – A review of research on benefits and costs* [Dublin, Department of Social, Community and Family Affairs]; James Q Wilson *et al* (1995) *Just a piece of paper?* [London, Institute of Economic Affairs]; Ed Straw (1998) *Relative Values* [London, Demos], and Barry Maley (2001) *Family and marriage in Australia* [Sydney, Centre for Independent Studies]

1201 See for example: Pope John Paul II (1981) *Familiaris Consortio – The role of the Christian family in the modern world* [The Vatican]; National Conference of Catholic Bishops (1988) *Faithful to each other forever* [Washington DC, NCCB]; Australian Catholic Bishops Conference (2001) *A common marriage policy for the Catholic Church in Australia* [Canberra, the Conference] and *Threshold* (2001) 70; 4-5

1202 Isabel Sawhill (2012) '20 years later, it turns out Dan Quayle was right about Murphy Brown and unmarried moms' *The Washington Post*, May 26

1203 William Clinton (1994) *The state of our union* [Washington DC, US Congress, January 25]

1204 Hilary Rodham Clinton (1996) *It Takes a Village* [New York, Simon and Schuster]

1205 See: Department of Health and Human Services, *Healthy marriage initiative* [Washington DC, The Department]; George W Bush (2002) 'George W Bush on supporting marriage' *Threshold* 72: 4; 'Bush puts marriage on the agenda' *Threshold* (2002) 72:3; and 'US: Support for marriage' *Threshold* (2003) 78: 34. See also Wade Horn (2004) 'Marriage, family and the welfare of children: A call for action' in D Moynihan, T Smeeding and L Rainwater (eds) *The future of the family* [New York, Russell Sage]; and Wade F Horn (2004) 'Promoting healthy marriages' *Threshold* 82: 32-34

1206 Barack Obama (2006) *The audacity of hope* [New York, Crown]

1207 Tony Blair (2001) *Speech*, Christian Socialist Movement, London, March 29. See also: The Home Office (1998) *Supporting families: A consultation document* [London, The Home Office]; 'Lords support marriage' *Threshold* (1999) 61:9; Penelope Gibb (1999) 'Supporting families' *Marriage, Family and Society Issues* 1: 15-16; 'UK funding boost for marriage support' *Threshold* (2000) 63: 8-10; 'UK: Government plan for marriage and relationship support' *Threshold* (2002) 73: 6-7 , citing the Lord Chancellor's Advisory Group on Marriage and Relationship Support (2002) *Moving forward together* [London, Lord Chancellor's Department]

1208 See for example: Iain Duncan Smith (2011) *Social justice: Transforming lives*, Cmnd 8314

1209 Frank Field (2010) *The foundation years: Preventing poor children becoming poor adults* [London, HM Government]; Graham Allen (2011) *Early intervention: The next steps* [London, HM Government]; and Graham Allen (2011) *Early intervention: Smart investment, massive savings* [London, HM Government]

1210 *To have and to hold* (1998) *supra*. Support was subsequently urged by the House of Representatives Family and Community Affairs Committee (2004) *Every picture tells a story. A report on the inquiry into child custody arrangements in the event of a family separation* [Canberra, Parliament of the Commonwealth of Australia], paragraphs 3.46, 3.52 and 3.67

1211 Eleanor Harding (2012) 'Senior judge starts campaign to "mend not end marriages"' *Daily Mail* Online, January 3

1212 Tim Simpson (2009) 'Only marriage can mend broken Britain, says top judge in attack on "pass the partner" society' *Daily Mail Online*, June 17

1213 See for example: Leah Ward Sears (2010) 'Far more benefit than harm in waiting' *Familyscholars.org* (June 18) and William J Doherty and Leah Ward Sears (2011) 'Delaying divorce to save marriages: The Second Chances Act' *The Washington Post*, October 20

1214 For example: The recommendation from the bipartisan *To have and to hold* report

et al.

in Australia for the provision of vouchers for marriage preparation was trialled, and although successful, never pursued. Similarly, the 1998 UK Green Paper *Supporting families* was shelved. See 'Editorial' *Threshold* (2002) 73: 2

1215 Richard J Neuhaus (1977) *To empower people* [Washington DC, American Enterprise Institute]

1216 John F Kennedy (1963) *Public Papers of the Presidents of the United States, 1962* [Washington DC, US Government Printing Office], 102-103

1217 SB Kamerman and AJ Kahn (1978) *Family policy: Government and families in fourteen countries* [New York, Columbia University Press]

1218 See: Kevin Andrews (2011) 'Civil society and the role of government' *Australian Polity* 2(2): 13-16; and Kevin Andrews (2012) 'Empowering civil society' *Australian Polity* 3(2):13-23

1219 Abraham Kuyper, 'Sphere sovereignty' in James D Bratt (1998) *Abraham Kuyper, A centennial reader* [Grand Rapids MI, Eerdmans], 472

1220 Kuyper, *supra*, 469

1221 Nathan Glazer (1988) *The limits of social policy* [Cambridge MA, Harvard University Press], 7

1222 Daniel Patrick Moynihan (1988) *Family and nation* [Boston MA, Harcourt]

1223 The Australian Government adopted a National Families Strategy in 1998 in response to the *To have and to hold* report. See (1999) 'National families strategy' *Marriage, Family and Society Issues* 2: 4

1224 Commission on the Family (1998) *Strengthening families for life*. Final report to the Minister for Social, Community and Family Affairs [Dublin, The Stationary Office] See also: Padraig O'Connor (1999) 'Strengthening families for life' *Marriage, Family and Society Issues* 3: 26-29

1225 The Canadian Province of Alberta adopted a Family Policy Grid in 1992. See The Premier's Council in Support of Alberta Families (1992) *Family Policy Grid.*

1226 Administration for Children and Families (2011) *Strengthening families and communities: 2011 resource guide* [Washington DC, US Department of Health and Human Services]

1227 'Europe's other crisis' (2012) *The Economist*, June 30-July 6, 56

1228 Steven Philip Kramer (2012) 'Depopulate and perish' *Australian Financial Review*, May 25, Review Section 3-4, reprinted from *Foreign Affairs.*

1229 John Daley *et al* (2012) *Game-changers: Economic reform priorities for Australia* [Melbourne, Grattan Institute]

1230 For a discussion of the interaction of the number of children a woman has and her workforce participation, see: Julie Moschion (2011) *The impact of fertility on mothers' labour supply in Australia: Evidence from exogenous variation in family size* [Melbourne, Melbourne Institute of Applied Economic and Social Research] Working Paper 17/11

1231 John Mueller (2010) *Redeeming economics: Recovering the missing element* [Wilmington DEL, ISI Books] 84-85

1232 See also: Allan Carlson (1993) *From cottage to work station: The family's search for harmony in the industrial age* [San Francisco, Ignatius Press], 70

1233 John Daley *et al* (2012) *Game-changers: Economic reform priorities for Australia* [Melbourne, Grattan Institute]

1234 MDR Evans and J Kelley (2002) 'Attitudes towards childcare in Australia' *The Australian Economic Review* 35: 188-196; and K Hand (2005) 'Mother's views on using formal childcare' *Family Matters* 70: 10-17

1235 Australian Bureau of Statistics (2011) *Childhood education and childcare*, Cat 4402.0

1236 Matthew Gray *et al* (2008) 'Parent-only care: A child care choice for working couple families?' *Family Matters* 79: 42-49

1237 See also: Jennifer Baxter and Matthew Gray (2008) 'Work and family responsibilities through life' *Family Matters* 79: 58-61

1238 Adam Smith *The Wealth of Nations*, Andrew Skinner (ed) [Middlesex UK, Penguin, 1970] 1.7, 173

1239 Paul Amato (2004) 'Tension between institutional and individual views of marriage' *Journal of Marriage and Family* 66: 959-965

1240 Amato (2004) *supra*, 963

1241 James Chapman (2012) 'One in five children from broken homes lose touch with one parent for ever' *Daily Mail Online*, January 25. Australian data reveals that 11 per cent of children post-separation never see their father: 'Mothers and children post separation' (2011) *Threshold* 101: 6

1242 Margaret Andrews (1994) 'Taking family seriously: A national strategy to enhance marriage and family' *Threshold* 44: 14-20

1243 Social Justice Policy Group (2007) *Breakthrough Britain: Ending the costs of social breakdown* [London, Centre for Social Justice] Vol 1, 48

1244 Michele Simons and Robyn Parker (2002) 'Relationship education services' *Family Matters* 63: 77-79, reporting on the Study of Australian Relationship Education Services.

1245 See for example: Mark Metherell (2011) 'Chlamydia rates rise among youth' *The Age*, September 27; and (2010) 'Chlamydia infections "at-time high" ' *The Age*, January 12 – showing infection reports had risen from 16,960 in 2000 to 74,305 in 2010.

1246 Judith Wallerstein (2011) 'What children of divorce do and don't learn' *Huffington Post*, December 7

1247 Marline Pearson (2008) 'Ignoring teens' romantic lives' *Threshold* 93: 6-7

1248 William Galston and Stephen Goldsmith 'Introduction' in Barbara Dafoe Whitehead and Marline Pearson, *Making a love connection: Teen relationships, pregnancy and marriage* [Washington DC, National Campaign to Prevent Teen Pregnancy], reprinted in Galston and Goldsmith (2008) 'Making a love connection' *Threshold* 93: 32

1249 Marline Pearson (2008) 'Relationship education for teens' *Threshold* 93: 8-11

1250 See for example: Mary Brown (2008) 'Developing healthy relationships program' *Threshold* 93: 30; and Tina Jack (2008) 'Loving for life' *Threshold* 93: 31

1251 See for example: National Campaign to Prevent Teen Pregnancy, *Tips for parents* [www.teenpregnancy.org]; 'Dating rules and parental happiness' (2008) *Threshold* 94: 3-4, citing the *Wall Street Journal*, June 27, 2008

1252 Frank Field (2010)*The foundation years: Preventing poor children becoming poor adults* [London, HM Government]

1253 For example: L Feinstein (2003) *How early can we predict future education achievement* LSE Centre Piece Summer; and L Feinstein (2003) 'Inequality in the early cognitive development of children in the early 1970 cohort' *Economica* 70: 73-97

1254 Geoffrey Gorer (1955) *Exploring English character* [New York, Criterion Books] cited by Field, *supra*, at 18

1255 Frank Field (2010) 'The biggest crisis facing Britain? Too many parents don't have a clue how to raise children' *Daily Mail* (August 10)

1256 Field (2010) *supra*, 19, and Frank Field (2003) *Neighbours from hell* [London, Politicos] US research also reveals that young people desire information about healthy relationships: Office of Family Assistance (2012) *School of thought: Healthy marriage and relationship education matters to our youth* [Washington DC, US Department of Health and Human Services]

1257 Field (2010) *supra*, 17

1258 James Chapman (2012) 'Ministers vow to drive down cost of childminders' *Daily Mail Online*, May 14

1259 See: Alan J Hawkins *et al* (2008) 'Does marriage and relationship education work? A meta-analytic study' *Journal of Consulting and Clinical Psychology* 76: 723-734.; and 'Marriage education works' (2009) *Threshold* 97: 30-31

1260 Parliament of Australia (1998) *To have and to hold* [Canberra, Parliament of the Commonwealth of Australia], 135. This was a conservative estimate.

1261 Australian Bureau of Statistics (2012) *Marriages, Australia, 2010* Cat 3310.0

1262 For example, the Catholic Bishops Conferences in Australia and the USA have formal policies encouraging marriage education. See: National Conference of Catholic Bishops (1988) *supra*; and Australian Catholic Bishops Conference (2001) *supra*

1263 See for example: Sally Cant (2007) 'Beliefs, attitudes, celebrants and ceremonies' *Threshold* 89: 17; Dally Messenger III (2007) 'The compact: Meaning in the civil marriage ceremony' *Threshold* 89: 18-20; and *To have and to hold* (1998) *supra*, 182-191

1264 Australian Bureau of Statistics (2010) *Marriages, Australia*

1265 Data provided by the Department of Families, Communities, Housing and Indigenous Affairs to the 2009 Australian Marriage Education conference would appear to confirm this conclusion.

1266 Scott M Stanley, Galena K Rhoades and Howard J Markman (2008) 'Implications for marriage education' *Threshold* 92: 12-13

1267 Thomas N Bradbury and Justin A Lavner (2012) 'How can we improve preventive and educational interventions for intimate relationships?' *Behavior Therapy* 43: 113-122

1268 Scott M Stanley, Marline Pearson and Galena K Rhoades (2008) 'Working with individuals: Within my reach' *Threshold* 94: 6-11

1269 'Major new study reveals that trained lay educators do best' (1999) *Threshold* 62: 11-13

1270 Eric Skattebo (2008) 'Using radio, the internet and conferences in MRE' *Threshold* 93: 15

1271 Rosalind Baker (2008) 'MRE at an introduction service' *Threshold* 93: 23, and Rosalind Baker (2012) 'Datings and introductions in the 21st century' *Threshold* 105 (forthcoming)

1272 Scott M Stanley, Marline Pearson and Galena K Rhoades (2008) 'Working with individuals: Within my reach' *Threshold* 93: 6-11

1273 Barbara Markey (2001) 'Cohabitation: Reacting or responding?' *Threshold* 68: 10-17

1274 Hawkins (2008) *supra.* See also JS Carroll and WH Doherty (2003) 'Evaluating the effectiveness of premarital intervention programs" A meta-analytic review of outcome research' *Family Relations* 53: 105-118

1275 VL Blanchard *et al* (2009) 'Investigating the effects of marriage and relationship education on couples' communication skills: A meta-analytic study' *Journal of Family Psychology* 23: 203-214

1276 Roger Harris *et al* (1992) *Love, sex and waterskiing* [Adelaide, University of South Australia]. A British survey revealed that 11 per cent of couples regretted getting married on their wedding day: 'Post nuptial remorse?' (2012) *Daily Mail Online*, July 17

1277 Kim Halford (2001) 'Forum' *Threshold* 68: 7-9

1278 Thomas N Bradbury and Justin A Lavner (2012) 'How can we improve preventive and educational interventions for intimate relationships?' *Behavior Therapy* 43: 113-122

1279 Kathleen M Walters (2006) 'The transition to parenthood' *Threshold* 96: 5-7

1280 Jay Belsky and John Kelly (1994) *The transition to parenthood – How a first child changes a marriage* [New York, Delecourte Press]

1281 Ted L Huston (2009) 'What's love got to do with it? Why some marriages succeed and others fail' *Personal Relationships* 16: 301-327

1282 M Carlson and S McLanahan (2006) 'Strengthening unmarried families: Could enhancing couple relationships also improve parenting?' *Social Service Review* 80: 297-321. See also: Rhys Price-Roberston, Diana Smart and Leah Bromfield (2010) 'Family is for life' *Family Matters* 85: 7-17

1283 M Carlson, S McLanahan and J Brooks-Gunn (2008) 'Coparenting and non-resident fathers' involvement with young children after a nonmarital birth' *Demography* 45: 461-488

1284 Carolyn Pape Cowan and Philip A Cowan (2006) 'Partners becoming parents' *Threshold* 86: 16-19 reprinting in an abridged form a presentation to the Peleg-Bilig Centre for the Study of Family Well-Being, Bar-Ilan University, Ramat Gan, Israel, 1999

1285 *Ibid.* Original emphasis.

1286 Carolyn Pape Cowan and Philip A Cowan (2006) 'The becoming-a-family study' *Threshold* 86: 8-13 reprinting in an abridged form a presentation to the Peleg-Bilig Centre for the Study of Family Well-Being, Bar-Ilan University, Ramat Gan, Israel, 1999

1287 See for example: Sean Brotherson (2006) 'The transition from partners to parents' *Threshold* 86: 20-23; David and Claudia Arp (2006) 'Partners or parents?' *Threshold* (2006) 86: 25-27;

1288 'Marriage education for couples becoming parents' (2006) *Threshold* 86: 28 – 29; and Denise Lacey (2006) 'Bringing baby home' *Threshold* 86: 30-31;

1289 Helena Deacon-Wood (2006) 'And baby makes 3' *Threshold* 86: 32-33

1290 'Ready, set, baby' (2006) *Threshold* 86: 34

1291 See: *To have and to hold* (1998) *supra*, at 217-225

1292 M Carlson *et al* (2005) *What do we know about unmarried parents: Implications for building strong families programs* [Washington DC, Mathematica Policy Research]

1293 Barbara Devaney and Robin Dion (2010) *15-month impacts of Oklahoma's Family Expectations program* [Washington DC, Mathematica Policy Research and

US Department of Health and Human Services]

1294 Robert G Wood *et al* (2012) 'The effects of building strong families: A healthy marriage and relationship skills education program for unmarried parents' *Journal of Policy Analysis and Management* 31: 228-252

1295 Australian Bureau of Statistics (2011) *Family characteristics, Australia, 2009-10* Cat. 4442.0

1296 Office for National Statistics (2007) *Social Trends*, 38: 22

1297 *Current Population Study* (2009)

1298 Margaret Howden (2007) *Stepfamilies: Understanding and responding effectively* [Australian Family Relationships Clearinghouse, Briefing No 6]; Lixia Qu and Ruth Weston (2005) 'Snapshot of couple families with stepparent-child relationships' *Family Matters* 70: 36-37. See also National Stepfamily Resource Center, 'Stepfamily fact sheet' www.stepfamilies.info. In Australia, stepfamilies were not counted by the ABS until 1986, and they are still not counted if children spend less than half the time with the stepparent: Steve Martin (2001) 'Understanding stepfamilies' *Threshold* 69: 12

1299 See chapter 7.

1300 Ron L Deal and David H Olson (2010) *The remarriage checkup: Tools to help your marriage last a lifetime* [Ada MI, Bethany House], citing US Census Bureau data.

1301 E Mavis Hetherington and John Kelly (2003) *For better or for worse: Divorce reconsidered* [New York, WW Norton]

1302 *To have and to hold* (1998) *supra*, 139

1303 *To have and to hold* (1998) *supra*, 269

1304 See for example: Margaret Newman (1994) *Stepfamily realities* [Oakland CA, New Harbinger], 1-4; Margaret Howden (2001) 'Stepfamily myths' *Threshold* 69: 16-17

1305 Deal and Olson (2010) *supra*

1306 These points are taken from Margaret Newman (1994) *Stepfamily realities* [Oakland CA, New Harbinger], 2-4

1307 See for example: Irene Gerrard (2001) 'Disenfranchised grief in stepfamilies' *Threshold* 69: 18-21; Margaret Howden (2001) 'Stepfamily complexity' *Threshold* 69: 13-14; and Irene Gerrard (2007) 'For better or for worse' *Threshold* 89: 22-25

1308 See: Irene Gerrard and Margaret Howden (1998) Making stepfamilies work: A course for couples – Leaders manual [Melbourne, Stepfamily Association of Victoria] reprinted in (2001) *Threshold* 69: 17; and Margaret Newman (1994), *supra*, 6

1309 See: 'Positive of living in a stepfamily' (2001) *Threshold* 69: 15 and the studies cited therein; and Irene Gerrard (2007) 'For better or for worse' *Threshold* 89: 22-25

1310 See: Steve Martin (1998) 'Stepfamily stages and the process of change' cited in Margaret Howden (2001) 'Stepfamily stages' *Threshold* 69: 22-23; Newman (1994) *supra*, 4 -5; and Robyn Elliot (2001) 'Factors which facilitate success in stepfamilies' *Threshold* 69: 23

1311 See also: Tony Kerin (1995) 'Preparing couples for remarriage' *Threshold* 46: 8-9

1312 Many of the pre 1998 studies are summarised in *To have and to hold* (1998) *supra*, 129-125.

1313 MH Butler and KS Wampler (1999) 'A meta-analytic update of research on the Couple Communication program' *The American Journal of Family Therapy* 27: 223-237; JS Carroll and WJ Doherty (2003) 'Evaluating the effectiveness of premarital prevention programs: A meta-analytic review of outcome research' *Family Relations* 52: 105-118; TL Hight (2000) 'Do the rich get richer? A meta-analysis of the methodological and substantive moderators of couple enrichment' (Doctoral dissertation, Virginia Commonwealth University) *Dissertation Abstracts International* 65: 3278B; and J Reardon-Anderson, M Stagner, JE Macomber and J Murray (2005*) Systematic review of the impact of marriage and relationship programs* [Washington DC, Urban Institute]

1314 AJ Hawkins, VL Blanchard, SA Baldwin and EB Fawcett (2008) 'Does marriage and relationship education work? A meta-analytic study' *Journal of Consulting and Clinical Psychology* 76: 723-734

1315 VL Blanchard, AJ Hawkins, SA Baldwin and EB Fawcett (2009) 'Investigating the effects of marriage and relationships education on couples' communication skills: A meta-analytic study' *Journal of Family Psychology* 23(2): 203-214

1316 Scott M Stanley *et al* (2006) 'Premarital education, marital quality, and marital stability: Findings from a large, random household survey' *Journal of Family Psychology* 20: 117-126

1317 Norval D Glenn (2005) *With this ring: A national survey on marriage in America* [Washington DC, National Fatherhood Initiative], 20

1318 Thomas N Bradbury and Justin A Lavner (2012) 'How can we improve preventive and educational interventions for intimate relationships?' *Behavior Therapy* 43: 113-122

1319 JM Gaubert *et al* (2010) *Early lessons from the implementation of a relationship and marriage skills program for low-income married couples* [New York, MDRC]

1320 Benjamin Karney and Thomas Bradbury (2010) *Intimate relationships* [New York, W W Norton], 530. See also: Kevin Andrews, Carmel Crawford and Marcella Reiter (2000) 'From wedding to marriage: Developing an integrated pre- and post-wedding programme' *Threshold* 63: 24-27

1321 'Media campaign launch in Bendigo' (1993) *Threshold* 41:1 and 4-7

1322 'Is love enough?' (1995) *Threshold* 46: 3

1323 'Relate campaign evaluation' (1999) *Threshold* 62: 4

1324 'Evaluation of the voucher pilot and *Two equals one' Threshold* 71: 26-27

1325 'Campaign looks to aid couples' (2007) *Threshold* 90: 4

1326 'Time to support marriage: UK report' (2007) *Threshold* 91: 4-6

1327 Norval D Glenn (2005) *With this ring: A national survey on marriage in America* [Washington DC, National Fatherhood Initiative], 12

1328 *To have and to hold* (1998) *supra*, 159

1329 David Popenoe (2008) 'Cohabitation, marriage and child wellbeing' *Threshold* 93: 20

1330 Zheng Wu (2000) *Cohabitation: An alternative form of family living* [New York, Oxford University Press], 143

1331 Horn (2004) *supra*

1332 Lucy Buckland (2011) 'New fathers could be forced to sign baby's birth certificate to make them take more responsibility' *Daily Mail Online*, December 19

1333 David Popenoe (2008) 'Cohabitation, marriage and child wellbeing' *Threshold* 93: 22

1334 Iain Duncan Smith (2012) *Social justice transforming lives* Cmnd 8314 [London, HM Government], 16

1335 US Department of Health and Human Services, Administration for Families and Children (2010) *Head Start impact study: Final report* [Washington DC], Executive summary, xxvi

1336 Aletha C Huston (22011) 'Children in poverty: Can public policy alleviate the consequences?' *Family Matters* 87: 13-26

1337 *Ibid.*, 17. Some programs, such as the Abecedarian study in North Carolina, Sure Start in the UK and Early Head Start in the US, have been shown to have more positive outcomes.

1338 Darcy Olsen and Jennifer Martin (2005) 'Assessing proposals for preschool and kindergarten: Essential information for parents, taxpayers, and policymakers' *Policy Report No 201* [Phoenix Arizona: Goldwater Institute]

1339 Graham Allen (2011) *Early intervention: The next steps* [London, HM Government], 3 (Original emphases)

1340 Toby Parcel, Lori Ann Campbell and Wenxuan Zhong (2012) 'Children's behaviour problems in the United States and Great Britain' *Journal of Health and Social Behavior*, May 10.

1341 Ilene Woolcott and Helen Glezer (1989) *Marriage counselling in Australia – An evaluation* [Melbourne, Australian Institute of Family Studies]

1342 Jay Folberg and Ann L Milne (eds) 1988 *Divorce mediation: Theory and practice* [New York, Guilford Press]; and Jay Folberg, Anne L Milne and Peter Salem, 'The evolution of divorce and family mediation: An overview' in Jay Folberg, Ann L Milne and Peter Salem (eds) *Divorce and family mediation: Models, techniques and applications* [New York, Guilford Press], 3-25

1343 Section 14 (5) of the *Family Law Act* provided: Where a court having jurisdiction under this Act is of the opinion that counselling may assist the parties to a marriage to improve their relationship to each other and to any child of the marriage, it may advise the parties to attend upon a marriage counsellor or an approved marriage counselling organisation and, if it thinks it desirable to do so, adjourn any proceedings before it to enable the attendance.

1344 William J Doherty, Brian J Willoughby and Bruce Peterson (2011) 'Interest in marital reconciliation among divorcing parents,' *Family Court Review* 49: 313-321

1345 *Family Law Act* 1975, s 14(6) which was subsequently replaced by s 44 (1B) in 1983

1346 s 37 (8)

1347 'Family Court Chief calls for more marriage education,' (1991) *Threshold* 34: 6

1348 Doherty, Willoughby and Peterson (2011) *supra*, 313

1349 I Woolcott, (1984) *Marriage Counselling services: Priorities and policy*, [Melbourne: Australian Institute of Family Studies], 29

1350 CA Everatt and RF Lee (2006) (eds) *When marriages fail: Systemic family therapy interventions and issues* [New York, Vintage]

1351 Parkinson (2011) *supra*

1352 Relationships Australia (Western Australia), *supra*, which found that 37 per cent of people regret their divorce five years later, and up to 40 per cent believe it could have been avoided.

1353 'Marriage popular, even after divorce' (2009) *Threshold* 97: 16-17, citing results of a US GfK Roper poll which indicated that 74 per cent of men and 86 per cent of women continued to believe in marriage post-divorce.

1354 Linda J Waite *et al* (2002) *Does divorce make people happy? Findings from a study of unhappy marriages* [New York, Institute for American Values]

1355 See: 'Happiness is U-shaped' (2011) *Threshold* 102: 6, and 'Commitment and satisfaction' (2011) *Threshold* 102: 6-7

1356 CA Johnson *et al* (2002) *Marriage in Oklahoma: 2001 baseline statewide survey on marriage and divorce* [Oklahoma City, Oklahoma Department of Human Services]

1357 See: Paul R Amato and Bryndel Holmann-Marriott (2007) 'A comparison of high- and low-distress marriages that end in divorce,' *Journal of Marriage and Family* 69: 621

1358 Norval D Glenn (2005) *With this ring ... A national survey on marriage in America* [Washington DC. National Fatherhood Initiative], 23. Surveys by Relationships Australia reveal that violence and abuse were cited as reasons for relationship breakdown in three per cent of cases in 2008, and five per cent in 2011: Relationships Australia (2011) *Issues and concerns for Australian relationships today*, Relationships Indicators Survey 2011.

1359 Bettina Arndt (2005) 'Better off wed,' *Threshold* 83: 33, citing Melbourne University research.

1360 Paul M de Graaf and Matthijs Kalmijn (2006) 'Divorce motives in a period of rising divorce: Evidence from a Dutch life-history survey,' *Journal of Family Issues* 27: 483-505. Sexual problems were a motive mentioned by 40 per cent; sexual infidelity by 37 per cent; and substance abuse by 22 per cent.

1361 'Work and marriage' (2006) *Threshold* 87: 4 (See also *Sunday Times*, March 13, 2006)

1362 Grant Thornton (2011) *For richer, for poorer?* Matrimonial Survey [London, Grant Thornton]; and 'Affairs no longer main cause of UK marriage breakdown' (2011) *Threshold* 103: 4. An Australian survey revealed that 'infidelity/losing interest/ meeting other people' was the reason for relationship breakdown in only 11 per cent of cases in 2011: Relationships Australia (2011) *Issues and concerns for Australian relationships today* [Deakin ACT, Relationships Australia], 11

1363 Bradbury and Karney (2010) *supra*

1364 Alan Booth and Paul R Amato (2001) 'Parental predivorce relations and offspring postdivorce well-being' *Journal of Marriage and Family* 63: 197-212, at 211. See also: Leslie R Martin *et al* (2005) 'Longevity following the experience of parental divorce' *Social Science and Medicine* 61: 2177-2189: "Dismantling a seemingly functional family may be more traumatic and have more significant long-term negative effects than the dissolution of a clearly troubled family."

1365 Frank Furstenberg Jr and Andrew Cherlin (1991) *Divided families: What happens to children when parents part* [Cambridge MA, Harvard University Press]

1366 Diane Vaughn (1986) *Uncoupling: Turning points in intimate relationships* [Oxford, Oxford University Press]

1367 Andrew Cherlin (2009) *The marriage-go-round. The state of marriage and the family in America today* [New York, Knopf]

1368 H Weineberg (1994) 'Marital reconciliation in the United States: Which couples are successful?' *Journal of Marriage and the Family* 56: 80-88; and H Weinberg (1995)

'An examination of ever-divorced women who attempted a marital reconciliation before becoming divorced' *Journal of Divorce and Remarriage* 23: 129-146.

1369 LA Morgan (1988) 'Outcomes of marital separation: A longitudinal test of predictors' *Journal of Marriage and the Family* 50: 493-498

1370 Doherty, Willoughby and Peterson (2011) *supra*, 318-319

1371 Paul R Amato (2005) 'The impact of family formation change on the social, cognitive, and emotional well-being of the next generation' *The future of children* 15: 88-89

1372 William J Doherty and Leah Ward Sears (2011) *Second chances. A proposal to reduce unnecessary divorce* [New York, Institute for American Values]

1373 *Ibid.*, 41

1374 William Galston (1990-91) 'A Liberal-Democratic case for the two-parent family' *The Responsive Community* 1: 23

1375 Hilary Clinton (2010) 'Transcript of Clinton on divorce waiting periods and counselling, Politics of divorce prevention' *The Family Law News Blog* (March 18)

1376 Thorsten Kneip and Gerrittt Bauer (2009) 'Did unilateral divorce laws raise divorce rates in Western Europe?' *Journal of Marriage and Family* 71: 592-607. See also Leora Friedberg (1998) 'Did unilateral divorce raise divorce rates?: Evidence from panel data' *American Economic Review* 88: 608-627

1377 'Delay divorce, says UK Minister' (2000) *Threshold* 65: 9

1378 Susan L Pollet and Melissa Lombreglia (2009) 'A nationwide survey of mandatory parent education' *Family Court Review* 46: 375-394

1379 Doherty and Sears (2011) *supra*, 33. The authors specifically propose that waiting periods be able to be waived in the case of domestic violence.

1380 Doherty and Sears (2011) *supra*, 34

1381 William Doherty and Steven Harris (2011) 'Discernment counseling for couples considering divorce' in *Reconciliation and couples on the brink, Roundtable Proceedings*, [Sydney, PMRC Australia], 7 See also: www.mncouplesonthebrink.org

1382 *To have and to hold* (1998) *supra*, 269

1383 Allan Carlson and David Blankenhorn (1998) 'Marriage and taxes' *Weekly Standard* (February 9)

1384 Barbara Dafoe Whitehead and David Popenoe (2006) *The state of our unions* [Rutgers NJ, the National Marriage Project]

1385 Adam Catasso and C Eugene Steurle (2005) 'The hefty penalty on marriage facing many households with children' *The Future of Children* 15: 157-175.

1386 John Humphreys (2009) 'Ending the churn: A tax/welfare swap' *Monograph* [Sydney, Centre for Independent Studies]

1387 Iain Duncan Smith (2102) *Social justice transforming lives* Cmnd 8314 [London, HM Government], 18

1388 This discussion is taken from (2008) 'Income splitting in OECD countries' *Australian Polity* 2: 27 which reprints OECD analysis and (2008) 'Income splitting under discussion' *Australian Polity* 2: 25-26 which reprints a New Zealand Discussion Paper.

1389 In some countries income splitting is restricted to married partners, while in other countries it is allowed for *de facto* partners and same-sex partners.

1390 OECD (2006) *Fundamental reform of personal income tax* [Paris, OECD Publishing], 55

1391 H Ault (1997) *Comparative income taxation: A structural analysis* [Amsterdam, Kluwer Law International], 273

1392 Virginia Haussegger (2002) 'The sins of our feminist mothers' *The Age* [Melbourne] July 23. See also Virginia Haussegger (2005) *Wonder women: The myth of having it all* [Sydney, Allen and Unwin]

1393 It is not my intention to discuss here the extensive debate that ensued. For a summary of the responses to Haussegger, see Natasha Campo 'Having it all' or 'had enough'? Blaming feminism in *The Age* and *The Sydney Morning Herald*, 1980-2004' *The Australian Public Intellectual Network* [www.api.com]

1394 Kate Bolick (2100) 'All single ladies' *The Atlantic* (November) 116-136

1395 www.genea.com.au/Library/Been-trying-for-a-while-/Infertility/Age-and-Infertility

1396 Julia Medew (2011) 'Mr Right "is not worth the wait"' *The Age* (Melbourne) October 19 quoting Monash IVF Director, Professor Gab Kovacs. US research revealed that conception occurred in only 18 per cent of cases involving frozen eggs from women under 30, and just 10.3 per cent of cases where the women was over 30. See also: Jenny Hope (2012) 'Women over 40 told: "Don't take IVF for granted" ' *Daily Mail Online*, April 6, quoting researchers at the Yale Fertility Center, and Ruth Weston and Lixia Qu (2006) 'IVF – a viable means of achieving delayed parenthood?' *Threshold* 86: 42

1397 Hannah Reid (2012) 'We wish we'd had babies in our thirties, admit 80 per cent of first-time parents in their forties' *Daily Mail Online* March 9. See also: K Mac Dougall, Y Beyene, and RD Nachtigall (2012) 'Inconvenient biology:' advantages and disadvantages of first-time parenting after age 40 using *in vitro* fertilization' *Human Reproduction* 27(4): 1058-1065. A 2012 survey of Australian women aged 18-44 found that having a baby was a number three priority after family and friends and their relationship with their partner: 'Australian women do not view having a baby as a top priority, a new survey has found' (2012) *The Australian Online*, April 22. Seventy per cent reported knowing at least one person having difficulties conceiving.

1398 Mary McConnell (2011) 'Women as young as 18 are resorting to sperm donors online as they give up the hunt for Mr Right' *Daily Mail Online*, October 10, reporting that women 25 and under make up a quarter of all registrants on some online donor sites.

1399 Haussegger (2002) *supra*

1400 Thornton and Young-DeMarco (2001) *supra*

1401 *Ibid*

1402 Andrew J Cherlin (2009) *The marriage-go-round* [New York, Vintage Books] 193

1403 Kerry Rubin and Lia Macko (2004) *Midlife crisis at 30: How the stakes have changed for a new generation – and what to do about it* [New York, Rodale Books], 10. See also: Lori Gottlieb (2010) *Marry him – The case for settling for Mr Good Enough* [New Yotk, Dutton]

1404 Sheryl Sandberg (2011) Speech at Barnard College, New York, May 17

1405 Anne-Marie Slaughter (2012) 'Why women still can't have it all' *The Atlantic*, July/August

1406 Helen Gurley Brown (1985) *Having it all* [New York, Pocket Books]

1407 *Bliss* magazine, cited in Willetts (2010) *supra*

1408 Malenie Christiansen (2009) 'More de factos end up divorcing after saying I do' *Courier Mail* (Brisbane) July 17, 9.

1409 Deborah Arthurs (2012) 'Marriage is overrated and health and happiness benefits for wedded couples are a MYTH' *Daily Mail Online*, January 18

1410 Copen *et al* (2012) *supra*

1411 Natasha Burton (2012) 'Cohabitation – divorce link? I don't think so' *Huffington Post* (US) April 16

1412 Nor do many people know about the demographic changes outlined in this book: see Pew Research Center (2010) *The decline of marriage and rise of new families* [Washington DC, The Center]

1413 Galena K Rhoades, Scott M Stanley and Howard J Markman (2009) 'Working with cohabitation in relationship education and therapy' *Journal of Couple and Relationship Therapy* 8: 95-112

1414 Stevenson and Wolfers (2007) *supra*

1415 See chapter seven. See also: Rose M Kreider and Jason M Fields (2001) 'Number, timing and duration of marriages and divorces' *Current Population Reports* 70-80

1416 Stevenson and Wolfers (2007) *supra*

1417 Shail Jain (2007) 'Lifetime marriage and divorce trends' *Australian Social Trends, 2007* [Canberra, Australian Bureau of Statistics]

1418 A Ambert (2009) *Divorce: Facts, causes and consequences* [Ottawa, Vanier Institute of the Family]

1419 Australian Bureau of Statistics, *Marriages and Divorces, Australia*, cited by Marriage Education Programme Inc, Melbourne, 2006

1420 Matthew D Bramlett and William D Mosher (2002) 'Cohabitation, marriage, divorce and remarriage in the United States' *Vital and Health Statistics* 23 (22) [Washington DC, National Center for Health Statistics]. The risks are calculated for women only.

1421 Ruth Weston, Lixia Qu and David de Vaus (2008) 'Cohabitation: Level of stability and post-cohabitation pathways' *Threshold* 92: 18-20

1422 Christian Smith *et al, supra*, 154. See also Paul Taylor, Cary Funk and April Clarke (2010) *As marriage and parenthood drift apart, public is concerned about social impact* [Washington DC, Pew Research Center] which reveals that 68 per cent of people living together expect to marry their partner, which is significantly higher than the proportion who actually do marry.

1423 *Ibid.*

1424 *Ibid.*, 123

1425 Tony Gee (2003) 'Grief and loss in divorce' *Threshold* 77: 26-29

1426 See the discussion in chapter eight.

1427 Whitehead, *supra*, 128-9

1428 Stein Ringen (1998) *The family in question* [London, Demos], 47

1429 Catherine A Surra and Christine R Gray (2000) 'A typology of processes of commitment to marriage' in Linda J Waite (ed) *Ties that bind* [Hawthorne NY, Aldine De Gruyter], 260

1430 David Popenoe and Barbara Dafoe Whitehead (1999) *Should we live together? What young adults need to now about cohabitation before marriage* [Rutgers State University, NJ, National Marriage Project]; also reprinted in *Threshold* (1999) 61: 10-18

1431 Mark Regernus and Jeremy Uecker (2011) *Premarital sex in America* [Oxford, Oxford University Press], 199-204

1432 Tony Kerin (1999) 'The myth of prêt-a-porter marriage' *Threshold* 61: 21-22. See also: Tony Kerin (2003) 'Inappropriately prolonged courtships' *Threshold* 76: 13-14

1433 See for example: Cheryl Dakis (2008) 'From cohabitation to marriage: The transitional process of "becoming married"' *Threshold* 92: 22-26; Margaret Andrews

(2008) 'FOCCUS and cohabitation' *Threshold* 92: 21; and 'Workshop on cohabiting couples and FOCCUS' (2008) *Threshold* 92: 30-31

1434 Sotirios Sarantakos (1996) 'The virtues of liberation' *Threshold* 53: 9-11; and Sotirios Sarantakos (1999) 'Trial cohabitation revisted' *Threshold* 61: 19-20

1435 Scott M Stanley, Galena K Rhoades and Howard J Markman (2008) 'Implications for marriage education' *Threshold* 92: 12-13

1436 See also: Linda J Waite (2003) 'Uncommitted cohabitation versus marriage' *Threshold* 76: 17-20

1437 Rhoades *et al* (2012) *supra*, 385-386

1438 Mark Gungor (2008) *Laugh your way to a better marriage* [New York, Atria Books], 97

1439 Gungor (2008) *supra*, 99

1440 Herbert Anderson and Robert Cotton Fite (1993) *Becoming married* [Louisville KY, Westminster/John Knox Press], 7

1441 *Ibid.*, 15

1442 *Ibid.*, 107-108

1443 Galena K Rhoades, Scott M Stanley and Howard J Markman (2009) 'Working with cohabitation in relationship education and therapy' *Journal of Couple and Relationship Therapy* 8: 95-112

1444 For example, Cheryl Wallis(1998) 'The challenge of cohabitation' *Threshold* 58: 6–7; and Tony Kerin (1998) 'Commitment: Marriage versus cohabitation' *Threshold* 53: 8-9.

1445 David Olson (1994) *Marriage and the family: Diversity and strengths* [Mayfield CA.] The checklist is reprinted in 'Is cohabitation the right choice for you?' *Threshold* 49: 24.

1446 Rhoades *et al* (2009) *supra*, 103

1447 Scott M Stanley, Galena K Rhoades and Howard J Markman (2008) 'Cohabitation: What we know' *Threshold* 92: 6

1448 Kevin and Margaret Andrews and Carmel Crawford (2003) 'An educational response to living together' *Threshold* 76: 25 –30. See also: Barbara Markey (2003) 'Quality marriage prep when cohabitors choose to marry' *Threshold* 76: 21-23; and Alan E Craddock (2009) 'A new inventory for cohabiting couples' *Threshold* 76: 23

1449 See: Kevin Andrews (1997) 'The age for marriage' *Threshold* 54: 10-11

1450 Lixia Qu and Grace Soriano (2004) 'Forming couple relationships' *Family Matters* 68: 43-49

1451 Larry L Bumpass, Teresa C Martin and James A Sweet (1991) 'The impact of family background and early marital factors on marital disruption' *Journal of Family Issues* 12: 22-44

1452 Paul R Amato and Stacy J Rogers (1997) 'A longitudinal study of marital problems and subsequent divorce' *Journal of Marriage and the Family* 59: 612-624; and Alan Booth and John N Edwards (1985) 'Age at marriage and marital instability' *Journal of Marriage and the Family* 47: 67-75

1453 Paul R Amato, Alan Booth, David R Johnston and Stacey J Rogers (2007) *Alone together* [Cambridge MA, Harvard University Press], 79

1454 Kathleen M Walters (2009) 'How young is too young?' *Threshold* 97: 18-20

1455 Mark Regnerus (2009) 'Say yes. What are you waiting for' *Washington Post*, April 26

1456 Norval D Glenn, Jeremy E Uecker and Robert W B Love Jr (2010) 'Later first marriage and marital success' *Social Science Research* 39.6: 787-800

1457 Jeremy E Uecker (2012) 'Marriage and mental health among young adults' *Journal of Health and Social Behavior* 53: 67-83

1458 Norval D Glenn (2005) *With this ring. . . A national survey on marriage in America* [Washington DC, National Fatherhood Initiative], 19

1459 *Ibid.*, 20

1460 www.genea.com *supra*

1461 Suzanne C Tough *et al* (2002) 'Delayed childbearing and its impact on population rate changes in lower birth weight, multiple birth, and preterm delivery' *Pediatrics* 109: 399-403

1462 Tony Kerin (2003) 'Inappropriately prolonged relationships' *Threshold* 76: 13-14

1463 Sharon Jayson (2009) 'With this doubt, I thee wed' *USA Today* (December 1)

1464 See: Lawrie Molony (2011) 'The decision to marry: Freedoms, constraints and individual rights' *Threshold* 102: 10-14

1465 Mark Regerus and Jeremy Uecker (2011) *Premarital sex in America* [New York, Oxford University Press], 249

1466 'Whatever happened to old-fashioned love?' (1990) Letter, *The Age* Melbourne, Australia, June 19.

1467 See *To have and to hold* (1998) *supra*, at 101; and Michele Simons *et al* (1994) *Pathways to marriage* [Adelaide, University of South Australia]

1468 Leo Tolstoy (1917) *Anna Karenina*, 1

1469 Bradbury and Karney (2010) *supra*, at 400-401

1470 Linda J Waite (2003) 'Uncommitted cohabitation versus marriage' *Threshold* 76: 17-20

1471 'Myths about marriage' (1999, revised 2003) *Modern marriage* [Melbourne, Threshold Publishing]

1472 Rosalind Baker (2009) 'Five myths that will kill any love relationship' *Threshold* 95: 24-25

1473 Social Justice Policy Group (2007) *Breakthrough Britain: Ending the costs of social breakdown* [London, Centre for Social Justice] Vol 1, 17

1474 'David Mace' (1991) *Threshold* 32:9

1475 Margaret Andrews (1996) 'Developing a national strategy of marriage and family education' in Bill Muehlenberg *et al* (eds) *The family: There is no other way* [Melbourne, Australian Family Association] 62-84

1476 R Harris *et al* (1992) *Love, sex and waterskiing* [Adelaide, University of South Australia]. In a survey of 1,698 people attending marriage education programs, 90 per cent reported that after attending a program they would seek professional help if problems arose in their marriage.

1477 SM MacDermid, TL Huston and SM McHale (1990) 'Changes in marriage associated with the transition to parenthood: Individual differences as a function of sex-role attitudes and changes in division of household labor' *Journal of Marriage and the Family* 52: 475-486

1478 Lawrence Kurdek (1998) 'The nature and predictors of the trajectory of change in marital quality over the first 4 years of marriage for first-married husbands and wives' *Journal of Family Psychology* 12: 494-510

1479 Justin A Lavner and Thomas N Bradbury (2010) 'Patterns of change in marital satisfaction over the newlywed years' *Journal of Marriage and Family* 72: 1171-1187

1480 JR Anderson, MJ Van Ryzin and WJ Doherty (2010) 'Developmental trajectories of marital happiness in continuously married individuals: A group-based modelling approach' *Journal of Family Psychology* 24: 587-596

1481 John Gottman (1999) *The seven principles for making marriage work* [New York, Crown], 131. See also: John Gottman (1994) *Why marriages succeed or fail* [New York, Simon and Schuster]; and Hilary Smith (2009) 'Making marriage work' *Threshold* 95: 8

1482 Kathleen M Walters (1998) 'Does active listening prevent marital distress?' *Threshold* 58: 10 - 12

1483 Walters (1998) *supra,* 10

1484 Walters (1998) *supra,* 10

1485 Walters (1998) *supra,* 10

1486 See: 'The top 10 everyday niggles and passion-killers' (2011) *Threshold* 102: 4

1487 John Gottman (2011) *The science of trust* [New York, WW Norton and Co]

1488 Benjamin Karney (2011) 'Keeping marriages healthy, and why it's so difficult' *Threshold* 101: 34-36. See also: Benjamin R Karney and Thomas N Bradbury (2000) 'Attributions in marriage: State or trait? A growth curve analysis' *Journal of Personality and Social Psychology* 78: 295-309; and LA Neff and BR Karney (2005) 'To know you is to love you: The implications of global adoration and specific accuracy for marriage relationships' *Journal of Personality and Social Psychology* 88: 480-497

1489 Ted L Huston (2009) 'What's love got to do with it? Why some marriages succeed and others fail' *Personal Relationships* 16: 301-327

1490 Walters (1998) *supra,* 10

1491 Walters (1998) *supra.* See also John Gottman *et al* (1998) 'Predicting marital happiness and stability from newlywed interactions' *Journal of Marriage and Family* 60: 5-22; and John Gottman and Robert W Levenson (2000) 'The timing of divorce: Predicting when a couple will divorce over a 14 year period' *Journal of Marriage and Family* 62: 737-745

1492 LM Papp, EM Cummings and MC Goeke-Morey (2009) 'For richer, for poorer: Money as a topic of marital conflict in the home' *Family Relations* 58: 91-103. See also: Thomas Bradbury (2010) 'Which conflicts consume couples the most?' *Threshold* 99: 36

1493 Paul R Amato, Jennifer B Kane and Spencer James (2011) 'Reconsidering the "good divorce"' *Family Relations* 60: 511-524. See also Paul Taylor, Cary Funk and April Clark (2010) *As marriage and parenthood drift apart, public is concerned about social impact* [Washington DC, Pew Research Center], 45 showing that 58 per cent of survey respondents thought divorce preferable to maintaining an unhappy marriage.

1494 Constance Ahrons (1994) *The good divorce: Keeping your family together when your marriage comes apart* [New York, HarperCollins], 2

1495 *Ibid.,* 3

1496 Bettina Arndt (2004) 'Better off wed' *The Bulletin,* November 24, 31, citing research by the Institute of Applied Economic and Social Research at the University of Melbourne.

1497 See for example, Pew Research Center (2010) *The decline of marriage and rise of new families* [Washington DC, The Center]

1498 See also: J Pryor and B Rogers (2001) *Children in changing families. Life after parental separation* [Oxford, Blackwell]

1499 George J Cohen *et al* (2002) 'Helping children and families deal with divorce and separation' *Pediatrics* 110: 1019-1022

1500 Alan Booth and Paul R Amato (2001) 'Parental predivorce relations and offspring postdivorce well-being' *Journal of Marriage and Family* 63: 197-212

1501 Amato, Kane and James (2011) *supra*, 520

1502 James Chapman (2012) 'One in five children from broken homes lose touch with one parent for ever' *Daily Mail Online,* January 25

1503 Amato, Kane and James (2011) *supra*, 518. See also: Alan Booth and Paul R Amato (2001) 'Parental pre-divorce relations and offspring postdivorce well-being' *Journal of Marriage and the Family* 63: 210; Brad Peters and Marion F Ehrenberg (2008) 'The influence of parental separations and divorce on father-child relationships' *Journal of Divorce and Remarriage* 49: 96-97; and Alan Booth and Paul R Amato (1994) 'Parental marital quality, parental divorce, and relations with parents' *Journal of Marriage and the Family* 56: 27

1504 Frank F Furstenberg Jr and Christine W Nord (1985) 'Parenting apart: Patterns of childbearing after marital disruption' *Journal of Marriage and the Family* 47: 893-904. See also: Judith A Seltzer (1991) 'Relationships between fathers and children who live apart: The father's role after separation' *Journal of Marriage and the Family* 53: 79-101; and David Popenoe (1996) *Life without father* [New York, the Free Press], 31

1505 'Mothers and children post separation' (2011) *Threshold* 101: 6, citing Australian Institute of Family Studies data.

1506 "In the parallel parenting cluster, non-resident parents had moderate levels of contact with children but low scores on discussions, influence, and helping to raise children. Resident parents reported little interference on the part of non-resident parents but a moderate degree of conflict and a low level of satisfaction. Nonresident parents in this cluster were involved with their children but communicated with resident parents infrequently and were perceived by resident parents as having a limited role in their children's lives. This cluster represented 35% of all families in the sample." Amato, Kane and James, *supra*, 517

1507 Amato, Kane and James (2011) *supra*, 520

1508 Amato, Kane and James (2011) *supra*, 522

1509 Jan Pryor (2011) 'Commentary on "Reconsidering the 'good divorce'" by Paul Amato et al.' *Family Relations* 60: 525-527. A contrary view is expressed by Constance R Ahrons (2011) 'Commentary on "Reconsidering the 'good divorce'"' *Family Relations* 60: 528-532

1510 L Laumann-Billings and RE Emery (2000) 'Distress among young adults from divorced families' *Journal of Family Psychology* 14: 671-687

1511 Adele Horin (2010) 'Separated couples diverge in views of relationship' *The Age* (July 5), quoting Australian National University professor, Bruce Smyth.

1512 Lianne Woodward, David M Fergusson and Jay Belsky (2000) 'Timing of parental separation and attachment to parents in adolescence: Results of a prospective study from birth to age 16' *Journal of Marriage and Family* 62: 167

1513 Valerie King (2002) 'Parental divorce and interpersonal trust in adult offspring' *Journal of Marriage and the Family* 64: 648; Paul R Amato and Juliana M Sobolewski (2001) 'The effects of divorce and marital discord on adult children's psychological well-being' *American Sociological Review* 66: 912

1514 Paul R Amato (2001) 'Children of divorce in the 1990s: An update of the Amato and Keith (1991) meta-analysis' *Journal of Family Psychology* 15: 355-375; Paul R Amato and Bruce Keith (1991) 'Parental divorce and the well-being of children: A meta-analysis' *Psychological Bulletin* 110: 24-46; and Yongmin Sun (2001) 'Family environment and adolescents' well-being before and after parents' marital disruption: A longitudinal analysis' *Journal of Marriage and Family* 63: 697-713

1515 Paul R Amato and Alan Booth (1991) 'Consequences of parental divorce and marital unhappiness for adult well-being' *Social Forces* 69: 895-914

1516 M Scott Peck (1978) *The road less travelled* [New York, Simon and Schuster], 23-24

1517 Council on Families in America (1995) *Marriage in America* [New York, Institute for American Values], 10

1518 See generally: David Popenoe (1996) *Life without father* [New York, The Free Press]; Kristian Moore *et al* (2002) *Marriage from a child's perspective: How does family structure affect children, and what can we do about it?* [Washington DC, Child Trends]; Susan Brown (2010) 'Marriage and child well-being: Research and policy perspectives' *Journal of Marriage and Family* 72: 1059-1077; Karin Grossman *et al* (2002) The uniqueness of the child-father attachment relationship: Fathers' sensitive and challenging play as a pivotal variable in a 16-year longitudinal study' *Social Development* 11:301-337; Kyle Pruett (1998) 'Role of the father' *Pediatrics* 102: E1, 1253-1262; and Cynthia C Harper and Sara S McLanahan (2004) 'Father absence and youth incarceration' *Journal of Research on Adolescence* 14: 369-397

1519 Deborah A Cobb-Clark and Erdal Tekin (2011) *Fathers and youth's delinquent behavior*, [Melbourne, Melbourne Institute of Applied Economic and Social Research] Working Paper 23/11

1520 Marcia L Carlson (2006) 'Family structure, father involvement, and adolescent outcomes' *Journal of Marriage and Family* 68: 137-154

1521 Mark D Regnerus and Laura B Luchies (2006) 'The parent-child relationship and opportunities for adolescents' first sex' *Journal of Family Issues* 27: 159-183. See also: Bruce J Ellis *et al* (2003) 'Does father absence place daughters at special risk of early sexual activity and teenage pregnancy?' *Child Development* 74: 801-821

1522 Anna Sarkadi *et al* (2008) 'Fathers involvement and children's developmental outcomes: A systematic review of longitudinal studies' *Acta Paediatrica* 97: 153-158

1523 Sue Shellenbarger (2011) 'The secret of dads' success' *The Wall Street Journal* (June 14) citing analysis in the journal *Behavioral and Brain Sciences*. See also: 'Do early father-infant interactions predict the onset of externalising behaviours in young children? Findings from a longitudinal cohort study', *Journal of Child Psychology and Psychiatry*, published online, July 19

1524 See for example: Frank Mott (1993) 'Absent fathers and child development: Emotional and cognitive effects at ages 5-9' cited in Mary Ann Powell and Toby L Parcel (1997) 'Effects of family structure on the earnings attainment process: Differences by gender' *Journal of Marriage and Family* 59: 419; and Anna Sanz-de-Galdeano and Daniela Vuri (2007) 'Parental divorce and students' performance: Evidence from longitudinal data' *Oxford Bulletin of Economics and Statistics* 69: 327

1525 Sharon C Risch, Kathleen M Jodl and Jacquelynne S Eccles (2004) 'Role of the father-adolescent relationship in shaping adolescents' attitudes towards divorce' *Journal of Marriage and the Family* 66: 55

1526 Kathleen M Harris, Frank F Furstenberg Jr and Jeremy K Marmer (1998) 'Parental involvement with adolescents in intact families: The influence of fathers over the life course' *Demography* 35: 201-216

1527 Richard Fletcher (2006) 'Fathers' connection to their infants' *Threshold* 87: 32-33. See also: Peter Little (2006) 'Big boys, little men ... the male parenting roadmap' *Threshold* 87: 34; Richard Fletcher (2003) 'Fathers as partners in change' *Threshold* 75: 12-13; Gary Dornau (2003) 'Dads and developmental health' *Threshold* 75: 18-19; Pete French (2003) 'Engaging men after separation' *Threshold* 75: 22-24; and Kyle and Marsha Kline Pruett (2009) *Partnership parenting* [Da Capo Lifelong Books]

1528 S Le Menestrel (1999) 'What do fathers contribute to children's well-being' *Child Trends Research Brief* [Washington DC, Child Trends]

1529 'A father's love is one of the greatest influences on personality development' (2012) *Science Blog*, June 12.

1530 The National Centre for Fathering (2000) *A call to commitment: Fathers' involvement in their children's learning* [Washington DC, US Department of Health and Human Services]

1531 Le Menestrel (1999), *supra*

1532 The National Centre for Fathering (2000), *supra*

1533 Quoted in 'Support for fathers significant' (2009) *Threshold* 97: 4-5, citing the *New York Times*, November 2

1534 David and Vera Mace (1987) *How to have a happy marriage* [Nashville, Abington]

1535 For example: Linda Waite (2006) 'What makes a healthy marriage?' *Threshold* 88:20; Cheryl Dakis (2006) 'What makes a relationship work? *Threshold* 88: 16-17; Stephen Leyden (2006) 'Partnership: The basis of a healthy relationship' *Threshold* 88: 21; Alan Craddock (2006) 'What makes a healthy marriage?' *Threshold* 88: 25;

Blaine J Fowers (2000) *The myth of marital happiness* [San Francisco, Jossey-Bass]; and Neil Clark Warren (2003) 'Active commitment' *Threshold* 76: 10-12

1536 See for example: Les and Leslie Parrott (1995) *Saving your marriage before it starts* [Grand Rapids MI, Zondervan]

1537 LA Neff and BR Karney (2005) 'To know you is to love you: The implications of global adoration and specific accuracy for marital relationships' *Journal of Personality and Social Psychology* 88: 489-497

1538 Robyn Parker (2002) *Why marriages last: A discussion of the literature* Research Paper No 28 [Melbourne, Australian Institute of Family Studies]. See also: 'Why marriages last' (2002) *Threshold* 74: 3

1539 Nicole Forrester (2011) '5 things men look for in a woman' *Huffington Post Canada*, September 22

1540 Nicole Forrester (2011) '6 things women look for in a man' *Huffington Post Canada*, October 2

1541 E Mavis Hetherington and John Kelly (2002) *For better or for worse: Divorce reconsidered* [New York, WW Norton], 25-33

1542 Karney (2011) *supra*

1543 Ted L Huston (2009) 'What's love got to do with it" Why some marriages succeed and others fail?' *Personal Relationships* 16: 301-327

1544 Karney (2011) *supra*. See also: L Hardoy and P Schone (2008) 'Subsidising "stayers": Effects of a Norwegian child care reform on marital stability' *Journal of Marriage and Family* 70: 571-584

1545 Thomas N Bradbury and Benjamin R Karney (2010) *Intimate Relationships* [New York, WW Norton and Co], 535-537 (Reprinted with permission of WW Norton and Co) Emphases added. © Thomas N Bradbury and Benjamin R Karney.

1546 Viktor E Frankl (1959) *Man's search for meaning* [Boston, Beacon Press] 36

1547 See also: Alexander Hamilton, James Madison and John Jay (1787-1788) *The Federalist* [republished Cambridge MA, Harvard University Press, 2009]

1548 George Washington (1789) *First inaugural address* [Washington DC, US Congress]

1549 Jonah Lehrer (2010) 'Beyond passion' *Threshold* 98: 25, reprinted from *ScienceBlogs*.

1550 See: Stephen Marche (2012) 'Is facebook making us lonely?' *The Atlantic*, May, 60-69

1551 Ted L Huston (2009) 'What's love got to do with it? Why some marriages succeed and others fail' *Personal Relationships* 16: 301-327

1552 Lawrence Stone (1977) *The family, sex, and marriage* [New York, Harper Collins], 425

1553 Blaine J Fowers (2000) *Beyond the Myth of Marital Happiness*, [San Francisco, Jossey-Bass]

1554 Tara Parker-Pope (2010) *For better – the science of a good marriage* [New York, Dutton], 284

1555 See for example, Don S Browning *et al* (1997) *From culture wars to common good – Religion and the American family debate* [Louisville, Kentucky: Westminster John Knox Press]. See also: Kevin Andrews (2000) 'One size does not fit all,' *Threshold* 66: 30-33

1556 Charles Murray (2012) *Coming apart: The state of white America 1960-2010* [New York, Crown Forum], 254

1557 Although Aristotle agreed that a happy life is pleasant, he did not consider gratification as a sufficient good for human happiness: *Nicomachean Ethics*.

1558 CS Lewis (1960) *The four loves* [New York, Harcourt, Brace and World]

1559 See: Blaine J Fowers (1998) 'Psychology and the good marriage' *American Behavioral Scientist* 41: 516-541

1560 See for example, Andrew J Cherlin (2009) *The marriage-go-round* [New York, Vintage Books] 139

1561 Blaine J Fowers, (2003) 'Marital happiness and commitment', *Threshold* 76: 7-9

1562 David Schweingruber *et al* (2004) ' "Popping the question" when the answer is known: The engagement proposal as performance' *Sociological Focus* 37: 143-161; Phillip Vannini (2004) 'Will you marry me? Spectacle and consumption in the ritual of marriage proposals' *The Journal of Popular Culture* 38: 169-185; and David Schweinruber *et al* (2008) ' "A story and a ring:" Audience judgments about engagement proposals' *Sex Roles* 58: 165-78

1563 'Even bridezillas get the post-nuptial blues' (2006) *Sunday Times*, New York (August 7). It was reported that the average wedding cost in Australia in 2007 was $39,114: 'Wedding costs rise' (2007) *Threshold* 89: 7. See also 'Brides go budget' (2009) *Threshold* 96: 5. The average cost of a wedding in the UK in 2012 was £18,500: Deborah Arthurs (2012) 'Rise of the runaway bride' *Daily Mail*, May 7.

1564 Lisa Ryan and Suzanne Dziurawiec (2001) 'Materialism and its relationship to life satisfaction' *Social Indicators Research* 55: 185-197

1565 Annie Dennis (2007) 'Some reasons people choose to marry' *Threshold* 89: 14-16

1566 See: 'AIFS abroad – Vancouver' (2003) *Family Matters* 66: 60-61

1567 Edward Westermarck (1922) *History of human marriage* [New York, Allerton] Vol 1.

AUTHOR INDEX

SUBJECT INDEX

About the author

Kevin Andrews has been a member of the Australian Parliament since 1991. He has served as an Australian Cabinet Minister, chairman of the Opposition Parties' Policy Committee, and chairman of the Parliamentary Committee that produced the report, *To have and to hold – strategies to strengthen marriage and relationships*. He currently serves as the Shadow Minister for Families, Housing and Human Services. He writes in the media regularly, publishes a policy magazine, and has spoken at many national and international conferences.

Kevin is married to Margaret, and they have five children. Together with a group of other couples, they founded the Marriage Education Programme in 1980. The Programme has provided pre- and post-marriage courses for more than 20,000 people.

www.maybeido.com

www.ingramcontent.com/pod-product-compliance
Lightning Source LLC
Chambersburg PA
CBHW051946270326
41929CB00015B/2551